Domestic Workers
in Saudi Arabia
and the Emirates

a socio-legal study on conflicts

Antoinette Vlieger

Human Rights and Culture Series

qp

Quid Pro Books

New Orleans, Louisiana

Published in 2012 in the United States of America by Quid Pro Books. Previously published in 2011 in The Netherlands by the author, in fulfillment of the requirements for the doctorate degree from the University of Amsterdam.

QUID PRO BOOKS

QUID PRO, LLC
5860 Citrus Boulevard, suite D-101
New Orleans, Louisiana 70123 USA

www.quidprobooks.com

ISBN/EAN: 978-1-61027-128-8 (pbk)
ISBN/EAN: 978-1-61027-130-1 (hc)

Also available in quality eBook editions.

Contents

Acknowledgments

My Dutch Protestant grandmother was angry her entire life at being removed from school at the age of eleven because she was a girl. She had wanted to become a doctor to cure people. My other Dutch Protestant grandmother thought that this research project was silly, that domestic workers should take care of their own problems and that I should stay at home and wait for a suitable husband to find me. Scholars generalize to better understand the world, but just as often, understanding is to be found in the rejection of generalizations. Just like the typical Dutch Protestant grandmother does not exist, there is no typical Muslim, no average Saudi or Emirati. Therefore, I dedicate this dissertation to those Saudi and Emirati employers who are open-minded, fair, and generous. They do exist and set an example in a place where others abuse the opportunities provided by the meager legal system. They lift entire families out of the poverty trap, where Europe simply closes its doors.

I thank Eleftherios Iakovou for inspiring me to go back to university to do a PhD, if only to prove I was not reading The Economist to impress him. I thank Destiny's Child, whose girl power songs (on my MP3 player hidden under a veil) kept me sane when chased by the religious police. I thank Allan, Grace, and Jan for their hospitality in Manila, Gita for her excellent interpretation work in Jakarta, The King Faisal Foundation for inviting me to Saudi Arabia and Mauritius for offering me a place to stay in Dubai when my funds were running low. Samar, Abdallah, and Madeha, by being amazingly warm and interested, saved me from becoming prejudiced. Hassan drove me around all of Riyadh, even though it scared him to death how I put him "in the eye of the government." I thank Paul Aarts for sharing his contact with me, and Menno Lenstra from the Dutch embassy in Riyadh for his support. Obviously, I am highly indebted to everyone who agreed to be interviewed, some of them at serious risk of deportation or job loss.

I thank Robert Knegt (legal sociologist), Evert Verhulp (lawyer), and Barbara Oomen (legal anthropologist) for joining forces to make this multi-disciplinary research a success. Robert, our discussions and email exchanges have inspired me enormously. Barbara, thank you for bringing my extended thoughts and ideas back into one picture, just by providing the books and theories I needed at the right moment. Heleen van Luijn, thank you for your advice, which made this dissertation coherent. Alexandra and Matthieu, thank you for your continuous support in my struggle with computers and printers.

I am heavily indebted to my mother, Maja, who taught me that nothing is impossible; there are only things that take more time. She raised me with the message: "You are a smart kid, now go save the world." I thank my sister for always standing beside me, for crying on my shoulder and for letting me cry on hers. I thank my brother for his wonderful laughter every time I told him about this silly academic world. Thank you all for making me who I am.

PART ONE

INTRODUCTION

1. Introduction to the research

Filipina domestic worker, employed in Riyadh: "Really they are good to me. If I say I need rest, they give me rest." (And if they were not so good to you, if you would have some problem with your employer, where would you go?) "Madam, I cannot go anywhere, I am not allowed to go outside. I cannot go to the embassy. I will just cry in my room and pray."

Indonesian domestic worker, previously employed in Dubai: "I also was a victim of trafficking. First in Dubai I was raped. Then my employer sent me to Iraq and I was forced to go into prostitution. I had no papers or anything so I couldn't get out. Through the internet and through friends I contacted the embassy, but they never helped me. Then I contacted the International Organization for Migration and they helped me to get home, but some of my friends are still in Iraq. I filed a report at the police here against the recruitment agency but so far they haven't done anything. It's a big corruption here. People in the government, they all become very rich from us."

These two short excerpts from interviews are examples of the facts that form the basis of this dissertation. It discusses the factors that influence the conflicts between female, migrant, live-in domestic workers and their employers, from the perspective of sociology of law. The results show (among other things) what these two examples illustrate: if a domestic worker is lucky, her employer is good to her; if she is not so lucky, she has nowhere to go. Under the best of circumstances a domestic worker in the United Arab Emirates or Saudi Arabia may be treated right, but she has no rights.

1.1 How the undertaking of this research project took shape
In the spring of 2007, Human Rights Watch (HRW) published a report on abuses against female Sri Lankan domestic workers in the Kingdom of Saudi Arabia, the United Arab Emirates, Kuwait, and Lebanon, stating the following:

> Migrant domestic workers are among the least protected workers of the labor force. They work in an unregulated and undervalued job sector and they are at high risk of abuse and exploitation. (...) They generally work excessively long working hours, get no rest days, and are paid discriminatory wages. (...) Sri Lankan women domestic workers also suffer physical, psychological, and sexual abuse, non-payment of wages, food deprivation, confiscation of their identity documents, forced confinement in the workplace, and limitations on their ability to return to their home countries when they wish to do so. In some cases, the combination of these pervasive workplace abuses create a situation in which women workers are trapped in forced labor.[1]

---

1 Report 9. Since not all reports have a clear author, the studied reports are listed after the bibliography and are referred to by number.

Female domestic workers are live-ins who perform tasks in private households, such as cleaning, cooking, childcare, and care for the elderly, in exchange for food, lodging, and money. Their nationality, gender, race, and economic status put them in the lowest stratum of the social hierarchy in many societies, which makes them vulnerable to discrimination. Such workers are even more susceptible to abuse because their workplace is within the protected private sphere of the household. The HRW report gives the impression that the situation in the Middle East is worse than elsewhere. So do, in comparison, reports 8, 17, 18, and 19.[2] Several interviewees from NGOs in Manila and Jakarta confirm that the situation is currently worse on the Arabian Peninsula than elsewhere, as did interviewees from the International Labour Organization (ILO), although no hard quantitative data are available to confirm this.

The HRW report and the reactions to it in the international press and forums focused on what was happening in these countries in terms of a relatively high occurrence of conflicts,[3] foregoing the question which factors influence these conflicts. When confronted with that question – and usually without wanting to say so publicly – several interviewed diplomats and scholars suggested that because most of the employers are Muslim, Islam must have something to do with it.[4] However, this explanation seemed unlikely in light of the fact that according to Muslims their religion – like most other religions[5] – is one of peace and justice. Secondly, although the position of domestic workers in for instance Indonesia is not good, it does not seem to be as bad as it is in the Middle East, although Indonesia has the largest Muslim population in the world. Therefore, Islam (alone) as the cause seemed unlikely, but without proper insight into the actual factors at influence, effective solutions cannot be formulated. Therefore, this dissertation aims to investigate factors that influence these conflicts.

---

2 Again, since not all reports have a clear author, the studied reports are listed after the bibliography and are referred to by number.
3 Instead of the term abuse, the term conflicts will be used throughout this dissertation, as will be explained in section 1.3.
4 For instance, one interviewee stated: "Of course the abuse has to do with Islam. I will never say that in public, but that is what I think."
5 Vergrote (1987) P79.

1.2 Socio-legal study

The research on these conflicts has been undertaken from the perspective of sociology of law, with many aspects of legal anthropology included and applied. Sociology of law (or legal sociology) is the systematic, theoretically grounded, empirical study of law and conflicts as a set of social practices. As such, it draws on the whole range of methods and theories generally associated with sociological research.[6] Legal anthropology scholars study legal systems, law and law-like social phenomena, and take as foundational that law cannot be meaningfully understood apart from the wider culture and society. Scholars in this area share a commitment to intensive and rigorous field methodologies requiring extensive involvement in the communities under study.[7] The next two sections describe what, for the purpose of this research, has been considered to be law and what has been considered a conflict.

Law as an object of research

In my own country The Netherlands, as in many other Western countries, the concept of law usually refers to governmentally enforced norms,[8] which is meant to imply that the norms concerned are applied more or less equally to everybody by higher authorities. As such, this Western concept of law is attached to the concept of the rule of law. In the Middle East this concept turned out not to be a workable definition; in both Saudi Arabia and the Emirates, enforcement by the government does not depend on the norm, but rather on the persons involved. Statutory norms, generally considered law, can in Saudi Arabia and the Emirates be (a) generally enforced, but not if broken by powerful individuals,[9] (b) enforced only if broken by powerless individuals,[10] or (c) not meant to be enforced at all.[11] As will be described further in chapter 9, there is no rule of law in either country. If it is not (only) the norm concerned but mainly the individual involved that determines whether a norm is governmentally enforced or not, the definition of law as norms enforced by political authorities, cannot be used. Furthermore, for Muslims, Sharia or Islamic law is the source of both legal and moral standards.[12]

---

6 Clark (2007) P1413.
7 Clark (2007) P68.
8 See for instance the general introduction to law from which I have been teaching at the University of Amsterdam – Law School: Brouwer (2004).
9 Royalty is not (not always? not severely?) punished for murder or torture. See for Saudi Arabia, for instance, chapter 2.2 under government, and for the Emirates among others http://www.uaetorture.com/ June 2010.
10 For instance the sponsorship regulations as described in section 7.2.2 are generally enforced on non-Western migrants, but not on nationals or Western migrants.
11 For instance the statutory norm in the Emirates stating that car drivers have to use a safety belt; interviewees from the government explained that this law was only intended to encourage drivers to use it. Moreover, the regulations on the retention of passports as described in chapter 10.4 (if they exist, which is not clear) are not meant to be enforced, but seem to have been written as some form of window dressing.
12 Clark (2007) P827 & Nasr (2004) P155.

Instead of the binary distinction regularly made between the two,[13] Sharia distinguishes five categories of acts: not permitted, not recommended, neutral, recommended, and obligated.[14] Thirdly, many Muslims claim that the validity of Sharia norms does not depend on recognition or enforcement by the government, but rather that the status of the government depends on Sharia.[15]

The understanding of the concept of law as being those norms that are governmentally enforced on (more or less) everybody, is therefore problematic to transpose onto Sharia-based legal systems or systems without a strong rule of law. It presented as such a difficulty in the delimitation of this research. One possible solution to the question of what is to be studied when one studies law in another culture, is the concept of law as what people locally refer to as law.[16] Yet this definition poses a problem in the philosophy of language: which word or words should be used in Arabic to ask what people refer to as law? Even the term Sharia has multiple meanings.[17] Do we include all or none of them, and do we limit legal research to Qanun, which usually refers to man-made law? Or, on the contrary, should we extend our research to 'Urf and 'Adah, which refer to customary rules but may be governmentally enforced?[18] In order to make such decisions, one needs predetermined concepts of what law is, and it is beneficial to express these precisely for objective research.

Therefore, for the purpose of this research, all norms have been studied that are either positive, society-organizing rules (organizing the production and distribution of goods, decision-making, and legitimization), or negative rules for the disposition and conduct of all responsible beings (which sanction the trespassing), and which can influence or are referred to in conflicts involving domestic workers. This definition resembles Petrazycki's concept of law[19] and includes (i) Kelsen's governmentally enforced norms[20] (ii) Malinowski's norms which are considered to be the obligations of one person and the rightful claims of another[21] (iii) Maine's status-based normative positions,[22] and (iv) rules which do not concern an ought to, but a way of *doing* in a legal institutional reality.

---

13 Of which legal norms are supposed to be governmentally enforced and therefore are considered to be law, while moral standards are supposed to be enforced only to the extent they influence or shape legal norms.

14 Nasr (2004) P126.

15 Schacht (1964) and Fadl (2001) P13.

16 Oomen (2005) used a comparable concept of law in South-Africa.

17 According to Hans Wehr's Arabic to English dictionary, the term Sharia is derived from the verb shara'a and relates to the ideas of "spiritual law" and "way of belief and practice."

18 Nasr (2004) P121.

19 Kurczewski (2009).

20 Brouwer (2004) chapter I.

21 Clark (2007) P70. Malinowski's work foreshadowed a generation of anthropological research on how order could be achieved in societies lacking central authority, codes and constables. This focus moved legal anthropology away from Western-based equations of law with formal institutional legal structures and towards a more functionally based interest in social ordering and control, however achieved, across different societies.

22 Maine (1913).

Based on this understanding, customary norms, contractual norms, Sharia norms, and formal legal norms, as far as they can influence or are referred to in conflicts involving domestic workers, have been examined.

Should we call part or all of these norms law? Merry states that research on legal pluralism (see chapter 3) has not made it easier to write a definition of law: "The literature has not yet clearly demarcated a boundary between normative orders that can and cannot be called law. I think one of the difficulties lies in the tremendous variation in normative orders and the diversity of particular situations."[23] The issue can be resolved, as Griffith[24] suggests, by giving up on the concept of law entirely. This concept suggests a distinction between law and other normative systems and focuses on definitional matters and the search for universal concepts rather than on data and analysis. This dissertation therefore purposefully does not describe law, but norms.

Conflicts as an object of research
The term conflicts is used throughout this dissertation, while the Human Rights Watch report writes on abuses. This last term is problematic for scientific research because it is a descriptive term that already implies a particular normative evaluation. Working for 200 dollars per month was considered abuse by some Western colleagues, while for most domestic workers this is ten times what they would earn at home. The use of the term human rights breaches does not solve this problem because the objectivity of human rights is contested; some scholars argue that human rights have a distinctive origin in Western philosophies and political experiences, which are grounded in the Western concepts of fundamental rights and equality.[25] Furthermore, many non-Western government officials claim that, contrary to the statement that the Universal Declaration of Human Rights (UDHR) is now considered *ius cogens*[26] and thus universal law, states are only bound to treaties after ratifying them.[27] Both Saudi Arabia and the Emirates have refrained from ratifying some of the most basic human rights conventions (see chapter 7), which means that according to the views of the Saudi and Emirati governments, there are few human rights breaches on the Arabian Peninsula. According to human rights activists, however, there are many.

To solve the issue somewhat objectively, the term conflicts is used, which for the purpose of this research is defined as a situation in which one party objects to the behavior of at least one other, in explicit or implicit reference to certain norms that (according to the first party) are being violated.

---

23 Merry (1988) P878.
24 In Michaels (2009) P250.
25 Clark (2007) P718.
26 Merry (2006b) P102 left side of the page.
27 Merry (2006b) P102 right side of the page.

The other party can justify its behavior using different norms or he can agree on the norms but nevertheless act otherwise. The objections can be overt, as is the case with employers deducting fines from salaries or domestic workers absconding, or as covert as a slower pace in cleaning activities.[28] For the purpose of this socio-legal research, this definition is effective; it focuses on norms to which parties refer.[29] Thus, in the case of the rape of a domestic worker, this definition focuses on the facts that both parties usually agree that rape is not permitted (reference to the same norms) and on the power (im)balances that enable one party to act in breach of the shared norms.[30] In the case of a salary conflict in which parties refer to different norms, the focus is both on the question of the origin of these differing norms and on the question of who has the power to enforce his or her own set of norms.

Since Llewellyn and Hoebel published *The Cheyenne Way* in 1941, conflicts have been perceived by anthropological scholars as a road to the discovery of law.[31] Inspired by Laura Nader in the mid-1960s, scholars moved still more decisively outside the formal boundaries of law and legal institutions to study disputes as part of wider social and cultural processes. For the purpose of this study on domestic workers, conflicts are approached as has been promoted by Nader: they are seen as events in a series of circumstances linking persons and groups over time. This focus on processes means that conflicts must be understood in their various phases, both before and after they reach a public conflict resolution arena; how do they come into existence and how are they (not) resolved.

1.3 Types of conflicts involving domestic workers

The types of conflicts in which domestic workers in Saudi Arabia and the Emirates regularly find themselves according to the data in this research, can be divided into three types. In the first type of conflict, there is disagreement from the outset about the norms that should apply. For instance, if a domestic worker expects to receive a salary of $400 per month and the employer claims to have agreed on $200 per month, the conflict is clearly connected to a preliminary disagreement on norms. In the second type of conflict, the conflicting parties disagree on behavior or preferred outcome and only thereafter disagree on the norms which should apply. For example in a conflict on the question if a domestic worker has the right to join her employer's family on a trip to Mecca, the parties do not seem to have had clear norms in mind at the start of the conflict; they merely have a clear goal or preferred outcome. It is not disagreement over norms that seems to lead to such a conflict.

---

28 See, among others, Moukarbel (2009) for symbolic violence and everyday forms of resistance.
29 Rather than goals, as many other definitions of conflicts do, as in Schwitters (2000) P202.
30 See Rooij (2011) for an overview of common definitions of power.
31 Clark (2007) P241-244.

Instead, the disagreement on behavior or outcome seems to come first, and both parties subsequently refer to norms as argumentative or justifying tools, while they had no clear perception of norms from the outset. In the third type of conflicts, both parties at first agree on the norms, but one acts contrary to these norms anyway. Thereafter, the party in breach of a shared norm regularly refers to norms that state that his behavior is a permissible exception to the norm. For instance, in cases of rape, the rapist will often agree (beforehand) that rape (in general) is not permissible. Upon or after the act, he may justify his action by referring to norms formulating an exception. For instance, if the domestic worker is re-categorized as a slave or property, then sexual intercourse without mutual consent is considered to be permissible.

In short, type one conflicts commence with norm disagreement. Type two conflicts commence without a clear conception of the applicable norms, and type three conflicts commence with norm agreement. This tripartite distinction is useful for data analysis, but it is important to note that conflicts do not always fall (or remain) within the same category. If both parties have clearly agreed on a certain salary but the employer's business is not doing well, he can lower the salary and refer to the norm that everyone in his family has to contribute to make ends meet. Although the domestic worker may agree on the norm that family members have to contribute, she can refer to the norm that she is a worker, not a family member, and therefore the contract should be upheld. Is this a type two or a type three conflict? That is not clear. So although the tripartite distinction is not fixed or rigid, it does create a useful division into different sorts of conflicts that can facilitate socio-legal research on the factors that influence conflicts.

The first type of conflict concerns many salary conflicts; as in the above example, domestic workers regularly claim that the salary they receive is not the salary that has been agreed on. Especially many Filipinas[32] claim to have been promised a salary of $400 and do not accept the payment of only half that amount. Employers in turn claim that an amount of around $200 has been agreed on with their agency. Moreover, the question of whether the domestic worker has a right to salary payments during the first three months regularly leads to conflicts, as does the question if payments should be made monthly or at the end of the two year contract. Other conflicts that are usually norm-conflicts concern the question of how many days a week the domestic worker has to work, how many hours per day, and what her specific tasks are or even if she is indeed supposed to work as a domestic worker (she may have agreed to become a waitress or nurse). Furthermore, domestic workers regularly disagree from the start with the norm of their employer that they are not permitted to leave the house – not on their own or not at all – or the norm that they also (occasionally or frequently) have to work in other houses.

---

32 See chapter 6 for the reasons hereto.

Acts that are by certain employers seen as acts of occultism, such as the collection of hair, is another conflict in which there is a clear disagreement on norms from the start; what seems to be perfectly innocent to the domestic worker, a habit she has grown up with, can be perceived as extremely dangerous and thus forbidden by her employer.

The second type of conflict concerns among others the question of whether a domestic worker has the right to have a boyfriend (whom she either frequents or calls). This is an issue rarely discussed either at the agencies in the countries of origin or destination, and usually does not come up in the domestic worker's mind until she actually has a boyfriend. This issue is connected to the question to what extent the domestic worker should be seen as part of the family or as a worker; how far does the authority of the employer over her acts reach and to what extent is she entitled to things that other family members are entitled to, such as protection, care, and the same food. To the contrary, the domestic worker may not want to be entitled hereto and prefer to be left more on her own, to cook her own food, to have privacy, and to decide for herself how she will spend her money. All these conflicts seem to depend not on norms, but on questions such as whether there is a mutual liking between domestic worker and the family she works in, whether she is lonely or homesick, whether she likes Arabic food, and whether the mutual trust between domestic worker and employer grows or fades away.

The third type of conflict concerns theft, child abuse, sexual relations (with mutual consent) with a married male employer (either with or without payments), and physical, psychological or sexual violence including but not limited to rape and murder. In these instances the reaction is frequently that all these acts are normally not permitted, but that this was an exception. Another issue which is usually a type three conflict concerns the question if the labor agreement can be ended prematurely or not. From the outset, both parties usually (though certainly not always) deny that this is the case, that the contract is for two years. Yet both parties can present exceptions to this rule, such as the fact that a close family member of the domestic worker has passed away or the fact that one of the employer's sons turns out to be in love with her.

Especially type three conflicts occasionally reach the Western press. For instance, they extensively reported on the case of Nour Miyati, severely abused by her employers to the point that she lost nine fingers due to gangrene. Her employers had to pay minor compensation only.[33] Shortly before finishing this dissertation, another extreme case reached the international newspapers: a Sri Lankan domestic worker had arrived back home with twenty four nails in her body, stuck in there by her employer as punishment for complaints over the work load.[34]

---

33 Among many: http://archive.arabnews.com/?page=1&section=0&article=110110&d=21&m=5&y=2008.
34 Among others: http://www.ad.nl/ad/nl/1014/Bizar/article/detail/507872/2010/08/26/Saoedische-baas-slaat-spijkers-in-lichaam-van-dienstmeid.dhtml September 2010.

Yet it is type one conflicts, especially salary conflicts, that are, according to interviewed diplomats of the labor sending countries, most common. It is unknown with what frequency the different conflicts occur. According to interviewees of the Emirati and Saudi governments, the number of conflicts is highly exaggerated and usually domestic workers simply abscond to earn more money on the black market. According to the HRW report and diplomats of labor sending countries, conflicts involving domestic workers are much more numerous and more severe than conflicts involving any other type of migrant worker. The truth is that there are no hard data available. Also this research has not been able to provide such quantitative answers. Extensive multi-sited, multi-method research would be needed to provide the correct answer (see section 12.4).

The focus of this research has been mostly qualitative; what influences the different types of conflicts? If a conflict concerns a type one conflict in which clear norm disagreement has led to the conflict, the factors which influence such conflicts and the possible solutions are different from those in type two or three conflicts, in which norms are better analyzed as normative tools. Nevertheless, as there were no data available on the question of which types the different conflicts concerned, research and analysis focused on the norms to which parties referred, not on the three types. Yet the subdivision does return in the analysis of the data and the discussion of possible solutions.

1.4 Aim and research question

The aim of this research is the following:

To increase our knowledge of the factors that influence conflicts between domestic workers and their employers in the Kingdom of Saudi Arabia and the United Arab Emirates, with the expectation that such knowledge may contribute to improving the position of domestic workers.

The central question of this research is the following:

Which factors influence the (emergence and character of) conflicts in the Kingdom of Saudi Arabia and the United Arab Emirates between domestic workers and their employers, the norms both parties (may) refer to, and the related (im)balance of power?

This research question entails the following sub-questions:

i.   In what way and to what extent do domestic workers and their employers refer to Islamic, customary, contractual, and formal legal norms?
ii. Do conflicts concern disagreement over norms or disputes regarding behavior contrary to the norms upon which both parties agree?
iii. Which factors influence the Islamic, customary, contractual, and formal legal norms that both parties (may) refer to in conflicts?
iv. Which party is able to enforce its own norms or to act contrary to norms on which both parties agree, and which factors influence this (im)balance of power?
v.   Which kinds of external conflict resolution methods are used, what are their usual outcomes, and which factors influence these outcomes?

Definitions and delimitations

The aforementioned Human Rights Watch report concerned four countries: the Kingdom of Saudi Arabia, the United Arab Emirates, Kuwait, and Lebanon. This research was restricted to Saudi Arabia and the Emirates for the following reasons: due to time and financial restrictions, it was not possible to study all four countries described in the report. The two selected countries were chosen because they are considered the most conservative and the most open countries respectively of the four.[35] The research concerns the question which factors influence the conflicts concerned. Factors refers to all societal factors: political, economic, and ideological, at micro, meso, and macro level.

On the Arabian Peninsula, domestic work is not officially considered labor and the term domestic worker is often not understood. The word generally used in English is maid. Because this term is often considered degrading, domestic worker is used here. Live-out domestic workers, male domestic workers, and private drivers have been excluded from this research because their labor position is quite different. Domestic workers in this dissertation thus refers to female migrant live-in domestic workers. The employer is known by many different names, of which the most common are baba, mother, madam, master or employer. Throughout this dissertation employer is used, as employment is the most general term for situations in which one person performs services over a longer period of time and receives payment for doing so. However, use of the term employer is not meant to imply that (Western) norms of employment either do or do not apply to the labor relation under investigation.

---

[35] Saudi Arabia is difficult to enter due to strict visa regulations, which has brought the world comparatively little information on the country. Dubai is an international hub with a large tourist industry. In Saudi Arabia women have to cover themselves, alcohol is not allowed, and punishments such as flogging still occur. In Dubai tourists openly walk around in bikini's, drink alcohol, and visit prostitutes.

1.5 Research methods

Multi-sited grounded theory methods
Methodologically, this research is based on a combination of mostly qualitative and some quantitative methods. They were applied during extensive periods of fieldwork throughout 2008 and 2009 in the Kingdom of Saudi Arabia and the United Arab Emirates and in two countries of origin of domestic workers, the Philippines and Indonesia.[36] Because the research question is an open one, the research was conducted with grounded theory methods. As Charmaz explains, grounded theory methods consist of systematic yet flexible guidelines for collecting and analyzing data to construct theories 'grounded' in the data themselves.[37]

Grounded theorists collect data to develop theoretical analyses from the beginning of a project. They immediately study the gathered data and separate, sort and, synthesize these data through qualitative coding and attachment of labels to segments of data. This coding process is combined with intensive memo writing. By studying data and writing memos, ideas are developed that best fit and interpret the data as tentative analytic categories. Inevitable questions arise and gaps in the categories appear, leading to a consecutive sampling aimed at theory construction rather than population representativeness (i.e., generalizability). The final step is diagramming of the codes and categories, which aims to lead to the formulation of theory.

In light of the fact that the research question concerns a very sensitive issue and that both countries have dictatorial regimes, the second guiding principle in the choice of methods for this research was whether methods were executable in practice. The determination of this question was always answered onsite, not beforehand. There was really no alternative. For instance, the initial plan had been to talk to domestic workers in the park, as other researchers had done before. But upon arriving in the Emirates, it became clear that because of a police crackdown on irregular workers they had disappeared from the parks and most regular domestic workers were not permitted to leave the house without their employers. Door-to-door research often created a situation perceived as unsafe by both the interviewee (especially domestic workers) and the researcher. Many candidates for interviews and questionnaires were available in embassy shelters, but as these women were all runaways, restricting the research to them would likely have biased the results. It was not until all these options had been considered, and considerable information had already been gathered, that it became clear that research needed to be done in countries of origin as well: both to interview domestic workers who were about to leave and those who just arrived back home from Dubai and Riyadh.

---

36 In 2008 and 2009, almost four months in the Emirates, three months in Saudi Arabia, four weeks in Manila and three weeks in Jakarta.
37 Charmaz (2006) P2-3.

According to grounded theory methodologists, data gathering needs to be continued until the data become saturated, until they no longer lead to new questions and ideas. This was not possible in this research; the researcher ran out of time, money, and energy. Yet in the final stages of analysis, the data were reviewed again with the goal of finding something that would disprove the analyses. Therefore, the entire process concerned open minded data gathering, inductive theory building, theory testing on-site through targeted sampling, and finally deductive theory testing through attempted falsification by review of the gathered data.

Quantitative methods
One-hundred-sixty questionnaires were completed by domestic workers in Manila and Jakarta who were about to leave for employment in Saudi Arabia or the Emirates, and who were contacted at different pre-departure orientation courses. As these courses are governmentally prescribed, the results of these questionnaires may be deemed to be fairly representative of Filipina and Indonesian domestic workers. They are less representative of domestic workers of other nationalities. One hundred questionnaires were completed by domestic workers who had been employed in Saudi Arabia and the Emirates, and who were contacted (i) at their embassies in Saudi Arabia, (ii) at the airport upon return to Manila and Jakarta, (iii) at government or NGO-run safe houses in Dubai, Manila and Jakarta, (iv) in offices where domestic workers arrange for their paperwork upon contract renewal, and (v) in the houses of their employers. These questionnaires are less representative as there is no knowledge of the number of Filipina and Indonesian domestic workers who finish or renew their contract, versus the number of runaways. Representativeness is further discussed in the chapters presenting the data concerned. Since not all interviewees have filled in all the questions, in the different tables presenting the data, n is always somewhat less than one-hundred-sixty or one-hundred.

Qualitative methods
The following individuals were interviewed in semi-structured interviews: 73 domestic workers, 33 employers (on the subject of domestic workers), 15 Saudi and Emirati women (on the legal system), 32 government officials, 9 lawyers, 6 persons from international governmental organizations, 17 persons from nongovernmental organizations, 26 diplomats, 11 lower-strata male migrant workers, 7 agency owners, 2 Saudi experts on domestic violence, 4 nurses, and 3 judges. This list is the result of the principles that (i) many different types of interviewees were approached to gather all relevant views on the conflicts, and (ii) that anybody who could provide useful data and who agreed on being interviewed, has indeed been interviewed. The lobbying work hereto continued until researcher's last days in the different countries.

In addition to the interviews, one focus group discussion was held in Dubai with a Bible study group of Filipina domestic workers. The proceedings of four conferences attended by government officials of Saudi Arabia, the Emirates, the Philippines or Indonesia were analyzed. The contents of about two dozen individual and standard labor contracts were studied. Several pre-departure orientation courses in Manila and Jakarta were attended and the material distributed there was studied. More work was done by looking at the media. Newspaper articles, columns, and blogs over a period of two-and-a-half years were scanned for anything relevant to the position of domestic workers. A number of novels on Saudi Arabia and the Emirates were read for this same reason. The internet was searched for relevant *fatwas*.[38] Several conflicts, adjudicated in official conflict resolution mechanisms, were monitored. The possibility of discussing domestic workers' issues in newspapers or on the radio in Saudi Arabia was tested. Little tests were done on the question of how difficult it was for domestic workers to find safe houses or hotlines, by asking taxi drivers and domestic workers to what extent they were able to find either. An extensive search was conducted on the availability of possible conflict resolution officers or shelters in both Saudi Arabia and the Emirates, by asking different interviewees about such places, and thereafter trying to locate and visit the places concerned to assert their actual existence.

Furthermore, informants were sent into fifteen agencies in Manila and Jakarta, and calls were made to four more agencies, to gather the information usually provided to prospective domestic workers.[39] The researcher visited thirteen agencies in Saudi Arabia and the Emirates, presenting herself as being in search of a domestic worker, to acquire the information usually given to prospective employers (more hereon below, under *ethics*). Visits were made to agencies where employers exchanged domestic workers, and to several governmental offices in Manila, Jakarta, Dubai, and Riyadh, such as their 'pick up' in Riyadh airport. Finally, reports, books, and articles (listed in the bibliography) were studied to compare the research results to the situation at other places or times to get a better understanding of the particularities of the situation in Saudi Arabia and the Emirates. The same process of coding was applied to this literature.

The scientific demands for this type of research require details on the interviewees, the days and locations of the interviews, or (at least) a numbering of interviewees to permit cross-referencing and to provide a minimum of verifiability. However, due to security issues, the threat of closure of shelters and deportation, and the possibility of lesser sanctions such as physical abuse and financial penalties, all interviewees were promised anonymity.

---

38 Religious opinions.
39 In Manila a Filipino male, who pretended to gather information for his niece, in Jakarta an Indonesian female, who pretended to gather information for herself and her younger niece.

Furthermore, there is good reason to believe that the Saudi and Emirati secret services monitored this research activity and may have accessed computer files. Therefore, as a precaution, all identifying information has been entirely removed from this dissertation to protect the safety of all individuals involved.

As a result of the researcher's difficulty in mastering Arabic, it was used only for small talk and most of the communication took place in English. Where the English of the interviewee was insufficient, interpreters were used for Arabic (in Saudi Arabia and the Emirates), Tagalog (in Manila), Bahasa (in Jakarta), and Singhalese (in a Sri Lankan embassy). All interpreters were urged to translate as literally as possible and to share their views on the wordings and communication style of the interviewees.

Process

The process of data gathering took place as follows. First, a broad range of information was gathered on the countries studied, on sociology of labor, and on domestic workers. Based on this information, a heuristic model was developed that placed potentially relevant factors into a matrix: economy, ideology, and power could have influence at the household, the society or the global levels. After this, the first versions of the questionnaires and interview questions were written. A list was made of persons who should be interviewed and places were listed where possible interviewees could be met, such as parks, beauty parlors, shopping malls, and shelters.

Fieldwork lasted a total of four months in the United Arab Emirates and three months in Saudi Arabia. Fieldwork in the Philippines lasted one month and fieldwork in Indonesia lasted almost three weeks. In the first weeks of the fieldwork, all the conversations were recorded. However, because many interviewees only really opened up after the recorder was switched off, recording was stopped. After that notes were made, which were typed out and completed as soon after the interviews as possible. The interviews and completed questionnaires immediately led to alterations in the material. For instance, because only one domestic worker was forced to cut off her hair, the question on that subject was removed, while the question asking whether a worker had signed a contract in a language she could read was later added. Certain questions turned out to be generally misunderstood and did not offer any information. For instance, most domestic workers responded on the questionnaires that they would not join a trade union, but in later interviews, it was discovered that they did not know what trade unions were. Other questions were very informative, not because of the answers given but because they caused unexpected visible emotions. In one such instance, a question concerning a comparison between daughters and domestic workers enraged several employers. The quantitative questionnaires were therefore used mainly as a research tool for the qualitative part of this research; unexpected answers led to new leads and new interviews.

Some research attempts failed for various reasons: for instance, permission to visit certain places (such as detention centers) was never granted. Many domestic workers were inaccessible because women who spoke for instance only Swahili, could not be interviewed due to the lack of an interpreter. Moreover, women who had an employer who paid them triple salary generally did not want to be interviewed, because they were too afraid to upset their employer. Considering that meeting employers in the malls or beauty parlors, as planned, turned out to be impossible, some interviews were conducted door to door in the Emirates. It was unclear if this was allowed, but it felt safe enough – for the researcher and for the employers, although not for all domestic workers. In Saudi Arabia, on the contrary, this method was deemed too dangerous, as Western women can become the targets of attack.[40] Therefore, in Saudi Arabia most of the interviewed employers were gathered through the snowball method, one employer referring to the next.

Discussion of methods
The problems of finding and gathering quantitative data were considerable. Auwal states hereon: "Political realities in this region limit the ability of individuals and groups to collect and publish solid 'scientific' data on labor issues. With broad quantitative data unavailable, qualitative inquiry and anecdotal analysis provide the best opportunity to develop an understanding of how migrant laborers are treated or victimized in this region."[41] In this research, the main hurdles were the inaccessibility of certain types of domestic workers and the unwillingness of most employers to be interviewed. These problems could not be solved within the given timeframe and budget. Thus, the questionnaires have been used largely in a qualitative way. Where the quantitative data were deemed reliable enough, they are presented as an indication of scale and possible generalizability. That is, quantitative data provide parameters in the discussion that address the extent to which results observed here might apply outside of the sample as well. Other qualitative results deemed less representative have been restricted in their presentation to broad categories, such as *many* and *some*.

It turned out that certain data could not be used (as is common in this type of research) and are therefore not presented in this dissertation. For instance, the questions concerning the level of education and age often appeared to be answered incorrectly because many domestic workers have considerable financial reasons for overstating both. Even the question about their religion received dubious replies; several women, possibly hoping to find employment in Europe through this research, stated that they were Christian, while telling their employer

---

40 After the bombing in 2003, Western expatriates further retreated within their compounds, most of which are guarded with walls, gunmen, watchtowers and tanks.
41 Auwal (2010).

they were Muslim. Therefore, these results were discarded, though it should be kept in mind that serious attempts have been made to gather them.

Sampling bias occurred due to language issues and location problems (runaway Filipina domestic workers gather in safe houses, but for many other nationalities such locations are not available). Furthermore, domestic workers who were content with their employer although they were not permitted to leave the house, were often inaccessible or unwilling to talk for fear of losing employment. Again, in analyzing the data, caution was applied by continuously questioning the consistency of the results, whether the results might be different for other groups and why this might be the case.

Researcher bias, the sensitivity of the topic, and the highly protected privacy of the average Saudi or Emirati household, severely limited the possibilities of participatory observation within the households. An extreme example of researcher bias is an employer who introduced his domestic worker in an amazingly gentle way, while she was visibly shaking with fear in his presence. It is impossible to determine what the day-to-day relation here looks like, but it is certain that it does not look the way it is presented to the outside world. Further researcher bias was created by the fact that the researcher, as a woman, had certain access to places where males could not enter, while there were many other places where only males could enter. In those (and all other) places, people reacted as they would react to any woman, which very likely altered the topics they addressed. Unfortunately, because it is mainly women who research domestic workers, the extent of this researcher bias is difficult to assess.

Ethics

Most people involved in this research were aware of the fact that they were being interviewed. The exceptions were (i) personnel of the agencies both in the countries of origin and destination, and (ii) several Saudi and Emirati men who knew about the research but who did not seem to realize that their confessions on sexual relations with domestic workers provided outside official interviews that would be used for this dissertation. Neither the agents (except for one, see below) nor the men concerned have been informed of this after the fact. Though some will deem this unethical, there is a scientific value in doing what is needed to uncover the truth. These two values sometimes collide, in the same way that legal principles do.

In such instances, lines must be drawn and choices must be made as to which value receives preference in which case. In light of the different sources pointing to malevolent agents as an important factor that influences conflicts and in light of the aim of this research and the plight of domestic workers, it was considered unethical not to find out which information agents actually give to both employer and employee. Both parties were in the interviews not very clear on the information provided to them, and the visits turned out to be a useful tool to gather data. The same applied, mutatis mutandis, to the issue of intimate relations and sexual violence: in official interviews this topic was usually denied or belittled, while in inside interviews useful information was regularly provided. Thus, between the colliding ethical principles of informing all interviewees and of trying to uncover the truth, preference has been granted to the latter, in light of the research aim. As to the fact that the persons concerned were not later informed: one Indonesian agent has been informed afterwards. He responded with a politely formulated but clear death threat. After that, no other agents have been informed.

1.6 Societal and scientific relevance

There are an estimated two million domestic workers in Saudi Arabia and the United Arab Emirates.[42] The societal relevance of this research, which aims to contribute to improving their position, thus seems self-evident. Yet the issue is larger than just these two million women. Many of the factors that influence the position of domestic workers in these two countries also influence the position of other migrant workers, such as limited access to justice. This also influences the position of women in general, as Emirati and especially Saudi women suffer from diminished citizenship. At the same time, the research can help to explain the position of domestic workers in other rapidly changing societies and in other oil states. The policy recommendations in the concluding chapter (§12.5), therefore offer suggestions to improve many lives.

As for the scientific relevance, most research on domestic workers is done by sociologists and anthropologists, not by legal scholars.[43] The focus on factors that influence conflicts, power differences, and norms was therefore underdeveloped in existing theories on domestic workers (for an overview of existing theories, see §3.1). Concerning methodology; several data gathering methods turned out to be fruitful, especially the unannounced visits to agencies, and the interviewing of domestic workers at the airport upon return in their home country. Hopefully other researchers will be able to gather more data using these methods.

A new concept introduced in this dissertation concerns the distinction between three types of conflicts: (i) disagreement on norms, (ii) conflicts concerning behavior without preliminary norms, or (iii) conflicts concerning behavior contrary to shared norms (§1.3). It turned out to be fruitful for this research and may therefore be of use to other legal-sociologists. Scholars of legal pluralism (§3.3.1) state that social actors maneuver between different coexisting legal systems or between contradicting norms within one system, to achieve the most satisfactory decision in an existing conflict, using norms as discursive tools. However, the data of this dissertation clearly show that especially contractual norms are not merely applicable as discursive tools in existing conflicts; they are also regularly the direct cause

---

42 Jureidini (2010) states 1.2M in Saudi Arabia and 0.6 in the Emirates, but the Saudi Ministry of Justice estimates 1.4M in Saudi Arabia and other sources estimate 2M in Saudi Arabia alone.
43 Santos (2005) P9 and section 3.1 of this dissertation.

of conflicts. As such the distinction in three types of conflicts builds on the theory of legal pluralism.

Another new concept is power slavery (§10.7) which describes the situation in which one individual holds extreme power over another, without holding property rights. This concept of power slavery has advantage over the concept of bonded labour, as it clarifies how connected the position of the domestic worker is to the position of women and children in these locations where the patriarch is considered to be the state within the private sphere of the household. New, also, is the distinction introduced in chapter II, in three types of otherness, which helps to explain why the marginal position of the domestic worker is particularly problematic in the two countries researched.

Also new is the hypothesis presented in §3.2, stating that normative models may be rather similar throughout different times and locations (despite vast cultural differences), because the average number of individuals with whom members of a society interact, is of influence on the question of whether the different normative models will or will not properly function. Chapter 5 introduces a related hypothesis on the question why legal protection diminishes during the transition between the status-based model and the contractual model. New, too, is the hypothesis that labor protection is not developing in the Arabian Gulf because the upper-class lacks incentives to help or protect the have-nots (§7.4). Connected to this hypothesis is a discussion on the societal factors that possibly diminish the implementation of the international treaty against human trafficking (Palermo Protocol), with suggestions for research hereon in §12.4.2.

Furthermore, this dissertation makes the connection between several existing, but previously not connected theories; chapter 5 connects the concept of anomie to legal pluralism and the status based position of Henry Sumner Maine. Chapter 8 makes the connection between theories on civil citizenship, access to justice, and the concept of negotiating in the shadow of the law. Chapter 9 connects the rentier state theory to the absence of the rule of law, and the difficulties of the lower strata of society. Through use of these theories, the most important factors that influence the conflicts between domestic workers and their employers are set out and connected in concluding chapter 12. This chapter furthermore contains a list of questions which came up during this research but which have not been answered. Hopefully they will form the incentive to and basis of further comparative research.

Chapter 4 on religious norms formed the basis of an article 'Sharia on domestic workers: legal pluralism and strategic maneuvering in Saudi Arabia and the Emirates' published in the Journal for Islamic Law and Culture.[44] The data of chapter 6 on contractual norms formed the basis of two further articles. One con-

---

44 Vlieger (2010).

cerned the distinction among three types of conflicts: 'Transnationalism, Legal Pluralism and Types of Conflicts: Contractual norms concerning domestic workers' has been accepted for publication in a special issue on transnationalism of the Dutch Journal *Recht der Werkelijkheid*.[45] The other article, 'Domestic Workers in Saudi Arabia and the Emirates: Trafficking Victims?' has been accepted for publication in the Journal of International Migration.[46] Chapter 8 on access to justice has been presented at the 2011 yearly conference in San Francisco of the Law and Society Association, and a (Dutch) article hereon has been accepted for publication in *Recht der Werkelijkheid*.[47]

1.7 Outline of the dissertation

This dissertation consists of five parts. The first part contains (1) this introducing chapter, (2) a chapter that provides background information on the two countries concerned, on migration, and on domestic work, and (3) a short overview of the existing literature on domestic workers and the framework of analysis for this dissertation. Thereafter, Part II (chapters 4 to 7) describes the different sets of norms to which parties refer: Islamic norms, customary norms, contractual norms, and formal legal norms. Part III (chapters 8 and 9) focuses on conflict resolution mechanisms, for domestic workers in particular and their availability in general. Part IV (chapters 10 and 11) describes the dynamics within the household: the lack of freedom of the domestic worker and her marginal position in the family, related to three forms of otherness. Part V, containing concluding chapter 12, places the research results in one framework of societal factors that influence conflicts in Saudi Arabia and the Emirates between domestic workers and their employers. Furthermore it offers suggestions for future research and discusses possibilities to improve the position of domestic workers.

---

45 Vlieger (2011 a).
46 Vlieger (2011 c).
47 Vlieger (2011 b).

2. Background information

This chapter provides a short introduction to the United Arab Emirates, the Kingdom of Saudi Arabia, labor migration, and domestic workers. It is meant for those unfamiliar with the two countries or the phenomena of the large flows of laborers, and female migrant live-in domestic workers.

2.1 The United Arab Emirates

The federation of the Emirates was founded in 1971 and consists of seven more or less independent states: Abu Dhabi, Dubai, Sharjah, Ras Al Khaimah, Umm Al Quwein, Ajman, and Fujairah. As a sovereign country, it is very young, yet its history dates back millennia. It reached its previous economic height before 1258, when the country's ports lost their central position in the Gulf due to the destruction of Baghdad.

At the beginning of the nineteenth century, the area was inhabited by several sheikhdoms. Local leaders were the male heads of the tribes that were most powerful at the time. The British Empire, in an attempt to make the Gulf safer from piracy, signed agreements around 1850 with the leading families, thereby largely consolidating the power distribution of that time. Both the nomadic and sedentary tribes gained income mostly from trade, pearls, and fishing.[48] In the twentieth century, competition from Japanese cultivated pearls ended the latter, but trade continued to grow, with many smugglers replacing pirates.

Both the economy and society drastically changed upon the discovery of a large oilfield in the 1960s and the subsequent investment of its revenues in infrastructure and marketing. In twenty years, the inhabitants became some of the richest people in the world.[49] While most oil is found in the soil of Abu Dhabi and some is found in Dubai, the other Emirates have profited as well. To prevent the economy from collapsing upon the exhaustion of the natural resources, the federal and state governments have been active (and internationally praised as visionary) in diversifying the economy and stimulating tourism.[50]

The country has been built at an unprecedented speed. Where forty years ago Sheikh Zayed Road was sandy and quiet, today it houses the Manhattan of the Middle East. Burj Al Khalifa is the highest building in the world and Burj al Arab, the famous seven star hotel, offers a view of the palm-shaped artificial islands. Large areas have been planned to become free zones, media cities, university cities, and parks. The harbor of Dubai has profited from the decline of Beirut as the commercial capital of the Middle East[51] and it has taken over Switzerland's position as the capital of black money.[52]

---

48 Davidson (2008) P1.
49 Sabban (2005) P2.
50 Tamini (2006) P2.
51 Rugh (2007) P7.
52 Davis (2006).

In the spring of 2009, it became clear that, especially in Dubai, many projects were built on a financial pyramid. Due to the world recession, many constructors faced bankruptcy, which lead to an exodus of migrant workers. However, new and very strict media laws prohibited proper media access to these issues. Therefore, the seriousness of the problems did not become widely known until the end of that year, when the Dubai bubble publicly collapsed[53] and big brother Abu Dhabi had to rescue the Emirate.[54]

Economy & labor force

The money needed for the economic boom (or bubble, as it is now also referred to) is as untraceable as the workers are nameless. About 95% of the workforce is now foreign, largely coming from Asia.[55] This has led to unrest, both from the workers who request better positions as workers or inhabitants and from the original population, which is uncomfortable with having become a small minority in its own country. The low-skilled workers are more visible in their protests and there have been large sit-downs on the country's main roads. According to the government, these were solved by the police in a peaceful manner; according to several interviewees, the protests were solved with large-scale, unnecessary violence and deportations. The citizens in general are pacified by the government with easy jobs in governmental offices, lucrative assignments, and social services.

Expatriates constitute around 95% of the working population and over 75% of the total population. Because the majority of these ex-pats are men, about 70% of the population is male.[56] Yet, this percentage would be much higher without the presence of the largely invisible female domestic workers. These statistics are highly sensitive and the government stopped publishing them in 1985; they are now based on estimates.[57] Since the beginning of the twentieth century, newcomers in the Arabian Gulf receive no citizenship – only residency permits that can be cancelled instantly, even after two generations. The tribal structure of the society is not very open to newcomers, but more importantly, neither government nor citizens are keen on sharing (power over) the natural resources of the country with outsiders.[58]

In light of the fact that Emiratis usually have cars and free time on their hands, they are more visible in the streets. Yet in certain places (for instance, the center of the somewhat poorer Emirate Sharjah), one sees almost nothing but Indian and Pakistani males in the street.

---

53 See for instance http://internationalpropertyinvestment.com/dubai-bubble referring already in 2008 to Dubai as a bubble, http://www.bt.com.bn/focus/2009/02/17/expat_exodus_as_dubais_bubble_bursts reporting in the spring of 2009 on the exodus of expats and http://middleeast.about.com/b/2009/11/27/is-bubble-bursting-dubai-bankrupt.htm on the near bankruptcy of Dubai and its effects on the world stock markets.
54 Ali (2010) P viii.
55 Report 3, P1.
56 Davidson (2008) P190.
57 Sabban (2005) P4-8.
58 Report 2, P69.

The police are very active in implementing restrictions on the freedom of association and gathering.[59] Newspapers and articles continuously point to the perceived
dangers of the current situation, as the population of domestic workers (including
cooks and drivers) already exceeds the population of citizens. The government has
tried to limit the influx of new migrants by raising the fees for new visas to around
a year's salary, but the effect has been minimal. Furthermore, rules have been introduced to limit the number of domestic workers per family (a core family with
two adults and two children can hire a maximum of six house workers), which has
created a thriving black market trade in domestic workers between poor and rich
families. The government does not take action on this, because the house workers
are part of an unspoken social contract in which no representation is (supposed to
be) demanded in exchange for social security, luxuries, and tax-freedom (see below under *government*).

Government

The British, who started the oil exploitation in the Emirates, paid part of the profits to the tribal leaders.[60] In doing so, the British and later the Americans changed
the political structure[61] of the previously egalitarian[62] society. Sheikhs used to be
the first among equals, but as they became less dependent on the support of the
indigenous population, this changed. Now that the original population has been
diminished to a small minority, their opinion matters even less, to the point that
they have become numerically, socially and politically irrelevant.[63] This creates
resentment.

Many Emiratis state to be happy with their political leaders. Interviewees talk of
vision and gratitude, they explain about leadership based on charisma and tell
how people cried when the late ruler of Dubai, Sheikh Rashid, passed away. Yet
there is another part of the population making comments such as: "The Emiratis
are not getting the better deal in all of this," and "Our country has been sold to
America." When Russia occupied Afghanistan, the Emirates sent troops to help
liberate the country. As in Saudi Arabia, they came back with knowledge of how to
fight unwanted power. In 2001, the World Trade Center was brought down by,
among others, two Emiratis. The government responded by openly arresting
many young men, while others (according to understandably anonymous sources) disappeared without a trace. Talk of politics at parties and receptions leads to
nervousness and warnings: "You could be charged with espionage you know, you
better be careful. We used to be a very peaceful country, but it's not like that anymore." Another interviewee admitted: "Many men shaved off their beards. We

---

59 Sabban (2005) P43.
60 The United States later took over the British position.
61 According to Davidson (2008) chapter 1, the political structure was changed on purpose; preferred clients were
strengthened.
62 Leezenberg (2002) P13.
63 Ali (2010) P x.

now wear baseball caps to be safe, but this doesn't mean we have become less conservative. On the contrary."

Dubai is run by the dynasty of the Maktoum family. The state is almost indistinguishable from private enterprise. Dubai's top managers simultaneously hold strategic government portfolios and manage major Maktoum-controlled real-estate development companies. The concept of a conflict of interests is barely recognized. Because the country ultimately has one landlord and myriad streams of rent and lease payments all flow to a single beneficiary, Dubai is able to dispense with most of the sales, customs, and income taxes essential to governments elsewhere. Dubai has furthermore been exemplary among the other Emirates in creating regulatory and legal bubble-domes tailored to the specific needs of foreign capital and ex-pat professionals. Meanwhile, oil-rich Abu Dhabi subsidizes the residual state functions, including foreign relations and defense, entrusted to the Emirates' federal administration – itself a condominium of the interests of the ruling sheikhs and their relatives.[64]

The governmental structure of the Emirates can well be explained through the rentier state theory.[65] This political science theory is most frequently applied to states rich in petroleum, as both Saudi Arabia and the Emirates are. The theory claims that states that receive substantial amounts of revenues (rent) from the outside world on a regular basis, combined with a relative absence of revenue from domestic taxation, tend to become autonomous from their societies, unaccountable to their citizens and autocratic. Such states fail to develop in the direction of the rule of law because in the absence of taxes, citizens have fewer incentives and abilities to pressure the government to become responsive to their needs. Instead, the government essentially 'bribes' the citizenry with welfare programs, salaries, and commercial assignments, becoming an allocative or distributive state.[66] The leading principle is thus 'no representation without taxation' instead of the democratic opposite of it, or as the former UK ambassador to the Emirates formulated it: "the social contract is that you get given things by the sheikh and in return you give the sheikh your allegiance."[67]

Society & culture
The economic achievements of the Emirates are unprecedented, but societal changes have not taken place with the same speed. At first glance, the Emirates have transformed into a completely different country. In many families, three generations live together. The grandmother is still full of beautiful stories about camel herds and pearl fishing; often she cannot read.

---

64 Davies (2006).
65 This theory was first proposed by Beblawi (1990) and improved and ameliorated in, among others, Aarts (2005).
66 Zakaria (2001), likewise Davidson (2008) chapter 5.
67 Ali (2010) P174-175.

Her daughter, the first generation profiting from the oil wealth, stays at home and is able to read some religious texts. The granddaughter, fluent in English, follows higher education and is interested in fashion.[68] Nevertheless, gender segregation and tribalism are still very much a part of everyday life.

Many Emiratis say that their country has not yet been organized the way they want it. The Emirates are not 'modern' enough: "Comparatively speaking, we are a very young country. (...) in the United Arab Emirates, we follow trends but we do not set them. If the status of domestic workers develops worldwide, we will be bound to follow. It may take longer here because our society is very new to modernization and human rights issues. However, we are changing."[69] On the other hand, there are many who say the developments are moving too fast, leading to a loss of traditional values. While the American University houses many Western-dressed boys and girls, the University of Sharjah has separate faculties for both sexes: one where boys dress in their white gowns and one for girls in their black *abayas*.

Dubai, specifically, is famously tolerant of Western vices, with the exception of recreational drugs. In contrast to Saudi Arabia, liquor flows freely in the city's hotels and ex-pat bars and no public objections are made against halter-tops or string bikinis on the beach. The Russian girls at the bars are the glamorous façade of a sinister sex trade servicing businessmen in five-star hotels. When ex-pats praise Dubai's unique openness, it is the freedom to party they refer to, not the freedom to organize unions or to publish critical opinions.[70]

Laws & legislature
An important body of law in the Emirates is Islamic law or Sharia, applied mainly in personal status issues and criminal cases. Yet its applicability creates confusion, as it is unclear to what extent its rules apply to non-Muslims. For instance, the rule that drinking alcohol is not permitted is generally expected not to be applicable to non-Muslims, as alcohol is served in practically all restaurants and bars in Dubai. However, anyone who comes into contact with the police (for instance, upon filing a complaint against a local for molestation, as one interviewee did), can face charges for alcohol abuse. Furthermore, Sharia is not a codified body of law (see chapter 4), which makes it difficult to determine what the exact contents of the Emirati version of this body of law are, what one's rights and duties are.[71]

Next to Sharia, there are increasing numbers of Swiss, English, and French law-oriented codes.[72] These include the Emirati 'Labor Law' which explicitly excludes domestic workers from its protection (see chapter 7).

---

68 Rugh (2007) P5.
69 Sabban (2005) P33.
70 Davies (2006).
71 Many expatriates complain about this.
72 See http://www.lexadin.nl/wlg/legis/nofr/oeur/lxweuae.htm for the English version of most important laws including the Labor Law.

Instruments of the International Labour Organization are generally not applied to domestic workers either. The government attempts to implement laws, but it is not always capable or interested thereto. An interviewed government official at a labor conference in Abu Dhabi admitted: "The labor inspectors thought that inspection meant checking the licenses. Now they do more than that: making sure that companies respect the rules, and respect the necessity for workers to be working according to the laws and the rules." Some laws, according to governmental interviewees, are not meant to be implemented; they are only meant as a hint towards what is considered proper behavior.[73]

To maintain harmony between the different Emirates, they were given the constitutional right to opt for joining the federal judicial system or to maintain their own independent system. Except for Dubai and Ras Al Khaima who maintain their own judicial systems, the other Emirates have joined the federal system. Its courts are organized to form two main divisions, civil and criminal, and are generally divided in three stages of litigation. Dubai and Ras Al Khaima initially organized their courts on two stages, but later Dubai expanded by the establishment of the Dubai Court of Cassation.[74] The jurisdiction of the federal third division, namely the Sharia courts, which initially was to review matters of personal status, was expanded in certain Emirates such as Abu Dhabi to include serious criminal cases, labor, and other commercial matters. In Dubai, the Emirates Labor Law is being applied by special labor courts, which are to be consulted if a mediation attempt by the Ministry of Labor has failed.[75] As domestic workers are excluded from the Labor Law (see chapter 7), they have no access to the courts administered to apply it (see chapter 8). The Emirates government has, in an attempt to better regulate the position of domestic workers, introduced a standard contract. The results hereof will be described in chapter 6 on contractual norms.

The judges in the different courts used to be mainly foreigners. For the application of Sharia, scholars have been invited into the country, mainly from Sudan, Egypt, and Pakistan. For the application of Western-oriented laws, retired Western judges have been invited.[76] The different systems seem to operate rather separated. All these judges, however, fall under the regulations of the sponsorship system (see chapter 7), which undermines their independence. Currently, more Emiratis are appointed as judges, but they are generally young and inexperienced. Recently, the first female judges have been appointed. Although the attempts to set up a proper functioning legal system are evident, not all courts and not all judges reach the standards of the inhabitants of the Emirates, as will be further described in chapter 9.

---

73 For instance a governmental interviewee stated that during the first years of the law concerned, the obligation to wear seatbelts while driving was only intended to promote, not to enforce such.

74 http://gulf-law.com/uae_judicial.html.

75 As explained by an interviewee from the Ministry of Labor.

76 As explained by several interviewees. As the labor courts never treat cases of domestic workers, these have not been researched and it is unknown what the nationalities of these judges are.

2.2 The Kingdom of Saudi Arabia

Although Islam began in Saudi Arabia, shortly after the prophet Mohammed passed away, the political center of the Muslim community was transferred to cities like Damascus, Baghdad, Cairo and Istanbul. In the nineteenth century, the Arabian Peninsula, although officially part of the Ottoman Empire, was largely ruled by local Emirs and Sheiks, who were the leaders of sedentary and nomadic tribes. As the Ottoman Empire collapsed in the First World War, the Arabian Peninsula became part of the British Empire's sphere of influence. With the financial and military support of this country, Ibn Saud united or conquered several regions of the Peninsula, which he united in 1932 in the current Kingdom of Saudi Arabia.[77]

Ibn Saud and his descendants adhered to the political agreement established in 1744 between religious leader Al-Wahhab and political leader Mohammed Ibn Saoud, forefather of King Ibn Saud. Al-Wahhab's goal was to create an ideal society that would be, as much as possible, similar to life during the time of the Prophet Mohammed.[78] The agreement divided power between the Saud family and religious scholars, most prominently the Al-Sheikh family. Mainstream Wahhabi[79] religious leaders (especially after their near annihilation in 1818 and the civil war in the second half of the nineteenth century) preach that absolute obedience to the political leader is a religious duty that prevents sedition (fitna) within the Muslim community.[80] This pragmatism has repeatedly led 'radical' Wahhabis, who demanded an uncompromising implementation of Wahhabi tenets, to oppose the religious establishment.

As in the Emirates, Saudi Arabia's economy, politics, and society changed immensely upon the discovery of oil in 1938. Saudi Arabia is currently one of the largest producers in the world. It is pivotal in the market because this country is relatively flexible in its oil production, through which it can influence the stability of prices. This makes Saudi Arabia of strategic importance to the oil-hungry United States. Adding complexity to that relationship is the fact that Saudi Arabia's largest oil fields are located in the part of the country where the Shi'a minority lives. The Shi'a are discriminated against by the Sunni majority and receive support from neighboring Iran, a nation in conflict with the United States.[81]

---

77 Abukhalil (2004) chapter 2.
78 Referred to as the Salafiyyah movement, or Salafism, meaning those who follow the early predecessors. See, among others, Nasr (2004) P102.
79 Wahhabis never refer to themselves as such and always use the terms Salafis or Ahl al-Tawhid.
80 Steinberg in Aarts (2005) P11 and 17: "Sixty years of a tyrannical imam are better than one night without him."
81 More on the Shi'a in Bradley (2005) chapter 4.

Economy & labor force

In contrast to the Emirates, Saudi Arabia has been less successful in diversifying its economy; the oil revenues still account for 75% of Saudi Arabia's budget revenues[82] that are redistributed throughout society and that, in turn, create vertical lines of loyalty. What Westerners perceive as corruption (buying loyalty) is the basis of the societal system. This purchase of loyalty and influence has led to protests from businessmen who are outside the inner circles, but nevertheless have enough power to be heard. The government is now trying to copy the economic policies of the Emirates and in 2005, significant reforms of the legal system were announced, so far – according to interviewees – with little results other than new buildings.

A problem that confronts Saudi Arabia (like many oil states, including the Emirates) is Dutch disease: the country's currency rises due to the sale of oil,[83] which makes other products from that same country too expensive to be exported. This then blocks other sectors of the economy from properly developing. This is less of a problem in the Emirates, by contrast, where the population is small enough to be taken care of by the government. In Saudi Arabia, however, a large portion of the population remains very poor. Approximately 60% of the population is below the age of twenty and more than 100,000 young Saudis enter the job market every year, where unemployment estimates range between 10% and 30%.[84] This includes young people who have received excellent educations in the United States or Great Britain, but who lack the proper tribal ties to rise in society.[85] Sociological research has shown that most crimes worldwide are committed by persons aged 15 to 25 and youth booms have contributed throughout history to the rise of revolutions.[86] Therefore, this army of young people, educated with relatively radical teachings[87] and largely unemployed, is worrisome for the stability of the country.[88]

The number of expatriates in Saudi Arabia is relatively smaller than in the Emirates. The Saudi Ministry of Labor estimated in 2003 that there were approximately seven million foreigners in Saudi Arabia, making up a little less than one-third of the kingdom's total population of 23 million,[89] although these estimates on both the population and the amount of foreigners varies widely.[90] Western workers largely reside in compounds, meant to keep the reality of tribal and segregated Saudi Arabia out, while shielding society from the perceived threat of Western 'decadence'. They have become highly secured since the bombings of 2003.[91] Non-Western expatriates live both in- and outside work camps.

---

82 Abukhalil (2004) P137.
83 Or natural gas, in the Dutch case.
84 Prokop in Aarts (2005) P77.
85 Al-Rasheed (2002) P113.
86 Levitt (2009) chapter 2.
87 More radical than their parents were raised: Kop in Aarts (2005) P61.
88 Likewise Bradley (2005) chapter 5.
89 http://www.migrationinformation.org/USfocus/display.cfm?ID=264 September 2010.
90 See among many others: http://countrystudies.us/saudi-arabia/19.htm September 2010.
91 Bradley (2005) chapter 6.

Government

After the Second World War, the British Empire lost power and influence within Saudi Arabia (as in the Emirates). At the same time, the United States grew in influence, mainly due to its involvement in the oil exploitation through Aramco.[92] Saudi Arabia moved to the center of the world's attention in 1973, due to the oil embargo. Following this, Saudi Arabia's oil wealth grew at an unprecedented rate. However, about 40% of the state's resources were and are spent on the royal family, who generally do not adhere to the conservative Wahhabi teachings that they prescribe to the rest of the country. The royal family members throw extravagant parties, and are by practically all interviewees considered to be entirely above the law, a statement supported by a variety of detailed stories concerning princes killing without punishment, and an apparent brothel near researcher's apartment, which could not be shut down as it was owned by a prince.

In 1979, the religious and political tensions became visible to the outside world when the mosque in Mecca was occupied by a group of conservatives.[93] The uprising was reportedly ended by French troops (who converted to Islam for the occasion) who flooded the mosques and electrocuted the insurgents.[94] Tensions between modernization and tradition, apparent in the battle between the powerful and the oppressed, became visible again during the 1990 Gulf War when the Ulema questioned the legitimacy of the rulers who welcomed American troops. This questioning led to reforms that had been promised for a long time.[95] Since the attacks of September 2001, in which fifteen out of the nineteen hijackers were originally from Saudi Arabia, both internal forces and the United States have been pressing for reforms. The Wahhabi teachings, which were useful to the ruling family in consolidating power, are now under attack. The Sauds[96] are looking for new legitimacy, no longer able to rely solely on their massive stockpile of weapons.

As with the United Arab Emirates, the rentier state theory is essential for understanding the Saudi governmental system. However, in Saudi Arabia, the concept of segmented clientelism[97] needs to be added: the royal family is not one power block, but is divided into clusters of princes who all have their own circle of supporters or networks of cronies.

---

92 The Arab American Oil Company, predecessor of state owned Saudi Aramco, currently the largest oil corporation in the world.
93 Steinberg in Aarts (2005) P28-29.
94 Fisk (2005) P1114.
95 Al-Rasheed (2002).
96 'Saudis' refers to the people of Saudi Arabia, whereas 'Sauds' refers to the ruling family Al Saud.
97 Hertog in Aarts (2005).

The King must unite and keep peace between (i) the different members of the vast royal family, who mainly want wealth and power; (ii) the religious fundamentalists, who demand wealth, power and a return to the past; (iii) the prominent, well-educated middle class that cries out for release from the stifling old traditions to gain more wealth and power; and (iv) the Bedouin tribes, who navigate between their romanticized nomadic way of life and the lure of the cities, but who strongly oppose increasing wealth and power for anyone not from their tribes.[98]

The relationship between the United States and Saudi Arabia has grown increasingly complex and co-dependent in recent years.[99] The United States' economy needs Saudi Arabia's oil and the royal family of the Sauds relies on American military support. For instance, in 1975, a private American firm (Vinnell, allegedly a cover for the CIA) was hired by the Pentagon to train the Saudi National Guard. Approximately one hundred thousand men swore to protect the royal family. Twenty-seven years later, Vinnell is still well entrenched in Saudi Arabia. This give-and-take relationship has made navigating the post-September 11 political waters difficult. Despite a lack of cooperation in the bombing campaign of Afghanistan and the investigation into September 11, Saudi Arabia remains the United States' chief ally in the Gulf. In response to the Saudi obstruction, United States senators have used strong rhetoric against the Sauds, calling the regime corrupt. Some have accused it of sponsoring terror, or at least doing nothing to abate it.[100] At the same time, others, both inside and outside Saudi Arabia, accuse the United States of actually causing the problems relating to Al Qaida. They believe Al Qaida should be perceived as a militant wing of the Saudi Arabian opposition to the regime which is considered illegitimate and unbearable and which is kept in power by the Americans.[101]

Society and culture
Many values and traditions from the Najd, the part of the country from which the ruling family stems, became the national standard upon the founding of the current Kingdom of Saudi Arabia in 1932. Similarly, the Wahhabi interpretation of Islam became the state religion. An important concept in Wahhabism is *khulwa*; even more than in the Emirates, the importance of gender segregation is stressed in Saudi Arabia. Women are not permitted to be in a place with a man who is not a *mahram* (an unmarriageable male, being a father, brother, son, or husband). This leads to the exclusion of women from the larger parts of public life. Although most are permitted to go shopping without a male guardian, they are not permitted to enter any government building.

---

98 Compare Sasson (2004) P20.
99 Abukhalil (2004) chapter 1.
100 Briody (2003).
101 Steinberg in Aarts (2005) P21. Fisk (2005) P840 even states that the American government appoints Ministers in the Saudi government.

Many men still prefer their wives, sisters, and daughters not to leave the house at all or to do so as little as possible. Society becomes visibly different as one is distanced from the center of Wahhabism around Riyadh. On the east and west coasts of Saudi Arabia, women play a more prominent role in public life. Religious police have little or no presence and bookstores sell more foreign literature,[102] while there also seems to be more direct interaction between foreigners and Saudi's.

Laws and legislatures

Although Wahhabism does not officially belong to any of the four schools of Sunni Islamic jurisprudence as it considers itself to be above them,[103] it largely supports the legal teachings of Ibn Hanbal (780-856), who is considered by some to be the prototype of the fundamentalist legal scholar. Ibn Hanbal stressed the importance of following the exact letter of the Quran and he rejected individual legal reasoning (such as analogy), philosophy, theology, and forbidden new things (*bid'a*).[104] This concept of *bid'a* is important in Saudi Arabia, where it is often used to stop unwanted developments. If the government actually wants a certain innovation, however, it will negotiate a *fatwa* (a legal authoritative opinion) with the religious establishment.

Throughout most Muslim countries, there is nowadays a de facto acceptance that the workings of Sharia should be limited to status, family, and inheritance law (to which banking and penal law are added in some countries). Governments have been allowed to write secular laws concerning public administration, taxes and (less regularly) penal law. Opposition to such laws arose in the fourteenth century from Ibn Taimiya, who stated that politics should take place entirely according to the Sharia. His work has had a great influence, especially within the Hanbali school of law followed in Saudi Arabia.[105] Wahhabism from the eighteenth century onwards built on his teachings, as well as on those of Salafism, the radical ideology of resistance as formulated by Sayyid Qutb, whose Egyptian followers were welcomed in Saudi Arabia.

Because the essence of all these movements is that the government should be subject entirely to the principles of Islam, they can only properly be understood as movements against the establishment. This is particularly true within the Kingdom of Saudi Arabia, where the Saud family is eager to gain legislative and judiciary power. There the religious leaders oppose the growing power of the Sauds' with references to the teachings of the aforementioned conservative scholars. The Ulema are closely connected to the Imams (see chapter 9), who have a considerable influence on public opinion through their preaching, both in the mosques and on television. Yet the Ulema are losing power to the Sauds. This

---

102 In the center of the country, the religious police seize all books, CDs and DVDs regarded as un-Islamic, see below.
103 Abukhalil (2004) P101.
104 Al-Zubaida (2005) P81.
105 Al-Zubaida (2003) P93

can be deduced from many small signs, such as the fact that for a long time the Quran – as interpreted by the Ulema – was considered to be the constitution,[106] while it now has been supplemented by the Sauds' Basic Law.[107]

Compared to the Ulema, the Mutawwa religious leaders were initially more focused on the daily rituals of Islam. In recent years, they have transformed into what ex-pats refer to as the 'religious police'. The Mutawwa, headed by the Committee for the Propagation of Virtue and the Prevention of Vice (CPVPV), are important to the implementation of certain aspects of Sharia. The Mutawwa presently consist of more than 3,500 officers in addition to thousands of volunteers, often accompanied by police escorts. They have the power to arrest unrelated males and females caught socializing. They can detain anyone engaged in homosexual behavior or prostitution, and can enforce Islamic dress codes and store closures during prayer times. The Mutawwa enforce Muslim dietary laws, prohibit the consumption or sale of alcoholic beverages and pork, and seize banned consumer products and media regarded as un-Islamic. (The latter include CDs or DVDs of various Western musical groups, television shows, and films.)

The Mutawwa have been criticized and ridiculed for the use of flogging to punish violators, banning Valentine's Day gifts and being staffed by ex-convicts, whose only job qualification is that they memorized the Quran to reduce their sentences. Perhaps the most serious and widely criticized incident associated with the Mutawwa occurred in 2002, when they prevented schoolgirls from escaping a burning school in Mecca. They based this deadly interdiction on the fact that the girls were not wearing headscarves and *abayas* (black robes), and were not accompanied by a male guardian. Fifteen girls died and fifty were injured as a result.[108] Apart from the work of the Mutawwa, the implementation of law in Saudi Arabia is very poor. Furthermore, while most judges are Saudi's and therefore do not fall under the sponsorship system, many lawyers are foreign. More information hereon will be provided in chapter 9.

There is comparatively little information available on laws and courts in Saudi Arabia, possibly because members of the legal-religious elite are generally – as researcher also found out during this research – not keen on granting anybody the right to interview them or access to courts and other legal institutions. Yet there is a Saudi Labor Law that just like its Emirati counterpart, explicitly excludes domestic workers from its protection (see chapter 7). The attached Labor Courts therefore rarely deal with cases involving domestic workers (see chapter 8). The Saudi government has written a draft law concerning the position of domestic workers, but that has been pending for years now. Instruments of the International Labour Organization (ILO) are generally not applied to domestic workers in Saudi Arabia

---

106 Abukhalil (2004) P86.
107 See http://www.mideastinfo.com/documents/Saudi_Arabia_Basic_Law.htm for an English translation of the Basic Law.
108 Kop in Aarts (2005) P64.

either. One ILO interviewee complained that so little can be achieved in this country that one wonders why it is a member state to the ILO. He explicitly stated that
this thought did not apply equally to the Emirates, while that country does not allow for trade unions either, and the ILO tripartite structure presumes some form
of representation of laborers in its states' members.[109]

2.3 Labor migration

In the twenty-first century, international labor migration, or the movement of people across borders for employment, is at the top of the policy agenda of many
countries, including countries of origin, transit, and destination. The (ILO) estimates that there are more than 80 million migrant workers. Ample positive effects of labor migration can be shown for both the sending and receiving countries, but there are also some serious downsides. On the upside, the sending
countries augment foreign exchange reserves through remittances that positively
affect the country's balance of payments, reduce poverty and unemployment, increase national per capita income, and develop an industry that services the recruitment process (recruitment agencies, travel agencies, health clinics, and other
related business ventures). Furthermore, because many women who migrate
send money home, status and power of women are augmented, whereupon sending
countries emancipate. In some cases, workers acquire new skills, which can be
utilized upon their return for the development of their home countries. Migration
also leads to an increase in income tax collection. Consumer markets enlarge and
migrant workers and their families spend their savings on home improvements,
machines and equipment, consumer durables, gifts, donations, jewelry, expensive
food items such as meat and fish, and children's education.[110]

The downsides of labor migration for sending countries can include growing
corruption to draw from the remittances, failure to provide employment at home,
brain drain, increased dependence on receiving countries, disrupted families and
– in cases of abuse – emotional and physical trauma, alienation, loss of self-esteem,
and the effects of these on other family members. For receiving countries, the positive aspects of labor migration include the fulfillment of vacancies (particularly
the unwanted low-skill jobs), economic growth, possibilities for women to develop
careers without the need for government-provided care centers for children and
the elderly and savings in human resource development. The downsides for receiving countries include growing racial and political tensions and, often but not
necessarily, growth of the hidden economy.[111]

---

109 Much more on Saudi Arabia can be read in among others Aarts (2005), Abukhalil (2004), Bradley (2005) and
Rasheed (2003 & 2007).
110 Licuanan in Heyzer (1994) P104.
111 Licuanan in Heyzer (1994) P112-113.

Due to social and political struggles, many receiving countries have closed their doors to permanent migration (or at least that of lower educated workers),[112] and switched to temporary contract migration to meet the labor shortage in certain types of occupations.[113] Labor-sending countries are not in a position to object, nor can they make any strong demands concerning labor conditions or salaries, as they compete with other countries for jobs for their nationals. They often offer lower wages while still trying to protect the overseas migrants in terms of wages and conditions of service.

Migration to the Gulf

An important flow of migrant labor was created by the growing oil production and derived industries of the Middle East, starting in the 1950s and rapidly expanding since the 1970s. The difference from the flow to the West (which regularly constituted a brain drain as also higher educated workers – if possible – often left permanently for the West), was that the Gulf States from the beginning wanted temporary workers only – particularly construction workers and, to a lesser extent, service workers. Another difference is that the governments of the sending countries were (and still are) encouraging this kind of labor export because of grown awareness of the remittances transferred by migrant workers.

In the Gulf, as elsewhere, patterns have emerged in the international flow of migrants. Workers from certain villages share their knowledge and contacts, or bring their family members directly to the Gulf. In this manner, large flows have come into existence to the Gulf from Kerala in India, Mindanao in the Philippines and the countryside around Jakarta. Other countries of origin include Bangladesh, Nepal, Pakistan, Sri Lanka, Vietnam, China, Egypt, and Morocco for lower-skilled workers. Higher-skilled workers come mainly from (again) India, Lebanon, Egypt, Europe, and the United States.

Some migration flows change over time. While India and Pakistan accounted for 95% of the Asian workers in 1975, by 1989 the South East and East Asian countries had become the main suppliers and India and Pakistan's share had decreased to less than 25%.[114] The world food crisis stimulated new flows from Somalia and Kenya. For several of these countries (especially the ones providing lower-skilled workers), remittances constitute the largest contributor to their Gross National Product, usually larger than development aid.

---

112 More on the distinction between lower and higher educated migrant workers and on the global politics of labor migration in Guild & Mantu (2011).
113 Raj-Hashim in Heyzer (1994) P119.
114 Lycklama a Nijeholt in Heyzer (1994) P8-9.

Causes of labor migration

Three determining factors in labor migration flows are (i) the 'pull' of changing demographics and labor market needs in many industrialized countries; (ii) the 'push' of pressures from overpopulation, unemployment, poverty, and political crises in less developed countries; and (iii) established inter-country networks based on family, culture, and history, which continue to fuel established movements for many years after.[115]

The flows of laborers from South Asia and the Horn of Africa to the GCC countries[116] are immense. To a large extent, the push and pull factors of migration are the same here as elsewhere. The main cause is a large difference in welfare; due to the oil riches of the Arabs and unemployment in many developing countries, millions take their chances. Billions of people worldwide live on less than two dollars a day and with a salary in the Middle East of at least $100 a month, the supply is unlimited. Due to modern communication technologies, knowledge of the opportunities spread fast.

Many workers leave mainly for the combination of adventure, the lack of employment opportunities at home and the desire for personal growth. Another factor stimulating flows is conflict at home; Lebanese workers are a particular example. Women often migrate because of the need to support children, especially if the father cannot or will not support them. Some women escape domestic violence, an unwanted marriage, or the difficulties of being in the position of a divorced woman.[117] It is estimated that female migrants make up almost half of migrant workers in the world today.[118]

2.4 Domestic workers

Female domestic workers are – as stated in chapter 1 – live-ins who perform tasks in private households, such as cleaning, cooking, childcare, and care for the elderly, in exchange for food, lodging, and money. In earlier historical periods, there was often a life cycle of domestic work: girls who worked as domestic workers during their younger years would hire one after marriage. Upon the introduction in Western Europe of the minimum wage, domestic workers became too expensive for the average household. Furthermore, other jobs became available for women and therefore paid domestic work almost vanished from many European countries. In the 1970s, several scholars therefore predicted the demise of paid domestic work,[119] but developments during the last two decades have proved them wrong; in both the Northern and the Southern hemispheres, the number of those engaged in paid domestic work has grown rapidly.

---

115 Maruah in Kuptsch (2006) P37.
116 Gulf Cooperation Council, consisting of Kuwait, Bahrain, Qatar, Oman, Saudi Arabia and the Emirates.
117 Report 22, P19.
118 Report 22, P29.
119 Moors (2003).

In some areas, such as China and India, intra-state migration is still predominant, but domestic work in most other countries has become essentially restricted to migrant women.[120] The late 1970s marked a watershed moment for the feminization of the migrant labor force. Since then, approximately 70% of the workers leaving from Indonesia for Saudi Arabia, Malaysia, Singapore, Hong Kong, Korea, and (for a time) Taiwan, have been women seeking employment as domestic workers.[121] Whereas in the 1970s women formed about 15% of the migrant labor force, in the mid-1990s they constituted in several countries the majority of migrant workers; almost 60% in the Philippines and approximately 80% in Sri Lanka and Indonesia. By the late 1990s, there were between 1.3 and 1.5 million Asian women working in the Middle East. Now there are more than 2 million domestic workers in Saudi Arabia and the Emirates alone.

Role and position in society
An emerging phenomenon for women in conditions of rapid economic development is that the rising costs of living necessitate their employment as wage workers. With undiminished domestic responsibilities, the result is a double burden of work and tasks at home. Due to cultural and societal configurations that prohibit both men and women from combining work life and family life without undue stress, distortions in economic and social life have occurred to enable women to cope with their double burden. One such distortion is the transfer of the domestic tasks to other women, often women from the Southern hemisphere.[122]

In countries of destination, domestic workers are often referred to as necessary but undesirable aliens. Domestic work is considered unskilled work. It is menial, has low prestige and is therefore usually performed by women from poor countries.[123] Despite this dismissive mischaracterization, domestic work is socially vital work requiring diverse skills.[124] Because of their nationality, gender, race, and economic status, in many societies these migrant domestic workers form the bottom stratum of the social hierarchy, which makes them vulnerable to discrimination. Because their workplace is the protected private sphere of the household, they are vulnerable to abuse. Their situation has been referred to as modern-day slavery[125] in those situations where they face unlimited work hours, employment in multiple households, forced confinement, verbal abuse, and other forms of maltreatment by employers.

---

120 Mourkabel (2009) P93.
121 Anggraeni (2006) P xi.
122 Lycklama a Nijeholt in Heyzer (1994) P37.
123 Alcid in Heyzer (1994) P169.
124 Lycklama a Nijeholt in Heyzer (1994) P32.
125 See for instance on internet in August 2010: http://gvnet.com/humantrafficking/UnitedArabEmirates.htm, http://socyberty.com/issues/modern-day-slavery-in-the-middle-east/ and http://www.migrant-rights. org/2010/03/02/modern-day-slavery-in-the-uae-unpaid-filipino-maid-beaten-and-starved-for-years/.

Initial entry into an alien society with no knowledge of the language or culture and no kinship support is an isolating experience in itself. Other factors such as lack of skills, low education levels, inexperience, and the lack of fallback positions (in their own national economy), combine to lower the (bargaining) position of domestic workers. These women's power to negotiate for better conditions is also limited by their youth: domestic workers have an average age between 15 and 30 years. Because they are not qualified for anything other than low-paying household jobs, they are vulnerable to employment pressures in an employers' market. Even 'veteran' domestic workers who migrate for a second time find that their occupational immobility makes their labor easy to exploit.[126]

In several countries of origin, such as Egypt, the existence of female migrant domestic workers is largely denied, because it is deemed shameful that the country's women must serve other men. In other countries, such as the Philippines, they have been dubbed 'modern day heroes' probably in an attempt to enlarge their numbers. Partly owing to its peculiar nature, this type of work has been the subject of many controversies, debates, academic analyses, and policy formulations. Yet the abuse of migrant domestic workers has continued over the years.[127]

Maid trade

Already in the nineteen eighties, the international labor migration of domestic workers had become big business, involving millions of women, billions of dollars, a large number of labor-sending and recruiting countries, and a multiplicity of agencies and intermediaries, such as recruitment agencies, banks, airlines, medical clinics, insurance companies, currency dealers, remittance services, and couriers.[128] It is for this reason that scholars and international organizations refer to the 'trade' in domestic workers, for there is indeed a full-blown economic reality benefitting families, businesses, and entire countries.[129] The magnitude of the maid trade is difficult to gauge accurately. Many official statistics underreport the actual number of workers involved, especially for illegal migrants.

Legal protection

As stated, domestic work is frequently perceived as non-productive work that requires little skill and is provided outside any form of company. Referring hereto, many of these workers are not protected by national legislation or the relevant legal institutions of receiving countries.[130]

---

126 Hossein in Heyzer (1994) P200-202.
127 Santos (2005) P4.
128 Heyzer (1994) P vi.
129 Lycklama a Nijeholt in Heyzer (1994) P32.
130 Santos (2005) P4. See chapter 7 for the lack of labor protection in Saudi Arabia and the Emirates.

The fact that domestic work is often transient, overseas employment involving temporary residency enhances the employer's power over the domestic worker, and makes it difficult or impossible for her to claim her rights. Often, only extreme cases of oppression, violence, and sexual harassment compel workers to resort to action against their employers. They are more dependent upon the employers' compassion than on the principles of justice.[131]

Given the increasing number of female migrant domestic workers seeking work over the past ten to fifteen years, and the growing incidence of exploitation and abuse many of them face, the International Labour Organization (ILO) decided in 1989 to focus on the plight of these women by undertaking research studies to understand the conditions under which they are employed. The studies also considered the legal position of domestic workers, and the extent to which they were covered and protected by national laws and regulations. The outcome of the studies would determine the actions required to protect migrant domestic workers at the national or international level, either through the adoption of appropriate rules of conduct, future international labor standards or other appropriate measures.

All of the studies[132] revealed the often harsh conditions under which foreign female domestic workers are employed. It is clear that they are a particularly vulnerable group of migrants who face difficulties and hardships unknown to industrial or service workers, who are protected by specific standards. As many countries do not consider domestic workers to be workers, and as the ILO has never been clear on the definition of workers, the ILO instruments are currently often not applied to them. Therefore the suggestion was made to improve their position through the establishment of a convention for the protection of foreign female domestic workers specifically. The Governing Body has proposed to work at the 2010 International Labour Conference on standards for domestic workers through a convention and an accompanying recommendation,[133] which resulted on the 16th of June 2011 in the adoption of the Convention on Domestic Workers.[134]

Domestic workers in Saudi Arabia and the Emirates
Like migrants to the Gulf in general, domestic workers migrate to Saudi Arabia and the Emirates in large numbers only since the 1970s.[135] On average, there is one domestic worker for each household in Saudi Arabia. The United Arab Emirates report a higher rate of at least one domestic worker for every citizen.[136]

---

131 Hossein in Heyzer (1994) P200-202.
132 Reports 1, 5, 6, 7, 22, and especially 24.
133 http://www.ilo.org/actrav/areas/lang-en/WCMS_DOC_ATR_ARE_DOM_EN/index.htm January 2011.
134 Thus far, no country has ratified the convention. September 2011.
135 Silvey (2006) P23.
136 Strobl (2009) P167 reports one to two. Others estimate this to be one domestic worker per citizen.

Of the estimated seven million foreign workers in Saudi Arabia, between 1.4 and 2 million are domestic workers.[137] The estimates for the Emirates range between two and five hundred thousand.[138] Embassies from labor-sending countries in both Saudi Arabia and the Emirates report that abuses against domestic workers account for the vast majority of the complaints they receive.[139] The women concerned come mainly from the Philippines, Indonesia, Nepal, India, Somalia, Ethiopia, and Morocco. Asian women are considered better than African domestic workers; they are reported to be relatively cheap, malleable, and willing to perform tasks deemed unattractive and menial by local women.[140]

The number of runaways is not small. All visited embassies report multiple requests for help on a daily basis. Most safe houses are overly full. For instance, the Jeddah deportation center houses 8,000 people in a facility designed for 5,500.[141] Tens of thousands of workers run away each year because of serious breaches of their rights, but most Emiratis and Saudis insist that the large majority of domestic workers is perfectly happy. There are runaways, they say, but these women mostly want to work on the black market because of the higher salaries paid there, or they – for no good reason – just changed their minds and wanted to go home. The reality is it hard to determine exactly how many runaways there are, who they are or why they run away. Only a combination of multiple research methods at many different locations can offer somewhat trustworthy results. Such research will remain difficult, however, because many domestic workers can be labeled trafficking victims (see chapter 7). One of the main reasons for the difficulties in research on trafficking is that this concerns 'hidden populations'. In the case of domestic workers they are not hidden because of the clandestine nature of their work as with prostitution, but because the workers remain within the privacy of family households where the state is reluctant to intervene.[142] Furthermore, the runaways do not really have a place to go in case of conflicts (see chapter 8), and are therefore difficult to research even after leaving the privacy of the household.

---

137 The deputy Minister of Labor stated 1.4, the Saudi Gazette April 15 2006 stated 2. Interviewees from the ILO presumed a number close to 2M.
138 Ali (2010) P95 estimates 450.000, which seems to be a relatively reliable estimate.
139 Report 18, P2.
140 Dias in Heyzer (1994) P135.
141 Report 18, P104.
142 Jureidini (2010) P155.

3. Theory

This chapter first provides a short overview of theories on domestic workers. Enlightening as all these studies on domestic workers may be, they offered no clear hypotheses on the question as to which factors influence the conflicts involving domestic workers particularly in Saudi Arabia or the Emirates. Although a number of studies have described why domestic workers worldwide have a less comfortable position in society, they seem to hold no explanation for international differences. Furthermore, they fail to explain issues which arrived from the data as gathered through a socio-legal perspective, with a focus on norms and conflicts. Therefore, several theories, most of which at first sight have little to do with domestic workers, have been used to analyze the data with a focus on the question to what extent they do or do not apply in Saudi Arabia and the Emirates. Section 3.2 first discusses the question to what extent it is appropriate to apply a Eurocentric perspective to the analysis of phenomena in the Middle East. Section 3.3 thereupon provides an overview of the theories as they have been used to analyze the data in this research.

3.1 Literature on domestic workers

Domestic work is a topic that has received scholarly attention mainly from economists, sociologists, anthropologists, and demographers.[143] The number of researchers focusing on this topic is on the rise[144] and the last two decades have witnessed an impressive growth in the academic literature relating to women, human rights and development, economic migration, trade, migration & globalization, transnationalism, immigration and racism, and the politics of caregiving. Socio-legal analyses of the status of migrant domestic workers are less common. Although human rights issues or conflicts inevitably arise in many of these works, the literature has thus far focused little on the factors that influence conflicts in specific countries. The review of the literature shows that the studies on domestic work can broadly be subdivided as follows:

Macro economics
The economics-based push-pull theory views migration as the outcome of poverty and the lack of employment opportunities in the countries of origin, which drive people to seek better opportunities in the destination countries. Hence, the push factors include economic, social, and political hardships in the poorest parts of the world. Pull factors are the comparative advantages in the more advanced nations – the promise of better living conditions, which lures prospective migrants.

---

143 Santos (2005) P9.
144 Moors (2003).

Macro socio-economic studies on the impact of the migration of domestic workers to their countries of origin and destination have been conducted by Prakash (1998), Chang (2000), Zachariah (2002), and Chammartin and Esim (2004). Anderson (2000), Anthias (2000), and Lutz (2008) focus on the macro economy of the countries of destination, where domestic help is often in demand to replace or supplement the help previously managed by the extended family and not provided by the state.

Micro socio-economics
Micro socio-economic studies on domestic workers focus on their backgrounds and the processes of emigration, re-migration, and the attached flows of remittances. Economic push and pull factors are similar for large groups of women, but nevertheless some migrate and others do not. An important theory explaining this aspect of the microeconomics of domestic work is the new household economics approach, or the new economics of migration theory. This theory suggests that migration decisions are not made by isolated individual actors, but by larger units of related people (typically families or households) in which people act collectively not only to maximize expected income but also to minimize risk. It is often the most adventurous who migrate, and for many such women the search for personal freedom and the accompanying rejection of traditional gender roles are as important as economic reasons. Momson (1999), Gamburd (2000), and Hochschild (2000) describe how domestic workers migrate to help their family financially, but also to evade physical abuse or unfaithful husbands. Others have studied the use of, and power over, remittances (Brochmann 1993).

Labor conditions and human rights
The hidden place of domestic workers within the privacy of the household, opens the door for exploitation and abuse, according to Anderson (2000) and Jureidini and Moukarbel (2004). Their occupation places these women in informal work situations with little access to networks and social support, leaving them increasingly vulnerable to discrimination and abuse. This abuse cannot be controlled, as the lack of formal regulations within many host countries allows basic human rights infringements to go unsanctioned. These labor conditions have been studied in Lebanon by Jureidini (2002), in Bahrain by Najjar (2002) and Najjar in Esim (2004), in the United Arab Emirates by Sabban (2002), and more generally in the Middle East by Esim & Smith (2004). Infringements on human rights have also been studied by Human Rights Watch.[145] In addition, a worldwide comparison of labor conditions and legal protections has been coordinated by the International Labour Organization.[146]

---

145 Report 8, Report 9 and Report 18.
146 Report 22.

Labor flows, trade & trafficking

Hochschild (2000) documented that Latina and Caribbean women work in the global care chain as domestic workers in the United States and Canada. Similar labor flows have also been studied by Hondagneu-Sotelo (2001), Romero (1992), Anderson (2000), and Bakan & Stasiulis (1997). Indonesians in other Asian nations and the Middle East have likewise been studied by Constable (1997) and Silvey (2006). Sri Lankans in Greece and the Middle East have been studied by Gamburd (2000) and Abu-Habib (1998) and Filipina women in more than 100 countries around the world have been studied by Parreñas (2001) who found that the work of caring for families in the North is performed mainly by women from the South. The maid trade, as described by Heyzer (1994), Mattar (2003), and Calandruccio (2005) has resulted in an international division of reproductive labor. It is also worth noting that the agents bringing domestic workers from their countries of origin to the countries of destination receive considerable fees, which regularly leads to practices that can be qualified as trafficking (Jureidini 2010).

Gendered and affective dimensions

Gendered and affective dimensions of domestic work have been studied by Rollins (1985), Parreñas (2001), and Moukarbel (2009). Gender is a term that refers to socially constructed differences between the sexes and to the social relationships between women and men. Gender-ascribed or gender-appropriate roles are different for men and women. Men typically have productive roles, while women's roles are of a reproductive[147] and domestic nature. Domestic work is regularly disqualified as real work and has been referred to as a labor of love by Romero (1992). According to Anderson (2000) domestic work is work at home and therefore not like any other job. Employers, according to Carling (2005) and Rollins (1985), are seeking the soft and personal qualities of affectionate care. The expectations that families have of the wife and mother are now placed onto the domestic worker but without the potential emotional rewards and the reciprocities involved in family structures, as reported by Anthias (2000). According to Hochschild (2000), working women delegate household responsibilities to other women employed as caretakers because they still have to deal with household chores. If a larger percentage of men participated more equally in chores and childcare, women would not need to resort to other lower class women from the global chain of care. Chang's (2000) overview provides a gendered analysis of how government policies regulate the lives of women in the increasingly global market.

---

147 Reproducing the productive labor force.

Transnationalism & identity

The reproduction of identity notions and belonging is inherent in migratory processes and the migratory experience. Home and destination are re-imagined in a
continuous process and thus changed, as noted by Gardner (1995). Migrants are
forced to question their preconceptions and rebuild their identities in an attempt
to adjust to their new situation (Buijs 1993). Live-in domestic workers often have
a harder time holding on to their cultural identities than other migrants.
Nevertheless, the migratory experience can also be very empowering: it can enhance women's authority and independence within their families and positively
affect gender roles (Brettell 2000 & Tacoli 1999). It can, however, also lead to
frustration and loss of self-esteem on the part of their husbands (Gamburd 2000).
Additional issues also arise from situations of transnational motherhood in which
female domestic workers migrate to take care of the children of others, thereby
creating a two-sided system of substitute mothering where their own children are
raised by others as well (Momsen 1999 and Hochschild 2000).

Class & status

Domestic workers are not hired solely to perform chores and to alleviate the double burden of working women. They are also hired to provide luxury and as status
symbols (Regt 2008, 2009). Hierarchies from the country of origin are often re-
created in the country of destination (Pattendath 2008), or as Romero (1992) explains, the relation between domestic worker and employer is a replication of the
contradiction between capitalists and proletarians. As the result of the above-men-
tioned empowerment, however, while the domestic worker might lose social status in the country of destination, she often simultaneously gains social status in
her country of origin (Anthias 2000; see more in Barber 2000, Ozyegin 2001,
and Moors 2003).

Citizenship

Another field of studies on paid domestic work has theorized citizenship status as
a new marker of inequality (Colen 1990, Bakan & Stasiulis 1995, Constable 1997,
Anderson 2000, Chang 2000, Parreñas 2001, and Lindio-McGovern 2003), connected to the national, class, and racial politics organizing domestic work
(Hondagneu-Sotelo 2001). The peculiarities of paid domestic work in the new global apartheid (Richmond 1994) lead to dependencies for domestic workers because of limited citizenship, which is related to the lack of sufficient legislative
protections to stand up against exploitative working conditions.

As stated above, all this work was interesting and insightful, but offered no clear
hypothesis on the question which factors influence conflicts between the domestic worker and the employer specifically in Saudi Arabia and the Emirates.

Therefore, several other theories have been used (as well) to analyze the data in this research, some of which make a comparison between the two countries concerned and Europe.

3.2 A Eurocentric perspective

Comparing the current situation in Saudi Arabia and the Emirates to issues in Europe's present or past is problematic in light of postcolonial theory, postmodernism and legal culturalism. Postcolonial theory concerns a (often Marxist) literary theory, mainly from Said, Spivak and Bhabha, that focuses on the legacy of colonialism and the question of how knowledge about the world is generated under specific relations between the (ex)colonizers and the (ex)colonized.[148] Comparing current normative patterns in the Middle East with such patterns in Europe's history is problematic in light of this theory. It suggests that the Middle East is behind in development compared to Europe, which would establish the supremacy of the latter over the former.[149] Instead, postcolonial theorists state that one should recognize the uniqueness of each culture's development. In this way, postcolonial theory resembles postmodernism, which states that there is no objective basis for knowledge (or at least not a knowable one). From this perspective, theories are merely human constructs that are never value-free and therefore postmodernism emphasizes diversity and relativism. The legal version of this development is legal culturalism, of which Pierre Legrand is the most important proponent. He states that legal systems cannot be analyzed outside of their historical and cultural context, and therefore comparisons in law are only possible by searching for differences.[150]

In the context of this study, one could assert that the economic, environmental, religious, and social changes that have taken place in Europe in the past are so different from the ones that currently take place on the Arabian Peninsula,[151] that similarities are suspect. Nonetheless, cross-cultural comparisons provide the advantage of fresh, outside perspectives from a participant-observer analytic scheme. Even so, the most important reason why such comparative research is particularly useful may be a mathematical one. Similarities can be defended because despite the differences in history and development, there is one paramount similarity in societal changes that can (partly) explain the similarities in normative patterns: the number of people with whom an average person interacts rises rapidly in the Middle East in the same way it has increased in Europe. It might be this number that primarily explains the similarities in changes in legal systems.

---

148 More on this subject in, among others, Ashcroft (1998) & Krishna (2009).
149 Visible also in the work of legal anthropologists, such as Hoebel's "evolution" in *The Law of Primitive Man*; see Gluckman in Nader (1969) P349.
150 Hesselink (2004) Chapter 2.
151 For instance, European handicraft guilds did not exist on the Arabian Peninsula, which moved from herding to oil industry.

Estimates of human group sizes from a variety of ethnographic and sociological sources suggest that there is a characteristic group size of about 125-200 that reappears with surprising frequency in a wide range of human societies. These organizations (such as villages in both horticultural societies and hunter-gatherer groups, the number of acquaintances a person has, and the basic military unit in most modern armies) all share one crucial characteristic: they consist of a set of individuals who know one another intimately because they interact on a regular basis.[152] In such groups, therefore, the status model and its enforcement are effective. This system can function in larger villages as well. Anthropologists have shown that towns regularly operate as conglomerates of small communities. For conflicts between persons of different sub-communities, judges, arbiters, or imams are appointed.

As an economy develops and traders arrive, the number of people with whom one interacts increases, but at first only for the traders themselves. The patriarchal system can continue to exist within the family, whereas the traders need other forms of protection in the form of, for instance, embassies; consuls deal with conflicts within their own communities and between their own and the host community. In these instances, group membership offers protection. In highly specialized economies, however, the number of people with whom one interacts becomes so large that even this group system may no longer function. Therefore, depersonalized objective norms that apply equally to everyone become necessary. Norms must be clear and guaranteed for every individual to allow rational decisions to be made.[153] In this way, a large economy can function properly. However, if no collective comes into existence to protect the position of individuals, individuals must pay high transaction costs to establish other forms of security or to create wider networks of protection through tribes or cronyism. In both Saudi Arabia and the Emirates, governments are in the process of creating a top-down, rights-based, depersonalized system. However, in society, this is obstructed by those who benefit from the current system. This leaves the bottom stratum of society, to which domestic workers belong, unprotected due to an absent or poorly functioning enforcement mechanism (more hereon in chapter 9).

This dissertation thus explicates a number of factors that influence conflicts involving domestic workers, often comparing the data to issues in the West and regularly with reference to theories developed in the West. Justification is provided by the fact that in both Europe and the Middle East, the average number of individuals with whom one interacts is on the rise, making adjustments to the normative system necessary. One could say that the rising number of individuals with whom one interacts causes communities to grow in size. Therefore, as entities, once they develop into a certain size, such communities need distribution, communication, and correction systems that smaller units do not need.

---

152 Dunbar in De Waal (2001) P181.
153 Max Weber.

In this light, the societies of Saudi Arabia and the Emirates can be viewed as communities that have grown extraordinarily rapidly and that are currently in need of, but lacking, certain socio-legal infrastructures that are typically developed amongst human systems of this size.[154]

3.3 Theoretical framework for this dissertation

This section provides the theoretical framework as used for the analysis of the three parts of this dissertation. The norms that parties refer to, as set out in part two, are analyzed through the concept of legal pluralism. The conflict resolution mechanisms, as set out in part three, are analyzed through the concepts of citizenship and access to law. The power (im)balance between the domestic worker and the employer, and the dynamics in the house, as set out in part four, are analyzed through the concept of slavery and monopsony versus the free labor market, and the concepts of otherness and expulsion.

3.3.1 Legal pluralism and four types of norms

The second part of this dissertation (chapters 4 to 7) describes and analyzes the norms to which domestic workers and their employers (may) refer in conflicts. The main framework of analysis for this part of the book is the concept of legal pluralism. Legal pluralism is generally defined as a situation in which two or more legal systems coexist in one social field. It is the existence of more than one legal order, based on different sources of ultimate validity and maintained by several forms of organizations in one social location, including (but not limited to) the state.[155] Such legal orders include the systems of courts and judges supported by the central government as well as non-governmental forms of normative ordering.[156] The different legal systems are not sharply defined but are interconnected and even mutually constitutive. Domestic workers in Saudi Arabia and the Emirates, as will be described in the following four chapters, work in such a state of legal pluralism. There are customary, contractual, religious, and formal legal norms applicable to them that can be (although they not necessarily are) enforced by social pressure and local, religious, or governmental authorities.

---

154 To an interviewee from the Shura, the advisory Parliament of Saudi Arabia, this hypothesis was presented as follows: "the societies of Saudi Arabia and the Emirates can be viewed as bodies which have grown the size of an adult, without the proper development of veins or bones." He found this an extremely accurate description of his country. For more on this type of theories, see Gommer (2011).
155 Benda-Beckmann (2001) P48.
156 Merry (1988) P870.

Legal pluralism scholars state that in such instances, social actors sustain their claims by use of arguments from the different coexisting legal systems – from religious, customary, contractual or formal legal norms. Legal concepts are part of a distinctive way of imagining, understanding or subdividing reality.[157] Legal concepts categorize, but because each category is connected through a norm to prescribed consequences, categorization is by no means a neutral activity. Whoever has the power to categorize can maneuver strategically to achieve desired consequences. Individuals who are more powerful can better profit from legal pluralism; a larger maneuvering space, or a larger reservoir of normative tools, allows them to enforce a larger range of by-them-preferred outcomes. Based on an analysis of disputes in a legally plural arena in Indonesia, Benda-Beckmann proposed a model of 'forum shopping' that provides a way of understanding how local dispute processes reshape legally plural situations. Disputants shop for forums for their problems and forums compete for disputes, which they use for their own local political ends.[158] External conflict resolution mechanisms are used very rarely in Saudi Arabia and the Emirates by either employers or domestic workers (as will be discussed in chapter 8). Forum shopping in this dissertation thus refers only to social actors maneuvering by referring in their arguments to different sets of norms, or to contradictory norms within one set, through the use of legal concepts.

Interviews with domestic workers and employers show that they often categorize a certain behavior or a certain situation to support their argument that a particular desired legal consequence is appropriate. Chapter 4 describes norms derived from Sharia that can be used in such manner. In general these religious norms do not lead to certain specific types of conflicts; they do not result in type one conflicts as discussed in chapter 1. The same applies to chapter 5 that describes customary norms; these norms are used for strategic maneuvering in existing conflicts (type two or three). Yet preliminary disagreement on customary norms also seems to cause (type one) conflicts. Chapter 6 describes contractual norms that primarily lead to type one conflicts; conflicts that start due to a preliminary disagreement on contractual norms. Chapter 7 describes formal legal norms, both national and international. The national norms generally provide normative tools for the employer, while the international norms generally provide tools for the domestic worker. These international norms largely have their origin in the West, where strong labor protection has come into existence. This chapter therefore analyses why this has occurred in the West and why not in Saudi Arabia and the Emirates.

---

157 Geertz (1973).
158 Merry (1988) P882.

Sharia as normative tools

When maneuvering, normative arguments are used as tools. This is clearly visible in chapter 4 on Sharia norms. According to certain historians, Sharia has been deduced from the Quran and narrations on the example of the Prophet Mohammed. These sources have been elaborated on, analyzed, interpreted, and added to throughout the centuries. The jurisprudence and resulting doctrine do not constitute a coherent set of rules, but a collection of moral principles, rituals, legal rulings, exegeses, and legal opinions,[159] that create considerable maneuvering space for Muslim judges and arbiters to settle conflicts in a matter deemed most suitable to the circumstances. From this perspective, Sharia forms a particular discourse referring to history and religion, which is used in negotiating discussions in a changing society. Islamic law is not only a legal system, but also a very strong discourse used in power struggles at all levels of society; it is a set of normative tools that may be used in conflicts within one family but also to either justify or attack entire regimes.[160] This view of Islamic law emphasizes that culture is hybrid and porous, and that the pervasive struggles over cultural values within local communities are competitions over power.[161] Chapter 4 discusses aspects of Sharia that can be used as normative tools by either domestic workers or their employers, in conflicts between them. It shows that Sharia is a resource in the power struggle between the two, which will do either good or harm to the domestic worker, depending on the situation at hand and the person with the power to choose which normative tool will be applied.

Customary norms in anomie

The plurality of norms and the strategic maneuvering are also clearly visible in the use of customary norms. Added for analysis to the concept of legal pluralism, is the theory of anomie, as introduced by Durkheim. This refers to a situation in which social or moral norms are confused, unclear, or simply absent due to rapid economic changes.[162] When this theory is placed within the theory of legal pluralism, the result is that according to Durkheim, legal pluralism and the possibilities for strategic maneuvering enlarge when a society's economy rapidly transforms. It is thus not only the multi-layered society of local, national, and international authorities that create legal pluralism; in light of the fact that law is living, is changing over time, legal pluralism is also caused by rapid societal changes.

Both in Saudi Arabia and in the Emirates, the economic changes of the last decades are not just significant, but unprecedented. The standard of living has increased massively in just a few decades, due to the discovery of oil and the rising prices per barrel.

---

159 See among others Zubaida (2003) P41.
160 Zubaida (2003) Introduction.
161 Compare Merry (2006) P9.
162 Durkheim (1897).

Pictures of Sheikh Zayed Road in Dubai tell it all. While in 1972 the dusty road was bordered by small mud houses, a mere thirty five years later the same spot has changed into a ten-lane highway, surrounded by skyscrapers. Durkheim argued that rapid economic changes, and the anomie that they cause, lead to a higher occurrence of suicide. Levels of suicide in Saudi Arabia are indeed high. A survey of students in Jeddah revealed that 65% of boys and 72% of girls showed symptoms of depression, and 7% of girls admitted that they had attempted suicide, twice the rate of the boys.[163]

Anomie can be detected in many aspects of society in both Saudi Arabia and the Emirates. Sachs phrases it as follows: "The transition to modern economic growth involves urbanization, changing gender roles, increasing social mobility, changing family structures, and increasing specialization. These are difficult transitions, involving multiple upheavals in social organization and in cultural beliefs."[164] In this respect, the current Gulf countries resemble Yugoslavia in transition, as described by Vera Erlich. Yugoslavia was at that time "simultaneously traditional and modern, backward and progressive, both to an extreme extent."[165] Under the patriarchal system, "rights and obligations had been clear and respected; there was consideration towards the weaker and violence was abhorred. But in the stage of decay of the system, relations became insecure, hence everyone fought for more rights."[166] As in Yugoslavia, in both Saudi Arabia and the Emirates extended families break up. Talented younger brothers no longer automatically accept the authority of older brothers, divorce spreads and domestic violence seems to increase.[167] This same conflict over norms seems to affect the domestic workers; different behavioral patterns can be recognized between and even within one family.

To show such, chapter 5 on customary norms extensively refers to the work of Rollins, who has summarized research on domestic workers mainly in Europe, throughout several centuries. She recognizes three stages which, from a sociolegal perspective, seem to indicate that in Europe, the labor relation involving domestic workers has changed from a patriarchal status model into a contractual model – a transition that according to the data in this research is currently taking place in Saudi Arabia and the Emirates as well.

Patriarchal status model
The first phase that Rollins deducts from the corpus of research on the history of domestic workers in Europe, is what will henceforth be referred to as the patriarchal status model. This model concerns the position of domestic workers in Europe before the changes caused by the industrial revolution:

---

163 Prokop in Aarts (2005) P73.
164 Sachs (2005) P38.
165 Erlich (1966) P5.
166 Erlich (1966) P91.
167 Reports of domestic violence increase, but it is unclear if this solely reflects more openness and a readiness to report or if the actual occurrence of domestic violence increases. Most interviewees thought the latter.

She (the domestic worker) was considered a part of the patriarchal household, expected to give the same loyalty and obedience and to receive the
same protection and guidance as would a family member, particularly a
child. This view of household relations was in the tradition of the Roman
patria potestas; the male had ultimate power over, and responsibility for all
the people in the house: wife, children, and servants.[168]

This is what Henry Sumner Maine[169] describes as the status model in an economy
described by Marx as kin-ordered production.[170] The reproductive tasks[171] that the
domestic worker has to perform are defined by the position she has obtained as part
of the family. They are therefore also referred to as relational rights, as this term indicates how the claims an individual can make are tied up with her position in society[172] or kinship. Kinship is a concept which does not (necessarily) involve biological
ties; it is a social construct.[173] Just as one can become part of the family by marriage,
so can one by agreeing to become a domestic worker. As soon as one has become
part of a family, the relationships are not defined by rights and duties, but by the patriarchal hierarchy in which every family member has a certain role to play. Just as
parents are supposed to do their best in raising a child regardless of the child's character or behavior, the domestic worker is supposed to do her best in fulfilling her
specific tasks regardless of the way she is treated by the master.

The denoting of the domestic worker as part of the family does not imply a position in the family hierarchy equal to, for instance, a daughter (as Patterson writes
concerning both servants and slaves).[174] Furthermore, at the top of the hierarchy,
the patriarch does not accept any higher authority:

The master wields his power with restraint, at his discretion and, above all,
unencumbered by rules, insofar as it is not limited by tradition or competing powers.[175] (...) Lest the reader romanticize paternalism, it should be
kept in mind that the master "wielding his power in restraint" could, and
often did entail brutality and degradation as well as protection. Punishment
for laxness, a transgression of deference, or insubordination was often
physical.[176]

---

168 Rollins (1985) P27.
169 Maine (1913) section 2.
170 Wolf (1990) chapter 3.
171 The term 'reproductive tasks' refers to everything that needs to be done to sustain and reproduce the so-called
'productive work force', such as having baby's (reproduction) and the preparation of meals. Working women, who
are still expected to perform these tasks, transfer part of these tasks to domestic workers.
172 Oomen (2005) P203.
173 Sally Falk Moore in Nader (1969) P374.
174 Patterson (1982) P62-64.
175 Rollins quoting Weber.
176 Compare Johnson (1997) P185 on physical violence of the patriarch: "often including the right to abuse, kill,
trade, lend, sell or otherwise dispose of children or wives."

Being a member of the family leads to a higher level of guidance, protection, or (as others would call it) interference. The employer was responsible for their morality, for their religious direction, for their total material welfare. In return servants were expected to give all of their time to their master, to relinquish all thought of having private lives. The traditional paternalistic relation between master and servant was, then, both consuming and protective of the servant, far more than the contractual arrangement that was its legal basis.[177]

Last but not least, because the status-based position does not concern interdependent rights and duties but rather proper roles one has to play, payments are not considered to be wages, but something like pocket money.[178]

Industrialization phase
The second phase in the labor relation of domestic workers, according to Rollins, took shape during the industrialization phase:

> Most nineteenth-century servants had excessive work demands placed on them, as middle-income families strove to meet the standards of the gentility (...). The degree of tension between employer and servant heightened for other reasons. A fundamental one was the newness of the majority of people in both groups to their positions; the men and women of the new middle class had not dealt with servants before, and the young people from rural areas had no training, nor models for appropriate servant behavior.[179]

In the patriarchal relation there is a hierarchical distance between employer and domestic worker that resembles the distance between a parent and a child, but this distance is larger in the industrialization stage: "Though most servants were of the same ethnicity and religion as their employers, distance between the two increased as the members of the new middle class strove to separate themselves from their domestics by drawing rigid class lines. Employers of the new middle class used their domestics to help define their new class identity."[180]

Sometimes, the hierarchical distance created between employer and employee was more extreme. With reference to their low morals, inadequate performance and lack of proper subservience, sometimes they were considered to be less than human.[181] This phenomenon of dehumanization is described[182] as the labeling of others as worthless, as a fundamental threat to cherished values and beliefs, as disposable, or as animals. These 'others' are thought not to possess the same feelings, thoughts, values, and purposes in life that we do.

---

177 Rollins (1985) P28.
178 Rollins (1985) P27. Compare to Chang (2008) P9 on domestic workers in Korea receiving pocket money.
179 Rollins (1985) P34-35.
180 Rollins (1985) P35 and Anderson (2000).
181 Rollins (1985).
182 Zimbardo (2008) P11, 222, 307 and 352.

The aim of this psychological process is for the domestic workers to lose their human status in the eyes of their employers, allowing these employers to suspend the morality that might typically govern reasoned actions toward others. Thus, dehumanization allows a person to have high moral standards and to behave evilly without cognitive dissonance occurring.[183]

Contractual model

The third phase in the development of the labor relation involving the domestic worker in Europe as described by Rollins is the contractual model. In this model, the employer and the domestic worker are (said to be) bound by what is stated in the contract, based on the fact that they have declared in freedom and knowledge that they want to be bound by it. Their respective rights and duties are interrelated, in the sense that the non-adherence of one party to its duties will cause that party to lose its rights. The labor relation is depersonalized; as long as rights and duties are all fulfilled, the personality and behavior outside the workplace are not important.

An example of this is a labor relationship involving domestic workers hired through a company. The employer considers the company, rather than the worker, to be the one with whom he has a contract. The worker is an anonymous creature who provides an anonymous service on behalf of someone else. The employer will not engage at all with the personality of the worker or with her behavior outside working hours. The worker is fully replaceable, which grants the domestic worker freedom but not protection, guidance, or care. This type can be found today in the United States, where large companies like Merry Maids supply clean houses, instead of workers. It is the service, not the person, that is being hired.

Addition to Rollins' model

As chapter 5 will show, some domestic workers adhere to the status-based position – or in the terminology of legal pluralism, they refer to the normative model of status based patriarchy to support their claims – whereas others prefer or use the contractual relation, but none of them would choose the relation of the industrialization phase. This type seems to be commonly acted out by employers in both countries, but is not referred to in their discourse. One of the aspects of this type of labor relation is a larger distance between employer and domestic worker, which sometimes intensifies to humiliation or even dehumanization. This dehumanization is regularly explained by the upward mobility of the employer; for a *nouveau riche* employer, his superiority is not self-evident and needs to be reasserted regularly.[184]

---

183 Fisk (2005) P680 contains an impressive list of examples of dehumanization.
184 Rollins (1985) P35 and 104.

Without denying the validity of this theory, the fact that the characteristics of the industrialization phase are acted out but never referred to as normative model, suggests that this dehumanization is contrary to the norms of both the employee and employer, and is only possible because there is a lack of enforcement of norms. The data from this research thus suggest that the behavior during the industrialization phase (as Rollins describes it) is not a type or model in itself, but a transition phase with shortcomings that lead to the possibility of dehumanization. When considering the ways in which rules or norms are (supposed to be) enforced in the status model and in the contractual model, what appears to have taken place in Europe and what is now taking place on the Arabian Peninsula, is a switch in enforcement from bottom to top. In the patriarchal society, the rules are formulated as proper roles one has to play. One plays the role of a good father, an eldest brother, or a servant. If someone in the system does not play his or her role correctly, enforcement takes place in the form of social pressure or punishment from someone higher but close in hierarchy. A father can punish his son for hitting a sister, or the women in a family might (more or less subtly) force the father to punish the son, or they can punish him themselves through disapproval.

There are two prerequisites for protection within this system. First, there has to be a person with some form of power, who has a reason (an incentive, a need, social pressure or expectations) to protect the specific individual. Second, such a person needs to know about the abuse or maltreatment. In smaller societies, this system can work well for a domestic worker; in a village where the daughters of farmers work in the house of a landowner, the master will think twice about abusing the domestic workers, because everyone in the village will be able to see her bruises at the market. The parents of the girl will complain and the church leader or imam will discuss it with the master. Shame is an important method in this type of enforcement of norms.

In the contractual system, enforcement is organized from the top, using a legal system with judges or arbiters who apply depersonalized rules or models of dispute settlement more or less equally to everyone. This is what is referred to as the rule of law: legal rules or models are to be applied to all. If rights are violated, a person can (ideally) demand protection in the form of enforcement of the rules. Whereas the enforcer in the patriarchal system knows the persons involved, the enforcer in the contractual system typically does not know either party. This theoretically guarantees the objective application of the depersonalized rules.[185]

Yet in the intermediate, industrial phase, problems occur and this could be caused by the fact that enforcement from the bottom diminishes, whereas enforcement from the top is not yet in place.

---

[185] This is the point where many Western legal scholars will start to speak of law, following Aristotle who said that appealing to a Judge is the same as appealing to law: *Ethica Nicomachea*, v. 5.

Both in Saudi Arabia and in the Emirates, the size of the average household has reduced, decreasing the amount of people who can keep an eye on each other. In Saudi Arabia, half the village used to be involved in each other's lives, as elder interviewees explained. Because this is no longer the case, the power of the patriarchal head of the family has actually enlarged considerably; he is no longer corrected by anyone. Furthermore, families have moved from tents or small houses to large houses with walls around them. The economy has made it possible for men to keep their wives at home, so abuse is now possible without neighbors knowing about it. This affects both weaker family members (mainly women and children), and domestic workers. Anyone with bruises can be kept inside until they heal.

For a domestic worker, an additional problem is the fact that her in-group does not live around the corner anymore. For instance, as two Indian interviewees explained: Indians who moved from their villages to a city would hire domestic workers from their village. Thereafter, some Indian families moved on to Dubai, continuing to hire women from their grandparents' village. Nowadays there usually is no connection between the employing family in for instance the Saudi town of Buraydah and the labor-sending family in Mindanao, Philippines. An abused domestic worker can be sent home to Ethiopia, upon which a new one can be ordered from Indonesia. If an abusive employer does not have to feel any shame from now unwitting neighbors, nor towards the distant family of the domestic worker, the patriarchal system has lost the power of shame. The answer to the question of why this industrial phase has so many problems, therefore, appears to be given by the explanation that it is a transitional stage in which there is a poor enforcement of norms.

These several concepts are combined in chapter 5; legal pluralism is enhanced by the fact that the economy is rapidly changing, which creates a situation referred to by Durkheim as anomie. Due to the growing number of individuals with whom one interacts, a new normative model is necessary, which stimulates a transfer from a patriarchal status based model to a contractual model. This change has taken place in Europe and is currently taking place in Saudi Arabia and the Emirates. The intermediate phase between the two normative models is problematic in light of the fact that enforcement mechanisms of one model are disappearing, while the enforcement mechanisms of the second model are not in place yet. As neither of the two models are properly enforced, ample opportunity is created for abuse and even dehumanization.

The data of chapter 5 furthermore show that although strategic maneuvering between the different models indeed takes place, some interviewees were adamantly convinced of the correctness of one model. In such instances, the differences between the models are not used as tools within (type 2 or 3) conflicts, but they actually cause (type one) conflicts. The data thus show that legal pluralism not only leads to strategic maneuvering *in* conflicts, but in certain instances also *causes* conflicts.

On contractual norms and the theory of consent

The introduction of the contractual model has led to the applicability of a third set of norms: contractual norms. These norms are connected to another acknowledged factor enhancing legal pluralism, namely the fact that domestic workers come from one legal order, their countries of origin, to work in another legal order, Saudi Arabia or the Emirates. Chapter 6 describes the contractual norms to which domestic workers and employers refer. First, the chapter describes where the domestic workers' ideas on contractual norms stem from and where the employers' ideas on such norms stem from. As the chapter shows, the two parties regularly receive completely different information on the contents of the agreed on contractual norms. These norms diverge to the extent that they regularly lead to type one conflicts, conflicts that start with a preliminary disagreement on norms. The chapter describes all types of conflicts which are connected to contractual norms, to show that, as with customary norms, legal pluralism not only leads to strategic maneuvering in existing conflicts, but in certain instances also causes conflicts.

The contractual norms that both parties refer to are so different that the Western theory of consent does not apply or barely applies. One of the central ideas of the capitalist labor market is that a laborer enters into a labor agreement with an employer. This labor agreement largely works like any other agreement, and the binding force of the agreement is consent. This has both an internal and an external aspect; one is supposed to declare what one wants, which refers to the internal aspect of free will based on knowledge. By declaring this free will (offer and acceptance, performance as an external aspect) parties create legal consequences.[186]

Consent in empirical reality is never a matter of being present or not-present, but a sliding scale of more or less consent. Legal systems partly recognize this, as no legal system using this theory of being bound by contracts because of consent is so radical as to state that parties are not bound if there is no full consent. Full consent rarely occurs, as humans do not have the mental capacity to fully comprehend all the possible consequences of agreements. Legal systems thus work with the fiction of consent and the question always is: how much (evidence of) real consent is needed to apply the legal concept of consent and its consequences, and if there is not enough real consent, what will the legal consequences hereof be? Considering the domestic workers, the research results show that the level of consent is usually very low. In both Saudi Arabia and the Emirates this low level of consent has no consequence; domestic workers are deemed to be bound to the contract, but usually only to the most basic stipulations: the obligation to work for two years as a domestic worker, for a certain salary, with the duty to obey the employer 24 hours per day. Contractual stipulations are disregarded on such a large scale that it is unclear what the purpose of the contract is.

---

186 Bix (2009).

On formal legal norms and game theory

Chapter 7 finalizes part 2 on norms, with a description of all the different formal legal norms. The fact that there are both national and international formal legal norms, according to legal pluralism theorists, enhances strategic maneuvering. In Saudi Arabia and the Emirates, as the chapter shows, national legal norms provide little normative tools to the domestic worker, while international legal norms – largely of Western origin – do. In Europe to the contrary, both international *and* national formal legal norms provide tools to the protection of workers. Furthermore, in Europe national formal legal norms regularly limit the strategic maneuvering space of the more powerful party, the employer, by stating that certain normative tools of the employer cannot override certain normative tools of the employee. For instance, in the Netherlands, the norm of contractual freedom (in the interest of the more powerful party the employer) cannot override the norms against arbitrary dismissal (which protect the less powerful party, the employee).

The chapter therefore analyzes why there is a difference here between Europe on the one hand, and Saudi Arabia and the Emirates on the other hand; why the national legal norms in Saudi Arabia and the Emirates provide little normative tools to migrant workers, and why they do not create a hierarchy in normative tools as is the case in Europe. The analysis is based on the theory of De Swaan, who contends that collective care for the lower classes came into existence in Europe, because they created problems for the more powerful part of society. He uses game theory[187] and the concept of collective goods to explain how the upper class improved the position of the underclass in its own interest. This theory can usefully be applied to low and unskilled migrant workers in Saudi Arabia and the Emirates, as they constitute the poor strata of both societies. While questions have been raised whether the data that De Swaan presented were sufficient to *prove* his proposition, the theory does offer interesting insights into the possible relation between flows of migrant workers and the (limited) development of protection of low-skilled workers.

De Swaan stated that the poor in Europe were perceived as a threat by the upper class because they could become beggars or, more dangerously, gangs of criminals. Poverty is a problem for the rich when large groups of poor people have the ability to milk cattle, appropriate stocks, set houses on fire, and abduct wives or children.[188] In certain periods of history, well-organized gangs of vagabonds constituted up to 20% of societies.[189] The poor – from the perspective of the rich – therefore needed to be pacified; they needed to be provided with a minimal standard of living to prevent them from taking whatever they wanted at their own initiative.[190]

---

187 Game theory is a branch of applied mathematics used in the social sciences, which attempts to capture behavior in strategic situations, in which an individual's choices depend on the choices of others.
188 Swaan (2004) P20-35.
189 Swaan (2004) P31.
190 Also Schwitters (1991) P289.

Already by the Middle Ages, initiatives were set up to provide basic aid. Although aid looks entirely different today, the dynamics of a modern democracy are the same. If you have six loaves of bread and three people want to divide them using the principles of democracy, game theory predicts that two of the three people will close a deal, so that they each get three loaves and the third gets nothing. In the long run, however, the third person will get angry and start a fight. Therefore, the first two will decide to provide everyone with at least half a loaf. Even in contemporary democracies, the 'haves' have an interest in pacifying the 'have-nots'.

The second reason why, according to De Swaan, protection of the lower classes came into existence is the fact that they were a threat to the higher echelons of society because they could carry and spread diseases. Especially during and after large epidemics, the fear of the lower classes, who were sick more often than the upper-class, grew. Garbage removal services were first privately organized by groups of individuals in certain neighborhoods, but they were eventually extended to the entire city because the rich and powerful understood that by improving the health of the poor, they could reduce the risks to their own health as well. Similarly, clean drinking water and sewage systems were collectively organized, first in the parts of town where the upper class lived and later in entire cities. Later, the rich and powerful organized health care for the lower classes to fight diseases that could spread from the poor to the rich.

Third, while the have-nots were dependent on the haves, the haves were also dependent on the have-nots for the proliferation of their wealth and privileges. They needed skilled and healthy workers, not just now, but also later on.[191] It was important to keep the poor workers somewhat in the neighborhood because they were necessary for both the next harvest and the harvest twenty years later. By raising the standard of living for laborers, the health and education of their children was improved as well. This was not just the result of direct government services for general education; it was also achieved by allowing laborers to invest in their children. Education provides knowledge of a shared language, the ability to count, shared norms, and values and discipline. Thus, even without specific vocational training, education makes the low classes much more suitable as employees of the rich. The early advocates did not have the jargon of modern economists, but their presentation of the contribution of labor standards to the creation of a healthier, better-educated and more productive working class and citizenry is still recognizable as an argument about the potential positive externalities of aid and protection.[192]

Fourth, even if the have-nots had jobs to provide for their most basic needs, they occasionally became angry about their fate, which led to either spontaneous uprisings or strikes that threatened the interests of employers.[193]

---

191 Also Veen (1994) P60 and the many works he quotes.
192 Also Humphries in Basu (2003) P84-85.
193 Swaan (2004) P160-162.

This situation deteriorated due to worsening conditions caused by changes in labor relations. The modern story of labor standards starts in England in the beginning of the nineteenth century. It can be seen as an attempt to offset the social costs that accompanied the development of industrialization.[194] As workers became better organized in unions, their power grew. The fear of the power of poor laborers grew to unprecedented proportions with the rise of communism in the second half of the nineteenth and the first half of the twentieth century.

A fifth cause posited by De Swaan for the development of labor laws came from the international community. With the growing importance of world trade, it became important to sign international agreements concerning labor law to create equal competition and a level playing field. The conventional dating of the start of the movement for international standards is 1818, with Robert Owen's moral call for the international application of standards to improve world welfare and the understanding that nations with high standards can prosper economically only if other nations are convinced to follow their lead.[195] Even earlier, however, the international economic level playing field influenced the abolition of slavery: many producers in the northern United States supported the abolition movement to prevent southern producers from gaining a market share by producing goods more cheaply using slave labor.[196]

There is resistance to De Swaan's claim that many collective goods to protect the have-nots have come into existence because of the interest of the haves. This resistance comes mainly from those who insist that these collective goods have come into existence because of Christianity or humanism. Yet this does not answer the question of why these two movements gained ground in Europe and not in the Middle East, as Islam heavily emphasizes protection of the poor and weak as well.[197] For instance, donating alms (*Zakaat*, an annual contribution of all liquid assets, not just annual income, to the poor, sick or suffering) is one of the five central pillars of Islam.[198] Differences in religion, therefore, do not explain the lack of labor law protection in the Middle East, while – as chapter 7 will explain – the phenomenon of large flows of circular migration and deportation does seem to explain this phenomenon. Nevertheless, for conclusive answers to this issue, comparative research in several countries on labor protection and the question to what extent the five causes set out by De Swaan exist – research that should include countries with different religions – would be necessary.

---

194 Also Engerman in Basu (2003) P10.
195 Also Engerman in Basu (2003) P37.
196 Also Molenaar (1953) P35.
197 Shadid (2003) P243.
198 Esposito (2007) P15.

3.3.2 Access to Justice

Part III of this dissertation, chapters 8 and 9, concerns conflict resolution mechanisms or institutions that could possibly resolve or mediate conflicts. Chapter 8 focuses on such institutions specifically for domestic workers, while chapter 9 places this into the larger picture of the entire legal system. The data gathered for these two chapters are analyzed by use of the theories on citizenship and access to justice, and the rentier state theory.

Citizenship

Section 3.1 on the literature concerning domestic workers mentions that lately several scholars have pointed at citizenship as an additional axis of inequality, along with race and class. As such, limited citizenship contributes to the weak position of domestic workers. Citizenship as necessary for rights to be effectively invoked, has been a primary topic of discussion since 1951, when Hannah Arendt published on the problem of individuals who are not members of a political community (persons but not citizens), and therefore are not granted access to the legal order.[199] Michael Walzer added that it is the political community whose members distribute power to one another and avoid, if they possibly can, sharing it with anyone else.[200] As the German philosopher Werner Hamacher formulates it, citizenship grants a *privi-le-gium*, a right to have rights.[201] Yet from this literature it did not become clear how limited citizenship could be more of a problem or a different problem to domestic workers in Saudi Arabia and the Emirates, than in for instance Canada as researched by Bakan and Stasiulis.[202] Nevertheless, the data of the research revealed that citizenship is indeed an important factor that influences the conflicts involving domestic workers, as can be analyzed by use of the theory of Bosniak.

As Bosniak rightfully states, a distinction needs to be made between the different types of citizenship.[203] She distinguishes three types of citizenship which are helpful in the analysis of the position of domestic workers: in the early days of most democratic countries, no mention was ever made of the fact that the right to vote would be limited to men, as this was presupposed. Women were not supposed to partake of public decision-making power, which can be referred to as political citizenship. Throughout history, women often lacked the rights to work outside the house and to strive for financial independence, which can be referred to as economic citizenship. Furthermore, in most countries, women (like children) were not supposed to defend their own rights, were not supposed to have an individual right to request governmental protection of their rights. This right to legal protection can be referred to as civil citizenship.

---

199 Arendt (1951).
200 Walzer (1983).
201 Hamacher (2004).
202 Bakan and Stasiulis (1995 and 1997).
203 Bosniak (2006).

Political citizenship is what most Saudis and Emiratis do not want domestic workers to gain. It is this type of citizenship that interviewees seem to have in mind when they say that the visa regulations (or sponsorship system) cannot be changed because of the number of migrant workers (over 90% in the Emirates). Yet this kind of citizenship has not been requested by any of the interviewed domestic workers.[204] Economic citizenship is not the issue here, either. Some scholars argue[205] that women in most countries can only join the political community and gain full citizenship by hiring a domestic worker. In other words, economic citizenship (the right to work outside the household) and political citizenship (the right to join in public decision-making) for working women is gained at the expense of the citizenship of domestic workers. This is true only concerning the political citizenship of domestic workers; they are paid laborers and thus economic citizens, but they are bound to the private sphere and thus excluded from public decision-making. Thus, their economic citizenship is not limited, and political citizenship is not what domestic workers seek. What they lack is civil citizenship, the right to legal protection.

Civil citizenship thus means legal protection by the government. Domestic workers lack this type of citizenship due to two separate causes. Bosniak makes a distinction between (i) those who lack citizenship based on their bureaucratic status or their lack of membership in a community, and (ii) those who lack citizenship based on a lack of membership in the public community. The first category contains illegal migrants who officially have no right to reside in a country. In many countries, they either have no rights or cannot enforce them, whereas in other countries they have limited rights. The second category contains those members of the community who have diminished membership in the public community, including women and all others whose lives are largely contained within the private sphere of the household, such as children and domestic workers.[206]

Diminished citizenship can thus be caused by bureaucratic status and by seclusion to the private spheres of the house. Both in Saudi Arabia and the Emirates, these two causes indeed strongly diminish civil citizenship of domestic workers. The first cause is the fact that they are migrants, working and residing under the sponsorship regulations as described in chapter 7 on formal legal norms. They do not, and will never, belong to the Saudi or Emirati state. This is the type of diminished citizenship to which Hannah Arendt referred. During World War II, stateless refugees (or indésirables) received no protection whatsoever from any state.

---

204 Likewise on migrant workers in the Emirates in general: Davidson (2008) P190.
205 Bosniak (2006) P15.
206 Bosniak (2006).

The second cause of limited civil citizenship is a status that domestic workers in Saudi Arabia and the Emirates share with domestic workers worldwide and, more generally, with all women worldwide: second-class citizenship. This is what led Marilyn French to argue that women's oppression has amounted to a form of slavery:

> What other term can one use to describe a state in which people do not have rights over their own bodies, their own sexuality, marriage, reproduction or divorce, in which they may not receive education or practice a trade or profession, or move about freely in the world? Many women (both past and present) work laboriously all their lives without receiving any payment for their work.[207]

'Slavery' is actually the word used by several interviewees to describe the position of domestic workers in both Saudi Arabia and the Emirates (more in chapter 10). It is also a term regularly used by interviewed Saudi women to describe their own position. Human Rights Watch calls them 'perpetual minors,' because, like children, women in Saudi Arabia are not supposed to protect their own rights, but are to be protected.[208] Whichever term one uses – minors or slaves – the essence is that in the Emirates and especially in Saudi Arabia, women (including domestic workers) suffer an extreme form of second-class citizenship.

Thus, the reason that domestic workers in Saudi Arabia and the Emirates suffer from a severe lack of enforceable rights is the fact that the two causes of diminished civil citizenship – visa regulations and the second class citizenship of women – are particularly severe in these countries. Moreover, female domestic workers, as migrant workers restricted to the house, suffer from both of these causes. To show that this is indeed the case, chapter 8 describes the lack of access to law from which domestic workers suffer. They lack civil citizenship, as they have no place to go, to ask for protection of their rights. The limitation of access to justice based on their status as migrant workers operates through the sponsorship system. The limitation based on their status as women operates through three concepts, which – as can be deduced with reference to chapter 4 on customary norms – are all concepts of the patriarchal system, not Islamic concepts. Both Saudi Arabia and the Emirates are still heavily patriarchal societies.

---

207 Johnson (1997) P15-16.
208 Report 21.

Rentier state theory

Chapter 8 thus describes the lack of access to justice of domestic workers, which leads to severely diminished civil citizenship. As chapter 5 on customary norms explains, both countries are in a transition from a status based patriarchal model to a contractual model, which demands a transition from a bottom-up implementation to a top-down implementation of norms. The chapter notes that this top-down implementation barely comes into existence; civil citizenship is thus problematic not only for domestic workers, but for many others both in Saudi Arabia and the Emirates. Chapter 9 therefore describes the general lack of access to justice and the absence of the rule of law. This situation can be explained through the rentier state theory.

As briefly explained in chapter 2, this political science theory states that governments that receive substantial amounts of revenues (rent) from the outside world on a regular basis, combined with a relative absence of revenue from domestic taxation, tend to become autonomous from their societies, unaccountable to their citizens and autocratic. Such states fail to develop in the direction of the rule of law because in the absence of taxes, citizens have less incentives and possibilities to pressure their government to become responsive to their needs. Instead, the government essentially 'bribes' the citizenry[209] with welfare programs, salaries, and commercial assignments, becoming an allocation or distributive state.

According to political scientist Friedman, the connection between the price of oil and the human rights situation is so strong that it resembles a mathematical equation that can be visualized graphically:

> According to the First Law of Petropolitics, the higher the average global crude oil prices rises, the more free speech, free press, free and fair elections, an independent judiciary, the rule of law, and independent political parties are eroded. (...) Countries that have a lot of crude oil but were well-established states with solid democratic institutions and diversified economies before their oil was discovered, would not be subject to the First Law of Petropolitics. (...) Political scientists have explored how an abundance of oil wealth in particular can reverse or erode democratizing trends: Michael Ross, using statistical analysis from 113 states between 1971 and 1997, concludes that a state's reliance on either oil or mineral exports tends to make it less democratic.
>
> First he argues, there is the 'taxation effect.' Oil-rich governments tend to use their revenues to relieve social pressure that might otherwise lead to demands for greater accountability from or representation in the governing authority. I like to put it this way: the motto of the American Revolution was 'no taxation without representation.'

---

209 Zakaria (2001).

The motto of the petrolist authoritarian is 'no representation without taxation.' Oil backed regimes that do not have to tax their people to survive because they can simply drill an oil well, also do not have to listen to their people or represent their wishes. The second mechanism through which oil dampens democratization, argues Ross, is the 'spending effect.' Oil wealth leads to greater patronage spending, which in turns dampens pressure for democratization.

The third mechanism he cites is the 'group formation effect.' When oil revenues provide an authoritarian state with a cash windfall, the government can use its newfound wealth to prevent independent social groups – precisely those most inclined to demand political rights – from forming. In addition, he argues, an overabundance of oil revenues can create a 'repression effect,' because it allows governments to spend excessively on police, internal security and intelligence forces that can be used to choke democratic movements. Finally, Ross sees a 'modernization effect' at work. A massive influx of oil wealth can diminish social pressures for occupational specialization, urbanization, and the securing of higher levels of education – trends that normally accompany broad economic development and that also produce a public that is more articulate, better able to organize, bargain and communicate, and endowed with economic power centers of its own.[210]

The rentier state theory has been elaborated on by many, with a very important contribution of Beblawi and Luciani.[211] The theory applies to this day:

> Orthodox 'rentier state theory' has been declared obsolete many times and each budget crisis in the Kingdom is closely followed by announcements that the Saudi distributional system has reached a breaking point, or is at least under immense pressure, pressure which leaves no choice but radical reform and a redefinition of the Saudi 'social contract'. Pressure to reform Saudi economic structures has indeed been mounting, but the outcome of reform efforts has been highly mixed, apparently without endangering the overall functioning of the system. Although the socio-economic fundamentals have changed significantly since the oil boom years, a true redefinition of the Saudi political economy has yet to happen.[212]

---

210 Friedman (2006).
211 Beblawi and Luciani (1987).
212 Hertog in Aarts (2005) P111.

The point that this dissertation adds to the rentier state theory is that because the governments of Saudi Arabia and the Emirates have an independent source of income and thus cannot be forced or stimulated into organizing a proper legal system, individuals have no choice but to protect themselves through ulterior systems including patriarchy, tribalism, cronyism, and corruption, which collectively determine somebody's *wasta* or clout, as will be described in chapter 9. Because domestic workers form the bottom stratum of society, they do not have *wasta* and are the ultimate victims of the oil revenues. This is not simply because the oil revenues have made their employers rich enough to hire domestic workers, but because the oil allows the governments to ignore abusive individuals, including (but not limited to) many domestic workers' employers.

Furthermore, chapter 9 explains the difference between Saudi Arabia and the Emirates referring to Montesquieu's division of power in three. In Saudi Arabia the legislative power and the judiciary are both run by an old and powerful class, a group of tribes that consider themselves to be nobility.

3.3.3 The power (im)balance and dynamics in the house
The fourth part of this dissertation digs into the power (im)balance between the domestic worker and the employer, and the resulting dynamics within the private sphere of the house. Chapter 10 first describes the lack of freedom on the side of the domestic worker, which is analyzed through the concepts of the free labor market, monopsony, and slavery. Chapter 11 describes the marginal position of the domestic worker within the household, as a stranger who is very close. This marginality or otherness regularly leads to tensions and conflicts that are generally ended by the employer by use of his power to instantly expel her.

On freedom and the labor market
In a balanced labor relationship, both employer and employee can resist, or take action against abusive behavior from the other party; the power is distributed in a manner that allows both parties to stand up against infringements of their rights. The minimum requirement hereto is the ability to leave the labor relation. Chapter 10 digs into the question exactly how much power the employer holds over the domestic worker, due to her lack of freedom to leave, caused by four different types of constraints: legal, economic, physical, and psychological. Based on this, it would seem incorrect to speak of a free labor market.

Then how should this situation be labeled? From the perspective of political theory, they suffer from severely diminished civil citizenship. Furthermore, the power is distributed unequally. Considered from an economic perspective, the result of these constraints cannot be labeled a free labor market. Although recruitment may, to some extent, have been free (though severe poverty can reduce this substantial freedom to nothing), as soon as the domestic worker arrives at the workplace, her freedom vanishes. The result is a phenomenon that economists call monopsony.[213] A monopsony (from Ancient Greek μονός (monos) 'single' + ψωνία (psonia) 'purchase') is a market form with only one buyer, called a monopsonist. He has the market power because he can affect the market price of a purchased good by varying the quantity bought.

Monopsonist theory recognizes that the phenomenon existed in the nineteenth-century company towns, which were isolated mining centers with only one employer (the mining company) for almost everyone. The company could unilaterally determine salary and working hours. Others suggest significant monopsony power in various contemporary labor markets, from baseball players and nurses to college professors. The economic effect is that it redistributes welfare away from workers to their employer, and it reduces the aggregate (or social) welfare enjoyed by both, because the employer's net gain is smaller than the loss inflicted on the worker.[214] In the situation of the domestic workers, this means that as soon as a worker has arrived in the household of an employer, she has no or almost no freedom to leave. This gives the employer the power, as sole buyer of her labor, to unilaterally decide on salary and the amount of hours to be worked. The welfare loss suffered by the domestic worker is larger than the gain of the employer, which is why this situation is considered Pareto inefficient.[215]

Is it modern-day slavery?
In the international press, the situation is not described as monopsony though, but as modern-day slavery. Chapter 10 discusses the question to what extent, based on the data in this research, is it correct to say that they are 'modern-day slaves' for a period of two years. Of course, the answer depends on the definition of slavery. The most frequently cited definition is the one given by the League of Nations committee on slavery: 'The state or condition of a person over whom any or all the powers attaching to the right of ownership are exercised.' This is what distinguishes slavery from all other forms of dependency and involuntary labor.[216] According to this definition, domestic workers are not slaves in either Saudi Arabia or the Emirates, because they are not officially the property of the employer. Another definition asks whether the person concerned lacks legal personhood: whether he is only an object of rights or can also be a subject of rights. Again this would imply that domestic workers are not slaves, because they can sign contracts.

---

213 Singh in Basu (2003) P125.
214 A broad and useful survey of both the theoretical and empirical literature on monopsony in labor markets may be found in Boal (1997). See also the large bibliography provided at the end of Manning (2003).
215 Pareto efficient is the situation in which the welfare of one party grows, while nobody's welfare diminishes. This situation is the contrary; the welfare of the domestic worker diminishes more than the growth in welfare of the employer.
216 Patterson (1982) P21.

Yet these definitions of slavery depend upon the concepts of ownership and property, concepts that are relatively new in history, while the institution of slavery is very old. The concept of slavery changed during the Roman Empire from a relationship of one person to another person, into the relationship between a person and a thing.

To put it simply, two thousand years ago, the *pater familias* had the right to make decisions about the things in his household (such as a horse) because he was the highest in the family hierarchy. Slaves used to be the lowest persons in this hierarchy and slavery was seen as a relationship between persons, as was the relation between the *pater familias* and his wife. Today, people have the right to take decisions about the things in their household (such as a car) because the person concerned holds a property right to that car. With the change in concepts concerning control, changing from a relation between persons into a relation between a person and a thing, slaves changed into things and became property.

In Roman law, this change took place with the alteration of the meaning of the word *dominium*. Originally, this word referred to the power of the *dominus*, which was the power of a man over his family or the power of a lord over his subjects (a relation between persons). Later on, *dominium* came to mean property (a relation between a person and a thing).[217] Through the changing doctrine of *dominium*, the condition of slavery was transformed from a condition of power *in personam* into a condition of power *in rem*.[218] Interestingly, in Arabic, the word *MaLiK* can mean king, ruler or tribal leader, but it also means 'owner'. The root *MLK* represents either ruling or owning, and *MiLK* can mean control or ownership. Although further research is needed, this could be a clue to the occurrence of the same development in Arabic lands as in Roman lands, in which ultimate control changed into ultimate ownership.

The United Nations has abandoned the concept of property in persons, but the organisation has not succeeded in eliminating the type of slavery that existed before the concept of property came into being: a power relationship in which one person has extreme control over another. Patterson states the following about what slavery is:

> Relations of inequality or domination, which exist whenever one person has more power than another, range on a continuum from those of marginal asymmetry to those in which one person is capable of exercising, with impunity, total power over another. (....) Slavery is one of the most extreme forms of the relation of domination, approaching the limits of total power from the viewpoint of the master and the total powerlessness from the viewpoint of the slave. Yet it differs from other forms of extreme domination in very special ways. If we are to understand how slavery is distinctive, we must first clarify the concept of power.

217 Van den Bergh (1988) P8-9.
218 Patterson (1982) P32.

The power relation has three facets. The first is social and involves the use or threat of violence in the control of one person by another. The second is the psychological facet of influence, the capacity to persuade another person to change the way he perceives his interests and his circumstances. And third is the cultural facet of authority, the means of transforming force into right and obedience to duty.[219]

Chapter 10 discusses that under this definition, domestic workers in Saudi Arabia and the Emirates are indeed slaves. But as the relation is not one of property but one of extreme power, it is usually referred to as bonded labour. Yet because it is akin to pre-Roman slavery, to slavery as it existed before the invention of the concept of property over persons, the labour relation can also be referred to as 'power slavery' as opposed to 'property slavery'.

Otherness
Chapter 11 digs into the marginal position of the domestic worker, of the stranger who comes close into the family. This position creates tensions that can lead to conflicts that are accompanied by a view of the domestic workers as 'others'. Such views of domestic workers are a common phenomenon, not limited to the Emirates or Saudi Arabia. Domestic workers are regularly viewed as fundamentally different: dirty and unreliable, yet indispensable, simultaneously attractive and dangerous. This reputation is related to their position on the fringes of the social order, just as slaves have always held a structurally marginal position.[220] This position involves a form of orientalization[221] which add to a fear of the other that is especially strong in the case of domestic workers because they are living inside the household. They are perceived as some sort of fifth column, a Trojan horse, a transgressor, who can bring the outside dangers inside, and the inside secrets onto the streets.

The domestic worker as outsider enters too closely within the intimacy of the family. Just as individuals have a personal space bubble that strangers may not pierce, so do families. For instance, in an elevator, worldwide, people "remain silent, avoid eye contact, immerse themselves in reading material or watch in awe as the floor numbers are illuminated from floor to floor. We do not acknowledge the existence of these strangers around us who, if we did, we would consider to have trespassed into our most private zone."[222] This same behavior is shown by entire families vis-à-vis the domestic worker who enters the families' space. She is ignored and kept at a distance, in glaring contrast to her daily proximity.[223]

---

219 Patterson (1982) P1-2.
220 Patterson (1982) P332.
221 A concept developed by Edward Said (2005), which is the Dutch translation of Orientalism (1978).
222 Borg (2007).
223 Rollins (1985) P32.

To manage this complicated situation, domestic workers are kept away from the family, as was also the case in for instance the industrializing United States: houses were designed with extra accoutrements to keep servants separate, including unnecessary servants' entrances, back stairs leading up to servants' attic rooms, kitchens separated from the main rooms by servants' pantries.[224]

The act of keeping domestic workers separated, is usually legitimized not through acknowledgment of fear of this outsider, but through the concept that domestic workers are dirty. The relationship between social status and cleanliness has been discussed extensively by Douglas,[225] who pointed out that persons and groups that reside at the margins of society are often seen as the carriers of pollution and disorder and therefore should be avoided.[226] Dirt is, according to Douglas, intimately related to the most fundamental conflict in the social order, the marginal person. This polluting person is always someone who has crossed a line that should never have been crossed or who brings together what should have remained entirely separate.[227]

To deal with the fact that this dirty outsider may turn out to be very attractive, they are commonly portrayed as lusty sexual devils.[228] This is problematic, however, because, though they are portrayed as unreliable, they are at the same time indispensable. This can lead to stress or agitation on the side of the employer.[229] As Patterson states, the marginal person, although a threat to the moral and social order, was often also essential for its survival.[230] Georg Hegel realized that total domination can become a form of extreme dependence on the object of one's power and total powerlessness can become the secret path to control.[231]

Chapter 11 analyzes the three different forms of 'otherness' of the domestic worker. She is the other in the sense that she is a stranger, somebody from a country far away. Secondly, she is the other woman next to the wife of the employer. Thirdly, she is the other in the sense that she is a woman, towards her male employer, who is a man. Although these three types of otherness are a phenomenon that can lead to conflicts anywhere in the world, there are several factors both in Saudi Arabia and the Emirates that contribute to a higher level of otherness, which as such influence the occurrence of conflicts.

---

224 Rollins (1985) P 52.
225 Douglas (1966).
226 Regt (2008) P5.
227 Patterson (1982) P322.
228 Schama (1988) P460.
229 Schama (1988) P457.
230 Patterson (1982) P46.
231 Patterson (1982) P2.

Expulsion

The three aggravated forms of otherness can lead to a variety of explosive situations, including rape and severe violence. In such situations, domestic workers are often instantly expelled from the household by the employer. This may take the form of physical violence, upon which the domestic worker herself leaves, but the most usual method of expulsion is an accusation. With the increasingly disenchanted worldview of the average Saudi and Emirati, accusations of either abuse of the children, theft, or having a boyfriend seems to have become more common. Yet sometimes the accusation concerns the practice of occultism, an accusation that, as Mary Douglas has shown, is a common practice for the expulsion of marginal women.[232] According to Douglas, accusations of magic and witchcraft are common against those at the margins and those whose position in the hierarchy is unclear: "Here are people living in the interstices of the power structure, felt to be a threat to those with better defined status. Since they are credited with dangerous uncontrollable powers, an excuse is given for suppressing them, they can be charged with witchcraft and violently dispatched without formality or delay."[233] The connection between an accusation of occultism and its ability to have a marginal person expelled resounds in the Arabic language: the Arabic word for excommunication is *Takfir*, which means calling someone a *Kafir*. This word can mean a non-believer, but it can also mean a disloyal person or even a communist. Through *takfir* or accusations in general, people are removed from a community regardless of the truth of the accusation.

More interesting for the analysis of the accusations is therefore not what has happened before, but what happens afterwards. It is crucial to note here that these four accusations do not differ as much as they would seem to, because they all have the same effect. Their result is always the immediate removal of the domestic worker from the household upon the instigation of the employer. This shows the employer's unlimited freedom to immediately terminate the work relationship, in stark contrast to the domestic worker's total lack of freedom, as described in chapter 10. Nevertheless, in light of the explosive situations that are the result of the otherness of the domestic worker, the freedom of the employer should not be limited.

Conclusion

Chapter 12 concludes this dissertation. The research question is: Which factors influence the conflicts in the Kingdom of Saudi Arabia and the United Arab Emirates between domestic workers and their employers, the norms both parties refer to and the (im)balance of power? In answer to this question, chapter 12 focuses on all the factors at influence and how they are connected.

---

232 Douglas (1966).
233 Douglas (1966) P102.

The following chapters thus present the data of the research which, through the above described theories, explain how certain factors influence the conflicts between domestic workers and their employers. Chapter 12 thereupon visualizes how these societal factors are interconnected. It extrapolates the results to other countries or other groups of individuals, offers suggestions for further research and provides policy recommendations.

PART TWO

NORMS

4. Sharia norms

4.1 Introduction

This chapter is the first of four chapters that discuss the three sub-questions: (i) In what way and to what extent do domestic workers and their employers refer to Islamic, customary, contractual, and formal legal norms? (ii) Do conflicts concern disagreement over norms or disputes regarding behavior contrary to the norms upon which both parties agree? (iii) Which factors influence the Islamic, customary, contractual, and formal legal norms that both parties (may) refer to in conflicts? Mainly because of this third sub-question, the chapters do not discuss the different sub-questions, but the different types of norms: Islamic norms, customary norms, contractual norms, and formal legal norms. This chapter discusses Islamic norms.

Several interviewees suggested that domestic workers may be in a difficult position on the Arabian Peninsula, because both the Emirates and Saudi Arabia are Muslim countries. An interviewed diplomat in Riyadh stated, for example: "Everyone says here that Islam is all-encompassing, that Sharia regulates every aspect of their lives and that they live accordingly. So obviously it also regulates the way they treat their domestic workers." Likewise an interviewee from the International Labour Organization in Geneva stated: "Of course the abuse has to do with Islam. I will never say that in public, but that is what I think."

Yet the results of this research show that this belief is incorrect. An active search for aspects of the Sharia that could influence the position of domestic workers and the conflicts they find themselves in, resulted in a list of factors that can theoretically influence their position, but that in reality have little effect. Sharia, from a certain perspective, as explained in the next section, offers a set of normative tools that can be used either by the employer or the domestic worker. As such, Sharia forms a good example of legal pluralism within one set of norms, a reservoir of tools that can be used to the defense of both parties in conflict. Sharia is both Dr. Jekyll and Mr. Hyde[234] in the sense that Islam is like a knife that can either do good or harm, depending on the person using it.

The chapter solely discusses Islamic norms, not Christian norms, or norms derived from any other religion that domestic workers may adhere to. This does not mean that all domestic workers are either Muslim or atheist; to the contrary. A large share of for instance Filipina domestic workers are Christian (while those from the Island of Mindanao are generally Muslim), but the percentages are difficult to assess. Not only are there no statistics available on the exact numbers of domestic workers, they are not available either on their respective countries of origin, or their religion. Furthermore, many of them travel on fake documents that regularly state a religion other than the one they really adhere to.

---

234 For a comparable but economy-focused conclusion, see Chang (2008) chapter 9.

For financial reasons, domestic workers may tell their employer that they are Muslim, while telling the researcher they are Christian, hoping for employment in Europe. Nevertheless, only Sharia norms are discussed in this chapter, because no interviewed domestic worker ever referred to other religious norms than Sharia and neither did any other interviewee (except for countless statements from Emirati and Saudi interviewees that Sharia is in many aspects the same as Christianity). To the contrary, domestic workers who convincingly stated they are practicing Christians nevertheless referred to Islamic norms in defense of their claims. As such, the reference to Islamic norms is a good example of strategic maneuvering as discussed in chapter 3.

The data for this particular chapter have been gathered through a literature study on Sharia and a search on the Internet, plus many interviews with Saudi and Emirati employers, domestic workers, government officials, and diplomats. As this is a socio-legal study, the method used for this chapter concerns primarily discourse analysis, not the traditional legal method.

4.2 Views on what Sharia is

Both in Saudi Arabia and in the Emirates (though to a lesser extent in the latter) the central legal framework is Sharia or Islamic law. There are different views on what Sharia is. One Muslim for example explained what Sharia is and its sacredness, by writing:

> God then is the supreme Legislator. Through His Laws, before which according to Islam all men and women are equal, human life is sanctified. The Divine Law embraces every aspect of life and removes the distinction between the sacred and profane or religious and secular. Since God is the creator of all things, there is no legitimate domain of life to which His Will or His Laws do not apply. Even the most ordinary acts of life carried out according to the Sharia are sanctified and persons of faith who live a life according to the Divine Law live a life immersed in grace, or what in Arabic is called barakah. Their life gains meaning and they move through the journey of life certain that they are following a road designed by God, a road that leads to salvation and felicity in the ultimate encounter with Him.[235]

In this view, Sharia is considered to be a set entity, something sacred and therefore unchangeable (by man). There are different interpretations (the four schools, *madhahib*), but in general Muslims believe that one interpretation is the right one, in the sense that there is one correct answer to legal questions, which is the answer that Allah would give.[236]

---

235 Nasr (2004) P119.
236 One interviewed judge stated that he tries to feel what Allah would have decided (and therefore it was not necessary to ask for evidence).

This answer needs to be deduced from the legal sources, but is seen as fixed. According to certain more liberal views on Sharia, these interpretations are less fixed, as the sources need to be read in light of the societal circumstances in different times. For instance, the rule that men are allowed to marry up to four wives, is viewed by most Muslims (in all four legal schools) as fixed. According to certain current liberal interpretations, men can nowadays marry only one wife, because in modern-day society men can never treat all four women equally, while Islam prescribes that they do. According to certain Muslims, Sharia thus cannot change over time, while according to others it can. Still, both agree on the divine origin of the rules.

According to certain historians, Sharia has been deduced from the Quran and the *Hadith*, narrations on the example (*Sunna*) of the Prophet Mohammed. These sources have been elaborated on, analyzed, interpreted, and added to throughout the centuries by religious scholars (*Ulema*) and legal scholars (*Fuqaha*). The jurisprudence and resulting doctrine (*Fiqh*), do not constitute a coherent set of rules, but a collection of moral principles, rituals, legal rulings, exegeses, and legal opinions (*fatwas*)[237] that create considerable maneuvering space for Muslim judges and arbiters to settle conflicts in a matter deemed most suitable to the circumstances. In this light, Sharia forms a particular discourse referring to history and religion, which is used in negotiating discussions in a changing society. Islamic law is not only a legal system, but also a very strong discourse used in power struggles at all levels of society; it is a set of normative tools that may be used in conflicts within one family but also to either justify or attack entire regimes.[238]

This – again according to these historians – has always been the case. From the start Islam was not purely a religion, but a political theory as well.[239] For instance, as discussed in chapter 2, the Wahhabi interpretation of Islamic law played an important role in the power consolidation in the Kingdom of Saudi Arabia from the eighteenth century on. Nowadays the ruling Saudi family still refers to the obligation of Muslims to follow political leaders, even if one does not agree with them. The King of Saudi Arabia calls himself Custodian of the two Holy Mosques. Political opponents, often declared Jewish spies, Communists or apostates,[240] try to enforce their claims stating that the royal family is un-Islamic. This criticism is countered by the proposition that attacking the leaders is itself un-Islamic because it creates *fitna* (internal strife) and therefore threatens the *umma* (community of Muslims).

Salafism is an Islamic doctrine that prescribes Muslims to follow the example of the first three generations of believers (known as the pious predecessors).

---

237 See among others Zubaida (2003) P41.
238 Zubaida (2003) Introduction.
239 Plato's 'The Republic' and 'The Laws', with their emphasis on the unchangeability and divine origin of laws, have been an important inspiration for this particular discourse of Islamic political philosophy. Leezenberg (2002) P36.
240 Calling somebody an apostate to end discussions and to demand obedience, was done frequently in seventeenth century Europe as well; Fisk (2005) P100.

The movement has been influenced by the radical ideology of resistance as formulated by the Egyptian Sayyid Qutb, who stated that statutory law is by definition contrary to Sharia, as only Allah can formulate laws. To follow these statutory rules is therefore idolatry. If governments of countries with adherents to Salafism (such as Saudi Arabia) nevertheless want to pass statutory laws, they do so by referring to the concept of *maslaha*, the common good or public interest. These concepts are thus used to either fight or support a specific law. Within families women claim rights based on Sharia, while their husbands claim that the same Islamic law appoints them as their *mahram*[241] giving them the power to decide what is best for the women.

Sharia in this interpretation is thus not a coherent and set entity, but a collection of contested normative arguments, a repertoire of ideas and practices that are not homogeneous but continually changing, because of contradictions, or because new ideas and institutions are adopted by members who use them as a mode of legitimizing claims to power and authority. This view of Islamic law emphasizes that culture is hybrid and porous, and that the pervasive struggles over cultural values within local communities are competitions over power.[242] This is the interpretation used in this dissertation, as it matches the theory of legal pluralism as described in chapter 3. Chapter 4 discusses aspects of Sharia that can be used as normative tools by either domestic workers or their employers, in conflicts between them. It shows that Sharia is a strong normative resource in the power struggle between the two, which will do either good or harm to the domestic worker, depending on the situation at hand and the person with the power to choose which normative tool will be applied. Inside the house, it is usually the employer who has that power, as will be described in chapters 10 and 11. Outside the house, it is the legal-religious caste that has that power, as will be described in section 11 of this chapter, and in chapter 8 and 9 on access to justice.

4.3 Belief in a panoptic God

An aspect of Islam that can positively impact the position of domestic workers is the view of Allah as a panoptic God, an all-seeing deity. In this respect Allah is the same as God, as Yahweh and the Egyptian God Osiris. They share the characteristic of being able to see and remember everything. After death, they judge us for our acts in life. The panoptic God, from the perspective of the sociology of law, is an incredibly powerful society-organizing phenomenon.[243] As briefly discussed in chapter 3, in very small societies social control is strong; it is difficult to steal someone else's horse because everyone will see you riding it. If you hit your wife and she walks around with black eyes, people will notice and judge you for it.

---

241 An unmarriageable male, being a father, brother, son, or husband, who operates as protector or legal guardian.
242 Compare Merry (2006) P9.
243 Vergrote (1987) P79-96.

As societies grow larger however, social control diminishes, which can lead to disorder and mayhem. From a functionalist[244] perspective, the belief in a panoptic God can be regarded as a (partial) solution to this problem by creating internal constraints. Even when no one is watching, even when nobody will ever be able to find out, the individual is constrained by the belief that God will punish him one day.

Many interviewees volunteered accounts of "bad" people compensating for immoral acts out of fear of Allah. Thieves who became ill returned the stolen goods; a violent interviewee who had a car accident offered compensation to the victim of his violence; an Emirati who seduced his secretary and later fired her, thought his business was failing because of these events and consequently donated large amounts to charities. Similarly, if an employer treats his domestic worker badly and later develops a headache, many of them see this as punishment for their treatment and repent for their acts.

The fact that Muslims perceive Allah as being able to see and hear everything and someone who will in the Hereafter reward or punish them, is sometimes used by domestic workers by use of Quranic verses or the Quran itself. Several teachers from pre-departure courses in countries of origin (see chapter 6) advise domestic workers to use Islam as defense: "We advise them to learn some parts of the Quran by heart and when her employers abuse her, she can recite these. Or she can carry a Quran with her and when they want to hit her, she can defend herself with the Book. Often this immediately stops the violence. People may not respect the domestic workers, but they do respect the Quran." Several interviewed domestic workers knew from experience that this sometimes actually works: "I told the madam that her husband grabbed me and she said I don't believe you, you are not clean. Then I said, get the Quran, get the Bible, make me swear and make your husband swear. So he came but he didn't want to touch the Quran, so then the madam knew I was speaking the truth." In such instances Sharia, or the idea that Allah will punish anybody not adhering to it, is a tool used by domestic workers.

4.4 Human rights, dignity, and equality
This functionalist perspective on the belief in a panoptic God as a society-organizing mechanism is usually not recognized by believers themselves. What Muslim interviewees did emphasize regularly was the centrality to Islam of justice, basic human rights, dignity, and equity. One interviewed diplomat from a labor sending country stated that many uneducated Indonesians from the countryside come to Saudi Arabia assuming that they will find an ideal society. "It is, after all, the country of Mecca and Medina, the homeland of Islam, the country where the holy law Sharia is applied and forms the constitution. ...

244 Structural functionalism, or simply functionalism, is a broad perspective in sociology and anthropology which sets out to interpret society as a structure with interrelated parts. Functionalism addresses society as a whole in terms of the function of its constituent elements; namely norms, customs, traditions and institutions. While some regard it as a school of thought, other regard functionalism as an interpretation method.

"They do not expect harsh treatment because they know their religion, Islam, as a belief of a morally superior lifestyle." Almost all books written by Muslims on their religion state the same. All interviewed Muslims agreed that the essence of Islam is equality, freedom, dignity, justice, and solidarity. Allah himself is referred to with many names, including the Infinitely Good, the All-Merciful, the Compassionate, the Just, and Bringer of Justice.[245]

According to several interviewees, the concept of human rights is not new to the Middle East; it was introduced by the Prophet Mohammed.[246] For instance, one interviewee from the Saudi National Society for Human Rights said: "Human rights and Islam are the same. I compared the Human Rights declaration of 1948 to Islam. It's all pretty much the same." Sociologists would say that this reflects the framing of modern human rights discourse in Islamic terms and that the current concept of rights did not exist at the time of the Prophet. Nevertheless, it is hard to deny that Sharia contains many rules concerning respectful and proper treatment.[247] In theory, Sharia, with its core of rights, dignity, and justice, should thus offer protection to domestic workers by providing argumentative tools that protect their interests.

4.5 Sharia on laborers

In addition to the general principles of Sharia that prescribe human rights and dignity, there are several Sharia rules specifically on the proper treatment of slaves and workers. Many interviewed employers made statements like, "People who are abusing their domestic workers are not real Muslims because Islam teaches us to treat servants as our brothers." Another stated, "Mohammed had a servant in the house. When one day there wasn't enough food, he didn't eat; he gave the food to the servant. That is what Islam teaches us." Many interviewees referred to the Prophet's sayings: "The wage earner should have his wage for the work he has done, before his sweat dries" and "The master shall pay fully for the services rendered and the servant shall work faithfully and honestly." Literature on Islam regularly states the same:

> The Holy Prophet said: they are your servants whom Allah has made your subordinates. He should give him to eat what he himself eats and to wear what he himself wears. And do not encumber them with labor that may exhaust them. And if you are obliged to put such a burden on them, you yourself should join them in the work. (...) It is the duty of the employer to take only such work from the employees as they can do easily. They should not be made to work as hard that their health gets impaired. (...)

---

245 Nasr (2004) P181.
246 Al-Rasheed (2002) P169 and Esposito (2007) P36.
247 See also Marzouqi (2001) and Kamali (2002).

If a Muslim abuses the power that Allah has given him over those who are under his care or authority, such as servants, workers or others under his care, then he should remember the power that Allah has over him. (...) The Prophet (peace and blessings of Allah be upon him) was the best of people in attitude towards his servants; he did not scold them and beat them, even if they went against his instructions.[248]

Muslim employers, according to Islam, should both treat their workers right and respect them: "None of you should say this is my slave and this is my slave girl. He should rather say, this is my man and this my maiden."[249] The almighty Allah himself has said, "And surely we have dignified the children of Adam. The Holy Prophet has instructed the master to treat them always as the members of the family." "Surely God has made you their masters and if He had willed He could have made you likewise in their possession as slaves."[250]

On a website where people can ask *fatwas*, a Muslim asked if it was (religiously) allowed to hire a servant. He received the following answer concerning the duties of the employer towards his domestic workers, based on the Quran and the Hadith: (1) He should give his servant the same food as he eats, (2) he should clothe him as he clothes himself, (3) he should not give him more to do than he is able for and if he does that he should help him, (4) he should pay him a wage that is appropriate to his work and his efforts, (5) he should not insult him or hit him, (6) he should treat him well and be kind to him and (7) he should overlook his mistakes and shortcomings.[251] All this provides normative tools for the domestic worker to improve her position.

4.6 Slavery
An aspect of Sharia that can be used as a normative tool to undermine the position of domestic workers is that Islam (according to some interviewees) emphasizes that everyone has been given a place in society by God (Allah), a place that there-fore must be accepted. The Quran states, "We have assigned their shares in this life, raising some of them above others in ranks, in order to let them serve one another."[252] In this light, domestic workers are seen as individuals who naturally take an inferior position in society. Some interviewees used this Sura to justify the fact that they have a very good life while their domestic workers do not, just as slaves did not.

---

248 Zubair (1989) P23 and beyond.
249 The Quran (4:25).
250 Ghazali's Ihya-Uloom-I-Din, chapter on Rights of Slaves, referred to among others at http://www.islamicity.com/articles/Articles.asp?ref=IC0609-3122 January 2011.
251 www.Islam-qa.com/en/ref/6314/pdf/dl January 2011. The site refers extensively to applicable Hadiths.
252 Sura 43 verse 32.

Slaves and domestic workers, according to this line of reasoning, must accept their inferior position because society is viewed as organized by a combination of the unchangeable laws of Allah (Sharia)[253] and customary rules that support societal order and that should not or cannot be changed.[254] Both of these types of norms are social rules that are like the rules of the universe in the sense that they cannot be altered,[255] which makes legal instrumentalism impossible. This is partly why slavery was abolished relatively late on the Arabian Peninsula: 1962 in Saudi Arabia[256] and 1963 in the Emirates.[257]

Despite the abolition of slavery, reference to Sharia was made by several Saudi and some Emirati interviewees, to defend the position that slavery in essence is not a bad thing (although abuse of slaves is). This view is by no means unique to Islam. In the West, many Christian clergymen used the Bible to defend slavery. Like the Quran, the Bible states that slaves must be treated well. However, what was an improvement in morality at the time of the scriptures later became a useful way to stop further improvement of the position of slaves; neither the Quran nor the Bible forbids slavery.[258] Likewise in Mauritania, one of the last countries to abolish slavery, a person cannot use the courts to file a complaint against someone who treats him or her as a slave because the courts apply Sharia, which does not contain rules on the abolition of slavery, and Muslim judges therefore claim not to have jurisdiction on this matter.[259] As such, Sharia is used as a normative tool to perpetuate existing power relations.

4.7 Islam and egalitarianism

Islam also offers rhetoric and normative resources that directly contradict the discourse that legitimizes and perpetuates inequalities. On the Arabian Peninsula, most people think hierarchically; tribesmen whose traceable ancestry goes back hundreds of years do not marry those whose ancestry is known for a shorter period of time, even if that time is a century.[260] This custom was prevalent before Islam and, according to other interviewed Muslims, Mohammed was against it. He emphasized the importance of the Muslim community (*umma*) instead of the tribes and provided rules for improving the position of certain groups lower in the hierarchy, mainly women, slaves and orphans. Anyone not believing in the divine origin of these laws could claim that Mohammed himself was a legal instrumentalist, who used the law as a tool to improve the position of the lower strata of society.

---

253 Zubaida (2003) Chapter 3.
254 Leezenberg (2002) P36.
255 Keesing (1981) P319.
256 Abukhalil (2004) P96 and http://www.hrw.org/mideast/saudi/labor/ February 2009.
257 Davis (2006).
258 Molenaar (1953) P13.
259 Bales (2004) P110.
260 Report 16, P12, supported by statements of interviewees that they would never marry somebody from a lower tribe.

More specifically in regard to slavery, scholars state that Islam emerged in a world in which slavery was practiced almost universally and it has aimed to improve the status of slaves since its inception.[261] The Quran and Hadith advise kindness and humane treatment toward slaves and even encourage the liberation of slaves.[262] Several interviewees stated that good Muslims should follow these injunctions. Therefore, while some claim that Islam obstructs improvement for those at the bottom of society, others say that this hierarchical thinking is a pre-Islamic *Jahilliya*[263] custom and anyone condoning slavery is a bad Muslim.

4.8 Domestic workers versus slaves

Another normative tool that theoretically can have positive impact on the position of domestic workers, is the emphasis placed by several interviewees on the distinction that Sharia makes between contemporary domestic workers and slaves or concubines. As an interviewee explained: "The servants who work in households do not come under the same rulings as slaves, whether male or female. Rather they come under the ruling of private workers who are hired to work for the employer and are like any other employee." This distinction creates a normative difference between a slave owner, who is permitted to have sex with his slave, and an employer, who is not permitted to have sex with his domestic worker. It is generally known that some employers do have sexual intercourse with their domestic workers,[264] but this is often described as giving a bad name to Islam. For instance, one interviewee said, "What some of these heads of households have done to these servants is not condoned by Islam; rather, Islam forbids it and warns against it. It is not permissible to use that as a means of attacking Islam or giving a bad impression of Islam, because these sins on the part of some Muslims are forbidden by Islam itself."

Nevertheless, some employers choose to regard their domestic workers as slaves (a view actively stimulated by certain agents, see chapter 6). For instance, the following question was found on a website publishing *fatwas*: "We made a contract that she would serve me because she agreed and I agreed with my side. Hence, this young lady still lives in her parents' home and is not married. She agreed I be her master so it gives me the rights to touch her and look at her." The answer he received was: "What you did with the servant woman is haram and is not permissible. A servant woman is not a slave woman whom it is permissible to touch and have intercourse with. A servant woman is free and is not permissible for you except through marriage, which is what you did, but unfortunately you did it late.

261 For instance, Marzouqi (2000) P431.
262 For instance, Nasr (2004) P181.
263 The "Period of Ignorance" from before the Prophet Mohammed.
264 See chapter 11.

The contract that existed between you and the servant woman was a contract of employment, which was to serve you in your house. It was not a contract that permitted you to have intercourse with her. You say that she agreed that you would be her master and she let you touch her and look at her and that you freed her from the contract, but this has no basis of validity in Sharia in the sense that you refer to. A free woman cannot become a slave unless she is a *kaafir*[265] woman from a state that is at war with the Muslims and the Muslims have captured her. This does not apply in the case which you are asking about."[266]

Yet despite the fact that Islam officially does not allow employers to treat their domestic workers as property or as concubines, in practice, some of them do; even if the domestic worker (contrary to the aforementioned young lady) does not agree to this. As will be further described in chapter 5, section 3 under purchase agreement, some employers use the discourse concerning concubines to legitimize rape. So although the discourse on the difference between slaves and domestic workers protects the latter, in practice it does not, as employers who do refer to them as slaves and as such rape them, are never punished for harassment and rarely for rape (more on this in chapters 8 and 11).

4.9 Position of women in Sharia

The argument offered most often by interviewees as to why Islam influences the labor position of domestic workers is the following: "Domestic workers are women, and women are generally treated badly under Islam." The problem with this line of reasoning is that it is based on territorial concurrence: the Middle East is Muslim; women (or domestic workers for that matter) are not always treated well there, so this must be because of Islam. Yet a closer look shows that men and women in the Middle East (as elsewhere in the world) are involved in a power struggle and, because they are Muslim, *both* men and women use the discourse of Islam to improve their position. This explains the absence of systematic differences in most Muslim countries between males and females in their support for Sharia as the only source of legislation.[267] Yet because men primarily communicate in the public domain, Westerners only hear the arguments of men; the voices of Muslim women rarely make their way into international public discourse.[268]

Just as Muslim men currently dominate public discourse, in the past, the rulers, theorists and judges who acted as the interpreters and guardians of Islam in the Middle East were usually males. Because they lived in patriarchal societies, they interpreted Islam through the lens of custom. They believed that any other interpretation would disrupt the continuity of the social order and its reinforcement of social cohesion, which, in their view, was congruent with 'the order of nature.'

---

265 Non-believer.
266 http://www.ahlalhdeeth.com/vbe/showthread.php?t=7421 January 2011.
267 Esposito (2007) P48.
268 Rapport 2, P100.

This predisposition became entrenched as the Quran was consistently read with a bias in favor of men. Arab tribal culture's discrimination against women has strongly influenced juristic interpretations that establish women's inferiority to men.[269]

Yet this is exactly what Muslim defenders of women's rights say the Prophet Mohammed did not want: "He (the Prophet) propounded the unheard-of dissertation that men and women were equal before God and that all religious duties and hopes applied to both alike. He even went so far as to declare, to the horror of all right-minded pagan Meccans, that a woman was a person in her own right and not merely by virtue of her relationship with men as mother, sister, wife or daughter and that she was therefore entitled to own property, to do business on her own and to dispose of her own person in marriage!"[270] There is a remarkable *Hadith* on which one of the first leaders of Islam commented: "When the Prophet was alive we were cautious when speaking and dealing with our women in fear that a revelation would come (from God) concerning our behavior. But when the Prophet died we were able to speak and deal with them (more freely)." This tradition reflects the social resistance to the early Islamic reforms regarding women. Nevertheless, these same early leaders were later believed when they stated that women must always obey their husbands, even though Quranic verses on the behavior of the Prophet toward his own wives suggest the contrary.[271]

Such interpretations that grant more rights and freedom to women have always existed and their influence on society depended on the large scale power structure of a particular country at a certain time; for instance in the 1980's, because of the deteriorating (world) economy, more and more people in Saudi Arabia proposed to let women work outside the house on a larger scale and to give them the right to drive cars so that Asian private drivers would no longer be necessary.[272] Yet in the nineties, under the influence of the American *kuffar*[273] armies being invited into the country and the following growth of Islamic extremism aimed against the authoritarian regime, the position of women worsened again; women were oppressed as part of the opposition against the regime and America.

At the same time in the Emirates, the original Emirati population changed into a small minority. As they also did not pay any taxes, their opinion mattered less and less. More important to the rulers were the Americans who advocated for emancipation leading to changes so fast, that many Emirati women (indeed usually encouraged by men) chose to decline the offered freedoms, to show their disgust over the practically naked women on their beaches.

---

269 Likewise, among others, Asad (2005) P285 and Esposito (2007) P27.
270 Asad (2005) P290-291.
271 Fadl (2001) chapter 7, specifically P223.
272 Al-Rasheed (2002) P152-153.
273 Arabic for (among others) non-believers.

Several female Emirati interviewees chose to remain veiled and stay at home as part of their opposition against the McDonaldization[274] of their world.

Yet although to a certain extent women do not want the rights and opportunities that men have, to a larger extent they resist the restrictions placed on them. In both countries discrimination by the legal community against women is still evident in the way judges use their discretionary authority to deliver lighter or harsher sentences in cases where a woman is one of the litigants. Especially in the Kingdom of Saudi Arabia, authorities essentially treat adult women as legal minors[275] who are entitled to little authority over their own lives and well-being. Adult women generally must obtain permission from a guardian to work, travel, study or marry. Male guardianship over women makes it nearly impossible for survivors of family violence to avail themselves of protection or redress mechanisms.[276] The woman is treated as a symbol of honor and virtue, as an object that needs to be protected for its childbearing functions, or that as a component of a family unit needs to be safeguarded against neglect.[277] In other words, women (according to most Saudi and Emirati men) need to be protected, not empowered to protect themselves, which undermines protection against the protectors.

Still there is movement. Outside court (male dominated) public discourse stimulates women to stay at home while at the same time there has recently been a lot of talk revolving around the rediscovery of early Islamic belief in equality between the sexes.[278] So while conservatives point out that the Convention on the Elimination of all forms of Discrimination Against Women (CEDAW) has been signed with the reservation of the prevalence of Sharia, modernists and Islamic feminists state that this treaty is merely restoring gender relations from the time of the Prophet, as the CEDAW concepts of equality are closer to the spirit of the religious texts than current practice.[279]

As with the position of women in general, the position of domestic workers is both attacked and defended through Islamic discourse. On the one hand, domestic workers are often denied access to courts because, as women, they need a *mahram*, a male relative or husband; as migrant workers, they usually do not have one around (see chapter 8). Yet, on the other hand, a domestic worker is like any other woman: an object to be protected as a component of a family unit that must be safeguarded against neglect. Many interviewed Emiratis and Saudis said: "People who treat their domestic workers like this, they are not real Muslims," exactly the way many say: "Men who treat their women badly, they are not real Muslims."

---

274 Americanization of especially visual culture.
275 Based on Sura 4 verse 34: Men are the protectors and maintainers of women, because God has given the one more (strength) than the other and because they support them from their means.
276 Report 21, P2.
277 Radtke (1994) P180 and beyond.
278 See also Report 10, P57. This discourse is used for decades now in countries such as Tunesia, while the last decade in gains ground even in Saudi Arabia.
279 Compare similar discourse in Egypt in Merry (2006) P96.

Just as many say that Islam grants rights to women in general, interviewees stated that Sharia grants rights to domestic workers. The result depends on who has the power to define Sharia, who has the power to choose the appropriate legal concept, to decide which normative tool will be applied.

4.10 Testimonies

Another argument regularly used to defend the proposition that Islam negatively influences the position of domestic women is that in the courts, a female witness only counts as half a witness under Sharia and that non-Muslims, in certain cases, are not permitted to testify at all. The special rapporteur on violence against women for instance, indicates in her report on Saudi Arabia that foreign women working as domestic servants "encounter severe obstacles in obtaining redress in the courts due to the strict evidentiary rules in the courts."[280] This is, according to the data in this research, theoretically correct but in practice not entirely true. The rule can indeed work to the disadvantage of domestic workers. Yet because of the discretionary authority of judges on the question whether or not to apply evidentiary rules of the Sharia, not the rule in itself is the main obstacle, but the judge. And he is prejudiced, as will be described below and further discussed in chapter 8.

Non-Muslim witnesses

Witnesses have always been and still are important in Sharia courts. Testimonies and confessions are often the primary evidence especially in criminal trials. What has been written can be forged, but oral lies are presumed to be impossible or at least unlikely.[281] Under Saudi Arabia's interpretation of Sharia a Muslim woman's testimony is not generally accepted in criminal cases and is worth only half the testimony of a man in civil suits. Furthermore, Saudi Arabia's interpretation makes the testimony of non-Muslims admissible only in cases of 'necessity'. Former chief judge of Saudi Arabia Salih Al-Luhaidan appeared to deny this possibility when he told Human Rights Watch that the requirements to be a witness include that "the individual must tell the truth and must be religious. The witness must be of the faithful (Muslim)."[282]

The reason given as to why Muslims are considered to be the most (or the only) trustworthy witnesses is the fact that witnesses have to take an oath. When discussing the possibility that male employers could be lying, a young legal scholar explained: "They have to take an oath you know, it's a very heavy oath and if you lie after this oath, you will get sick and you will get into accidents. Everyone knows this, so after taking the oath, nobody lies." Many interviewed Muslims stated they believe that whoever does not believe in an all seeing God, has no reason not to lie. Therefore testimonies of non-believers are considered to be less trustworthy, or not trustworthy at all. On the other

---

280 Report 15, Addendum P12 no. 14.
281 Zubaida (2003) P44.
282 Report 17, P88-89.

hand, though, several other Muslim interviewees stated that they did not believe this. They claimed that this line of reasoning is only used in conflicts with non-Muslims; without using this exact wording, they explained that the rule can be either used or disregarded as a strategic maneuver.

Female witnesses

The reason why women are not considered to be trustworthy witnesses is twofold. First, they are perceived to be very emotional. Because of that, they are considered not to be able to recall exactly what has happened. An interviewed Sharia scholar said: "And it is good that the testimony counts only half. I have seen on the television that also Western scientist they have proof that when a women talks, only half her brain works. The other half doesn't. But when a man talks, then both his brain halves work. It's true you know, you can check it on the Internet." Similarly, a website publishing *fatwas*[283] answered the question about why the statement of two women is considered to be equal to the testimony of one man: "a woman may forget or get confused, so the other woman can remind her. Allah has commanded the testimony of two women so as to be sure that they remember, because the mind and memory of two women takes the place of the mind and memory of one man. This does not mean that a woman does not understand or that she cannot remember things, but she is weaker than man in these aspects – usually. Scientific and specialized studies have shown that men's minds are more perfect than those of women and reality and experience bear witness to that."

Secondly, women's testimony is less accepted because of the division between the public and private domain; as the lives of many women – especially in Saudi Arabia – are largely restricted to their parents' household, their own household and their children's, almost the only matters their testimony could be asked about concern family matters. In such matters their testimonies are not expected to be trustworthy, for the same reason why in most Western countries people have the right to refuse to testify when it concerns family matters: one is not expected to tell the truth if exposure of the truth negatively affects a loved one.

The problem with 'women being emotional' is concept validity; how can emotionality be objectively defined? In interviews with both Emiratis and Saudis things that I did not consider to be emotional were labeled as being emotional and vice versa. For instance, Filipina president Gloria Arroyo was perceived by several Saudis as being very emotional in her dealings with events in Afghanistan, while George W. Bush was not perceived as emotional but as rational in his quest for power and money, masculine in vindictiveness or prone to retribution. The second problem with 'women being emotional' is the fact that if individuals are treated as emotional all their lives, in general they become emotional.

---

283 http://www.islam-qa.com/en/ February 2009.

This is what is called the Rosenthal effect.[284] Several female interviewees both in Saudi Arabia and the Emirates agreed that they were very emotional and therefore agreed that their testimony should count only half.

4.11 Norms versus implementation

The fact that female witnesses count only half and that non-Muslims are considered less trustworthy, in theory definitely creates a problem for domestic workers. If an employer rapes them without any witnesses being present, then in theory she would lose a court case if it is his word against hers. Yet in practice things work differently. First of all, a judge – especially a more powerful one – can convict somebody if he wants to, even without having enough witnesses due to his maneuvering space. The famous case of the Qatif girl concerned a young woman in Riyadh who was raped by seven men.[285] She did not seek help until a week later and did not decide to make a case until four months later. By that time there was not much other evidence of what had happened apart from her narration. Theoretically she would have lost the case against the seven accused men. Yet the court ruled that due to the meager evidence and the absence of confessions, the men did not get the death penalty, but they were all sentenced to jail for up to seven years. So while theoretically it was not possible to sentence them at all, they got sentenced.

Secondly, a judge does not have to convict anybody if he does not want to, even if there are enough witnesses. In another high profile case, Indonesian domestic worker Nour Miyati had been repeatedly beaten up by her employers. She was taken to the hospital where nine fingers and parts of her feet had to be removed because of gangrene. Her lip and ear were damaged and she had many bruises. Several doctors and nurses were prepared to testify that the gangrene had been caused by the severe beatings of her employers who, on top of all that, had not permitted her to see a doctor. Her employers confessed. Nevertheless, the male employer received no punishment and the female employer was sentenced to lashes, but this punishment was later withdrawn.

According to Sharia the only guaranteed way to obtain a rape conviction is if the accused confesses or if there are four adult male witnesses to the act of penetration[286] yet in the rape case of this Saudi woman, severe convictions followed. But in the case of the Indonesian domestic worker where there was enough evidence, no conviction followed other than a very meager financial compensation. It is not the evidence that made the difference here, but the individuals involved.

284 Psychologist Robert Rosenthal from Harvard proved in 1966 that the school results of students who were treated as intelligent improved, while results of students who were treated as less intelligent deteriorated, even though they had been divided into two groups at random.
285 See http://en.wikipedia.org/wiki/Qatif_girl_rape_case, for basic facts and references. The case received much international attention as the victim was sentenced to ninety lashes for being alone with a man who was not a relative, a sentence which was doubled after her attorney contacted the international press.
286 Report 18, P91.

The cases are typical (see chapter 9), especially for Saudi Arabia; the evidentiary rules are followed if the judges concerned decide to do so. So, in the end the result does not depend on the evidentiary rule, but on the judge. Schacht, an expert on Islamic law notes: "As for the witnesses and women counting half; there are loads of tricks around Sharia rules, but this is something they do not want to find a trick for; they are perfectly happy with this rule"[287] – depending on the woman involved, it seems.

A distinction therefore needs to be made between the norm, or the normative tool, and its implementation. Sharia norms can in theory either undermine or improve the position of domestic workers, but whether they do so or not depends on the question of whether the persons with the power hereto choose to apply them. As stated in the second section of this chapter, inside the house, the employer has the power to decide which norm will be implemented. Outside the house, the judiciary has that power and this implementation is usually not in favor of the domestic worker, as in the given example on evidentiary rules. This can largely be extended to all Sharia rules. As will be elaborated on in chapters 8 and 9, domestic workers stand a very small chance of seeing the norms applied that are in their favor. Judges usually side with those who have *wasta*, those who have the right tribal connection, the right friends or the deeper pockets. This is especially the case in Saudi Arabia, where most judges are member of a legal-religious caste, which appears to be more concerned with its own position in society than with a just application of Sharia. More hereon in chapter 9.

4.12 Summary

This chapter discussed how Sharia can be seen as a collection of rhetorical tools or arguments that are used in power struggles throughout all strata of Islamic society, including conflicts between domestic workers and their employers. The result depends not on the many norms and concepts of Sharia, but on the question who has the power to decide which legal concept or normative tool will be applied. Such is the case with the position of domestic workers, but also with the position of women in general: it is both under attack and defended through the use of Islamic discourse. Another argument regularly used to defend the proposition that Islam negatively influences the position of domestic women is the fact that female witnesses under Sharia only count as half and that non-Muslims, in certain cases, are not permitted to testify at all. In practice, however, the evidentiary rules are followed if the judges concerned decide to do so. Thus, in the end, the result does not depend on the evidentiary rule, but on the judge. A third aspect of Islam that can theoretically worsen the position of the domestic worker is that Islam (according to some interviewees) emphasizes that everyone has been given a place in society by God (Allah) – a place that has to be accepted.

---

287 Schacht (1964) P177.

Nevertheless, as with the position of women, Islam offers rhetoric or normative resources that directly contradict this discourse that legitimizes and perpetuates inequalities. Furthermore, there are several aspects of Islam that can theoretically positively impact the position of domestic workers. The first is the view of Allah as a panoptic God who constrains the individual through the belief that God will one day punish him for sins that no one witnessed. Another aspect of Islam that Muslim interviewees regularly emphasized was the centrality to Islam of justice, basic human rights, dignity and equity. According to several interviewees, the concept of human rights is not new to the Middle East. It was introduced by the Prophet Mohammed. In addition to these general principles of Sharia that prescribe human rights and dignity, there are several Sharia rules specifically about the proper treatment of slaves and workers. If all Muslims on the Arabian Peninsula followed these rules, the domestic workers would fare rather well. Another potentially positive aspect of Islam is the emphasis that contemporary domestic workers are not slaves or concubines. This distinction means that although slave owners are permitted to have sex with their slaves, employers are not permitted to have sex with their domestic workers. In practice, however, employers are never punished for harassment and are rarely punished for rape.

Because domestic workers are migrants, their knowledge of Arabic is usually poor or nonexistent. Because many are not Muslim, their ability to convince a decision maker by using Sharia rhetoric is very limited. In courts, domestic workers usually lose (see chapter 8). Within the household, the employer has far more power than the domestic worker (see chapters 10 and 11). Therefore, the employer can easily enforce the interpretations of Sharia that are more convenient for him and use the normative tools that defend his preferred outcome. The conflicts between domestic workers and their employers in Saudi Arabia and the Emirates are therefore not directly influenced by Sharia, but rather by power relations.

5. Customary norms

5.1 Introduction

This chapter describes customary norms and the attached behavior of domestic workers and their employers. Customary norms are norms that regulate day-to-day behavior and are not prescribed by a secular or supernatural authority. They are enforced by social pressure or local leaders and regularly influence other norms. Because they are used or referred to in everyday behavior, they are closely connected to the political and economic structure of a community. 'The way things are done' often becomes 'the way things should be done'. In a developing economy, the way things are done changes, leading customary norms to change.[288] Therefore, to describe customary law, often a term is used which has been introduced by Ehrlich: living law.[289]

This chapter describes such customary norms and compares them to customary norms pertaining to domestic workers in Europe over the last several centuries, as they can be deduced from a summary by Rollins of research on domestic workers.[290] Section 5.2 shows how domestic workers and employers in both Saudi Arabia and the Emirates, make statements about the normative position of domestic workers, which very much resemble the three phases in the development in Europe as described by Rollins and summarized in chapter 3. Section 5.3 digs deeper into the question of how parties try to maneuver strategically, using the tools provided by the different normative models. As the data show, Rollins' first and third phase are referred to as normative models, while the second phase is only acted out by employers, but never normatively referred to. Yet while strategic maneuvering does take place, some interviewees seemed adamantly convinced of the correctness of one model. In such instances, if the other party is convinced of another model, type one conflicts due to preliminary disagreement on norms may occur. The data for this particular chapter have been derived entirely from interviews with domestic workers and employers.

5.2 Characteristics of the three phases

Both in the Kingdom of Saudi Arabia and in the United Arab Emirates, there are striking overlaps in the way domestic workers and their employers describe their respective positions and the way Rollins sets out the three phases (chapter 3): the phase of the patriarchal status model, the intermediate phase, and the contractual phase.

---

288 Clark (2007) P375, 379 and 380.
289 Oomen (2005) P201.
290 Rollins (1985) Chapter 1.

Patriarchal status model in the Gulf

The characteristics of the status model as described by Rollins are that (i) the domestic worker is seen as part of the employer's family; (ii) within which the patriarch is the ultimate decision maker and discipliner who accepts no interference from another authority, such as the government; (iii) the domestic worker is considered to need guidance on proper behavior and protection the way children need this; and (iv) payments should be seen as (voluntarily given) pocket money instead of (obligated) wages, as the status model lacks the notion of interdependent and individual rights and duties, but instead defines interdependency in terms of proper roles one must play.

The first characteristic of the status model as described by Rollins is that the domestic worker is seen as part of the employer's family. This aspect is common in the discourse of interviewed domestic workers and employers. In both the Kingdom of Saudi Arabia and the United Arab Emirates, calling the man of the house 'Baba' is quite common and the woman is often called 'Ummi,' which is Arabic for 'my mother', or 'Mama'. Some domestic workers are called 'aunty', but when describing the domestic workers out of earshot, they are regularly referred to as 'children' or 'girls'.

More than half of the interviewed employers stated that the domestic worker was either part of the family, or part of the family with a somewhat different position. Only a small minority considered it a working relationship. In the questionnaire, 58% of domestic workers stated that they were part of the family, 15% said they were part of the family with a somewhat different position and 26% claimed to be workers. Yet in the interviews, neither the employers nor the employees turned out to be entirely consistent on this topic, as will be further discussed in section 5.3.

The second characteristic is that the patriarch is the ultimate decision maker and the discipliner who accepts no interference from another authority, such as the government. Inside the home, he is the state.[291] In both Saudi Arabia and the Emirates, this is an argument regularly used by employers and by government officials to explain why the domestic workers cannot be regulated through a labor law. Many interviewed employers claimed to consider it absolutely forbidden for the 'competing power' of the government to interfere in domestic matters: "It's something from our house and it's not for somebody from outside to judge. Also, the government, they have nothing to do with us. The labor law cannot cover them; the rules cannot go in the house." According to a somewhat smaller group, the government is also not allowed to draft rules concerning physical violence.

---

291 Compare Sasson (2004) P29: "The authority of a Saudi male is unlimited; his wife and children survive only if he desires. In our homes, he is the state."

It is important to note that the non-interference demanded from the government concerns not only domestic workers, but all family members: "Even if there is a problem with my father like if he would beat me, even then, they have nothing to do with it; it's our house."[292]

The third characteristic is that a domestic worker, because she is subordinated to a child-like status, needs guidance and protection. Several employers made statements like: "They are alone here, without family; we need to advise them, to guide them," or "They need to be protected, like I protect my own." This guidance seems to encompass all aspects of life: religion, education about how to handle money, smoking, boyfriends and all other contacts with people outside the house. The reason given by interviewed employers for this oversight is twofold. First, because the domestic worker is considered (in some respects) a child, she needs education and protection. In addition, being considered part of the family means she could bring shame on the entire household through her indiscretions.

Another characteristic of the patriarchal status model is that payments should be seen as (voluntary) pocket money instead of (obligated) wages, because one cannot speak of interdependent rights and duties, but rather of proper roles one has to play. In both Saudi Arabia and the Emirates, interviewed employers regularly stated as much. A highly ranked Emirati echoed several other employers: "It's not a labor relation; the girls are working in our houses. Therefore you cannot speak of salary." The same was said by European men when they were requested by feminists to pay their wives salary for household work: Why should a housewife receive any payment, if she gets everything she needs? In this same line of reasoning, in the patriarchal relation salary is not considered a right of the domestic worker.

According to interviewees at the Filipino embassy in Riyadh, at the Indonesian embassy in Abu Dhabi, at several NGOs and at the National Society for Human Rights, non-payment or underpayment is the number one problem for domestic workers. Most of the interviewed runaways did not receive salary, sometimes not for several years. However, some interviewed employers claimed to offer gifts instead of a salary, worth more than that salary. This type of employer considered gifts to be more appropriate than payment for household work.

---

292 Early Anglo-American Law was the same in this respect. Levit (2006) P180: "The notion of women as property also meant that men could never be guilty of raping their wives because men could treat their possessions, or 'chattel' in nearly any way they wanted. Indeed, the doctrine of 'chastisement' allowed husbands to beat their wives, in 'moderation' to make them obey. (...) When feminists challenged the laws on chastisement during the Reconstruction era, judges invoked the public-private distinction, reasoning that the legal system should not interfere in cases of wife beating, to protect the privacy of the marriage relationship and to promote domestic harmony."

Intermediate phase

The main characteristics of the labor position of the domestic worker during the European phase of industrialization, here referred to as the intermediate phase are – as can be deduced from the work of Rollins – as follows: (i) work demands increased heavily to meet the standards of the new gentility; (ii) as the phenomenon of domestic work spread, often neither the domestic worker nor the employer were acquainted with domestic work; (iii) hierarchical distance between the domestic worker and the employer grew, sometimes immensely, as employers of the new middle class used their domestics to help define their new class identity; and (iv) humiliation in certain families deteriorated into dehumanization.

The first characteristic of the labor position of the domestic worker during the European phase of industrialization is that work demands increased significantly. This happens in many families in Saudi Arabia and the United Arab Emirates as well: the standards of the gentility place a heavy burden on many domestic workers. In Saudi Arabia and, more noticeably, in Dubai, cleanliness is an important virtue.[293] Interviewed domestic workers stated that many employers ordered them to clean the entire house every day: "The children have to look clean, the cars have to be spotless, the pavement in front of the house needs to be swept and the windows must shine." Almost all domestic workers complained of the workload, with workdays varying from a rare eight hours to a sleep-depriving twenty hours.[294]

Keeping a house clean in a desert country is not an easy task. Because younger employers have never done any cleaning themselves, they do not seem to realize the magnitude of the task. This brings us to the second characteristic: as the phenomenon of domestic work spreads, often neither the domestic worker nor the employer is acquainted with domestic work. This applies to a large part of the households in the Emirates and Saudi Arabia; many employers are new to having a domestic worker in their household. The standards of living in both Saudi Arabia and the Emirates have risen at an unprecedented pace. Most families now have a domestic worker, but not many had one a generation ago. In Dubai, all houses have a 'maid-room', but cities can now be built at a speed that exceeds the time needed to educate an entire population on phenomena that are new to them. The Emirates, in particular, used to be quite egalitarian,[295] and the new differences in hierarchy lack the decorum that is elsewhere utilized to make power differences more acceptable, or more bearable. For instance, the principle of *noblesse oblige*[296] that has developed in Europe as a corrective mechanism to large power differences seems to be unknown to most Saudi and Emirati employers.

---

293 Compare Holton (2007) P176.
294 Compare Anderson (2000) P141.
295 With small differences in wealth, there are usually smaller differences in power.
296 Privilege creates responsibility.

Based on the theory of sociologist Elias, a possible explanation is the fact that such forms of internalized self-restraint have not yet developed, but are likely to develop soon, as society both in Saudi Arabia and the Emirates used to be small scale, but with an unprecedented speed, now form increasingly complex networks of social connections.[297]

An ambassador of a labor-sending country stated: "You have to keep in mind that Saudi Arabia only recently was a very tribal society with slavery. Their own lower class was treated badly and they are the ones who are treating the workers the worst now. They have money now and they have no idea how to deal with that." Yet being less used to a labor relationship seems to be an issue on the side of workers as well. Visits to shelters, and interviews there, revealed that runaway domestic workers in the safe houses are comparatively young and in their first contract, whereas domestic workers are generally older and go back to the Middle East for repeated contracts. Although further research is needed here and other explanations could be formulated, it might be an indication that first time domestic workers, especially the ones who have grown up in pre-industrial extended families, are as little used to labor relations as their employers and are therefore more prone to end up in a conflict and run away.

The third characteristic of the European industrialization phase is that the hierarchical distance between domestic worker and employer increased, sometimes significantly, as employers of the new middle class used domestics to help define their new class identity. In the Emirates and Saudi Arabia, many middle-class employers use their domestic workers to position themselves in the social hierarchy. Positions in the social hierarchy have become so important that some families hire a domestic worker even though this might be neither necessary nor economically feasible.[298] In these instances wage conflicts might occur, but this appears to be for a different reason than in the families with patriarchal behavioral patterns.

In the hierarchy, employers seem to copy not only Saudi and Emirati upper class behavior, but also that of the former colonial powers. They use French and English instead of Arabic; the female employer is regularly referred to as 'Madam'. The men, including young boys, are called 'Sir'. This appears to express a larger distance than the previously discussed 'Ummi' and 'Baba'. In Saudi Arabia and the Emirates, skin color[299] is another important determining factor in the social hierarchy. This is a common phenomenon: for centuries and throughout the world, it has been the general pattern that darker-skinned people are considered to be of lower status than lighter-skinned people. In the labor relationship of the domestic workers, this means that, in general, darker-skinned domestic workers would serve the lighter-skinned mistress.[300]

---

297 Elias (2001).
298 Likewise in Yemen: Regt (2008).
299 Holton (2007) P156 describes the wish in the Emirates to have lighter skin many decades ago.
300 Rollins (1985) P7 and still visible in films and TV series.

This might create tension when employees are fair-skinned and working for a somewhat darker employer. If lighter-skinned workers are Christian (like many Filipinas), according to interviewed domestic workers, this was sometimes used by their employers to bolster their superiority; Islam is deemed to be a higher stage in the development of religions.[301]

In Saudi Arabia and the Emirates, as elsewhere, domestic workers are by many employers considered to have very low morals, inadequate performance and a lack of subservience. Many interviewed employers stated that their domestic workers were uneducated, young, in need of guidance, vulgar and ignorant. But it can get worse than that: they are sometimes considered less than human.[302] This brings us to the fourth characteristic, humiliation, which might deteriorate into dehumanization through extreme forms of otherness (more on perceived otherness in chapter 11).

Answers that were frequently given to the question of what domestic workers would like to see changed in the behavior of their employers included, "They must treat the worker as a human being, not like an animal," or "They talk to me like I am a dog." The behavior that leads to remarks such as these is not only humiliation, but also a denial of basic human needs like eating and urinating. In one instance, a domestic worker was not permitted to use the bathrooms; her employer unlocked the door three times a day, so she could pee in the garden. Several domestic workers made statements like, "And they never think about the fact that I also have to eat and drink, that I also have to go to the toilet sometimes." Several interviewed domestic workers reported having been locked in the bathroom without food when the employers left the house for a few days.

Contractual relations in the Gulf

Characteristics of this contractual relation thus are the following: (i) the rights and duties of the employer and domestic worker are interdependent; (ii) if one does not adhere to the agreed terms, the other may end the contract; and (iii) the essence of the agreement is the work and therefore the personality of the domestic worker is less important, leading to (iv) less interference, but also less protection.

Characteristics of such contractual relations involving domestic workers are recognizable in both the United Arab Emirates and the Kingdom of Saudi Arabia, although to a somewhat lesser extent than the characteristics of the other two phases. What exists on a larger scale, both in Saudi Arabia and the Emirates, is the freelancer. This term is used by domestic workers when referring to someone who does not work in one household, but who works for several different households every week. Like social scientists, freelancers refer to live-in domestic workers as 'contract workers', because the live-ins are deemed to be bound for two years by a written contract, whereas the freelancers are free to leave the employer.

---

301 Compare Prokop in Aarts (2005) P57-81.
302 For references to the dehumanization of domestic workers in The Netherlands, see Jansen (2008) P147.

Yet it is the freelancer whose labor relation is more contractual, whereas the position of the live-ins is more status-based and patriarchal. This confusion in terminology is related to the fact that laymen usually regard the freelancer as not having a labor agreement, because she does not sign a contract. According to jurists, however, her oral agreement to work constitutes a labor agreement, which is legally defined as an oral contract.

Because these freelancers are not dependent on one employer for their income, they usually have the freedom to quit if they do not like how they are being treated. This freedom certainly has advantages, although there are also disadvantages: the workers have to arrange for their own housing, food, transportation, and medical care. To some domestic workers, this is enough reason not to become a freelancer: "I don't want to be a freelancer. Too much headache you know, with transportation and the house and all. I am good where I am." Some interviewed domestic workers ran away and became freelancers, but they gave this up when they faced problems they considered too large to deal with themselves. They later returned to the Middle East as live-ins again. In addition to not wanting to freelance, many domestic workers simply would not be able to work as a freelancer. Freelancing requires a level of independence, language skills and knowledge of the country in which they work that many lack.

Another situation where the traits of the contractual labor relation seem to be stronger is within the large households of the upper classes. Although here the freedom to leave is restricted, the labor relationship is certainly more impersonal. Most palaces have been designed to minimize the contact between domestic workers and employers. The personality of the worker matters little, because the emphasis is placed on the work the employer is paying for; the house must be clean and the food must be cooked. Yet live-in domestic workers will probably never have a fully contractual labor relation. Their workplaces are the private domain of the household, in which patriarchal thinking influences the behavior of the persons in it.

5.3 Strategic maneuvering between models
As discussed in chapter 3, the economies of Saudi Arabia and the Emirates are developing at an unprecedented speed. According to Durkheim, such developments lead to a phenomenon he refers to as anomie: a situation in which social or moral norms are confused, unclear, or simply absent due to rapid economic changes.[303] When this theory is placed within the theory of legal pluralism, the result is that legal pluralism and the possibilities for strategic maneuvering enlarge when a society's economy transforms. In the discourse of domestic workers and their employers such strategic maneuvering between the patriarchal status model and the contractual model is clearly visible. Yet Rollins' second phase (during industrialization in Europe) is never used as a normative tool.

---

303 Durkheim (1897).

Therefore, this dissertation suggests that the second phase is not a model in itself, but an intermediate phase. A closer look furthermore reveals that the contractual model can be subdivided into different types of contracts that have contradicting normative consequences. Domestic workers and their employers not only use the two models as normative tools in their strategic maneuvering, but also several subtypes of contracts to support their claims.

The patriarchal status model
The first model to which both employers and domestic workers refer is the patriarchal status model, regularly referred to as a status contract, although it only marginally resembles the modern concept of a contract, as discussed in chapter 3. A status contract is an agreement through which one party takes a position in an existing hierarchy – in this case, the patriarchal family structure. The status contract, like a marriage, makes a person part of an (extended) household. Thereafter, it is not the content of the contract but the patriarchal relationship that regulates their relations.[304]

Many of the employers interviewed for this research used the status model to justify paternalistic behavior and the right to set behavioral rules that have little to do with the tasks expected, but which instead resemble a parent-child relationship. Participation in the family structure demands a high level of loyalty towards the family, so emphasizing a domestic worker's position in the family reduces the risk of family secrets being revealed to outsiders. Furthermore, employers used this particular line of reasoning to justify their demand for love and care. Domestic workers are not only supposed to dress and feed the children, but are also usually expected to offer emotional involvement as well: "Take care of the children like they are your own." This discourse is used by domestic workers when they demand care and protection.

The status model is also used to reject the claim of domestic workers to certain rights. Most commonly, it is used to justify why a labor law cannot be applied to domestic workers. Particular rights are denied through this model, such as the domestic workers' right to proper contact with their own families[305] or contractual agreements concerning household tasks: "I told them I didn't want to serve at all their parties. I told her they are not my employers, all these people. So I said, 'This is not in the contract, Madam.' She says, 'Why you always refer to the contract! You are in our family now.'"

Contractual models
A second model referred to by the interviewed domestic workers is the contractual model, though a closer look reveals that it is actually several subtypes of the model which are used as a normative tool.

---

304 Maine (1913).
305 Compare Anderson (2000).

The first subtype, the labor contract, is here defined as a contract between two parties in which one (the employer) accepts the obligation to pay a salary, while the other (the employee) accepts the obligation to perform tasks under the instruction of the employer. The rights and duties of both parties are regarded as interdependent. These terms of this relationship are used by domestic workers mainly when demanding timely payment of their full salaries. It was also used to reject paternalism or (overly strong) demands for emotional involvement: "I applied for a job, not a family." Furthermore, it was used to reject sexual advances. For instance, one domestic worker said, "My employer said: you are so beautiful. I told him that I offer my service, that doesn't include my body! I didn't sign anything to offer my body!"

A second subtype of the contractual model, referred to mostly by employers, is the servitude contract. The servitude contract (as defined for this analysis) is a labor contract in which the employer has paid an amount of money in advance, causing the employee to lose the right to leave prematurely. The payments made to the agency – and all other expenses – are relabeled as debts of the domestic worker to the employer, which must be paid back by fulfilling the obligations of the contract for the full two years. Domestic workers are sometimes forced to pay this money back even when the labor relation is terminated prematurely by the employer. For instance, one domestic worker related how her employer had to go back to India for family reasons. By withholding her passport, he forced her to pay back part of the costs he had incurred. The fact that she was not the one who had received that money in the first place did not matter to him.

A third subtype is the service contract. In their contact with the agencies, both the employers and the domestic workers use the discourse of the service contract, here defined as a contract in which one party must organize or arrange a certain task or service for the other party. The person who actually performs the task is of little or no importance, as long as the task is performed properly. The employer can claim to have acquired two different services: one is the 'delivery of a good domestic worker' against payment; the other is 'cleaning and caretaking for two years'. Most agencies offer the option to exchange the domestic worker for another one within three months if she does not comply with justified expectations. Several employers do so, even though this is incompatible with the status contract discourse, which states that the domestic worker has become part of the family. The domestic worker uses the discourse of the service contract when claiming to have rights towards the agency, primarily the agency in the country of origin: the agent was supposed to find her a good employer in exchange for a certain amount of money. This discourse is used when the employer does not provide the domestic worker with what she believes she is entitled to. This often concerns salary payments, but it also regularly concerns matters that (according to Western law) are cases of criminal law. For instance, one domestic worker who had been raped by her employer told me she was planning to sue her agency back home: "They promised me a good employer, but he wasn't." Sometimes the domestic workers contact the agency in the country of destination, as they (correctly or incorrectly) understand this to be the representative of the agency in the country of origin. The domestic worker uses the discourse of the service contract and the right to a 'good employer' toward this agency when she is unhappy with her employer and has decided to stop working entirely, within the three-month probationary period.

A fourth subtype of the contractual model, used only by certain employers, not by domestic workers, is the purchase contract. This is a contract in which one person acquires ownership over an object from another person. The object can – apart from goods – be a person, or the labor of a person. Several researchers note that the payments made when hiring a domestic worker create a feeling of ownership.[306] This discourse has become politically incorrect since the abolition of slavery, but is still used by employers mainly when addressing third parties.[307] This is due to the fact that ownership creates (almost) absolute rights over the object that has been purchased, rights that can be upheld against all other individuals, including those with whom one does not have any contract. Therefore it is used towards people other than the domestic worker or the agency. As several interviewees in shelters explained, when domestic workers run away to a shelter, employers frequently search for them and say things like: "Give me back my maid. I have paid a lot of money for her."

Another reason why this discourse is used by employers is that Islam states that it is not permissible to have sex with a domestic worker, but it is permissible to do so with a slave or concubine. The discourse is thus used to claim a right to sexual intercourse that cannot be claimed under the employment, service, or servitude contracts. A domestic worker told Human Rights Watch[308] that her employer said: "I want to tell you how I got you from the agency. I bought you for 10,000 Riyals," upon which he raped her. Likewise, a website publishing fatwas[309] received a letter from a man saying that he needed someone "for comfort and support and to fulfill my jobs." He made an agreement with a woman that she would be his slave: "So it gives me the rights to touch her and look at her."[310] This discourse seems to be more common in Saudi Arabia than in the Emirates. In Saudi Arabia some people offer their domestic worker for sale on TV through SMS services; an interviewed agent stated that domestic workers are slaves, and far more interviewees stated that certain employers regard domestic workers as property.

---

306 Among others, Guzman (2003).
307 And by certain agencies, as explained in chapter 6.
308 Report 18, P42.
309 Religious opinions.
310 http://www.islamqa.com/en/ref/26067 March 2010.

Five contradicting normative tools

In the preceding analysis of the discourse of the employers and the domestic workers, two different models with several subtypes can thus be recognized. They are often incompatible and are referred to depending on the situation, to whom one is talking and what one is trying to achieve. Because the employer is in a more powerful position than the domestic worker, he has numerous options for strategic maneuvering. When demanding loyalty and care, he can treat the agreement as a status agreement. When telling the domestic worker she does not have the right to leave the house before the end of the contract, he can refer to the servitude agreement. When he is tired of her, he can take her to the agency to replace her, referring to the service agreement. Legal pluralism and the attached maneuvering space caused by the rapidly changing economy, is theoretically in the interest of both parties, as they both have more normative tools. In practice it is not in the interest of the party with less power, which in this case is the domestic worker; she cannot enforce her preferred argumentative tools, while the employer can.

The data furthermore show that there are two normative models co-existing with several subtypes, to which both domestic worker and employer can refer to support their claims. Yet the intermediate phase, as explained in chapter 3, is not a model in itself.

5.4 Conflicts due to incompatible expectations

The previous section should not be interpreted to mean that both domestic worker and employer are endlessly opportunistic in their choice of model, in their choice of normative tool. There does seem to be some level of preliminary belief on what is the 'right' model. Although no hard conclusions can be drawn, the data seem to suggest that those persons who more strongly refer to the status based patriarchal model tend to be older employers or more inexperienced domestic workers from rural areas. As such, the results furthermore suggest[311] that conflicts can arise if the domestic worker is expecting a labor relation, or a normative model, that the employer is not offering. In other words, while legal pluralism enables strategic maneuvering in existing conflicts, it may also create conflicts in cases of preliminary disagreement on norms.

To people entirely used to thinking in the patriarchal status model, the concept of rights turned out to be difficult to grasp. This was evident when talking about enforcement. When asked what human rights are, both employers and employees gave answers such as: "Human rights means to have respect." When asked if one could go to a judge to demand respect, they replied negatively.

---

311 It was very difficult to find families in which both the employer and the employee could be interviewed. In most cases, domestic workers talked about the behavior and discourse of their employer, whereas employers from other families talked about the behavior and discourse of their domestic workers. Therefore, I state that the results suggest that a mismatch makes conflicts likely. Only extensive interviews with both parties in the same family could prove this.

Similarly, an interviewed employer said: "Many domestic workers do have rights; they are treated kindly." When asked if they could do anything if they were not treated kindly, he responded that they could not. Likewise, for anyone accustomed to contractual relations, it is hard to grasp how a domestic worker thinking in the patriarchal status model does not see the need for reciprocity in behavior. Several interviewed domestic workers claimed to have completed their full contractual period despite severe abuse, because they felt it was the role they had to play. A bad master was, as they said, just a matter of shame and of fate.[312]

Many interviewed domestic workers entirely rejected the status model and the thought of being part of the family. One Filipina in Dubai powerfully summarized this view: "I applied for a job, not for a family!" Others specifically focused their criticism on the aspect of guidance: "We ask if we can have the day off. But they will not allow this. Because they say maybe we will do a problem outside. But if we have problems, it is our problems, not their problems." This type of domestic worker usually came from a town instead of a village and comparing Indonesia to the Philippines, they were more likely to have come from Manila.

Other domestic workers who did not receive this status-based position explicitly asked for it. They wrote on the questionnaires: "They must treat the housemaid as his real family!" This type of worker was more likely to come from the countryside, especially the Indonesian countryside, where the patriarchal system still regulates entire villages[313] and some women did not even understand the Bahasa word for contract.[314]

The troubles resulting from this mismatch of expectations should not be underestimated: "Part of being a domestic worker was acting like the person the employer wanted her domestic to be. The better the performance, the greater the probability of the domestic worker receiving more than the minimum in material and emotional rewards. And like employers, domestics have definite preferences."[315] But even within one family different models are often expected; the grandmother regularly demands a patriarchal status-based labor relation. Her daughter (who probably never worked) more likely behaves like a nouveau riche, whereas the granddaughter, who teaches computer skills, is fully accustomed to the contractual relation. In such families, one can see the grandmother share the kitchen with the domestic worker, whereas the mother says demeaning things about her from the sofa and the daughter explains the respective rights and duties at Starbucks.

---

312 On the conditions under which people are likely to make the switch to rights-based thinking, see Merry (2006) P215: "If their experience of claiming rights is positive, in that institutional actors support and validate these claims, they are more likely to see themselves as rights-bearing subjects and to claim rights in the next crisis."
313 Very informative on this matter was an organization for women's rights in Jakarta.
314 Bahasa is the official language of Indonesia. My attentive interpreter explicitly told me whenever an interviewee did not seem to understand certain words.
315 Rollins (1985) P140.

For a domestic worker this situation can be confusing[316] and even dangerous when the granddaughter is not concerned or just curious if the domestic worker has a boyfriend, while the grandmother thinks the rules of honor killings should apply.

The situation becomes even more complicated when some individuals insist on one model, while others refer to different models at different times. Employers refer to the patriarchal status model when denying a day off ("My wife doesn't have a day off, either"), but refer to the contractual model when enforcing a salary deduction ("The contract states she has experience, but I can see from her ironing that she doesn't, so I lowered her salary"). Domestic workers refer to the patriarchal model when demanding care and protection, but to the contractual model when demanding a weekly day off. So on the one hand, the co-existence of the different models creates maneuvering space in existing conflicts. On the other hand, the co-existence sometimes causes (type one) conflicts in cases in which the two parties have a preliminary contradicting conviction on what is the appropriate model.

5.5 Summary

This chapter describes customary norms and how they change due to the rapid economic changes taking place in both the Kingdom of Saudi Arabia and the United Arab Emirates. In the last fifty years, both countries have undergone a process of industrialization[317] in which production was moved from extended family units into companies and factories outside the family. This same transformation has taken place in Europe, but over a much longer period of time and in a different manner, which makes similarities unlikely. Nevertheless, the similarities between Europe and the Gulf in customary norms pertaining to domestic workers are striking.

Rollins[318] describes three phases in the development of the position of domestic workers in Europe that, if placed in the corpus of sociology of law, can be framed as a development from the status model to the contractual model. Domestic workers and employers in both Saudi Arabia and the Emirates make statements about the position of domestic workers, which very much resemble these three phases. The difference between Europe on the one hand and Saudi Arabia and the Emirates on the other is that due to the speed of economic changes, the three phases can be recognized concurrently between families, within families, or even in the discourse of one employer. At the same time, domestic workers expect or demand either a status-based or a contractual relation, depending upon where they come from and on the issue at hand. The speed of the changes and the co-

---

316 Compare Heyzer (1994) P71 on contradictory demands leading to anxiety and tension.
317 Clark (2007) P736: Industrialization is a process of economic and social change in which societies increase levels of productivity by changing what, where and how they produce. The production takes place in small, medium or large enterprises, often centralized in urban areas.
318 Rollins (1985) Chapter 1.

existence of different normative models can be referred to as anomie, as described by Durkheim.

Yet although both employer and employee maneuver between a status model and a contractual model, the intermediate phase is never referred to as normative model or ideal to be followed; it is only acted out by certain employers, in the sense that it merely describes the actual situation in certain relationships. Therefore an adjustment of Rollins' theory is proposed. Whereas Rollins presented her findings as three phases in the development of labor relations, the results of this research suggest that there are only two normative models: the status model and the contractual model. The intermediate phase concerns a labor relation in which humiliation is possible, because the enforcement mechanisms of the status model are disappearing, whereas the enforcement mechanisms of the contractual model are not yet in place. Rollins' description of three phases is thus redefined as two models with an intermediate phase, in which degradation and dehumanization are possible because the safeguards of the status model have disappeared, whereas the safeguards of the contractual model are not yet in place.

The data in this research furthermore show that the strategic maneuvering does not simply take place between the two models, but also between different subtypes. Furthermore the data suggest that if parties have a preliminary contradicting conviction on what is the appropriate model, this sometimes causes (type one) conflicts; not only are the models used in conflicts, they also cause conflicts.

6. Contractual norms

6.1 Introduction

Contractual norms are norms that are considered to be binding on parties, because parties have in freedom and knowledge agreed to them and wanted to be bound by them. Contracts create *in personam* rights or relative rights, meaning rights that are binding only on contracting parties, not on third parties. They are distinguished from absolute rights that are binding on all individuals: everyone has to observe, for instance, somebody else's property right, but can largely ignore somebody else's contract. Contractual norms are furthermore distinguished from statutory norms, as contractual norms are self-imposed, while for instance tort law is not.[319]

Contractual norms are a third type of norm to which domestic workers and their employers refer in conflicts. They concern everything that parties agreed on during the recruitment process, both by the domestic worker in the country of origin and by the employer in the country of destination. Furthermore, as views on what has been agreed on can vary between parties, it concerns everything parties think they have agreed on. As the data in this research show, there are large differences of opinion between employers and domestic workers on this type of norm and this regularly results in type one conflicts, conflicts that concern preliminary disagreement on norms.

Section 6.2 therefore starts with the description of the perspective of an average employer and employee, to show how their expectations on contractual norms can lead to conflicts. Section 6.3 describes where the perceptions of the domestic workers concerning what has been agreed on stem from. These perceptions result from the contact with the agency, the contract and the pre-departure procedures and courses. Section 6.4 describes the information that agencies provide in the countries of destination, that shape the perception of the employers on what has been agreed on. Section 6.5 provides an overview of the type one conflicts that result from the preliminary disagreement on contractual norms. Section 6.6 discusses that the Western theory of consent does not apply.

The data for this particular chapter have been gathered through questionnaires, mainly filled in by domestic workers who were about to leave for the Middle East, but also by domestic workers who had been working in Saudi Arabia and the Emirates already. Other sources were unannounced visits and calls to agencies in Saudi Arabia, the Emirates, Indonesia and the Philippines, visits to pre-departure orientation courses, about two dozen written contracts, and interviews with domestic workers, employers and government officials.

---

319 Clark (2007) P290.

6.2 Perspectives of an average employer and employee

The international press usually blames the employer for all conflicts between domestic workers and their employers.[320] This judgment however is not always correct. To explain such, this section describes the point of view of an average Saudi or Emirati employer: he visits an agency located somewhere in the part of town where he is living and formulates his wishes: "I want a domestic worker to take care of the house and my four children. We want her to have work experience and we prefer a Filipina." The agency replies that the going rate for Filipinas is $200 a month. The man does not agree, as many people pay a monthly salary of $100. The agency explains that he can currently get a Nepalese for that money, but for Filipinas the price has gone up. They agree on a Filipina and the man has to pay $1.600 to the agency for travel expenses and paperwork. The man is told that for the first two months he does not have to pay any salary (her contribution to the travel expenses) and that it is best not to allow her to talk to anybody and to keep her inside the house.

Three months later, he is notified that his domestic worker has arrived. He goes to the airport to a special place to pick her up and brings her to his wife, who will explain her all the work to be done. Soon the problems start. For starters, she does not want to take care of the children, but after some discussion she gets to work. It soon becomes clear, however, that she does not have experience, as she has no idea how to iron an *abaya*, the traditional Arab dress. The next problem is that she wants to leave the house, but this is not permitted in Saudi Arabia. At the end of the third month, she erupts in anger when he hands her the agreed $200. That night she runs away. The man is very upset, as this has cost him a lot of money and his wife will be without help for another 3 months.

From the perspective of an average Filipina, however, the story is very different. She has heard from friends at home that one can earn big money in the Middle East as a domestic worker. Some of them are in Dubai and she wants to go there as well. She goes to an agency and pays them $260 to find her a good employer in the Emirates. She is told that the salary for Filipinas in the Middle East is $400 per month. The agency does not give her a written contract, because they say that the work and the salary are the same everywhere. From then on, she has to remain within the compound of the agency. During her 2 months there, she receives a 3 hour lesson on how to operate electronic devices and she follows a 3 day crash course in Arabic and Middle Eastern culture, but she understands only half of it.

She is brought to the airport where a man from the agency in the capital, whom she has never met, hands her a sealed envelope that contains her contract. He then gives her a ticket and she finds out that she is not going to Dubai, but to Riyadh.

---

320 In the studied media coverage, abusive employers were usually mentioned and the meager legal protection facilitating such abuse was sometimes mentioned, but no mention was ever made of the agencies misinforming the domestic workers.

As she does not know anything about the Middle East, she does not realize that life will be different there. Upon arrival, she has to wait in a room for three days, where she has to sleep in a chair. Eventually somebody hands her a black dress and a veil that she is expected to wear. Finally, a man who does not even introduce himself, comes to pick her up. Apparently, he is her master now. After arriving at the house of the family, in poor English she is told to take care of children. She is angry about that, because she agreed to become a domestic worker and according to her, this entails only cleaning and cooking. In addition, she has to prepare all the food. She gets to eat the leftovers, but as the taste is so different, she cannot stand it and is continuously hungry. The worst part is that she is never allowed to leave the house! She is terribly homesick and when at the end of the third month her employer pays her only $200, she snaps. She cannot take it anymore. During the night she climbs out of the window and runs away.

6.3 Contractual rights as perceived by domestic workers

Many domestic workers thus have very different ideas from those of their employers as to what the agreed labor conditions are. How does this situation develop? To understand this, the process of recruitment of domestic workers has been researched to examine where and to what extent both parties gather information on contractual norms.

6.3.1 The recruitment process

Domestic workers enter their labor relation through a variety of channels, often used in combination. As interviewed domestic workers explained, they are often approached in their villages by middlemen or recruiters.[321] Others approach these recruiters themselves, after hearing stories from friends or family members about making 'big money' in the Middle East. In larger cities, women can simply walk into job agencies. Middle men usually ask for a placement fee; the domestic workers never question them about this amount, as it is presented as fixed, while it is not. Many agencies in the capital no longer ask for a placement fee for the Middle East – as revealed by the questionnaires filled in by domestic workers who were about to leave for the Middle East.[322]

In Manila, a male informant hired for the purpose of this research visited seven recruitment agencies. He pretended to gather information for his cousin from the countryside, who wanted to work in the Middle East as a domestic worker. A female informant researched three additional agencies by phone.

---

321 Many of these middle men recruit for jobs abroad. If for some reason the papers required cannot (immediately) be obtained, the domestic worker will work in the city (first).

322 This seems to be the successful result of both governments in their attempts to reduce debt bondage. For instance in the Philippines nowadays the placement fee cannot be over one month's salary of the employment contract, with some exceptions. Maruah in Kuptsch (2006) P41.

The ten agencies investigated were partly Filipino and partly Arabic. The answers given were very inconsistent (in contrast to the answers given in Jakarta). Three agencies said that they no longer sent women to the Middle East because of the danger of imprisonment or because of the many salary conflicts. Of the remaining seven agencies, five did not allow the informant to see the contract. One agency provided two different contracts and required both to be signed; the contracts stated different salaries, and one granted free days, whereas the other did not. Two agencies stated that salary and days off depended on the employer. First, the domestic worker was required to sign a contract, and then she would be informed of the conditions. Six agencies said nothing about workers not being permitted to leave the house or not having any days off. The salary offered was generally around $200, but one agency offered $400. Some requested valid identity documents and police clearances, while others did not. None of them requested permission from family members. Six agencies refused to answer certain questions posed by the informant.

In Jakarta, a female informant investigated eight agencies, pretending to want a job as a domestic worker in the Middle East and to inquire for her younger (undocumented) niece. The responses were very consistent and all of the agents she talked to were Indonesian. In none of the agencies was she permitted to read the contract before deciding if she wanted to sign or not. None of the agencies requested a birth certificate or passport; they all stated that they could provide (false) documents for the younger niece. Yet they all demanded a letter from the parents or husband with permission; this permission may be prescribed by the government, but according to several interviewees this was not because of a lack of full legal capacity of the women, but because the society is still very patriarchal, more so than in the Philippines. No information was provided voluntarily about days off, but upon being questioned hereon, half the recruiters replied there would be no days off and half replied that it depended on the individual employer. No information was provided voluntarily regarding the segregation of men and women in the Middle East or on the fact that most domestic workers are not permitted to leave the house. Upon the question concerned, they replied that it depended on the employer, or that there would not be any place to visit anyway.

All of the agencies offered a salary of around $200. Most agencies said they would decide which country the domestic worker would go to. One agent asked after five questions from the informant: "Are you sure you want to work?" Several of the agencies' guards offered money and protection in exchange for mentioning to the recruiter that the informant had come to the agency through the guard. Afterwards the informant said: "They were mostly very intimidating and condescending. They seem to think you do not need to know anything."

Neither the agents in Manila nor the agents in Jakarta are thus very generous in providing information during the recruitment process. Some information given is incorrect, such as the salary of $400 per month. Other important information is simply not provided, such as exactly what the work entails, how many days or hours per week the domestic worker has to work and the fact that most domestic workers are not permitted to freely leave the house. Many agencies do not allow the domestic workers to read the contract or they do not give a contract and often they do not have answers to important questions. Thus, the recruiters are not informing the domestic workers correctly on the labor conditions.

6.3.2 *Written contracts*

A second factor that influences the perceptions of what domestic workers have agreed on, is written contracts. These contracts have been researched through the use of questionnaires that were completed by 160 domestic workers[323] who were about to leave for the Middle East.[324] Furthermore, a number of the domestic workers that were interviewed also provided copies of their contracts.

Table 6.1 Written contracts (n= 155)

	Jakarta	Manila
Yes, I signed a contract	91%	77%
Yes, I signed a contract I could read	89%	70%
Yes, I got a copy of the contract	73%	58%

These percentages were all lower when the same questions were asked to returning domestic workers (overall 73% had a contract, 58% could read it and 35% received a copy). The policy of both Saudi Arabia and the Emirates to obligate a written contract, mentioned by interviewees from both governments, therefore seems to have effect. Interesting is the fact that most NGOs both in Manila and Jakarta believe that the recruitment process is better organized in Manila, while these data shows the opposite concerning written contracts. (Other aspects were indeed better organized in Manila, such as the possibility to return to the same employer after finishing a 2 year contract without having to pay an agency again).[325] Several domestic workers who were interviewed upon their return in Asia made statements such as: "There was a contract, but the signature wasn't mine." One of them explained that her agent had signed both her false passport and her contract. Furthermore, many domestic workers in the interviews made statements like: "They made me sign all these papers, I don't know what."

---

323 As not all domestic workers replied to all questions, n is always somewhat lower than 160.
324 Sometimes these data are compared to 100 questionnaires filled in by domestic workers who had left their employers, either because of a conflict or after finishing the two-year contract.
325 Compare Anggraeni (2006) P36 and 42.

Fraud and contract substitution

One domestic worker interviewed in Riyadh stated that she had signed a contract stating that she was going to earn 400 dollars per month, but the Arabic version turned out to state 400 Riyal, which is only about 90 dollars, and that is what her employer paid her. Likewise a journalist wrote on his blog:[326] "A lot of people I've met in Dubai prepare a contract with a quite reasonable English version and a quite unreasonable Arabic version and rely on the fact that, in a UAE[327] court, the English has absolutely no standing." The Emirates government later on blocked this website stating that the author is lying, but an interviewee from the Dubai Ministry of Labor admitted: "The problem is that many domestic workers think they are going to earn 600 dollars per month, which turns out to be only 600 dirham" (about 135 dollars).

Another problem is the fact that several agencies switch the contracts upon arrival in the Middle East, which is called contract substitution. The new contracts contain clauses stating: "agreed and signed by both parties without interference or pressure from any party." This is problematic considering that the judges tend to read contracts literally and ignore the possibility of fraud, as will be further discussed in chapter 8. Interviewees from the Filipino embassies both in Saudi Arabia and the Emirates state that contract substitution is widespread: "When they arrive here, they are pressured to sign another contract and then that is the one that counts, so our contracts are never applied. It is hard for them to say no and also many of them are too trusting; they think the agents know what they are doing or they just don't want to go back, because they will be discredited."

Governmental standard contracts

The Emirati government has written a standard contract that is enforced through the Naturalization and Residency Department. Here, papers are only processed if the Emirati standard contract has been signed by the employer. A Dubai government official stated that "the core of the new contract is transparency in the relationship between the employer and the worker, while ensuring that both parties' rights are protected". This Emirati governmental standard contract is problematic as it provides a weekly day off for all those who have entered the country on this new contract. This news spread quickly and many other workers (with older contracts) believed that they also had the right to this day off, which created conflicts. These conflicts should be solved in 2 years when all domestic workers are supposed to have the new contract.

---

326 http://secretdubai.blogspot.com/ February 2008, currently blocked by the Emirati government; see also Ali (2010) P58.
327 United Arab Emirates.

More serious is the fact that neither the Saudi nor the Emirati government recognizes the conditions that have been offered to the workers pre-departure. Therefore, in the Emirates it is actually the government that practices contract substitution. As some countries of origin also have written a standard contract, some domestic workers have three different contracts. This seems to be most problematic in the case of Filipina domestic workers because their government currently uses a standard contract demanding $400 salary per month, plus a weekly day off.[328] The Filipino government claims to enforce its own standard contract, but in reality they are not very consistent. Several governmental offices process the paperwork of domestic workers who present a contract with a far lower salary. Also the government's pre-departure courses do not contain any information on the standard contract or the minimum wage. Furthermore during this research in both Saudi Arabia and the Emirates there were some indications that the embassies themselves 'replace' runaway domestic workers in other families for a salary of $200 per month.

Most employers in Saudi Arabia and the Emirates do not recognize the standard contracts of the countries of origin – if they are aware of their existence. An interviewed Filipina domestic worker stated: "In the embassy they make the employer sign the contract with the 400 dollar and the day off. But then if they come back to the house they throw that away." An interviewed employer said: "We signed a contract with the agency and with the embassy, but we stick to the first." As the conditions are quite different especially for the Filipina workers (half the salary), many are to be qualified as trafficking victims, but neither government recognizes them as such. Neither government recognizes the labor conditions as they have been agreed on in the countries of origin, nor do they recognize the workers concerned as trafficking victims (more on this issue in chapter 7).

Other standard contracts
Apart from the governmental standard contracts (both from countries of origin and destination) certain agencies both in Saudi Arabia and the Emirates work on standard contracts. These bilingual standard contracts are sent to their counterpart in the countries of origin, with the request to have the domestic worker read and sign this contract. These contracts contain clauses like: "The employer shall treat the employee in a just and human manner. In no case shall physical violence be used upon the employee" and "It shall be unlawful to deduct any amount from the regular salary of the employee". But these contracts contain other stipulations that can cause problems. The most important one is the rule on the travel expenses of the domestic worker for the trip returning home. The employer has to pay this, as interviewees explained, both according to customary rules and these contracts.

---

328 Saudi Gazette 19-06-2009 reported on Sri Lankan prescribed contracts with a minimum salary and the same large scale problem of contract substitution.

Yet the employer is released from this duty in two cases: if the domestic worker is doing something wrong and if the domestic worker decides to end the work relation prematurely for personal reasons. Interviewing runaways, it turned out that the behavior of certain employers heavily deteriorates close to the end of the contract, to force the domestic worker to run away in order to have others pay for her return ticket.

Another group writing standard contracts is formed by the unions of agencies. Sometimes these standard contracts are agreed on and sometimes the unions in the countries of destination try to prescribe them. In September 2008 the largest union of agencies in Manila was upset about a contract that Saudi unions tried to prescribe. It was a strange contract indeed, because it mainly described rights and duties of agencies, while it was supposed to replace also the contracts between employer and employee. Nevertheless the agreements contained no clause stating that the agencies signed as a legal representative of the employers or employees. The right of the agencies to bind third parties seemed to be implied. In this respect the contract seemed inspired by the patriarchal thought that richer or more powerful individuals have the right to make decisions for poor and less powerful individuals, without the latter giving consent. The fact that somebody needs help or protection provides enough legitimization. Every time when Saudis or Emiratis were questioned about the legal weaknesses of these contracts, they immediately evaded the topic by giving examples of 'bad' domestic workers.

But government officials in countries of origin also regularly refer to the stereotype that domestic workers are not fully capable of handling their own affairs. In Indonesia, workers are currently provided with medical insurance, although the policy which seems to be necessary to actually receive help is given to the agency, not to the worker. In Manila, domestic workers who returned from overseas in distress (sick, traumatized or simply broke) are sheltered in the capital, but they are not permitted to leave the premises. In Jakarta, returning domestic workers arrive at a separate terminal, which they are not permitted to leave freely; they have to pay the government to bring them home. All of these regulations are presented as being established to help the workers, but they also create ample opportunity to abuse migrant workers.

In summary, many domestic workers either do not have a contract or they have several contracts. For others contracts have been signed by agents, while it is not clear if this is based on a perceived sense of representation or a method to deceive the workers. Governments and other organizations use different standard contracts without agreement on which contract should be binding or on the legal base of these actions.

6.3.3 Preparations & Courses

In addition to the recruitment talk with the agent or recruiter and the oral or written agreements, a third factor that affects expectations concerning working conditions is the information given to the domestic workers during the waiting period and preparations.[329] Both in Manila and Jakarta the governments require and organize seminars. The courses focus mainly on language, culture and relevant legal rules. They are intended to properly prepare the domestic workers, but this research revealed that frequently incorrect information is provided concerning work conditions and rights.

Some parts of the booklets handed out during the courses imply that the domestic workers have rights that go beyond what any of the studied or discussed contracts state. For instance, it states that: "You may terminate your contract without just causes by serving one (1) month in advance written notice to the employer." No contract has been found that allows the worker to leave within 2 years without just causes. No employer or agent agreed to domestic workers having that right. Another teacher handed out booklets printed by the Saudi government, that were intended for workers going to Saudi Arabia who were covered by the labor law, while the women concerned as domestic workers are not. One school showed a film that stated that the workers have the right to one month holiday per year, while in reality the domestic workers do not have that right.

In some cases domestic workers were told that they do not have rights, while they actually do. Some teachers stated, for instance, that domestic workers do not have the right to bring mobile phones, while in neither Saudi Arabia nor the Emirates there is such a law. Several teachers made statements such as: "Don't ever run away from the house. If you run away, people who say they help you, can sell you into another country. You have to be obedient. You can be sued as a witch if you are disobedient and then you will be in troubles." But the most frequent problem was teachers simply being too vague about rights and duties. They stated, for instance, that the women have the right to rest and to sleep, without stating how much rest or sleep. Other remarks were certainly useful, such as "Don't ever sign a blank paper or don't put your finger print on any paper. They will use it to say you got your salary." Or "Don't gather any hair, the employer will think you do magic" or "stay away from men, if you get pregnant you go to jail!" (More on occultism and sexual relations is found in chapter 11.)

None of the teachers was very clear about what to do if these rights were violated. One teacher stated the following, which is a good example of the attitude of teachers towards rights: "Your salary is about 800 Riyal, but you have to be prepared for the reality. ...

---

329 After signing, domestic workers usually do not have the right to leave the agencies' dorms anymore. If they change their minds, the agents press them to stay, with expositions on the large investments they have made in order to get the papers for the women concerned processed.

"Many only give 600, so what do you do? Do you want to go back home? If you accept you continue your work well and you have to be nice to them so you can carefully try to persuade them to pay you the 800 as they have agreed to in the contract. If they refuse, you can try again after a year. You have to work well, so hopefully they pity you and they raise your salary. But it is against the law, so you can also refuse it. Then there are 2 possibilities. If the agency decides to send you to another family, but you will be illegal after that. You can also go home. It is not easy to persuade the Arabs to pay what is in the contract. It's sad but the reality is that sometimes you do have to accept this." So the teachers in general do not stimulate rights awareness, but acquiescence.

In case of serious problems, all the teachers and booklets advise the workers to go to their embassy. Phone numbers are handed out, though many domestic workers in the Middle East complain that these lines are rarely answered. Nobody handed out addresses or phone numbers of Saudi or Emirati authorities. No teacher or booklet said anything about rights vis-à-vis the agencies or where to go in case of a conflict with the agents or middle men, while this would have been very useful information.

In general, the domestic workers were not very receptive to the information given. One teacher was very clear when she showed a contract on a screen and pointed out all the conditions it should contain. While she explained that the contract had to state that the employer is responsible for medical fees, nobody reacted, even though contracts with such provision are very rare. Likewise, a teacher said that they had the right to a weekly day off, which triggered no response from the workers although it is likely that at least some of them have heard otherwise from domestic workers in the dormitories where they were staying (below). They did not state that they did not understand their contracts, nor did they ask questions or state that their contract or agent did not provide for these rights.

Some information is given to domestic workers in the dormitories in which they usually stay for about two months before departure. It is provided by other workers who have been to the Middle East before. This information tends to be more accurate than any other source, more accurate than information from friends and family members, who tend not to say anything about negative aspects. The 'dorm' information usually creates more realistic expectations about work conditions, but it is provided after, not before, the contract is signed.

Employers from their side expect a well-trained worker and both in Manila and Jakarta the women usually receive some form of training, although in practice this regularly comes down to keeping the offices or houses of the agents clean without receiving payment. Some admit that this is the case: "They practice by cleaning our offices." Other agencies say they prepare the women very well: "We have a whole manual of all the training the domestic workers should go through (...). 50% of our program is Arabic language lessons. The rest is how to handle babies, how to do beds, use a blender, a gas oven, how to clean an airco filter and all they have to do at the airport." When asked how it was possible that I had not met any domestic worker who had told me about a proper preparation this same agent said: "We have no choice. The training is expensive and if we would follow our own manual, we wouldn't be able to compete anymore." Several NGOs stated that in the capital there is indeed some minimal training given at the agencies, but in the countryside there is nothing. Domestic workers confirm this: "I was in the capital only one day. I never had any training or course."

During their training domestic workers thus receive information that is incorrect, information that is vague and information that should have been provided to the worker prior to her committing to the job offer. As for the training that the laborers are supposed to receive, usually they are not properly trained.

6.4 Contractual rights as perceived by employers
Both in Saudi Arabia and the Emirates, several agencies were visited by the researcher, presenting herself as looking for a domestic worker in order to hear what the agents tell employers about work conditions.

Emirati Agencies
In the Emirates on the border of Sharjah and Ajman[330] fees to be paid to the agency depended on nationality and experience, ranging from $340 for an inexperienced Ethiopian, to $1.370 for an experienced Indonesian. Everywhere the salary was around $200 monthly, never the $400 that the Filipino government demands. None of the 6 agencies said that the domestic workers sign a contract before departure. They all stated that the workers sign a contract upon arrival in the Middle East. None of the agents permitted potential employers to read the contract. They said it was not important; all an employer needed to know was that she would stay for 2 years, what the salary would be and the fact that there were no days off or maximum work hours.

I had to be persistent in all agencies to receive more information on further costs. Sometimes medical examinations and visas were included in the fee and sometimes they were not. The fee always included a one way ticket for the domestic workers and the employer would have to pay the return ticket, but no agency voluntarily offered that information. The fee to be paid to the agency, turned out to be nonrefundable, but if an employer was unsatisfied with the worker, he could exchange her for somebody else within the first 3 months. When asked who would pay the cost if the domestic worker would get sick, several agents stated that she would not get sick. When insisting ("what if she gets cancer or something?"), they said the domestic worker should be sent home. Some were aware of the existence

---

330 I haven't been able to find agencies in Dubai proper, which suggests a difference in law or enforcement per Emirate, but I haven't been able to find out more information thereon.

of health insurance or a health card, but most said it was better to put her on a plane.

Other remarks the agents made were: "Don't allow her to go outside on her own. Don't allow her to have a mobile phone. And it is not allowed for her to talk to the neighbor housewife or the neighbor maid. That is the law here." When asked why the domestic worker should not be allowed to go out, she (a Filipina agent) replied the domestic worker would get pregnant. When asked if instead of locking her up, maybe she should be given condoms, they insisted that she should not be given any freedom: "She will only abuse your kindness, as they always do with foreigners."

The agencies near the Omani border were visited by many Omanis (easily recognized by their different head coverings). In the street where all the agencies were located, about a third of the cars was Omani, while in the next street where there were no agencies, there were no Omani cars at all. An Indonesian diplomat explained that some domestic workers are immediately offered to Omani employers. Others run away from their employer to the agency after which the agents then offer them a second chance across the border. According to this diplomat, not all these domestic workers are aware that they are brought to another country.[331]

Saudi agencies
In Saudi Arabia 8 agencies were researched in the capital Riyadh and 3 in Jeddah. They were hard to find in Jeddah, and locals (both nationals and migrant workers) explained that this is due to the fact that many workers arrive on a visa for Mecca, to overstay their visa in search for work. Most of these illegal workers do not move on to Riyadh, although the salary is higher there, because migrants in Jeddah know about the stricter conditions in Riyadh and the severely diminished freedom of movement this entails.

To the agencies in Riyadh a fee of $1.580 to $3.840 needed to be paid, depending on nationality, experience and waiting period; for an additional payment somebody could start the next day. Diplomats explained that these workers had been 'bought' from their former Saudi employer and were therefore more expensive as the agencies wanted to earn a second premium on the worker. Other information, as in the Emirates, was not voluntarily given, but had to be pulled out of the agents. The financial arrangements were very much the same as in the Emirates: a non-returnable fee to the agency, responsibility of the employer for the return ticket and – officially – responsibility for medical expenses. Here as well many agents stated that the worker would not get sick or if she would really get sick, she should be sent back home. Several agents stated salary would not have to be paid for the first two months, either because the domestic worker had already received this or because this was her contribution to the ticket.

---

331 This is not unlikely in light of the fact that researcher herself crossed that same border pretending to be asleep in the car, while a friend signed papers for her.

Some offered a card on which the domestic worker was supposed to print her finger every month, as evidence she had received her salary. Others suggested not to pay her at all until the day she was going to return home. One agent advised not to take a Filipina as they all want to know exactly what hours they have to work: "You better take an Indonesian."

In response to the questions if the domestic workers signed a contract before they leave the home country, half the agencies said no and the other half stated yes, but that this contract is disregarded in Saudi Arabia. One agent stated: "She works all the time, every day. You pick her up from the airport and then you put her in the house and lock the door and after 2 years you open the door again." Another said: "That is there and this is Saudi Arabia and here we have our own rules and the rules are that she has no rights. I am sorry to say, but when she comes to your house, she is your slave. No need for contracts, that is nothing." And although the domestic workers are not covered by the labor law, one agent stated: "Well, there is the labor law but that, we don't use in practice. I don't know what it says, but it is not important really, nobody looks at the labor law."

The agencies in Jeddah were slightly different in this respect as nobody advocated ignoring the law. Here the central issue seemed to be the amount paid to the government in order to legalize a worker who had overstayed the visa for Mecca. One agent admitted to the existence of the Filipino standard contract demanding 400 dollars and a work day of 8 hours maximum. If I would want her to work more, maybe I could pay her a little extra.

In Saudi Arabia the business cards of several agents stated a second job as a civil servant in either the Ministry of Labor or the Ministry of Internal Affairs / Migration. Although this was not the case with the business cards in the Emirates, several sources confirmed that many agents here as well have a second job in a government office where they can influence the processing of the papers they request or influence political decisions on issues concerning migrant workers. When I asked Emiratis about a conflict of interests, they all agreed that this issue is not considered problematic by locals.

All agencies
One thing the agencies in the countries of origin and destination all had in common was that they were not willing to provide the names of their counterparts. If there were problems, these were always attributed to the counterpart. If, for instance, the domestic worker had been misinformed about her salary, the agencies in the Middle East blamed the agencies in Asia, while the agencies in Asia blamed the agencies in the Middle East. Yet nobody wanted to give phone numbers or names of these counterparts, except for one agency that volunteered the name of a very large well-connected agency.

In summary, the agencies in the countries of destination provide a great deal of incorrect information to the employers. They generally deny that the domestic worker has signed a contract pre-departure and often employers are not permitted to read the substitute contract. Agencies actively encourage the employers to restrict the domestic workers' rights and freedoms. Furthermore, according to other sources than this particular research, many domestic workers claim to have been (threatened to be) beaten up by agents, as among others Human Rights Watch discovered.[332]

6.5 Conflicts

Due to the myriad of contracts and the incorrect information provided by the agencies on both sides, many domestic workers have conflicts with their employer over the most essential labor conditions:

Salary
The salary is the topic that causes the most conflict. Many domestic workers do not know the salary at the moment they decide to go to the Middle East. Either they have been promised big money by a middle man or agent, or they have heard success stories. The going rate for both Filipina and Indonesian domestic workers is around 200 American dollars per month. The questionnaires from leaving domestic workers revealed the following results:

Table 6.2 Verbally promised salary　　　　　　　　　　**(n = 156)**

	Jakarta	Manila
Don't know	19%	28%
Up to $210	80%	36%
More than $210	1%	36%

Table 6.3 Salary according to contract　　　　　　　　　**(n = 153)**

	Jakarta	Manila
Don't know	23%	51%
Up to $210	76%	20%
More than $210	1%	29%

---

332 Report 9.

About a third of the Filipina women and a fifth of the Indonesians did not know what their salary would be. Yet the literature shows that in other countries there are many more who leave without agreement on this particular point: in Bangladesh, regardless of the channel of recruitment, around half did not know the wages they could expect.[333] Yet even if an oral agreement on this point had been made, many did not receive this amount; almost a third of the Filipinas according to these data were misinformed about their salary. This is problematic for the employer as well: "When I worked in Riyadh, I had a domestic worker who was very well educated. She had been told that she was going to earn $750 per month. Of course I didn't have that kind of money. I paid her a lot less; I paid her what I had agreed to, but the result was a very unsatisfied worker."

The embassies insist that if the worker does not receive this higher amount, she can claim the difference from the agency. In light of the fact that almost nobody receives this promised salary, this would cause most agencies to go bankrupt. According to NGOs in Manila, laborers very rarely succeed in winning a case against an agency due to the fact that (i) workers are intimidated not to start a case, (ii) the cases take too long and the worker has to move on into new employment, and (iii) both agencies and judges tend to ask for evidence that the worker has not received her (full) salary, while giving evidence that something has not happened is usually impossible.

Fees
Connected to the issue of the salary is the question of who pays the transaction costs. Most middle men and some agents ask for a placement fee, usually to be paid in cash. Placement fees seem to depend on the middle man, the age of the domestic workers and the necessity of false identification documents. Sometimes a salary deduction is agreed on, instead of a placement fee. Yet very often further deductions take place that the domestic worker never agreed to. This often amounts to 2, sometimes 3, months' worth of salary. The result is that she will not receive any salary until the end of the third or fourth month. If the domestic worker and her employer get into a conflict thereafter, the employer cannot, under Saudi or Emirati law, go back to the agency to either get a worker who has not been misinformed about work conditions, or to get (part of) his fees back. So by telling the employer that the first 2 months do not have to be paid for, the agencies in the countries of destination prevent problems for themselves. Some employers deduct further amounts, for instance for the *abaya* (traditional Arabic dress) or work clothes. The contracts usually do not contain rules against this practice, but if they do, few agencies or judges stop the employers from doing it, especially in Saudi Arabia.[334]

---

333 Report 6, P11.
334 As stated by interviewed diplomats from labor sending countries, who accounted of cases in which they had tried to settle salary conflicts, not only for domestic workers, but also for other migrant workers. In The Emirates there appear to be more restrictions on the sometimes unlimited deductions though.

Other employers have been told to pay 2 months' salary to the agency for the worker in advance, "so she could buy things she would need for the journey. But they didn't give her the 2 months' salary. It's actually what she had paid to the agency herself."

Days and hours
Two more issues leading to frequent conflicts are weekly days off and the amount of hours per day. Contracts regularly state that there will be days off, while hardly any domestic worker actually enjoys this. Most contracts do not state the amount of hours that have to be worked per day, but some state a maximum of 8 or 12 hours. The average amount of hours reported by the respondents is 17 hours per day, which is concurrent with research from the ILO and HRW. Several domestic workers who had run away told me they had decided to do so for the simple reason that they were exhausted. According to diplomats, this is also the reason why during Ramadan the amount of runaways in their shelters doubles; many are not given the time for sufficient sleep during this month.

Most domestic workers in the Middle East work 7 days per week (like many do in their countries of origin). But the following had been agreed to:

Table 6.4 Verbally agreed to work days per week   **(n = 154)**

	Jakarta	Manila
Don't know / no answer	33%	50%
5 or 6 days per week	24%	27%
7 days per week	43%	23%

Table 6.5 Contractually agreed to work days per week   **(n = 154)**

	Jakarta	Manila
Don't know / no answer	36%	63%
5 or 6 days per week	31%	26%
7 days per week	33%	10%

   These numbers are slightly better for the domestic workers who had already been in the Middle East. Several domestic workers were asked if they felt they had the right to a day off and if yes to explain why. Some answered that right was given by the laws in the countries of destination (which is not true). Others stated that the right came from the laws in the countries of origin (which is not true either). Still others answered that the rights had been acquired in previous work contracts. Yet most Indonesians answered they did not have the right to a day off and found that completely natural, as there is work to do in the house every day.

Confinement
Another important matter in which disagreement arises is the fact that most domestic workers are either not permitted to leave the employer's house at all, or not on their own. Although it is not unusual for domestic workers in the countries of origin to not be permitted to leave the house on their own and although many agencies do not allow the women to leave the dorm, many domestic workers complain about this aspect of their job. The results from the questionnaires show the following:

Table 6.6 Knowledge about confinement (n = 145)

	Jakarta	Manila
They told me I will not be allowed to leave	80%	39%
They told me I will probably not be allowed to leave	13%	12%
They said nothing about that	5%	25%
They told me I will be allowed to leave	1%	24%

Table 6.7 Upset if confined? (n = 150)

	Jakarta	Manila
No, it would not upset me	71%	38%
I do not know	14%	24%
Yes, it would upset me	15%	38%

In Saudi Arabia, the only two domestic workers who indicated they were permitted to leave the house were working for Lebanese and European employers. In Dubai more people were permitted to leave the house, but not many: of the 9 people in Dubai who were permitted to leave the house whenever they did not work, 6 were working for foreigners. Of the 6 who were permitted to go outside on their day off, all 6 were working for foreigners.

Yet here the results are likely not be representative of all domestic workers, as the questionnaires were largely filled in by runaways. In Saudi Arabia most domestic workers are not permitted to leave the house; they are not permitted to drive a car, there is no public transport and they are not seen walking in the street. But in Dubai, domestic workers can be found on the streets. On Fridays the parks and churches are visited not only by beauticians and waitresses,[335] but also by some domestic workers. So the fact that the questionnaires say most domestic workers were not permitted to leave the house, does not prove that the Emiratis are just as strict; it can indicate that not being permitted, creates a higher rate of runaways.

As for the reason why they are not permitted to leave the house, it is important to note that many wives and daughters are not permitted to leave the house either, especially in the most conservative part of Saudi Arabia, the Najd. Agents state that the concept of not being permitted to go outside for 2 years cannot be explained to uneducated young women. The women themselves claim to understand it very well and those who decide to go back to the same employer certainly agree to it. Many Saudis and Emiratis claim that all domestic workers know and thus agree to it, as it has been like this for over forty years; they must have heard about it from family and friends. But this is not true as the first contract workers usually do not realize that the women they see on TV in the streets of Dubai are largely beauticians and waitresses, not domestic workers.

Age, experience and training
Another issue that causes regular conflict is the experience or age requested by employers. Even if a worker is known to lack experience, they expect her to have received proper training. As discussed above, domestic workers usually receive very minimal training. Concerning age: in Saudi Arabia and the Emirates as in many other countries there is an official minimum age of 23 years old. Older domestic workers are expected to be more mature and better able to manage difficult work situations and consequently, cause fewer employment-related problems.[336] But many low-skilled workers have not been registered at birth; it is estimated that more than 7 in 10 children in the world's least-developed countries do not have birth certificates or other registration documents.[337] They buy fake birth certificates at a town hall after which a passport can easily be acquired.

---

335 All migrants, as the Emirati's in general refuse to perform these serving and low paid jobs.
336 Anggraeni (2006) P115.
337 Report 27, P32.

Others use the identification papers from elder siblings or the agency supplies the workers with the documents needed. Several interviewees in Manila explained that fake birth certificates can be acquired anywhere, even across the street from the Department of Foreign Affairs. According to somebody from the ILO in Jakarta, it is quite normal for people to have several identification documents such as passports or drivers licenses readily available in case they may be needed.

If false documents are acquired, their official age is usually altered because of circumstances at home: these women usually do not have the means to follow education beyond the age of 10 or 12. They come from agrarian villages where, due to modern techniques and smaller lots of land per family, they simply do not have much work to do either. On top of that, as the families are poor and need cash to be able to participate in the market economy, they all want to work. Therefore even if they can read and have read the data in their own documents and know these to be false, they do not report this. Some employers are unhappy with under-aged workers because they don't have the appropriate skills, they aren't strong enough to complete the work and they are not emotionally strong enough to stay away from home for two years. Yet other employers do not have a problem with these workers as they do not return them to the agency within the 3 month probation period. While nobody wanted to admit to being aware that his or her domestic worker was under-aged, some interviewed employers stated that young girls are by many (others) thought more obedient or more attractive.

The number of domestic workers that are under-aged can only be guessed. During the research, when asked about their age and year of birth, many women gave contradicting or confusing answers to these questions. Many faces looked much younger than the stated 25 years. Both in Manila and Jakarta the interpreters guessed that 5% to 20% of the domestic workers were under-aged, but NGOs in the Emirates guessed these numbers to be higher for countries of origin such as Nepal. Interviewed diplomats agreed with these estimates. Yet these under-aged women comprised a large percentage of the population in the shelters in Saudi Arabia. There are several possible reasons for this: (i) younger workers run away more often as they might be less capable to do the work, to function in a labor relation (see chapter 3), to communicate on problems or to deal with homesickness, (ii) younger workers are abused more often, or (iii) older workers run away as often and are abused as often, but they do not end up in the shelters as they have been to Saudi Arabia before and have built up a network of acquaintances that they can go to for help (more hereon in chapter 8).

Country of destination

Many domestic workers do not know what country they will work in, or they are brought to a country different from the one they agreed to. Several interviewees, even after up to 2 years, still did not know in what country they were working. For many women from Kerala 'Dubai' stands for the entire Middle East. This to some does not seem like a serious problem, but actually it is for a number of reasons: (i) Some of the women expect to be close to family members who could be contacted in case of problems. (ii) If family members back home do not know where they are, they are untraceable in case of emergencies. (iii) These domestic workers leave with the wrong telephone numbers (embassies, hotlines) in their luggage. (iv) Some domestic workers specifically want to go to Saudi Arabia to be able to do the Hajj, while (v) others specifically do not want to go to Saudi Arabia, as they know about the confinement and religious police.

An even more serious problem forms the cases in which women are brought across the border to be forced elsewhere into prostitution. There are numerous rumors about female migrant workers being brought to countries such as Iraq. The large flow of workers from the Emirates into Dubai through Al Ain-Buraimi is less problematic from the perspective of the workers, as many seem to agree to this. Yet some are forced to go there by a fake first employer who pretends not to want them anymore, or they are brought across the border illegally (with or without fake identity papers), which makes them vulnerable to abuse.

In conclusion: the recruitment process leads to many conflicts on the most basic working conditions; salary, transaction costs, deductions, weekly days off, hours to be worked per day, confinement, tasks, experience, age and even the country in which a domestic worker will be employed. In many of these conflicts both the employer and the employee feel that they are only demanding the agreed upon labor conditions, while the other party is in breach of the contract. Both in the Emirates and Saudi Arabia, the employer is usually in a position to enforce his view of the agreed-on labor conditions (see chapters 10 and 11 on power relations).

6.6 Contract law and consent

The initial source of Islamic contract law is the Quranic revelation "ye who believe! Fulfill (all) obligations". This verse is the basis of the sanctity of a wide variety of obligations, including those that are spiritual, social, political, and commercial,[338] and has been elaborated on in the Jurisprudence of Transactions. It is the basis for the rule that in matters of civil or commercial dealing, any agreement not specifically prohibited by Sharia is valid and binding on the parties and could be enforced by the courts.[339] Sharia jurisprudence states that consent is an essential part of the contract; a marriage closed without consent for instance is invalid. But the range of situations in which the level of consent is deemed to have been insufficient is limited. For instance, there appears to be little theory on 'abuse of circumstances.' If a domestic worker is forced to sign a new contract

338 Mohammed (1988) P116.
339 Habachy (1962) P459.

upon arrival in The Middle East and she gets to work even one day, she is deemed to have consented to the new contract, no matter what her reasons may have been to do so.

Many Muslims and scholars state that Sharia – including its contract law – is complete, infallible and valid equally throughout the centuries. Others state that it may be assumed that, at the time that Islamic contract law started taking its shape in the seventh century, commerce was limited to a market of goods that consisted of surplus farm products and handicraft. They state that Islamic contract law therefore reflects and addresses the transactional reality of that period.[340] This may explain the absence of a well developed theory on consent; the concept may not have been necessary by lack of too many contracts concluded without consent.

There are other explanations thinkable. In Europe the theory of consent was not generally accepted until the nineteenth century. By that time, dietary improvements had raised the average IQ and combined with better education, this had created a situation in which most individuals indeed bound themselves in what could be referred to as free will. Currently in many villages where domestic workers stem from, the average IQ and education do not seem to have reached that level, but that is disregarded in Saudi Arabia and the Emirates. A third hypothesis is that the theory of consent was – also in the West – never developed to protect those that had entered an agreement without consent, but to bind those that could not prove that there was no consent. A fourth explanation could be the theory discussed in chapter 7, that the theory of consent has been developed because the upper classes had incentives to protect the lower classes, which is not the case in the Middle East.

Whichever is the correct theory, the research results of chapter 6 show that the level of consent is usually very low. First, there is often no consent because many domestic workers are not capable or not permitted to acquire knowledge on the conditions of the agreement.[341] Second, there is often no alternative to signing; many families are extremely poor and have no alternative to gather financial means. Third, many domestic workers are more or less forced by their (especially male) family members into signing; they take the decision to send daughters and wives overseas "to earn well, save and give their family a bright future."[342] In addition, they are regularly minors, and last but not least, some do not even have an understanding of the concept of an agreement, as they have been raised in a patriarchal society with status-related concepts of rights and obligations (see chapter 5).

---

340 Mohammed (1988) P117.
341 In many countries of the world women have more problems gathering proper knowledge of labor market conditions due to their position in the respective societies.
342 As stated by several NGOs in Manila & Jakarta; see also Heyzer (2006) P48-49 and Report 22 P36.

In both Saudi Arabia and the Emirates this low level of consent has no consequence; domestic workers are deemed to be bound to the contract, but usually only to the most basic stipulations: the obligation to work for 2 years as a domestic worker, for a certain salary, with the duty to obey the employer 24 hours per day. Contractual stipulations are disregarded on such a scale, that it is unclear what the purpose of the contract is. One option could be to satisfy the international community and press, who complain about the poorly organized labor market in the Gulf. Another option could be the fact that after signing the contract the domestic workers feel that they have lost the freedom to leave their employer.

As discussed briefly in section 4 of chapter 6, the Western concept of legal representation is not applied, and this paragraph shows that the Western concept of consent is not applied. Both can be explained with the patriarchal model in which a more powerful person represents and protects a less powerful person. Consent in this model is not necessary; the fact that a woman walks into an agency in need of a job, shows that she needs a more powerful person to handle her affairs and from then on this more powerful person makes all the decisions for her. Domestic workers never complain about agents not having the right to legally represent them. They rarely state to have the rights to certain conditions based on their contract, nor do they refer to the interconnectedness of their rights and the rights of the employer (as discussed in chapter 5). Rather they think that they deserve a certain treatment in light of the fact that they performed their duties well: if one behaves as a good worker, one deserves proper treatment. If they do not receive the salary that has been promised to them, most attribute this fact to fate. This is also one of the reasons why upon returning to their home country, they do not warn others of possible lies told by the agencies; it is just a matter of fate who gets a good salary and who does not.

6.7 Summary
Due to a lack of information or lies, domestic workers and employers often have a very different perception of the contractual norms that have been agreed on. This leads to many conflicts and it raises questions about the binding force of the contracts, conflicts that can hardly be blamed on either party. In The Philippines and Indonesia middle men or agents do not provide important information such as exactly what the work entails, how many days or hours per week the domestic worker has to work and the fact that most domestic workers are not permitted to freely leave the house. Domestic workers from these two countries regularly have to sign contracts they cannot read, contracts they are not permitted to read, multiple contracts or they have no contracts at all. Governments and other organizations use different standard contracts without agreement on which contract should be binding or on the legal base of these actions. During their training domestic workers receive information that is incorrect, information that is simply

too vague and information that should have been provided to the worker prior to her committing to the job offer. As for the training that the laborers are supposed to receive, usually they are not properly trained.

Agencies in Saudi Arabia and the Emirates do not perform any better. They provide a great deal of incorrect information to the employers and deny the fact that the domestic worker has signed a contract pre-departure. Often employers are not permitted to read the contract either. On top of that, agencies actively encourage the employers to restrict the domestic workers' rights and freedoms. The result is a broad range of conflicts caused by disagreement on the applicable contractual norms. Such conflicts concern the most basic working conditions: salary, transaction costs, deductions, weekly days off, hours to be worked per day, confinement, tasks, experience, age and even the country in which a domestic worker will be employed.

7. Formal legal norms

7.1 Introduction

This chapter provides an overview of formal legal norms, either written or ratified by the Saudi or Emirati government. Section 7.2 examines statutory law. Domestic workers are explicitly excluded from the labor laws. They are included in the sponsorship system, a set of immigration regulations. The chapter then addresses the most relevant rules of international law (§7.3). It describes the Universal Declaration of Human Rights, the Arab Charter on Human Rights, the Convention on the Elimination of all forms of Discrimination Against Women (CEDAW), ratified international labor agreements and the Palermo Protocol against Human Trafficking.

These two sections show that national formal legal norms provide normative tools to the advantage of the employer, while international formal legal norms provide tools to the advantage of the domestic worker. In Europe, the situation is different. Here both national and international legal norms provide tools for the protection of employees. Furthermore (as discussed in chapter 3), formal legal norms regularly create a hierarchy between different norms, which limits the maneuvering space and thus the advantage of the more powerful party, the employer. De Swaan has provided a theory explaining that in Europe the haves had five different interests in providing means and protection to the have-nots. Section 7.4 therefore moves on to the question to what extent the upper-class in Saudi Arabia and the Emirates share these same interests. It shows that they do not, which is a good explanation for the question why little formal legal protection for the lower strata of society has come into existence in the two countries. This situation would improve upon removal of the sponsorship system and implementation of the Palermo Protocol. Section 7.5 therefore discusses specific obstructions to alterations of the sponsorship system and to the implementation of the Palermo Protocol.

The data for this particular chapter stem mainly from interviews with government officials, but also with employers, diplomats and lawyers. Other sources were discourse used at international conferences, the laws and conventions themselves and internet newspapers.

7.2 Statutory norms

7.2.1 Excluded from the Labor Law

In both Saudi Arabia and the Emirates, domestic workers have been explicitly excluded from the protections of the statutory labor law.

Saudi labor law, article 7:

> The following shall be exempted from the implementation of the provisions of this law:

(1) The employers family members, namely, the spouse, the ascendants and descendants who constitute the only workers of the firm.

(2) Domestic helpers and the like.

(3) Sea workers working on board of vessels with a load of less than five hundred tons.

(4) Agricultural workers other than the categories stated in Article (5) of this Law.

(5) Non-Saudi workers entering the Kingdom to perform a specific task for a period not exceeding two months.

(6) Players and coaches of sports clubs and federations.

The Ministry shall, in coordination with the competent authorities, draft regulations for domestic helpers and the like to govern their relations with their employers and specify the rights and duties of each party and submit the same to the Council of Ministers.[343]

Emirati labor law, article 3:

The provisions of this Law shall not apply to the following categories:

- Employees of the Federal Government and of governmental departments of the emirates of the Federation, employees of municipalities, other employees of federal and local public authorities and corporations, as well as employees who are recruited against federal and local governmental projects.
- Members of the armed forces, police and security.
- Domestic servants employed in private households, and the like.
- Farming and grazing workers, other than those working in agricultural establishments that process their own products, and those who are permanently employed to operate or repair mechanical equipment required for agricultural work.

Most interviewed employers agree with the fact that domestic workers have been excluded from the labor law, stating that it is absolutely forbidden for the government to interfere in domestic matters.[344] Exclusion of domestic workers from labor laws is by no means particular to the Middle East.[345] In many countries, this was (or still is) the case.[346] The idea that a domestic worker's welfare, including salary, lies beyond the scope of public business, partly originates from the capitalist division of labor into the productive and reproductive spheres, where the notion of work is a "production process that contributes to capitalist accumulation and exchange."

---

343 Under this last provision, the Saudi government has been working on a draft law concerning domestic workers for years now, but thus far it has not entered into force.

344 See also section 3.3.

345 Compare, for instance, Anggraeni (2006). Hong Kong does, but Singapore does not, offer foreign domestic helpers protection under the labor laws.

346 See also Report 24.

In contrast, domestic work falls within the "process of reproduction, essential to the survival of the family and society, but does not directly lead to the process of accumulation and exchange." Thus, it is not customarily considered work and it converts the status of domestic workers into non-workers.[347]

Concerning the implementation of a labor law within the house, an interviewed government official stated: "It would be very difficult to police what's happening there, from a public-private point of view." Arabs consider the house too private to open their doors to inspectors: "The house is sacred. Inspectors who just walk in would not be accepted ever! An inspector has the right to ask whatever question he likes. He can come to the *maglis*[348] and he can talk to the maid there, but he can never enter the house!" Part of the problem in this respect is gender segregation: women are not permitted to be in a space with other men without a *mahram*.[349] In Saudi Arabia, where this principle is applied very strictly, this means that a woman who is alone cannot call the police if there seems to be a burglar in the house. The policemen will not enter the scene unless the woman leaves to go to a female neighbor's house. One group that does enter the house in Saudi Arabia is the *Mutawwa*, or religious police. Yet – as can be deducted from many letters written to newspapers – this is not socially accepted either.

Although the protection of the private sphere is more extreme in the Middle East, it seems to be a universal rule that legal instrumentalism is less effective and more unwanted in the private domain. Vilhelm Aubert conducted research on the effectiveness of the Norwegian domestic workers law and determined that the law was largely disregarded. For instance, almost half the employers admitted to letting their domestic workers work more than the maximum of ten hours per day (without financial compensation). The law was unknown or unclear to many, but it was also not enforced. There were no inspections arranged and prosecution was only possible after repeated infringements and upon complaint by the domestic worker. The Norwegian government felt that enforcement mechanisms, such as unannounced visits, were inappropriate for the house and that any form of external intervention would deteriorate labor relations[350] – just as several interviewed Saudis and Emiratis stated.

---

347 Guzman (2003).
348 A kind of living room (usually right behind the front door), a space considered to be between the outside and the inside, between public and private.
349 An unmarriageable male, being a father, brother, son, or husband.
350 Griffiths (1996) P113-135.

7.2.2 *The sponsorship system*

One part of the formal legal system that is actively enforced by both governments (unlike many other norms) is the sponsorship system, or the immigration regulations. According to these norms, foreign workers cannot enter Saudi Arabia or the Emirates for work without a local guarantor, either an individual or a governmental or private institution. The system does not allow foreign workers to move from one institution to another or from one employer to another without the approval of the employer/sponsor. The main difficulty for the domestic worker is the rule that as soon as the labor contract is no longer in place (for whatever reason), the visa automatically becomes invalid and the worker has to leave the country. If labor laws do not offer sufficient protection against arbitrary dismissal, or if labor laws do not apply (as is the case with domestic workers), these regulations give immense power to the employer, who can have the worker deported at will.[351]

Furthermore, the worker can only leave the country with the employer's signature. A labor agent in Saudi Arabia explained that after the first three months of employment, domestic workers who wish to end their contract early require an exit visa and a court order to do so. "In Saudi Arabia, the maid goes to the embassy and the embassy takes her to court and the judge has to decide whether to release her from the contract. The employer signs and then the Ministry of Foreign Affairs stamps the contract; this is called legalization." Running away from the employer risks punishment by detention or deportation.[352] An interviewed ambassador explained: "According to the law, running away is a crime, even if the employer severely abuses you." The sponsorship system thus severely limits the freedom of the domestic worker, as will be further discussed in chapter 10. It also severely limits her abilities to claim any rights and this diminishes her civil citizenship, as will be discussed in chapter 8.

7.3 International law

International law can be divided into international conventions (or treaty law), customary law and general principles common to the major legal systems of the world.[353] According to some, customary international law is binding regardless of ratifications; according to others, it is not binding.[354] Conventions become binding on states upon ratification.[355]

---

351 Emirati scholar at Abu Dhabi Dialogue, January 2008 and Report 22, P35.
352 Esim (2004) P21.
353 See among others: Restatement of the Law (3d) Foreign Relations Law of the United States, articles 102 on sources of International Law, and article 38 of the UN treaty that establishes the International Court of Justice and looks at the sources the Court can use to decide its cases.
354 Such statements most commonly are made by dictators that do not wish to be bound by human rights law.
355 Plus often some form of internal confirmation by – usually – the parliament, depending on the constitution of the country concerned.

Thereupon governments are obliged to take action on non self-executing norms, while self-executing norms become incorporated either directly or indirectly into the national legal system, depending on the system chosen by the country concerned. In monistic systems, national and international law are regarded as one legal system. The act of ratification (by itself, or ratification plus approval by the national parliament if required) immediately incorporates the rules concerned into national law and citizens can directly invoke them in court as national law. Dualists emphasize the difference between national and international law and require the translation of the latter into the former. Without conversion into national laws, citizens cannot invoke the rules of the ratified treaty and judges cannot apply them.[356]

In the Emirates, some governmental interviewees claimed to have a dualistic system. However, the somewhat vague article of the Constitution that is said to regulate the matter is somehow absent from many English translations.[357] It states:

> Article 125: The Governments of the Emirates shall undertake the appropriate measures to implement the law promulgated by the Union and the treaties and international agreements concluded by the Union, including the promulgation of the Local Laws, regulations, decisions and orders necessary for such implementation. The Union authorities shall supervise the implementation by Emirate's Governments of the Union Laws, decisions. Treaties, administrative and judicial authorities in the Emirates should forward to the Union authorities all possible assistance in this connection.[358]

In Saudi Arabia, most interviewed government officials claimed to have a monistic system (one official added that it is not monistic when someone is in conflict with the government), whereas others considered it dualistic. Internet sources on the Basic Law itself are not conclusive either; some sources state:

> Article 70: Any international treaty or agreement approved by a Royal Decree and its provision shall be valid and effective and shall directly be referred to by the courts in passing their judgments.[359]

---

356 For instance The Netherlands have a monistic system, while the USA and the UK have dualist systems (although with EU law a new normative order has been created which no longer allows for a dualist approach towards its self-executing norms).

357 For instance, http://www.worldstatesmen.org/uae_const.doc March 2009.

358 Official translation, see http://www.uaecabinet.ae/English/UAEGovernment/Pages/constitution_1_7.aspx September 2011.

359 See for instance the first report on human rights conditions in the Kingdom of Saudi Arabia: www.nrhr.org.sa/nsfiles/22.doc (December 2010).

Other sources state:

> Article 70: Laws, treaties, international agreements and concessions shall be issued and modified by Royal Decrees.[360]

If both systems are dualistic, international treaties should be transferred into national law, but they rarely are.[361] Even lawyers and judges do not know if they can appeal directly to international law in court. The Saudi National Society for Human Rights, for instance, claims to appeal to both Sharia and treaties in court, but it could not say on which basis the claims were acknowledged or rejected.

As Merry rightfully states, countries ratify or comply with international law because of reciprocity, desire for membership in the international community, the wish to appear 'civilized', pressure from other countries for trade agreements and myriad other forms of indirect pressure. Less powerful countries are more vulnerable to this pressure, whereas some of the most powerful countries (such as the U.S.A or oil-rich states like Saudi Arabia and the Emirates) refuse to be bound by some aspects of international law at all.[362] Realists claim that states comply only when it is in their self-interest. This self-interest is currently creating a growing need for both countries to ratify (some) international law, as they both hope to attract foreign direct investments to diversify their economies.[363] Moreover, certain international organizations demand ratification of certain conventions in exchange for wanted benefits, such as the World Trade Organization and the European Union. Saudi Arabia and the Emirates have therefore ratified a number of treaties, but their number is low and compliance even lower. This is because, although they may have an incentive to ratify treaties, they do not have too many incentives to implement them, as will be explained in section 7.4.

7.3.1 Universal Declaration of Human Rights

Articles 13, 23 and 24 of the 1948 Universal Declaration of Human Rights are being violated daily against foreign domestic workers in the Middle East. [364] These articles state the following:

> Article 13:
> (1) Everyone has the right to freedom of movement and residence within the borders of each state.
> (2) Everyone has the right to leave any country, including his own, and to return to his country.

---

360 See for instance http://www.ilo.org/wcmsp5/groups/public/---ed_protect/---protrav/---ilo_aids/documents/
legaldocument/wcms_125883.pdf (December 2010).
361 CEDAW, for instance, is not.
362 Merry (2006b) P100-101.
363 See section 2.1.1 for the Emirates and 2.2.2 for Saudi Arabia.
364 Jureidini (2010) P146.

Article 23:

(1) Everyone has the right to work, to free choice of employment, to just and favorable conditions of work and to protection against unemployment.

(2) Everyone, without any discrimination, has the right to equal pay for equal work.

(3) Everyone who works has the right to just and favorable remuneration ensuring for himself and his family an existence worthy of human dignity, and supplemented, if necessary, by other means of social protection.

(4) Everyone has the right to form and to join trade unions for the protection of
his interests.

Article 24: Everyone has the right to rest and leisure, including reasonable limitation of working hours and periodic holidays with pay.

7.3.2 *The Arab Charter on Human Rights*

Several Islamic countries have criticized the Universal Declaration of Human
Rights for its perceived failure to take into account the cultural and religious context of Muslim countries. This has lead to the writing of the Arab Charter on
Human Rights (The Charter). The Charter, as revised in 2004, entered into force
on 15 March 2008 (which is after the start of this research). It received criticism
from the international community because agreeing to a regional treaty that set
standards below the universal human rights values set out in UN treaties, was
considered to be inconsistent with States' obligations under international human
rights law.[365] However, the Charter also contains several affirmations of current
international human rights standards. It states:

> Article 43: Nothing in this Charter may be construed or interpreted as impairing
> the rights and freedoms protected by the domestic laws of the States parties or
> those set forth in the international and regional human rights instruments
> which the States parties have adopted or ratified, including the rights of women,
> the rights of the child and the rights of persons belonging to minorities.

Furthermore, the preamble states:

> (...) reaffirming the principles of the Charter of the United Nations, the
> Universal Declaration of Human Rights and the provisions of the
> International Covenant on Civil and Political Rights and the International
> Covenant on Economic, Social and Cultural Rights.

---

365 http://hrlr.oxfordjournals.org/content/10/1/169.short?rss=1 September 2010.

Since not all member states have signed and ratified all these covenants, this preamble is an important step forward for countries such as Saudi Arabia and the Emirates. Important for the position of domestic workers is the following article:

Article 3:
(1) Each State party to the present Charter undertakes to ensure to all individuals subject to its jurisdiction the right to enjoy the rights and freedoms set forth herein, without distinction on grounds of race, colour, sex, language, religious belief, opinion, thought, national or social origin, wealth, birth or physical or mental disability.
(2)The States parties to the present Charter shall take the requisite measures to guarantee effective equality in the enjoyment of all the rights and freedoms enshrined in the present Charter in order to ensure protection against all forms of discrimination based on any of the grounds mentioned in the preceding paragraph.
(3) Men and women are equal in respect of human dignity, rights and obligations within the framework of the positive discrimination established in favor of women by the Islamic Sharia, other divine laws and by applicable laws and legal instruments. Accordingly, each State party pledges to take all the requisite measures to guarantee equal opportunities and effective equality between men and women in the enjoyment of all the rights set out in this Charter.

The Charter thus refers to individuals, not to citizens. Furthermore, the Charter states:

Article 8:
(1) No one shall be subjected to physical or psychological torture or to cruel, degrading, humiliating or inhuman treatment.
(2) Each State party shall protect every individual subject to its jurisdiction from such practices and shall take effective measures to prevent them. The commission of, or participation in, such acts shall be regarded as crimes that are punishable by law and not subject to any statute of limitations. Each State party shall guarantee in its legal system redress for any victim of torture and the right to rehabilitation and compensation.

Article 12:
All persons are equal before the courts and tribunals. The States parties shall guarantee the independence of the judiciary and protect magistrates against any interference, pressure or threats. They shall also guarantee every person subject to their jurisdiction the right to seek a legal remedy before courts of all levels.

If implemented, the Charter would thus provide proper legal protection to domestic workers.

7.3.3 UN Convention on the Rights of Migrant Workers

Neither Saudi Arabia nor the United Arab Emirates has ratified the UN Convention on the Protection of the Rights of All Migrant Workers and Members of Their Families. This convention entered into force in 2003 and has now been ratified by around forty – mainly labor sending – countries. Neither Saudi Arabia nor the Emirates is likely to ratify it any time soon, as government officials and citizens generally agree that migrants, even third generation migrants, should not have any rights, let alone the members of their families. The larger flows of migrant workers who arrive on two or three year contracts are not even considered to be migrant workers. They are consistently referred to as contract workers, to emphasize the return to their home country. Furthermore, even if these two countries would ratify the convention, the regulations would not be applied to domestic workers as they are not considered to be workers.

7.3.4 CEDAW and the reservations to it

In 2000, Saudi Arabia ratified the Convention on the Elimination of All Forms of Discrimination Against Women (CEDAW) and in 2004 the Emirates did the same. The convention states:

> Article 1:
> For the purposes of the present Convention, the term 'discrimination against women' shall mean any distinction, exclusion or restriction made on the basis of sex which has the effect or purpose of impairing or nullifying the recognition, enjoyment or exercise by women, irrespective of their marital status, on a basis of equality of men and women, of human rights and fundamental freedoms in the political, economic, social, cultural, civil or any other field.

Article 2 thereupon adds that states parties condemn discrimination against women in all its forms and agree to pursue by all appropriate means and without delay a policy of eliminating discrimination against women. By prohibiting any distinction which has the *effect* of impairing the rights of women, CEDAW prohibits both direct and indirect discrimination. Because almost all domestic workers are female, excluding them from the protections of the labor law based on the argument that this is the private sphere of the household seems tantamount to indirect discrimination. Human Rights Watch states:

> The exclusion of domestic workers from national labor laws, while neutral on paper in its focus on a form of employment, has a disparate impact on women and girls since the overwhelming majority of domestic workers are female. The lesser protection extended to domestic work, reflects discrimination against a form of work usually performed by women and girls and

that involve tasks associated with traditional female domestic roles such as cleaning, childcare and cooking. No legitimate reasons exist for these exclusions. Therefore the unequal protection of domestic workers under national laws constitutes impermissible disparate impact discrimination on the basis of sex.[366]

Furthermore the concepts of *khulwa* and the *mahram*, concepts that – as will be described in chapter 8 – severely limit the access of women to justice, constitute direct discrimination. Yet there has never been a court ruling on any of these matters. Therefore it is not officially established to what extent the limitations to the rights and access to justice of domestic workers are indeed contrary to CEDAW. Furthermore, they may or may not fall under the reservations made by both countries to this convention, while these reservations may or may not be permissible or acceptable.[367] The Convention permits ratification subject to reservations, provided that the reservations are not incompatible with the object and purpose of the Convention (article 28). A number of States have entered reservations to particular articles on the ground that national law, tradition, religion or culture are not congruent with Convention principles, and purport to justify the reservation on that basis.[368] The reservations that Saudi Arabia and the Emirates have made (and that may concern the position of domestic workers) are the following: [369]

Saudi Arabia:
1. In case of contradiction between any term of the Convention and the norms of Islamic law, the Kingdom is not under obligation to observe the contradictory terms of the Convention.

United Arab Emirates:
The United Arab Emirates makes reservations to articles 2 (f), 9, 15 (2), 16 and 29 (1) of the Convention, as follows:
Article 2 (f)
The United Arab Emirates, being of the opinion that this paragraph violates the rules of inheritance established in accordance with the precepts of the Sharia, makes a reservation thereto and does not consider itself bound by the provisions thereof.
Article 15 (2)
The United Arab Emirates, considering this paragraph in conflict with the precepts of the Sharia regarding legal capacity, testimony and the right to conclude contracts, makes a reservation to the said paragraph of the said article and does not consider itself bound by the provisions thereof.

---

366 Report 3.
367 See Clark (2011) on permissibility and acceptability of reservations to CEDAW.
368 http://www.un.org/womenwatch/daw/cedaw/reservations.htm September 2011.
369 http://www.un.org/womenwatch/daw/cedaw/reservations-country.htm September 2011.

As stated, it is unclear to what extent these reservations cover the limitation of rights and access to justice of domestic workers, as there has been no court ruling on the matter in either of the two countries. In light of the conclusions of chapter 4, it is unlikely that Sharia would indeed be a solid basis for the limitations concerned. Furthermore, even if Sharia scholars would conclude that the limitations to the rights and access to justice of domestic workers are indeed prescribed by Sharia and that CEDAW can therefore not prevail, questions can be raised about the permissibility and acceptability hereof.

The CEDAW Commission does not accept all reservations to the Convention. Article 28, paragraph 2 of CEDAW adopts the impermissibility principle contained in the Vienna Convention on the Law of Treaties. It states that a reservation incompatible with the object and purpose of the Convention shall not be permitted. Although the Convention does not prohibit the entering of reservations, those which challenge the central principles of the Convention are contrary to the provisions of the Convention and to general international law. Article 2 is considered by the Committee to be a core provision of the Convention. The Committee holds the view that states parties which ratify the Convention do so because they agree that discrimination against women in all its forms should be condemned and that the strategies set out in article 2, subparagraphs (a) to (g), should be implemented by States parties to eliminate it. Neither traditional, religious or cultural practice nor incompatible domestic laws and policies can justify violations of the Convention.

The United Arab Emirates have never filed a report with the CEDAW commission. The Kingdom of Saudi Arabia has done so in 2008. The report basically states that women have unlimited access to justice.[370] Legally that may be true (based on article 47 of the Basic Law that grants equal access to justice to all citizens and residents) but in practice this is not the case because of the concepts of *mahram* and *khulwa*.

---

370 Report 32, P8.

7.3.5 International Labor Law

Saudi Arabia and the Emirates have ratified the following ILO conventions:

	Saudi Arabia	Emirates
C1 Hours of Work (Industry) Convention, 1919	X	X
C14 Weekly Rest (Industry) Convention, 1921	X	
C29 Forced Labor Convention, 1930	X	X
C30 Hours of Work (Commerce and Offices) Convention, 1930	X	
C45 Underground Work (Women) Convention, 1935	X	
C81 Labor Inspection Convention, 1947	X	X
C89 Night Work (Women) Convention (Revised), 1948	X	X
C90 Night Work of Young Persons (Industry) Convention (Revised), 1948	X	
C100 Equal Remuneration Convention, 1951	X	X
C105 Abolition of Forced Labor Convention, 1957	X	X
C106 Weekly Rest (Commerce and Offices) Convention, 1957	X	
C111 Discrimination (Employment and Occupation) Convention, 1958	X	X
C123 Minimum Age (Underground Work) Convention, 1965	X	
C138 Minimum Age Convention, 1973		X
C174 Prevention of Major Industrial Accidents Convention, 1993	X	
C182 Worst Forms of Child Labor Convention, 1999	X	X

Because neither country recognizes domestic workers as workers, these conventions are not applied to them. The ILO has never been clear on its definition of workers, nor on the question of whether domestic workers may be excluded from national labor laws or ILO conventions.[371] If the ILO believes that this is not allowed, then the convention that it is considering to write concerning the position of domestic workers could be limited to one single rule: "Domestic workers are workers and therefore cannot be excluded from the protection of labor laws."

7.3.6 Palermo Protocol on human trafficking

The Protocol to Prevent, Suppress and Punish trafficking in Persons, especially Women and Children (the Palermo Protocol) is a protocol to the Convention against Transnational Organized Crime. The United Nations Office on Drugs and Crime (UNODC) is responsible for implementing the Protocol. It offers practical help to states with drafting laws, creating comprehensive national anti-trafficking strategies, and assisting with resources to implement them. The phrase 'human trafficking' makes most people think of women forced into prostitution. Yet the definition is much broader in the Palermo Protocol, or the supplement to the UN convention against transnational organized crime, in which 'trafficking in persons' is described as follows:

(a) The recruitment, transportation, transfer, harboring or receipt of persons, by means of the threat or use of force or other forms of coercion, of abduction, of fraud, of deception, of the abuse of power or of a position of vulnerability or of the giving or receiving of payments or benefits to achieve the consent of a person having control over another person, for the purpose of exploitation. Exploitation shall include, at a minimum, the exploitation of the prostitution of others or other forms of sexual exploitation, forced labor or services, slavery or practices similar to slavery, servitude or the removal of organs;
(b) The consent of a victim of trafficking in persons to the intended exploitation set forth in subsection (a) of this article shall be irrelevant where any of the means set forth in subsection (a) have been used;
(c) The recruitment, transportation, transfer, harboring or receipt of a child for the purpose of exploitation shall be considered 'trafficking in persons' even if this does not involve any of the means set forth in subsection (a) of this article;
(d) 'Child' shall mean any person under 18 years of age.[372]

---

371 Confirmed by interviewed ILO personnel.
372 Protocol supplementing the United Nations Convention against transnational organized crime, article 3.

The UNODC suggests that this definition can be split up into three parts:

(i) The act of recruitment, transportation, transfer, harboring or receipt of persons;
(ii) by means of threat, use of force, coercion, abduction, fraud, deception, abuse of power or vulnerability, or giving payments or benefits to a person in control of the victim;
(iii) for the purpose of exploitation, which includes, at a minimum, sexual exploitation, forced labor or services, slavery or similar practices or the removal of organs.[373]

It is important to note that based on this definition, legal workers as well as illegal workers may be trafficking victims. As the above definition of trafficking shows, it concerns acts (i) for the purpose of exploitation and (ii) by means of among others fraud and deception. Based on this, many domestic workers should be considered victims of trafficking under the Palermo Protocol, as exploitation, forced labor and practices akin to slavery are unfortunately no exceptions, but general market conditions on which they have not been properly informed.

As described in chapter 6 on contractual norms, most domestic workers are not permitted to leave their employer's household for the duration of their two year contract – not on their own or not at all, and not even if they have a conflict with their employer. This changes their labor into forced labor, in those cases in which the domestic workers have not agreed to, and object to this condition. Even if domestic workers are aware of the condition they cannot leave the premises at all, it remains problematic as it severely restricts their access to justice (as will be described in further detail in chapters 8 and 10). Adding to the fact that the position of domestic workers regularly constitutes a situation of forced labor, is the fact that most employers confiscate the passport of the domestic worker (see chapter 10). Thirdly, the visa regulations tie the legal position of the domestic worker to her employer. The combination of forced confinement (including locked doors), confiscation of passports and visa regulation which force the domestic worker to choose between continuation of her job or deportation, often result in a situation which should be labeled as forced labor. Forced labor constitutes exploitation. The second reason why many domestic workers should be considered victims of exploitation is the fact that most workers are on call 24 hours per day.

---

[373] http://www.unodc.org/unodc/en/human-trafficking/faqs.html September 2010.

They work average days of around 17 hours and do not have days off for the duration of their two year contract (as described in chapter 6 on contractual norms). Further reasons which are regularly addressed as adhering to exploitation, are other forms of abuse such as physical, psychological and sexual abuse (see chapters 5 and 11).[374]

Exploitation or culture?

Confinement and excessive work hours are thus so widespread, that exploitation should be regarded as the general market condition. Jureidini carefully poses the question: "Is the treatment of domestic workers by employers (that includes long exploitative hours, low pay, restrictions of freedom and abusive behavior) so accepted in some countries that neither trafficking, nor criminal intent is present, but rather a cultural norm?"[375] He asks in other words: can it be exploitation and can it thus be trafficking, if it is culture? This resembles the cultural defense often used regarding the treatment of women in the private sphere of the house. For a long time, international law was also in the West considered to be a rights framework belonging to the public, not the private sphere.[376] Only fairly recently has domestic violence been reframed as a human rights issue, based on the fact that victims of domestic violence are primarily women and that therefore punishment only of violence committed in the public sphere would constitute discrimination. In the same line of reasoning, a lack of protection of workers in the private sphere would constitute discrimination by both the state and the international community, and therefore a human rights breach. Cultural defense, just like it can no longer be used to defend the oppression of women, cannot be used anymore to defend exploitation or trafficking of domestic workers.

Deceit, misleading and failing to warn

Domestic workers are victims of trafficking if they are brought to the Middle East for exploitation by means of fraud or deception. The data in this research show that domestic workers are often misinformed or deceived about the most important work conditions. As described in chapter 6, especially a large share of Filipina domestic workers are not aware of the fact that most domestic workers are not permitted to leave the house of their employer. Secondly, many domestic workers are deceived or misinformed about their salary and the payment of transaction costs. They are frequently misled about weekly days off and the number of working hours per day. The agencies in the countries of destination actively encourage employers to restrict the domestic workers' rights and freedoms and as such actively encourage exploitation and forced labor.

---

374 Jureidini (2010).
375 Jureidini (2010) P157.
376 Romany (1993) P87.

Therefore the acts of the agents can often be qualified as human trafficking. Contrary to statements from interviewees in the Emirati and the Saudi governments, this concerns agencies in both the countries of origin *and* the destination countries.

Delphi Indicators
A new tool to help determine whether individuals are victims of trafficking – and which supports the statement that they often are – is called the Delphi Indicators.[377] As the ILO states, without clear operational indicators there is a risk that researchers and practitioners might not recognize trafficking when they see it or might see trafficking where it does not exist.[378] Because of uncertainty about the meaning of terms such as 'coercion,' 'deception,' 'fraud,' 'abuse of power or of a position of vulnerability,' 'control over another person' and 'exploitation,' there was a risk that without further clarification, interpretations of these terms could diverge widely between and within countries and researchers.[379] The ILO states that somebody is a victim of trafficking if two strong indicators apply, one strong and one medium indicator, or three medium indicators (weak indicators are disregarded here). The Delphi indicators support the statement that many domestic workers in Saudi Arabia and the Emirates are victims of trafficking, based on the following indicators:

Strong indicators:
- Deception about the nature of the job, location or employer
- Excessive working days or hours
- Confiscation of documents
- Isolation, confinement or surveillance
- Violence against victims

Medium indicators:
- Deception about working conditions
- Deception about wages/earnings
- Poor living conditions
- No respect for labor laws or contracts signed
- No social protection (contract, social insurance, etc.)
- Withholding of wages
- Dependence on exploiters
- Difficulty living in an unfamiliar area
- Relationship with authorities/legal status

377 http://www.ilo.org/global/Themes/Forced_Labour/lang--en/docName--WCMS_105884/index.htm November 2010.
378 http://www.childtrafficking.com/Docs/ilo_09_operational_beings_1009.pdf October 2010.
379 According to an ILO interviewee, the indicators are currently being used in different contexts, e.g., for national surveys or law enforcement, but the ILO does not keep track of all the countries using them. They were used in the pilot trafficking survey which we implemented in collaboration with national bureaus of statistics in Moldova and Armenia. They have been recently used by some national research institutes in Portugal, Finland and Germany.

It is noteworthy that the Delphi Indicators do not require an intent aimed specifically at exploitation. They do acknowledge several factors in the Emirates and Saudi Arabia which add to the status of trafficking victims: the confiscation of documents is problematic, while most employers confiscate the passports of their domestic workers (in cooperation with the authorities). Secondly, the relationship with the authorities and legal status are deemed an indicator, while in the Gulf, based on the visa regulations, the domestic worker is deemed to be a criminal and subject to deportation the moment she leaves the premises of her employer, regardless of the question why she left. Trafficking victims are also all minors as they cannot be regarded as capable of assessing the exploitative labor conditions and the attached risks.

There is a Filipino Act against trafficking[380] under which confinement makes one a trafficking victim; possible consent to confinement is not mentioned. When the union representing about 80% of all Filipino agencies was confronted with the question of whether this makes almost all domestic workers in the Middle East trafficking victims, it replied: "So it is state sanctioned trafficking, because POEA[381] has processed all the papers. And the agencies are legal." Interviewed agents typically stated that if the paperwork is correct, the domestic worker is not a trafficking victim. Lack of consent, fraud or abuse of circumstances are of no consequence to them. Surprisingly, however, all interviewed government officials agreed with these agents, or they believed that only women who are brought into prostitution can be trafficking victims. The Dubai police stated in a newspaper article that no one had ever been convicted of trafficking; therefore, it does not exist.[382] Even the ILO does not include these domestic workers in their trafficking estimates[383] and most interviewees from NGOs stated that it is of "no use" to define them as such.

But article 6 of the Palermo Protocol obligates states to offer assistance and protection to trafficking victims and articles 5 and 9 obligate them to criminalize and prevent trafficking:

Article 6: Assistance to and protection of victims of trafficking in persons
(1) In appropriate cases and to the extent possible under its domestic law, each State Party shall protect the privacy and identity of victims of trafficking in persons, including, inter alia, by making legal proceedings relating to such trafficking confidential.
(2) Each State Party shall ensure that its domestic legal or administrative system contains measures that provide to victims of trafficking in persons, in appropriate cases:

---

380 Republic Act no. 9208, May 26 2003: Act to institute policies to eliminate trafficking in persons, especially women & children.
381 The Filipino government office concerned.
382 7 Days Newspaper, as quoted on http://secretdubai.blogspot.com/.
383 Report 22, P49 states that around 800,000 persons are trafficked into non-sexual forced labor worldwide. This is lower than the estimates of this research that 1,000,000 domestic workers in Saudi Arabia and the Emirates are trafficking victims under the Palermo Protocol.

(a) Information on relevant court and administrative proceedings;

(b) Assistance to enable their views and concerns to be presented and considered at appropriate stages of criminal proceedings against offenders, in a manner not prejudicial to the rights of the defense.

(3) Each State Party shall consider implementing measures to provide for the physical, psychological and social recovery of victims of trafficking in persons, including, in appropriate cases, in cooperation with non-governmental organizations, other relevant organizations and other elements of civil society, and, in particular, the provision of:

(a) Appropriate housing;

(b) Counseling and information, in particular as regards their legal rights, in a language that the victims of trafficking in persons can understand;

(c) Medical, psychological and material assistance; and

(d) Employment, educational and training opportunities.

(4) Each State Party shall take into account, in applying the provisions of this article, the age, gender and special needs of victims of trafficking in persons, in particular the special needs of children, including appropriate housing, education and care.

(5) Each State Party shall endeavor to provide for the physical safety of victims of trafficking in persons while they are within its territory.

(6) Each State Party shall ensure that its domestic legal system contains measures that offer victims of trafficking in persons the possibility of obtaining compensation for damage suffered.

Article 5: Criminalization

(1) Each State Party shall adopt such legislative and other measures as may be necessary to establish as criminal offences the conduct set forth in article 3 of this Protocol, when committed intentionally.

(2) Each State Party shall also adopt such legislative and other measures as may be necessary to establish as criminal offences:

(a) Subject to the basic concepts of its legal system, attempting to commit an offence established in accordance with paragraph 1 of this article;

(b) Participating as an accomplice in an offence established in accordance with paragraph 1 of this article; and

(c) Organizing or directing other persons to commit an offence established in accordance with paragraph 1 of this article.

Article 9: Prevention of trafficking in persons

(1) States Parties shall establish comprehensive policies, programs and other measures:

(a) To prevent and combat trafficking in persons; and

(b) To protect victims of trafficking in persons, especially women and children, from re-victimization.

(2) States Parties shall endeavor to undertake measures such as research, information and mass media campaigns and social and economic initiatives to prevent and combat trafficking in persons.

(3) Policies, programs and other measures established in accordance with this article shall, as appropriate, include cooperation with non-governmental organizations, other relevant organizations and other elements of civil society.

(4) States Parties shall take or strengthen measures, including through bilateral or multilateral cooperation, to alleviate the factors that make persons, especially women and children, vulnerable to trafficking, such as poverty, underdevelopment and lack of equal opportunity.

(5) States Parties shall adopt or strengthen legislative or other measures, such as educational, social or cultural measures, including through bilateral and multilateral cooperation, to discourage the demand that fosters all forms of exploitation of persons, especially women and children, that leads to trafficking.

By actively and publicly defining half the domestic workers in Saudi Arabia and the Emirates as trafficking victims, the international community could call on both governments to account for their lack of proper action against the agencies and the lack of assistance to trafficked domestic workers. Yet there are specific obstructions to the implementation of the Palermo Protocol that will be described in section 7.5, after a general explanation on the poor protection of the lower strata of society both in Saudi Arabia and the Emirates.

7.4 Why so little labor protection?

As the previous two sections show, international formal legal norms provide ample normative tools for the protection of domestic workers, while national formal legal norms do not. In Europe, this is not the case; there is ample statutory law protecting laborers, including migrant domestic workers. Neither do Saudi or Emirati national formal legal norms provide for a hierarchy between normative tools, to delimit the maneuvering space of the more powerful party, the employer. In these two countries, one of the reasons for poor legal protection is the fact that both societies are halfway through the rapid transformation from a patriarchal, status-based society to a society based on contractual relations (as described in chapter 5). One of the characteristics of patriarchy is that the master "wields his power with restraint, at his discretion and, above all, unencumbered by rules, insofar as it is not limited by tradition or competing powers."[384]

---

384 Rollins (1985) quoting Weber.

This most strongly affects the private sphere of the household, as patriarchs try to hold on to the status-based system that offers them more power than the contractual system. This has been the case in Europe as well, but legal protection of domestic workers has nevertheless slowly come into existence there. Are Saudi Arabia and the Emirates just a few decades behind in this development (as interviewees from the government claim) or are there other societal causes as well?

One additional reason given by interviewees for limited protections under labor laws is the argument generally maintained against labor laws: labor should (as much as possible) be left to market mechanisms. As the Deputy Minister of Labor of Saudi Arabia stated in an interview: "Minimum salary – no, we do not interfere in this, it is the free market, it is up to the people. They decide, they agree." Many Saudi and Emirati government officials have been trained in the United States, the largest proponent of the free market mechanism, which is likely to have influenced them. On the other hand, this free market line of reasoning is frequently used in Europe as well, but there the need for laws that compensate for the weaker position of employees is now the *communis opinio*.[385] There is some labor protection in the U.S., although it is more limited than in Europe. Again, the question arises: are Saudi Arabia and the Emirates behind the United States and Europe in development, or are there ideological and legal differences between the continents due to societal differences? As described in chapter 3, according to Abram de Swaan[386] legislation protecting laborers and the required changes in society's underlying belief system[387] came into existence because it was in the interest of the upper-class to improve the position of the underclass. This is not the case in Saudi Arabia or the Emirates.

7.4.1 Five interests largely absent

The five interests which the upper-class had in Europe to create means and protection for the lower classes, as discussed in chapter 3 are: (i) fear of beggars, thieves and gangs, (ii) fear of contagious diseases carried by the lower classes, (iii) the positive effects of means and protection on the availability and skills of the current and future labor force, (iv) anxiety for riots and revolutions, and (v) the need to coordinate efforts in order to create or maintain level economic playing field.

These five interests currently exist on the Arabian Peninsula to a limited extent only, because poor laborers are generally migrant workers who can be 'imported' and 'deported' at will.[388] Beggars, thieves and gang members can be jailed or deported and usually it is the latter. Sixteenth-century European communities could expel their poor as well, but as other communities did the same, this practice created gangs that roamed the country from one village to the next.

---

385 Compare Humphries in Basu (2003) P85 and Schwitters (2000) P93.
386 Swaan (2004).
387 Engerman in Basu (2003) P30.
388 Based on the sponsorship system as described in section 7.2.

Soon the rich in Europe realized their interest in the rule that each community had to take care of its own poor. Nowadays, however, strict border controls have emerged that allow wealthier countries (the haves) to permanently expel unwanted individuals (the have-nots). Therefore, the same 'deal' of non-expulsion does not apply.

Secondly, the Emiratis and Saudis are not likely to provide proper healthcare for their workers, as the rich do not suffer the same threat from the poor as they did in earlier times in Europe. Before flying to the Arabian Peninsula, all migrant workers have to undergo extensive health checks and no one who is sick is permitted to fly in. Furthermore, as soon as an individual is found to be sick he is usually instantly deported, not treated. Iris scans prevent not only irregular migrants from returning, but also those workers who have been found to carry contagious diseases like tuberculosis or HIV/AIDS. Even employers who are willing to pay for the treatment of their employees cannot stop their deportation and banishment for life.[389]

The third reason that these conditions are less prevalent on the Arabian Peninsula is that allowing workers to invest in themselves and their children to create a healthier and better-educated work force, is not in the interest of the Saudis or Emiratis. Although the migrant workers in both countries do invest heavily in the education of their children,[390] the new generation of workers prefers not to go to the Arabian Peninsula. This is especially true for domestic workers; if they gain enough wealth, their children will pursue vocational training, for instance, to become nurses. If possible, they will apply for jobs in Western countries that offer higher salaries and better working conditions. Even if domestic workers do not succeed in seeing their children complete a proper education, the salary from the Middle East will likely be used for family members to pay placement fees for countries that offer higher salaries for domestic workers, such as Hong Kong or Singapore. Thus, while host countries benefit from foreign workers and the freedom from capital investment,[391] the downside is that they do not benefit from investments in these workers and therefore have no interest in raising their standard of living.

Concerning the threat of strikes and worker uprisings, it benefits the Saudis and the Emiratis that communism is no longer viewed as an attainable ideal by the majority of laborers. Therefore, the upper class is less wary of the danger of radical labor movements that need to be averted with a generous social contract.[392] Anyone who goes on strike for better labor conditions is arrested and deported.

---

389 See for instance http://secretdubai.blogspot.com/2007/07/story-of-badal.html.
390 Having to pay for family members, especially children, was a reason frequently given by domestic workers why they would not be able to go home, as discussed in chapter 10.
391 Licuanan in Heyzer (1994) P109.
392 Swaan (2004) P12.

They are treated the same way as thieves and workers whose visa have expired: they are all perceived as criminals, as became clear in several interviews with government officials. The oppression of labor movements has also become considerably easier with weaponry available to the Emirati and Saudi security forces, which the nineteenth-century European police forces could only dream of. Certain groups within the security forces are even trained by the American CIA.[393]

The fifth interest in the West – pressure from the international community to create a level economic playing field – does not have much of an effect on the Arabian Peninsula either. The international pressure is rather poor, because there is little need for a level playing field. The exports from both Saudi Arabia and the Emirates consist largely of oil and oil-related products. The more powerful players in the international field either do not produce these same products, or they do produce oil, but, in light of the world economy, have no interest in raising Saudi and Emirati production costs. The lack of international economic-based pressure is even more severe for domestic workers. Because they produce nothing tradable on the monetary market, they do not form a competitive import sector that requires an international level playing field.[394]

Thus, the five interests that have existed in Europe to raise the standard of living for workers barely exist in Saudi Arabia or the Emirates. On the contrary, keeping the workers cheap is in the best interest of both governments, because cheap laborers provide for wealth and luxury, which keeps their citizens fairly content. As Fareed Zakaria states, this is part of the 'deal' between the upper class and society: legitimacy by means of luxury.[395] Both governments have written Labor Laws, and Saudi Arabia works on a specific domestic workers act, but in light of the foregoing, it is not surprising that these initiatives seem to be taken primarily in the interest of Saudi and Emirati employers. For instance, when discussing the Saudi draft Domestic Workers Act, the Saudi Shura[396] suggested that the employer should have a legal right to withhold portions of salaries to prevent domestic workers from absconding. One member explicitly stated that the Act as proposed would do more harm to citizens than good.[397] This preoccupation with the employer-citizens rather than with the employee-migrants can also be seen in other labor-importing states, such as Singapore.[398] A comparative research on the question to what extent the five causes given by De Swaan are absent or present, comparing countries with different cultures, would therefore be interesting (more hereon in chapter 12).

---

393 Briody (2003).
394 Basu (2003) P4.
395 See chapter 2, citing, among others, Zakaria (2001).
396 A sort of Consultative Parliament.
397 http://www.gulfinthemedia.com/index.php?id=461628&news_type=Political&lang=en& later removed from the internet.
398 Anggraeni (2006) P115.

7.4.2 Labor protection and civil society

This situation of the near absence in Saudi Arabia and the Emirates of De Swaan's five upper-class interests, is slowly changing though. Yet to the extent that the causes now come into existence, they can have little effect due to the absence of civil society. This section first describes the changes in society that, based on De Swaan, may be expected to lead to protection of the poor. Thereafter it describes how in Europe they came into existence as bottom-up movements or spontaneous collective actions, for which the *conditio sine qua non*, civil society, is absent in the Middle East.

First, the number of poor migrants that live in both countries illegally and invisibly is on the rise. As explained by several interviewees, Saudi Arabia especially is struggling with large groups of migrants that enter the country on an *Umra* visa (for Mecca), after which they disappear into illegality. These invisible migrants are becoming better organized each year and they slowly begin to resemble the groups of vagabonds that made the German forests unsafe several centuries ago. Although the Emirates are better in controlling the entrance of migrants into their country, they suffer the same problem with the appearance of gangs. Several Emirati interviewees in Dubai said they were afraid of 'mafia' groups that apparently steal, rob and even abduct people. These groups are growing and thus far, neither government seems capable of finding and deporting all of these individuals. If this continues, in due time it could lead to a change in attitude similar to what occurred in Europe; that these groups of individuals would not steal, rob, or abduct if given a chance to earn a living legally.

Second, there is a growing problem, mainly in the Emirates, of a dependence on migrant workers. This dependence has become quite large, as about 90% of laborers are migrants.[399] Although individuals can be deported, this cannot be done on a large scale, as this would halt the entire economy. During the general amnesty several years ago that permitted irregular workers to leave the country without paying a fine, so many people left that many construction companies faced serious problems in continuing their projects. This engendered anger towards the government (and, according to several interviewees, is the reason why Labor Minister Al Kaabi had to pack his bags), but it also raised awareness about just how dependent the economy had become on foreign workers. While strikes had previously been seen as a costly nuisance, they are now increasingly perceived as real threats.

Several Emirati interviewees complained that things have gotten out of hand and that it would be better if all migrants would leave; people would lose wealth, but life would be safer again. Others complained that the workers must be treated better, or one day they will emerge from their camps of 50,000 men cramped together to take whatever property or women they can get their hands on.

---

399 See chapter 2.

Therefore, the awareness that grew in Europe about the need to appease the have-nots with certain minimum living conditions seems to arise in Saudi Arabia and the Emirates as well. Still, collective action to achieve better labor conditions for the workers is not likely to occur anytime soon, because another societal aspect that was necessary in the West is not present in the Middle East: civil society.[400]

Labor protection as bottom up collectivized good
In Europe, as De Swaan describes, many collective goods came into existence not as initiatives from the government, but from small, powerful groups within society. Governmental bodies regularly came into existence as a way to fulfill collective tasks that were earlier performed at a lower level, but were later lifted to a national level. For instance, one of the first and most important tasks to be collectivized was defense against external threats. This defense was often first organized at the village level, by the inhabitants themselves. Later, deals would be closed with cities before they began to be organized at a state level. Garbage collection was set up by small groups that organized themselves, or by individuals who offered paid subscriptions; it later became state organized. Social security was started by laborers deciding to set up collective funds for themselves; they later developed into state-run welfare systems (solely, or in competition with private funds). In so-called friendly societies[401] the first sewage systems were initiatives by individuals in the richer parts of town, but they became a town and later a state responsibility. Even the police started as neighborhood security forces. All of these initiatives were started by private individuals, not by governmental bodies. Those bodies were only created later, when the collective action was lifted to a higher, governmental level.[402]

Many collective goods were provided for by the state in exchange for taxes, which used to be the contribution paid to the garbage company, trade union or friendly society. The government was given money in exchange for collective goods beginning with villages paying taxes to towns and later to kings, in exchange for security and other collective goods. With the growing financial needs of the governments and the diminishing wealth of the old nobility (as the land they owned lost value compared to labor and capital), higher taxes were requested and were paid voluntarily in exchange for properly organized collective goods, participation in the way they were organized and the possibility to remove poor organizers. This is part of the story of how democracy developed in the West.[403] Workers and unions advocated further reforms as they became more powerful, partly because of the strength from nineteenth-century legislation that permitted the formation and exercise of some forms of collective power by unions.[404]

---

400 Civil society is composed of the totality of voluntary civic and social organizations and institutions, as opposed to the structures of the government (regardless of that state's political system) and commercial institutions of the market.
401 Also Schwitters (1991) P12-20.
402 Compare Berger & Neuhaus in Eberly (2000) P166.
403 As described by the proponents of the rentier state theory. More hereon in chapters 2 and 9.
404 Engerman in Basu (2003) P22.

In the United Arab Emirates and the Kingdom of Saudi Arabia, the emergence of the state followed an entirely different course. Although both countries had tribal and religious leaders, larger governmental bodies did not come into existence until the discovery of oil, when the political leaders with whom Western oil companies had signed their agreements, gained an independent source of income. Money under this model does not flow up, from society to the government, but down, from the government to society. It is strategically used to buy loyalty through the provisions of wealth and luxury. Collective goods thus come into existence only if the government – not a group within society – decides that this is necessary.

To the extent that an individual in either society would nevertheless be inclined to do something, they face the problem that Saudi Arabia's and the Emirates' governments severely limit the possibility for individuals to unite or to express their dissatisfaction with aspects of society that they consider poorly organized. This is sometimes taken to extremes. For instance, as one interviewee reported, in Saudi Arabia a woman who set up a micro-finance initiative was arrested for causing *fitna*, internal strife. Migrants who try to set up initiatives or who express their views on the necessity of governmental action are usually deported from both countries immediately. According to interviewees from the Emirati government, individuals are not permitted to privately set up shelters or centers for battered women. The overall discourse of the government in interviews and official statements, is that individuals are not permitted to organize such matters; if they are necessary, then the government should organize them. If they are not really necessary, they should not be organized at all (with the government, of course, deciding what is and what is not necessary).

Civil Society

Civil society concerns organizational units other than the government or the market. It consists of families, neighborhoods, voluntary associations, charities, lodges, fraternal orders, houses of worship and an endless variety of civic enterprises that emerge as people join forces, work toward common purposes and, in the process, learn the habits of collaboration and trust, but also develop accountability mechanisms. Many of the social reform movements in history, whether focused on morality, justice for women and children or the eradication of poverty and suffering, were orchestrated by voluntary associations.[405]

In the Middle East, however, non-governmental organizations are state-controlled or nonexistent,[406] except for organizations in and around mosques.[407]

---

405 Eberly in Eberly (2000) P3 and 7. Also Bayly (2005) P72.
406 Esposito (2007) P40.
407 Zakaria (2001).

De Toqueville's famous phrase 'voluntary associations' expresses the idea that liberty is of the essence to civil society.[408] Thus, under extreme conditions of state oppression there can be no question of the power of civil society.[409] Both Saudi Arabia and the Emirates are absolute monarchies that prohibit all political parties, unsanctioned private associations and NGOs.[410] The emergence of the modern authoritarian system played a significant role in curtailing the growth of civil institutions. The restrictions on basic freedoms left their mark on the nascent civil society that found no accommodating public space. In the absence of a viable civil society that could protect citizens' interests, exposed individuals turned their backs on the institutions of civil society and sought the rude shelter of the tribal and clan systems, with their feudal and organic bonds.[411]

This lack of a civil society is even worse in the Emirates, where the citizens constitute less than 10% of the population.[412] Because a large part of the remaining 90% of the population has no rights and no intention of staying in the country for a longer time, they have no incentive to become involved in issues that could be improved by civil society actions.[413] As an interviewee summarized it: "The organizations of the ex-pats are not involved in anything. They are just here to make money and then they go home. It's comfortable; they don't pay taxes. And also there is no communication between the different communities, so how will this come to a shared civil society?"

Van Doorn is thus correct when he comments on the work of De Swaan (previous section) that large differences between the haves and the have-nots are not enough for protections for the poor to come into existence. Civil society is needed and its effectiveness depends on the organization and power of the proletariat and the nature and characteristics of other societal coalitions.[414] Likewise, the corporate social responsibility movement[415] cannot arise due to the lack of freedom of expression. The quality of news reporting is poor in both Saudi Arabia and the Emirates. To the extent that newspapers do write about the situation of laborers in general or domestic workers in particular, they usually focus on descriptions of individual cases. Overall analyses and quantitative data are lacking. Thus, the absence of systematic investigation by the media creates the impression that abuse of workers and problems related to their unenviable positions are rare. This has also been the case with domestic violence against women and children. Domestic violence was long believed to be an issue of regrettable, isolated incidents, not a problem occurring on a large scale in all societal strata.

---

408 Himmelfarb in Eberly (2000) P95.
409 Eberly (2000) P65.
410 http://www.google.com/hostednews/afp/article/ALeqM5ieWR1y4we-axmf3a4fAxntX075DA and report 28.
411 Report 10, P166.
412 See chapter 2.
413 Likewise, Davidson (2008) P190-193.
414 Van Doorn (1990).
415 Which is a combination of civil society and market; producers supporting social goals.

This image changed only with a large government-backed campaign in 2007 and 2008, but the image of the abuse of domestic workers remains as it was: a matter of isolated incidents.

All Saudi and Emirati interviewees responded with disbelief when presented with the quantitative results of chapter 6 of this dissertation. Several attempts to publish these results in a newspaper in Saudi Arabia were fruitless, and on the (English-speaking, more liberal) Saudi radio, the researcher was permitted to state the topic of her research, but not to discuss the results. Presentation of these results at a gathering of Arab and European human rights organizations caused vehement reactions. In my experience, the topic of abuse of domestic workers is thus not discussable. Likewise, in the Emirates the results of chapter 6 were denied with the argument that many runaways find employment on the black market. The possibility was not accepted that irregular employment could be the effect rather than the cause of large-scale absconding. That same presumption is also published regularly in Saudi newspapers: that domestic workers run away solely to earn more on the black market, not because of possible abuse or false promises from agents. The result is that many citizens, although they know that abuse occurs, are unaware of its scale and causes and will remain unaware until the media are granted greater freedom of expression.

In summary, the five interests that, according to De Swaan, contributed to the development of aid and protection of the lower strata of society in Europe, barely exist in the Middle East. This is due to the phenomenon of circular migration. To the extent that these five causes do come into existence now though, they cannot be expected to have much result, as both governments are dictatorial and therefore do not allow for the development of civil society. As there is no freedom of expression, not enough people become aware of a problem to ignite collective action and to the extent that there would be enough people, they do not enjoy the freedom to unite.

7.5 Specific obstructions

7.5.1 *Obstructions to abolition of the sponsorship system*

The regimes in Saudi Arabia and the Emirates are, according to the rentier state theory, likely to become less authoritarian, less oppressive, and more sensitive to the needs of both inhabitants and economy, when the oil runs out.[416] Citizens will gain more freedom to unite, more freedom of expression, both necessary for the proper functioning of civil society. Little can be done to hasten this process.

---

416 According to contested estimates, oil reserves worldwide could run out in less than 40 years: http://www.independent.co.uk/news/science/world-oil-supplies-are-set-to-run-out-faster-than-expected-warn-scientists-453068.html. More optimistic sources say for Saudi Arabia it is about 70 years: http://en.wikipedia.org/wiki/Oil_reserves or even 90 years: http://www.saudi-us-relations.org/energy/saudi-energy-reserves.html. Other studies raise doubt about Saudi's reserves: http://www.iags.org/n0331043.htm.

Nevertheless, the haves could gain more interest in protecting the have-nots, and particularly migrant workers, if the sponsorship system would be altered to mitigate circular migration and its consequences. This is actually a topic of discussion currently in both countries. Yet the possibilities for change have to be considered in light of the reasons people give why the current system cannot simply be abolished. According to interviewees, the reasons are the following:

Transaction costs

The most important reason given by employers as to why workers are not permitted to leave and why the sponsorship system cannot be abolished is the fact that employers pay large fees (from $700 to $2.700)[417] to agencies, governmental institutions and other parties[418] when hiring a worker.[419] Employers do not want domestic workers to leave and work for someone else who has not paid these fees, and who would therefore be willing to pay a higher salary. An interviewed employer, when asked if he would allow his domestic workers to leave and work for another family, said: "No, we paid a lot for them to come here!" But when asked if he would allow them to leave if there was a rule that the next sponsor or employer would have to pay a percentage of what the first sponsor paid in fees, answers were given such as: "Well, if there was that rule, then maybe we could change the other rules as well."

Neither governments nor agencies ever return (part of the) fees and the domestic worker can only be 'exchanged' in the first three months if (for whatever reason) she does not satisfy the employer.[420] After that, it is the employer's loss. As the Arab News formulated it: "They [the employers] shoulder the burden, expense and risk. If a maid's performance is not satisfactory, there is little option but to simply send her back to her home country and write off the costs." These costs are usually perceived as debts from the domestic worker to the employer,[421] which must be repaid by serving the full two years of the contract, even though it is not the worker but the agency that benefits. Around half of the fees paid by the employer to the agency is spent on a one-way ticket, of which the worker no longer profits the moment she is deported. To the contrary, a considerable profit appears to be made by the agency,[422] profit it cannot lose as there are no fee-restitution rules or habits.

---

417 In the Emirates, for instance, employers pay the agency a fee of $350 for an Ethiopian and $1.250 for a Filipina. Government fees for ex-pats are around $1.150. In Saudi Arabia, an agency supplying domestic workers without waiting lists (probably bought from their previous employer) asked for $2.700.

418 For instance, doctors for health certificates or criminals for false passports.

419 Likewise Report 18, P29.

420 See chapter 6; all visited agencies in Saudi Arabia and the Emirates stated such. Interviewed employers confirmed this was the rule, although it does not seem to have been written done anywhere.

421 Even by interviewees from the Human Rights Commission in Saudi Arabia.

422 A fact that might be deduced from the extremely expensive cars driven by most agency owners, although further research hereon is needed. Yet this will be difficult as cooperation of the agency owners is not to be expected.

Criminality

Another financial reason to retain the sponsorship system is given by business-men, as explained by an interviewee: "It was mostly businessmen who are in support of the sponsorship law. They say that it is there to protect them in case an employee – such as an accountant – runs off with their money." Many interviewed employers and government officials stated that if workers were permitted more freedom, they expected that the workers would leave to become criminals: "Because you have to understand, if we give them the passport, they can go anywhere and it will be a big mess. You cannot know where they are, where they go. They go to Mecca, go to Medina, there are thousands of them, they go into prostitution, they sell alcohol, thievery." An employer said his domestic worker was not permitted to leave the house, because the only place to go was the mall: "She will meet her mafia friends there who will stimulate her to run away and to become a prostitute."[423]

No Saudi or Emirati interviewee[424] seemed to consider the possibility that foreigners who smuggle drugs and alcohol or go into prostitution, maybe do so because they do not have the option of getting a legal job, precisely because of the sponsorship regulations. A person who runs away from an abusive employer, and who cannot go home because of debts incurred to come to the Middle East or because she lacks passport or release documents, generally has no choice but to work in criminal activities. According to interviewees, especially in Saudi Arabia there are many princes who "import" workers, take their passports and send them to the streets to make money for the prince. This also forces the workers concerned into criminal behavior because the workers do not have the opportunity to apply for jobs with other employers. Thus, the sponsorship system seems to be creating the problems it is supposed to prevent.

Detention for private debts

A third reason given by employers for why the sponsorship system cannot be abolished is the fact that in these countries, individuals can be (and, indeed, regularly are) jailed for indebtedness. An interviewed Emirati government official stated: "We need to change this sponsorship system, but you have to keep in mind that it was well intended. If you get into troubles with the police and you have to pay a large fine, somebody has to be responsible for you; otherwise, you will be in jail for the rest of your life. Locals have family members to pay for them, but the laborers do not have a family here and therefore they need a sponsor."

Private debt as grounds for detention is prohibited under international human rights standards, as it is considered akin to debt bondage or slavery.[425]

---

423 Compare Esim (2004) P80.
424 Contrary to several Bahreini's who did recognize this possibility.
425 Report 17, P53.

Specifically, Article 11 of the International Convention on Civil and Political Rights provides:

> Article 11: No one shall be imprisoned merely on the ground of inability to fulfill a contractual obligation.

But neither the Emirates nor Saudi Arabia is a member state of this convention. The rules on detention for private debts are sometimes ascribed to Arab culture: "for several centuries, private property in Islam was so well protected that a debtor's person, rather than his assets, answered for his debts. A Muslim judge could order seizure and imprisonment of a recalcitrant debtor to force him to pay his debts, but he could not order foreclosure of his proprietary wealth to satisfy his unpaid creditors."[426] Yet this statement is incorrect as detention for private debts used to be common in many parts of the world including the West and according to some it still is.[427] Furthermore, the Arab Charter on Human Rights explicitly forbids this practice:

> Article 18: No one who is shown by a court to be unable to pay a debt arising from a contractual obligation shall be imprisoned.

Migration and the sponsorship system

A non-financial reason given by interviewees for why the sponsorship system cannot be abolished is fear that immigration will grow even larger and the workers will no longer leave the country and will eventually "take over the country." The current sponsorship regulations allow the Saudis and Emiratis to deport foreign workers instantly (upon running away or dismissal, visas become invalid instantly). Annulment would only be accepted if the system were to be replaced by another system limiting the residency rights of the immense groups of foreigners, such as the 3+3 residency cap discussed in the spring of 2008.[428] If this proposed law were passed, unskilled workers would be permitted to work in Saudi Arabia or the Emirates with a three-year labor contract that can only be renewed once.[429] The governments thus put a maximum on the number of years that certain foreign contract workers can stay in their respective countries, which appears to be a preliminary step to adjustments of the sponsorship system.

---

426 Report 17, P72.
427 See for instance http://www.nakedcapitalism.com/2010/06/jail-for-unpaid-debt-a-reality-in-six-states-strategic-default-pushback-watch.html, on detention for private debts in the USA.
428 It was discussed among others at the Abu Dhabi Dialogue.
429 For more information on this labor rotation system or time-limited circular migration, see, among others, http://emirateseconomist.blogspot.com/2007/11/un-charter-and-gcc-labor-rotation.html.

Possible adjustments

Based on these lines of reasoning, abolishing the sponsorship system is currently not an option for either the Emirati or the Saudi government. Yet adjustments to the system are possible. Apart from the residency cap, two alternatives for the sponsorship system are being discussed. Both entail a transfer of sponsorship to a larger organization. In the Emirates, the plan is to put sponsorship in the hands of the government. The Minister of Labor has sketched a blueprint of new procedures that would require laborers wishing to work in the Emirates to go through the Ministry of Labor, rather than through recruiting agencies. In contrast, in Saudi Arabia, a limited number of agencies is to become sponsor, turning these contracted agencies into labor pools. They are expected to recruit large numbers of foreign laborers, enabling employers to hire a worker on the spot without the 60-120 day delay currently experienced by sponsors in Saudi Arabia. These workers would be given a three-month probationary period, during which both parties in the working relationship could withdraw from the agreement. In the event of dissatisfaction, the foreign worker simply would flow back into the Ministry's or agency's labor pool and the employer would be provided with another worker.

These systems grant more freedom and therefore more power to the worker. Yet they are not perfect and therefore not uncontested. If the worker gets into a conflict with the Ministry (in the Emirates) or the agency (in Saudi Arabia), he would be just as powerless in the event of a conflict with the employer, as he is currently. However, because the relation in these scenarios is not one-on-one, the level of abuse might be lower. An interviewee in Riyadh clearly saw this, stating: "It is better to find a job in a large company, because in a one-man company usually the employer gets very abusive." Furthermore, these labor pool systems could possibly be better than a completely free market (which is demanded by certain interviewees) because of transaction costs. These costs actually diminish the freedom of migrant workers, as will be discussed in chapter 10. In concluding chapter 12 the proposed alteration of the sponsorship system will therefore be defended.

7.5.2 Obstructions to implementation of the Palermo Protocol

An additional issue that needs to be tackled to improve the position of migrant workers in order to provide the haves with incentives to protect the have-nots, is better regulation of the trade in migrant workers. If the sponsorship system is improved, but still many migrant workers arrive on false promises, conflicts will continue to arise. If they continue to arrive on false documents, they will remain within the power of the individual employer. Better regulation would be necessary, which simply comes down to proper implementation of the Palermo Protocol. However, there are currently several obstructions to the implementation of this protocol.

Jureidini states that, as trafficking is difficult to assert, the use of civil and criminal laws to address exploitation and abuses, may be more appropriate legal means for prosecution and redress than trafficking regulations.[430] But the lack of prosecution is not caused by a lack of clarity on legal concepts such as trafficking or exploitation, but rather by societal issues. There are currently several obstructions to the implementation of the UN's Palermo Protocol. Primarily, the human trafficking business is estimated to be about as large as both the illegal arms trade and the drug trade combined.[431] This kind of money can buy a lot. In all four countries visited for this study (Saudi Arabia, the Emirates, Philippines, and Indonesia), interviewees stated that a legal case or action against a rich and powerful man cannot be won. For instance, an interviewed government official in Manila said: "No, who is this government officer that is going to file a complaint against a big man?" There is some government action, such as the Philippines Act on joint liability of agents and middlemen, but according to interviewees, this Act has not led to significant results. Sometimes an agency's license will be temporarily suspended, but afterwards either the suspension is cancelled or the agent concerned simply starts a new agency under a different name. Government officials are said to be bribed regularly or are connected to the agents by family ties. Possible penalties can be changed into fines low enough not to deter anyone.

Moreover, governments of labor-sending countries are more concerned with employment and remittances, which constitute a very large portion of their GNP.[432] Moreover, the IMF and the World Bank apparently use remittance flows in their calculations of sustainable loans, and credit rating agencies such as Moody's, Standard & Poor's, and Fitch do the same for their decisions on certain bond ratings.[433] The governments of labor-sending countries do not want these remittances to diminish and therefore do not make a strong stand for their overseas workers.

Muslim countries like Indonesia struggle with an additional problem: if they complain excessively about the treatment of their workers, they might not continue to be provided with visas for visiting Mecca.[434] This is a very effective threat to the government of the country with the largest Muslim population in the world. Additionally, the Indonesian military dictatorship only lost power in 1998. A spokesperson for an NGO explained, "The big agencies, these owners are high in the army; they run the department at the airport where they process the migrant workers. The army and the agencies, they are one. They are also the ones in the

---

430 Jureidini (2010) P147.

431 Among others, the International Conference on Gender, Migration and Development, Mr. Richard Evans. For estimates on the profit per domestic worker, see Heyzer (1994) P56.

432 See for instance http://blogs.worldbank.org/eastasiapacific/remittances-and-the-philippines-economy-the-elephant-in-the-room, for a World Bank estimate of 10% of GNP for the Philippines, November 2010.

433 Are workers' remittances relevant for credit rating agencies? Avendaño, Gaillard & Nieto Parra, at www.oecd.org/dataoecd/13/14/42728791.doc June 2010.

434 Confirmed by several interviewees, including an interviewee at an official human rights organization in Saudi Arabia.

government. It is all interconnected. That is why nobody ever goes to jail." An Indonesian diplomat called the agents from his country "mafia": "Really, they are too powerful for us to do something about them."

In the Middle East, many agents have another job within the government that allows them to get papers processed smoothly and to prevent action against their agency. When an Emirati government official was asked if it was possible that the Ministry of Labor would set up an internet site with the names of good and bad agents, he laughed and said the Ministry of Labor and the bad agents are one and the same. In Saudi Arabia, an important leader of the union of agents is one of the top officials of the Ministry of Labor. There are also agency owners who have a second job in the embassy of their country of origin to process all the paperwork there. This explains how women can be lured to Riyadh as salespeople only to be forced into domestic work upon arrival. The government officers involved are undoubtedly aware that women in Saudi Arabia are not permitted to work in sales.

Furthermore, the domestic workers are a small part of the legitimacy of both governments. Oil revenues are either redistributed among loyal citizens or used to provide luxuries to appease the population.[435] Domestic workers are part of these luxuries; keeping the employment of domestic workers unregulated helps to palliate employers and keep both governments popular (enough). Thus, the government pretends that the domestic industry is a private industry with which it will not interfere, but meanwhile it deals with countries such as Nepal for cheaper workers when the prices of Filipinas rise to the point that the lower-class Saudis and Emiratis can no longer afford them. Furthermore, because the state has an independent source of income, the government cannot be forced to properly organize anything, including the legal system. This state model, referred to in political science as the rentier state theory,[436] works mostly to the disadvantage of the lower strata of society, including domestic workers.[437]

An interesting aspect of trafficking is that the U.S. Department of State, according to its trafficking reports, thinks that the Emirates are doing better in their fight against trafficking than Saudi Arabia, giving them second and third tier rankings, respectively.[438] Unfortunately, this research has not provided any evidence that supports this view. Although in December 2006 the Emirates government passed a comprehensive anti-trafficking law prohibiting all forms of trafficking (with prescribed penalties ranging from one year to life imprisonment), the government did not prosecute any cases. Although the Ministry of Labor imposed some fines on labor recruiters for fraudulent practices,[439] the Ministry of Justice did not pursue criminal prosecutions of those facilitating trafficking.

---

435 Beblawi (1990), Aarts (2005) and especially Zakaria (2001). See also sections 2.1 and 2.2.
436 See paragraph 3.3.2.
437 Publication of the author (expected Spring 2011).
438 http://www.state.gov/g/tip/rls/tiprpt/.
439 Usually practices in breach of the sponsorship regulations.

The government also did not produce evidence that it prosecuted employers for using intimidation to force employees to work. Similarly, the Emirates does not consider laborers forced into involuntary servitude to be trafficking victims if they are over the age of 18 and entered the country voluntarily. Many cases of forced labor are therefore not investigated. There are no formal mechanisms to identify women who are trafficked into domestic servitude, and the Emirates does not offer victims asylum, residence or legal alternatives to immediate deportation to source countries. Therefore, the difference between Saudi Arabia and the Emirates with respect to trafficking seems to be based solely on Emirati marketing talent.

Thus, neither the countries of origin nor the countries of destination do much about the trafficking issue. At international conferences, the countries of destination state that the agencies in the countries of origin are the problem, whereas the countries of origin state that the agencies and employers in the countries of destination are the problem. The result is that the trafficking agencies continue their business untouched. With the amount of money and political interests involved, this cannot be expected to change unless measures are taken to make action against these agencies possible by the international community in neutral countries, as will be discussed in chapter 12.

7.6 Summary

This chapter provides an overview of formal legal norms concerning domestic workers, either written or ratified by the Saudi or Emirati government. In both Saudi Arabia and the Emirates, domestic workers have been explicitly excluded from the protections of the statutory labor laws. The sponsorship system is a set of immigration regulations that allows for deportation of the domestic worker upon the wishes of either employer or government. Thus far the international protests against this system have been without much result, as the sponsorship system provides substantial financial means to both governments and several other parties. Moreover, it is perceived by Saudis and Emiratis as providing safeguards against the dangers of the large migration flows. Nevertheless, two alternatives for the sponsorship system are currently being discussed. Both entail a transfer of sponsorship to a larger organization. In the Emirates, the plan is to put sponsorship in the hands of the government. In contrast, in Saudi Arabia, a limited number of agencies is to become sponsor, turning these contracted agencies into labor pools. These labor pool systems could possibly be better than a completely free market, because of transaction costs. This will be further discussed in concluding chapter 12.

Both Saudi Arabia and the Emirates have ratified several ILO treaties, but because neither country recognizes domestic workers as workers, these conventions are not applied to them. The most relevant other rules of international law are the

Palermo Protocol against human trafficking and the Convention on the Elimination of all forms of Discrimination Against Women (CEDAW). By prohibiting any distinction which has the effect of impairing the rights of women, CEDAW prohibits both direct and indirect discrimination. Because almost all domestic workers are female, excluding them from the protections of the labor law seems tantamount to indirect discrimination. Yet there has never been a court ruling on this matter. The Palermo Protocol obligates states to offer assistance and protection to trafficking victims and to criminalize and prevent trafficking. However, this does not take place, probably because there is too much money involved in the maid trade. This cannot be expected to change unless measures are taken to make action against agencies possible by the international community in neutral countries, as will be discussed in concluding chapter 12.

The situation in which parties can refer to four different types of norms (as described in chapters 4 to 7 – Islamic, customary, contractual and formal legal norms), can be referred to as legal pluralism. It creates maneuvering space, in which mainly the more powerful party can tactically choose which norms to apply in a certain situation. A larger maneuvering space, or a larger reservoir of normative tools, allows them to enforce a larger range of by-them-preferred outcomes. This maneuvering space could be limited by a formal law, such as a labor law to protect the weaker party (the domestic worker). One of the important features of the position of domestic workers in Saudi Arabia and the Emirates, however, is that they are excluded from the existing labor laws.[440] But even if they were to be covered by the existing labor laws, their protections would be minimal; the formal legal protections for laborers are overall rather limited in both Saudi Arabia and the Emirates. This chapter discussed, based mostly on the work of De Swaan,[441] how Western labor law can be perceived as a collective good that was developed by the haves to protect the have-nots in their own interest. Under this analysis, labor laws emerged in Europe because the upper class was confronted with problems created by the poor state of the underclass, being crime, contagious diseases, the threat of strikes and revolutions, the need for (new) laborers to perpetuate wealth and the need for a level economic playing field. By improving the state of the underclass, the upper class improved its own position as well.

On the Arabian Peninsula, though, most of the lower class laborers are migrants who are generally deported for every possible (perceived) shortcoming. Thus, the societal factors that stimulated the upper class in the West to take protective steps toward the underclass barely exist on the Arabian Peninsula. This made effective labor laws unlikely to come into existence over the last decades. Currently the societal stimuli for the upper class to protect laborers do – partly – come into existence.

---

440 Chapter 7.
441 Swaan (2004).

Still, changes cannot be expected, as the absence of civil society further blocks the development of protective labor laws. The governments of Saudi Arabia and the Emirates are both dictatorial states. As such, they do not recognize the freedom to unite, the right to collective action, or the freedom of expression. Yet these are all necessary to create collective goods such as protective laws. Therefore, even to the extent that the societal circumstances which would stimulate labor protection of the poor, do come into existence, this process cannot take place due to the lack of a civil society.

This leads to an interesting connection. The discovery of oil has lead to an unprecedented growth in wealth, which created a demand for domestic workers. Yet the circularity of the labor flows prevent the same mechanisms that created labor protection in the West, from happening in the Gulf. Furthermore, the discovery of oil created a dictatorial (because financially independent) state, which vehemently curtails the freedom to unite and the freedom of expression. Therefore civil society and many collective goods cannot or do not come into existence. As such, oil is both the cause for the fact that domestic workers are working in Saudi Arabia and the Emirates, and for the fact that they are not protected by formal legal norms.

PART THREE

INSTITUTIONS

8. Access to Justice

8.1 Introduction

As discussed in chapters 4 to 7 of this dissertation, all four legal subfields provide for unclear or contradicting norms. This creates an extensive maneuvering space that is especially useful to the more powerful party in the labor relation, the employer. He can choose which norms to apply and does so depending on his own interests and the situation at hand. Formal legal norms could curtail such a maneuvering space, but – as described in chapter 7 – neither government takes serious action hereto, because the phenomenon of circular migration does not give them an incentive to do so. As far as citizens would have the incentive, they cannot as there is no freedom to unite or freedom of speech. Therefore, labor protection of domestic workers cannot be expected to develop any time soon. This lack of formal legal protection could be compensated by conflict resolution mechanisms that otherwise grant protection to the less powerful party, the domestic worker. The third research sub-question therefore is: which kinds of external conflict resolution methods are used, what are their usual outcomes and which factors influence their outcomes. This chapter describes in answer to this third sub-question, the places domestic workers can turn to when conflicts occur.

As explained in chapter 3, domestic workers suffer from heavily diminished civil citizenship. Briefly, civil citizenship means legal protection from the government. Domestic workers lack this type of citizenship due to two separate causes: (i) they lack citizenship based on their bureaucratic status or their lack of membership in the Saudi and Emirati community and (ii) they lack citizenship based on a lack of membership in the public community, as they are in their movements restricted to the house of their employer. Thus, the reason that domestic workers in Saudi Arabia and the Emirates suffer from a lack of enforceable rights is the fact that the two factors diminishing civil citizenship – visa regulations and the second class citizenship of women – intersect.

The title of the chapter is *Access to Justice* but this concept refers to more than just the availability of free legal aid.[442] Following Llewellyn and Hoebel,[443] this study considers the availability of any kind of dispute resolution procedure for conflicts (including negotiation, mediation, arbitration and adjudication) and the question to what extent domestic workers can realize there what they perceive as their rights. Section 8.2 considers several official enforcement or conflict resolution mechanisms in Saudi Arabia and the Emirates (police, courts and legal aid). Section 8.3 describes other possible norm enforcement and conflict resolution mechanisms (friends and family, agencies, shelters, NGOs, and embassies).

---

442 Clark (2007) P13-14.
443 Clark (2007) P241-244.

It also describes possibilities for redress in two researched home countries: the Philippines and Indonesia. Section 8.4 examines the concept and necessity of access to justice and the consequences of its absence for domestic workers in Saudi Arabia and the Emirates. Section 8.5 digs deeper into the two causes to diminished civil citizenship: the legal status of migrant workers and the gender of domestic workers. This paragraph shows that the three concepts that limit citizenship of women are all patriarchal, not Islamic concepts.

The chapters focuses mainly on conflict resolution mechanisms available to domestic workers – not their employers – for two reasons. First, within the house the employer usually has the power to enforce his own version of the applicable norms. Secondly, if he is no longer satisfied with the situation, he can have the domestic worker deported at will – and regularly does so, as will be explained in chapter 11. The employer rarely requests involvement of an external conflict resolution mechanism. To the extent he does, this is discussed in section 8.2 on police and courts.

The content of this chapter is based on interviews with and questionnaires responded to by domestic workers. This mostly concerned the explicit question where, in case of a conflict, they had turned to or would turn to. Furthermore, there were specific questions if they would go to the police, embassies or the Saudi or Emirati government and if not, why not. Government officials, diplomats, NGO members and lawyers have also been asked what the available conflict resolution mechanisms were. Many locations have been visited: labor offices, a police station, lawyers, shelters, embassies, the governor's office. Last but not least, as several domestic workers stated to have asked (taxi) drivers for help, several drivers have been asked where they would bring anybody asking for help. Several locations turned out to have a different function from the one officially stated, others turned out not to exist (yet).

8.2 Official conflict resolution mechanisms
Domestic workers are excluded from the Saudi and Emirati Labor Laws and therefore they officially have no access to the labor offices that, according to these Labor Laws, are designated to deal with conflicts between employers and employees.[444] Other conflict resolution mechanisms do not compensate for this exclusion, as will be shown in this chapter.

8.2.1 Police
In the event of a violent conflict in Europe, one would usually refer first to the police, although illegal foreign workers would be less likely to call the police because of deportation concerns. In Saudi Arabia and the Emirates, however, neither legal nor illegal domestic workers are eager to go to the police.

---

444 See also chapters 2 and 6.

Out of 72 questionnaire respondents in these countries, only 12 said that they would go to the police in the event of a problem. Of these respondents, half were legal and half were illegal.[445] There were no differences in the responses between workers in Saudi Arabia and the Emirates.

Expressed reasons not to go to the police
When asked why they would not go to the police, many domestic workers claimed to be afraid of the police. Several domestic workers made statements such as: "Because I am afraid of the policemen here in Saudi Arabia. I don't know whether the policeman is good or not. There is news that policemen here sometimes rape domestic workers who are trying to escape from their employer." "Even the police are not good; also, they might do something wrong to me, so I don't trust them." The second reason domestic workers are afraid of the police is that they fear being thrown in jail.[446] The detention centers in Saudi Arabia and in the Emirates are not very pleasant. As described by an interviewee who had stayed there, the Dubai female detention center has about thirty mattresses for about seventy women. In the evening, the doors are locked and the guards go home. The interviewee reported that the women were afraid of what would happen if there was a fire while they were locked in alone. Some women stay in the detention center for months. Workers brought in for being pregnant and unmarried sometimes give birth there, still waiting to see a judge.

A third reason that domestic workers may not go to the police is the fact that they are not familiar with the rules and regulations of the countries in which they are working, as these interviews pointed out: "Because in this country they have different rules," and "I don't know the rules and law here in Dubai." These remarks seem to imply that domestic workers think they might be doing something contrary to the law without being aware of it. Indeed, this is a common problem. Most domestic workers do not know much about the sponsorship regulations, the *khulwa* rules prohibiting them from being in a room or a car with a man who is not a relative, rules and suspicions about witchcraft or laws about certain prescription drugs that may be considered illegal narcotics on the Arabian Peninsula.

A fourth reason given is that domestic workers do not think the police are actually going to help them. The fifth reason is that they do not expect to be believed. Potentially, it is possible that this fear (or simple distrust) has nothing to do with the police on the Arabian Peninsula.

---

445 They might have been illegal from the start, they might have become illegal while working on the black market, or they might be illegal because their employer continues to refuse to sign an exit permit after the domestic worker has sought refuge at the embassy.

446 Other sources report the same. See, for instance, Asia Pacific Mission for Migrants News Digest, Sept 2003, on a woman who was allegedly raped by an Emirati. She was hospitalized for ten days and subsequently pursued a case against him. However, she was the one jailed on trumped-up charges of having an illicit relationship (adultery) and being under the influence of alcohol.

It could be caused by poorly functioning police forces in the countries of origin. Yet there is considerable evidence to the contrary. Police officers regularly return domestic workers to their employers because the sponsorship regulations forbid workers to run away (without asking why they have run away). Both governments state that they have stopped the police from doing so, yet in both countries, interviewed diplomats acknowledged that this continues to happen. The National Society for Human Rights in Saudi Arabia has reported[447] several cases of policemen assaulting, beating or detaining foreign workers for days without lawful justification. Several interviewees that participated in this study reported the same. How often women are raped by the police is not known, but accounts of it are common, and they seem to effectively prevent women (both citizens and migrant workers) from asking the police for protection against men.

The fear of the police has a direct effect inside the household. About a third of the domestic workers interviewed in the embassies' shelters who claimed to have been raped or assaulted said that their sexually abusive employers were (or claimed to be) policemen. One added, "Yes, often it's policemen. And if we run to the police, we will be raped there." Although further research is needed, the data give the impression that policemen abuse their position because they do not expect their colleagues to take action against them. Alternative explanations are that policemen are more prone to rape (for instance because they choose this job as they enjoy having power?) or that rapists falsely claim to be policemen to prevent their victims from going to the police.

A problem in Saudi Arabia specifically is that, officially, women are not permitted to go to the police on their own. They are supposed to go with a *mahram*, an unmarriageable male, being a father, brother, son, or husband. Because most domestic workers do not have a *mahram* in the country where they work, some policemen will not talk to them. The language barrier presents yet one more problem. As an interviewed diplomat stated, "Sometimes they go to the police, but these people, they only help Saudis, you know. Already because we don't speak Arabic very well; they don't speak English. When you try to explain what happened, they just say *iskut inta!*"[448] Other research confirms that poor knowledge of the language limits migrant workers' possibilities to protect themselves from exploitation.[449]

The last problem with the police is that going to the police is, for many people from a 'culture of shame', unthinkable. As one Saudi interviewee stated: "We want to solve everything domestically; no outsiders are wanted. It is the culture of shame. We don't want to be seen in a police station or in a court. We will try every means to fix it; first, mediation. However, because of this, many women are suffering. They

---

447 Report 2.
448 Shut up, you!
449 Pool (2011) P215.

are forced by their family to accept the unacceptable." Many domestic workers come from the same type of culture; some will not ever tell anyone that they have been raped.

Potential improvements

The Emirates in particular are currently re-training their police force and this seems to have resulted in some improvement. Some of the domestic workers know this: "Sometimes the police, they are so bad. I hear from friends and sometimes I read in the newspaper. But now, when you go to the police, the police will take action now. Even if you are in hospital, the police will come asking what has happened because the police will think maybe the employer they beat you. Maybe slowly, slowly, there will be changes." Sometimes the police mean well, but their role is misunderstood. In the West, where there is a separation (though not absolute) of legislative, judiciary and executive power, the police are generally expected to research and report, but not to make decisions. On the Arabian Peninsula policemen easily step into the role of mediators or even judges. Furthermore, many conflicts that Westerners perceive as matters of penal law are private law issues under Sharia, which can be settled by paying compensation to the victim. If a policeman makes a well-intentioned mediation attempt and proposes a certain amount of money to be paid, migrants sometimes interpret this as police corruption.

Sometimes policemen say that their hands are tied. Several interviewees stated something like: "The police told me they cannot do anything because my employer is a rich man." Other researchers have found the same: "When I went to the police station, they told me: you are a housemaid, you are from Sri Lanka. He is from this country, he is a wealthy man, you can't argue with him, it's better that you go back to your country."[450] The workings of the police force can thus be expected to improve only if the overall legal system is improved as well. Yet, currently, judges and other conflict resolution mechanisms are barely accessible to domestic workers, as will be explained in the next section.

8.2.2 Conflict resolution mechanisms in Saudi Arabia

In the rare cases that domestic workers' conflicts are dealt with through official conflict resolution mechanisms, they are represented by diplomats from their countries. This seems to always be the case, even though in the Emirates there does not seem to be an official rule requiring this. In Saudi Arabia, there is an official rule, as will be described below.

Domestic workers are officially not permitted to turn to the labor offices in case of a conflict because they are explicitly excluded from the labor laws. Nevertheless, the Saudi Arabian labor offices sometimes accept the cases of domestic workers, although these cases seem to be exceptions.

---

450 Report 18, P109-110.

The Human Rights Commission stated in the *Universal Periodic Review* of 2009 that domestic workers have the right to go to the labor offices.[451] However, the office in Riyadh was unaware of this; it claimed not to accept cases from domestic workers and explicitly stated that women in general were not even permitted to be there. The regulations of this office make exceptions and accept cases involving a domestic worker only through the intervention of a male diplomat. One such male diplomat working in the very conservative province of Al Qasim stated: "If there is a problem in Al Qasim with any type of worker, first we talk to the employers and to the community leaders, only then to the labor offices. The people in the labor office in Riyadh, they have received some form of training, but not in Al Qasim. The chance of winning a case against an employer is close to zero there."

With no access to the labor offices, some domestic workers write letters to the governor's office, the National Society for Human Rights, or to the Human Rights Commission.[452] All three seem to function as ombudsmen. These institutions may officially take action by contacting the employer to ask for unpaid salary, passports, exit visas, or plane tickets. When researched, the governor's office (or Imara) reacted with hostility to the presence of non-Saudi visitors. This could possibly be because the office prefers written requests, but another interviewed diplomat denied the possibility of foreigners writing letters to the governor's office.

At the Human Rights Commission, a governmental body that officially claims to handle many cases concerning domestic workers, several persons made statements such as, "Domestic workers, they don't have problems, they are problems," and "Indonesian domestic workers are prostitutes, all of them." They were also not able or willing to show evidence of cases in which they had actually settled a conflict. The National Society for Human Rights, an institution working directly under the King, is the only institution with some indication[453] that occasional actions are taken on behalf domestic workers.

Another possibility in Saudi Arabia would be to refer to the Shari'a courts. Because domestic workers are not permitted to go to the labor offices based on the argument that they are part of the family, it would make sense to refer to the court that applies family law. Yet many Shari'a judges, according to interviewed diplomats, refuse to look into cases concerning domestic workers. The courts and the Ministry of Justice were approached for interviews, but all declined the request. The fact that there are no courts available is contrary to the Saudi Basic Governance Act:

---

451 http://lib.ohchr.org/HRBodies/UPR/Documents/Session4/SA/A_HRC_WG6_4_SAU_1_E.PDF section 38.
452 All three are governmental institutions, although the National Society for Human Rights seems to be slightly more independent.
453 Some newspaper articles report that these actions occur, although no domestic worker, diplomat or lawyer was able to confirm this. Such confirmation is necessary because the lack of press freedom and proper education of journalists makes Saudi newspapers unreliable sources.

Article 47: Both citizens and foreign residents have an equal right to litigation. The necessary procedures are set forth by the law.

It is also contrary to the Arab Charter on Human Rights:

Article 12: All persons are equal before the courts and tribunals. The States parties shall guarantee the independence of the judiciary and protect magistrates against any interference, pressure or threats. They shall also guarantee every person subject to their jurisdiction the right to seek a legal remedy before courts of all levels.

Article 13:
(1) Everyone has the right to a fair trial that affords adequate guarantees before a competent, independent and impartial court that has been constituted by law to hear any criminal charge against him or to decide on his rights or his obligations. Each State party shall guarantee to those without the requisite financial resources legal aid to enable them to defend their rights.
(2) Trials shall be public, except in exceptional cases that may be warranted by the interests of justice in a society that respects human freedoms and rights.

Most interviewed Saudis openly agreed that their legal system has severe shortcomings, with ramifications extending beyond domestic workers. This will be described in further detail in chapter 9.

8.2.3 Official conflict resolution mechanisms in the Emirates

In the Emirates, as in Saudi Arabia, domestic workers are excluded from the protections offered by the labor law and are thus not permitted to refer to the labor offices that adjudicate conflicts between employers and employees. The offices in the Emirates do not make exceptions (unlike the ones in Saudi Arabia). No interviewed diplomat had been able to file a case for a domestic worker at a labor office. Officially, during a conflict, domestic workers are supposed to turn to the mediation offices under the Ministry of the Interior because the domestic workers are regulated under the sponsorship system, not under the responsibility of the Ministry of Labor. As an interviewed Dubai government official explained, "Most cases turn out to be visa issues. We send that to migration; usually the employer wants the worker to leave the country and the worker wants to stay. That is usually the case. They can't stay then."

In Abu Dhabi, the conflict resolution office of the Ministry of Interior existed. In Dubai, it did not. Although it officially existed, in 2008 the Ministry of the Interior's reception desk had no idea of this office or its function and requests for access were sent to the media department, which also lacks adequate informational resources. The media office did mention the existence of a human rights department, but other interviewees stated that this department is preoccupied with things like the rights of policemen to receive proper pension funds.

When an attempt was made at the Ministry of Interior to file a case for a be-friended domestic worker, the researcher was sent from one desk to another, until someone finally provided a map of Dubai, showing where to go. The place was la-beled as "Imigrtion Brison." Domestic workers asking for help are thus given a map to the prison. That is probably enough to stop them from seeking justice. Continuing the search, however, "brison" turned out to concern a few young men who tried to get the name and telephone number of the domestic worker who dared to complain instead of just turning to her embassy. In short, the mediation department for domestic workers in Dubai did not exist. By 2009, however, ac-cording to several interviewees something had been set up, although nobody thus far had successfully filed a complaint on behalf of a domestic worker there. In Abu Dhabi, the dispute office at the immigration office does exist and according to in-terviewed diplomats functions fairly well. Nonetheless, not one of the domestic workers who were interviewed or completed questionnaires for this study were aware of the existence of this office.

Emirati Sharia Courts
Diplomats in the Emirates reported to occasionally take cases to the Shari'a Court or the attached reconciliation committee if a rule of religious law has been broken. However, they all complain about the very meager chances of winning a case. This is illustrated by statements from an interviewed Dubai Shari'a judge:

> Basically, there are three kinds of cases involving domestic workers: (1) they steal from you, (2) they have boyfriends or (3) they abuse the children. [*Are there no cases concerning abuse of domestic workers?*] No, if such an accusation is made, this domestic worker is lying. [*And how does it work with evidence in such cases? If the employer accuses her of having a boyfriend and if she denies, than it is his word against hers. So what kind of evidence do you request in such cases?*] We ask all kinds of questions and if I feel she stole then I punish her; if I feel she didn't steal, then I don't punish her. [*Well isn't it possible that it is the employer who is lying?*] No, I, as an employer, I pay 7,000 to the agency, I pay salary. We don't make stories like that. [*So if the employer says she has a boyfriend, then that is evidence enough?*] Yes, that is enough. We make him swear on the Quran, but why he would lose his time to come to court, to pay the fee in the court? So, therefore, if he tells me this in court, then I believe it is true that it is done. If he takes all this time to go to court then this lady does like this: she steals or she has a boyfriend. He can send her next day to her country so if he goes to court, he must speak the truth.

On evidence, an interviewed diplomat in Abu Dhabi stated:

> You can win a case in Shari'a court, but it is not easy. Evidence is difficult, but if you have it, you do stand a chance of winning. But you have to realize that only a very low percentage of cases go to court or even the reconciliation committee. Only ten to twenty percent. Usually we go to the dispute resolution office at the immigration department. Cases on work pressure are impossible, there is no evidence, we never win. Beating, sexual abuse, often there is no evidence and we rarely win. They say that sexual abuse is exceptional only, not a structural problem, but it is exceptional only that we can prove it. And the biggest problem is that it takes time to solve a conflict. And after a few months, they get depressed and they just want to go home. They don't care about the salary anymore and that is exactly what the employer wants.

The matter of evidence is thus problematic. Most domestic workers, according to interviewed diplomats, are not aware that they have to gather evidence or are not in a position to do so. They are sometimes forced by employers to sign salary receipts, or they are not aware that the paper in Arabic on which they had to press their inked finger was a receipt. In the case of rape, time usually passes before the worker is able to escape the household, during which time the bruises usually disappear. Even if the physical damage is still visible or traceable, the police (as diplomats and lawyers complain) are not pro-active in gathering evidence. They often (accidently or deliberately) forget to take pictures and, in the case of unwanted pregnancies, they only very rarely do DNA testing.

Prejudiced judges

Overall, all interviewed diplomats, both in Saudi Arabia and the Emirates, painted the same picture; for murder, employers are rarely sentenced to jail. For rape or physical violence, there are hardly any convictions. In the event of salary conflicts, most domestic workers receive only part of the payments due, usually less than half. Interviewed caseworkers stated: "Sometimes there are cases and we wait for the first hearing and then all of a sudden we get a call that the judge has ruled that he has to pay a small fine, but we were never informed of anything; we were never heard." Another interviewee said: "I have been handling cases for eight years now. Nobody has ever been convicted. One time we came very close, but he just paid some money and was released again. So now we don't even try anymore; we settle cases amicably, try to get some money out of it for the domestic worker." In the rare event that a domestic worker does win a case, she is confronted with the next problem: several interviewees explained that neither the Emirates nor Saudi Arabia has properly functioning sequestration laws; even if domestic workers have won a case, there are no legal procedures to force the other party to actually pay.

8.2.4 Lawyers or other forms of legal aid

The evidentiary problems in the Shari'a courts, the language problems and the lack of knowledge of the legal system could be alleviated, in part, by lawyer representation, but there is practically no legal aid available to domestic workers. The main reason for this is that they usually do not have any money (many conflicts concern non-payment of salaries) and there is no free legal aid. This is often justified by the argument that domestic workers do not pay taxes; no one (officially) pays taxes, and no one receives free legal aid. An average case, such as a divorce, costs about 15,000 Saudi Riyal (according to a Saudi lawyer), which is approximately the entire amount a domestic worker can expect to earn during her two-year contract.

What is important to note here is that, in general, there are not many lawyers available in either the Emirates or Saudi Arabia. Lawyers were considered by most interviewees to be bad people. The usual reasoning is that if you are innocent, you do not need a lawyer and if you are guilty, you are not entitled to one: "Lawyers only make right what is wrong." When confronted with the concept that 'bad guys' also have the right to an attorney – for example, to ensure that they do not receive a punishment greater than the legal maximum – interviewees did not seem to think that this argument was unacceptable but it was simply a new perspective on legal aid to them, something they had never thought about.

However, the jurists who have been educated on the Arabian Peninsula are generally not familiar with this line of reasoning either. Human Rights Watch interviewed a high court judge who stated: "Legal representation is allowed in case of evidence proving innocence. Take for example the case where a drunkard is accused of consuming alcohol. If he can prove that no alcohol was consumed and if he can provide witnesses and if he did not confess to the crime, then a lawyer can represent him in court."[454] Because witnesses are often accused of being accomplices,[455] alcohol tests are practically never used and torture is not uncommon to obtain confessions,[456] essentially no one has the right to an attorney.

Lawyers are also rare, because historically they were not as necessary as they are now. Until some American lawyers, working for Aramco and trained in the Sharia made their appearance, there were no lawyers in the Sharia courts in the Western sense, although the parties could be (and often were) represented by individuals experienced in legal court proceedings. The procedures of the Sharia courts were intentionally made as simple as possible, to enable all ignorant and uneducated people to come out of the desert, lay a complaint before the court and be given a fair hearing.[457]

---

454 Report 17, P86.

455 According to the same report (17) and the diplomats and lawyers interviewed for this research.

456 One Saudi interviewee explained how his friend had received extensive training on how to make suspects confess through torture. I asked him if he felt this was okay. He responded that as they were all guilty, it was okay to torture them. I asked how he knew they were all guilty. He responded that there was evidence. I asked – if there was evidence – why the confession was necessary. He responded that he had never thought about it like this, but that he understood where I was leading him; that if there is enough evidence, confessions are not needed, while if there is no evidence, suspects may be innocent. It was a new perspective to him.

457 Baroody (1980) P116.

There are additional hurdles for migrant workers, and procedures have become more complicated. The average Filipina domestic worker could send a request for help to the Riyadh governor's office, but she would need someone to tell her that this is a place that she could go for help because the labor courts are not intended for her. A Somalian or Nepalese domestic worker from a small village who can barely read or write would definitely need help, because cases never start without something on paper. Fifty years ago, this situation would not have existed; family structures and tribal ties would have provided for a higher educated, more experienced or better connected representative in conflicts. However, in the current situation of migrant workers, these family structures and tribal ties are absent.

The lack of legal aid creates problems especially for domestic workers in Saudi Arabia, where women are not allowed to represent themselves in court. Some judges even insist that women must be represented by a *mahram*[458] (more hereon below). The fact that many domestic workers do not have such a person in the country does not affect this rule. Most judges are so strict on this rule because, according to the Wahhabi interpretation of Islam, women are not permitted to show their faces to anyone but men they cannot marry. Therefore, without a *mahram*, women cannot be identified in court. The obvious solution would be for the court to appoint women to identify them in a separate room, but the Saudi government considers this too expensive and contrary to the general belief that women should not work outside their own household.

The situation in the Emirates is better, not only because women are permitted to both appear and practice in court but also because judges sometimes appoint lawyers to work certain cases for free. The difference between the Emirates and Saudi Arabia is due to the fact that the Emirates does not have an old and powerful judicial nobility like Saudi Arabia. Furthermore, in the Emirates, legal aid is necessary to help domestic workers with language problems and those who are not Muslim and therefore are not familiar with Shari'a courts. Most of all, legal aid is necessary to support domestic workers whose home country lacks an embassy in Saudi Arabia or the Emirates or whose diplomats are too few in number, too corrupt or too uneducated (as is often the case, unfortunately; see next section).

Potential improvements
Saudi Arabia has recently begun to seriously consider the role of defense lawyers (which may be due to American influence, but I found no evidence or indications hereon). The 2001 Code of Law Practice sets forth the rights and duties of the legal profession.

---

458 an unmarriageable male, being a father, brother, son, or husband.

Both Saudi Arabia and the Emirates have something of a Bar Association now, although it is not (yet) fully developed. They have not written proper rules of conduct for their members, nor licensing procedures, and they have no process in place to ban corrupt or incompetent lawyers from the profession. Nevertheless, such a process is greatly needed.

A problem with the existing corps of lawyers is that many are not Saudi or Emirati. As the nationals do not have the proper education in sufficient numbers, the market has attracted many foreigners. In Saudi Arabia, these incoming lawyers are primarily Arabic-speaking lawyers from countries like Lebanon and Iraq. The Emirates also attracts lawyers from Lebanon and Iraq as well as lawyers from Europe, America and South Africa. This Western group is almost exclusively concerned with more lucrative fields of corporate law and contract law. The other international lawyers also generally come to these countries to earn more money than they can at home. Saudi Arabia is not a particularly pleasant country to live in and lawyers do not generally move there to provide free legal aid.

Even lawyers who would want to provide free legal aid would probably not be able to, because lawyers are also subject to the sponsorship regulations (as described in chapter 6). An interviewed Egyptian worker explained: "Not many lawyers would do anything for a worker. Most of them are not Saudis and if they take a case against a Saudi employer, maybe they lose their sponsorship. Also with the judges; they used to be mainly foreigners, and they gained a lot of money; they do not want to be sent home." Not many sponsors in an authoritarian and corrupt society[459] would take responsibility for a do-gooder, so most foreign workers think that hiring a lawyer is a waste of money, as they are not considered to be independent at all.

8.3 Where else to go?

This section describes other possible places a domestic worker can go to in case of a conflict with her employer. These places are, consecutively: friends or the black market; agencies; shelters and hotlines; embassies; and organizations in the countries of origin.

8.3.1 Friends or the black market

If domestic workers have poor or no access to official conflict resolution institutions and mechanisms, where do they go for help? According to research in the Philippines, a country of origin for many domestic workers, the majority of domestic workers who encountered a conflict claimed to have turned to family and friends for help.[460] In contrast, workers who turn to friends and family in the country of destination for help in a conflict are difficult for a researcher to find.

---

459 See Chapters 2 & 9.
460 Report 4, P69-70.

Many use their connections to return home or to 'disappear' on the black market. If the latter is the case, they sometimes show up later at embassies and deportation centers. They are then treated as 'not genuine runaways' or as 'illegitimate runaways,' who have lost their rights to receive help or to get money from either their employer or the embassy for a plane ticket. Therefore, many will not tell the embassy personnel or a researcher that they first turned to family and friends, which makes it difficult to determine whether this has provided any way of exercising (part of) their (perceived) rights.

Presumably, family and friends would be unable to force the employer to cooperate. The only way of realizing one's rights by going to family and friends seems to be either to accept one's losses or to take justice into one's own hands. Several interviewed employers complain that "runaways have stolen" from them upon departure. It is unknown to what extent domestic workers perceive this as stealing or as taking what is rightfully theirs; one interviewed domestic worker claimed to have stolen exactly the amount she thought the employer owed her for 'unfair' salary deductions. Others admitted to taking more, not only because they needed it, but also as a punishment for the employer's bad behavior. Of course, interviewees who have stolen without a (perceived) reason are not likely to admit this to a researcher.

Other information on the self-established help networks suggests that they seem to improve over time, despite the fact that in both Saudi Arabia and the Emirates all interviewees emphasized that one may face large fines or even imprisonment for helping runaways. A Filipino interviewee in Saudi Arabia described the underground circuit as follows:

> "Of course only migrants are punished for helping migrants. And because of the fines, they always presume we help others for the money. Ladies running away, they can arrange for a marriage with somebody to be able to stay with that person. It's not just the Filipinos who do this, every nationality does. They rather do that, without telling their family, than telling them that they are in troubles. They feel they have to send the money home. But if they get pregnant they have a problem. So then they may go to a shelter, or they may try to have an illegal abortion. You can buy abortion pills on the black market; they work until you are two or three months pregnant, but they cause big medical problems. When people run away, if they have no friends or relatives, they will go to the embassy, but they will try friends and family first because the embassies are so bad. People who want to go home, either for a vacation or permanently, they have to pay either money or alcohol to the people working at the embassy, otherwise they will make you wait forever. And also the women in the shelter are largely under-aged. You have to marry somebody to be able to live somewhere and the women who

have never been married, they don't want to do this; they would rather go home. But the women who are married, who have children to feed, they will arrange a fake marriage. To find help, before the women run away, they will talk to drivers, they will talk to other domestic workers, ask for phone numbers of anybody who can help. But things are changing really, the Saudis they are changing, so now at least many can have a mobile phone and they are less lonely and it's easier to find help. Also, some just go to Batha[461] and ask men of their own nationality in the street for help. Or sometimes they try to get into the compounds and they hide there; they try to get work there and never leave the compound. They get the marriage papers at the black market; if somebody is going home, they bring them. My brother for instance, he is a mayor in a village, so he can get me all the papers I want him to write; birth certificates, wedding certificates, all that. When you go on holidays and you arrange these papers, they pay you and you get the holiday for free. And the man that she lives with then, sometimes he will take part of her salary, but usually it's only for sex. Also sometimes they contact the old sponsor and he will sell her: they find a new employer who will buy her from the old sponsor and then the payment will be deducted from the salary. 80% of the runaways runs away for problems in the house. Only 20% runs away for the money. It's much more difficult outside, so if they are in a good family, usually they will stay, even if the salary is higher on the black market. It's dangerous. Some stay underground for five or six years. Then they get tired of hiding all the time so they go to Jeddah and call themselves Fatima, say they just arrived on the Umra or Hajj. Then the government sends you home."

This description of the black market has been confirmed by other interviewees who said that in the event of trouble, many of them know which part of town to go to in order to find other migrant workers of the same nationality for help. Similarly, many ask drivers and other domestic workers for helpful phone numbers. Several drivers, in turn, confirmed having helped runaways and employers confirmed having found workers on the black market through their drivers. Two interviewees said that they had married a fellow-countryman in the country of destination after having run away; both had left the country several years later after getting into trouble (pregnancy and health problems, respectively). Some of the embassies visited for the purpose of this research display pictures with a statement asking if anyone objects to the marriage of the persons concerned. It is not known to what extent these marriages form part of the black market arrangements.

---

461 A part of Riyadh (capital of Saudi Arabia) where primarily migrants live.

In both Saudi Arabia and the Emirates, the police and secret services attempt to fight these irregular support networks. Migrants (especially drivers and cleaners who visit many places) can earn extra money by providing information on irregular migrants. According to interviewees at NGOs, some drivers earn money by helping runaways *and* by providing information to the secret services.

8.3.2 Agencies

Most domestic workers signed a contract with an agency in their country of origin. Nevertheless, sometimes when they find themselves in conflict with their employers, they turn to the agency with which the employer signed an agreement (the agency in the country of destination). They seem to regard this as the legal representative of the agency with which they signed the agreement. According to many sources, domestic workers are regularly physically or mentally abused at these agencies. For instance, an interviewee from the Human Rights Commission in Riyadh stated: "If they go to the agencies here, often they will just hit them to force them to go back to their sponsors." In the Emirates an interviewed government official stated: "The workers who come here through offices, they are victim because the offices are their first contact, they make them afraid; they create all these psychological barriers to ask for help."

Another interviewee stated: "Some agencies also try to catch their workers before they reach the shelters. So when she runs away, the employer calls the agency and the agency will put somebody at the door of the shelter, to stop you from going in. Some agencies have shelters or dormitories, whatever you want to call it. If they run away, they may also go to the agency and hide there. The agency then sells them to somebody else." An interviewed employer supported this: "I didn't want to wait three months to get a new worker, so the agency introduced me to a woman who had run away from her previous employer. She didn't talk a whole lot of English and no Arabic. I tried to explain to her that I had only one child, that it wouldn't be a hard job. When she didn't reply, the man at the agency started to yell at her. (...) The first night she ran away. I went to the deportation center to find her. She told me that at the agency they had beaten her up real bad. She was so terrified to be beaten up like that again, that all she wanted was to go home."

An interviewed domestic worker stated: "We were brought to the agency and there they beat us up. So we escaped and went to the police, but they just brought us back to the agent." This corroborates Alcid's findings: there are no channels for seeking redress in a majority of the receiving countries. Generally, the response is to leave the matter to the recruitment agency. Governments rely on recruiters to mediate between employers and foreign domestic workers, but there appears to be a contradiction here; labor recruitment agents exist not to serve or protect the rights and welfare of workers, but for profit.[462]

---

462 Alcid in Heyzer (1994) P170.

8.3.3 Shelters

Saudi Shelters

There are two government shelters in Saudi Arabia, in Riyadh and Jeddah. One interviewee mentioned a third shelter in Dhammam, but this has not been confirmed. In Riyadh, the shelter is run by the Ministry of Social Affairs, referred to by domestic workers as the deportation center. Exit visas are processed here for domestic workers who are unable to secure their employer's consent. Unfortunately, permission to visit this shelter was not granted despite repeated requests. Human Rights Watch was granted permission to visit the place, but only after everyone who had been there longer than a few days (the majority) had been removed. There were only a few dozen women left, while there are usually hundreds of women, some of whom have been there for months.[463] Many domestic workers are not allowed to enter the shelter if they have a cold, fever, or other sickness or are pregnant. The staff confiscates mobile phones and prevents domestic workers from contacting their families or making independent calls to consular officials. Without the freedom to leave the locked facilities, many domestic workers who have been there believed they were in a women's prison or detention center.[464]

Another shelter is in Jeddah. This shelter was originally set up to help repatriate pilgrims who had lost their documents or overstayed their trips to Mecca. As their only way out of the country, migrants often pay bribes to enter this deportation center, which is referred to by interviewees as 'the back door.' Non-Muslims have to assume Muslim names and pay higher bribes to enter the facilities (as an interviewee explained: "They go to Jeddah and call themselves Fatima"). Because the inflow into this deportation center has become very large, many are now refused entrance and these individuals end up under the flyovers of Sitteen Street. Here, hundreds of irregular migrant workers sleep in the street for months without proper access to sanitary facilities, which is a serious threat to the health of the babies who sleep there as well. The nights are dangerous on Sitteen Street, especially for women. Some are said to use the opportunity to earn money to bribe policemen for access to the deportation center. According to interviewees, life is not much better in the deportation center, but it is the only way home for these women. For instance, one interviewee stated: "The deportation center in Jeddah is very bad. Everyone sleeps on cartons on the floor, even me and my baby, and there are no pillows or anything. And it smells and there is trash everywhere and big rats running around. And the food is really bad. But most people stay for about two weeks and then you are sent home."

---

463 Report 4, P10.
464 Report 4, P97 and further.

Dubai Shelters

In Dubai, there is an official government shelter on the road to Al Ain. This shelter is unknown to most domestic workers, at least among the group of respondents interviewed in this study. The people organizing this shelter proudly show Westerners around, telling them, "We want this to become the largest shelter in the GCC[465]" and, "All is without taxation, it is free, it is all free services provided on humanitarian grounds." The center used to be a facility for drug addicts, and the organizers tell visitors that this is why there is barbed wire and watchtowers around the place.[466]

The main problem with this shelter is that the rules for admission are so strict that despite the thousands of runaways, the shelter is practically deserted, while the shelters run by embassies are very full. For example, one interviewee, a Russian girl who thought she had been married, did not find out that the marriage contract was fake until she had two children and her husband had disappeared. Now officially the mother of two children born out of wedlock, she was a criminal (according to the Emirates law) and therefore not allowed to enter the shelter. More recent newspaper articles created the impression that the shelter was no longer intended for runaway domestic workers but had been transformed into a place for victims of trafficking. However, the Emirati government continues to deny the existence of trafficking, and the shelter remains almost empty.

An illegal (but condoned) shelter that was the best known to Westerners, was one run by an American woman.[467] This was a comparatively small shelter and several people questioned the good intentions of the management. Interviewed abuse victims who stayed there have accused the founder of selling their stories for cash, and interviewees from the Emirates government suspected corruption. The founder herself claimed that this was just slander intended to stop her from damaging the image of Dubai. Yet several people staying in the shelter stated that they would rather not be there, but they had nowhere else to go. They reported being shouted at, prevented from leaving, and obligated to sign a contract never to talk to the police or the press, no matter what happened. A year later, the government leveled accusations at the founder the moment she went abroad. She decided not to come back to the Emirates. The place was then run by three people under 25 years old,[468] with no experience or training relevant to the running of a shelter.

---

465 GCC stands for Gulf Cooperation Council, constituting of Saudi Arabia, Kuwait, Bahrain, Qatar, the United Arab Emirates and the Sultanate of Oman.

466 Contrary to promises, the barbed wire and towers have yet to be removed after two years. Combined with the permanently closed and guarded entrance, these characteristics contribute to the feeling that the building is a prison, not a shelter.

467 It was probably condoned despite the suspicion of corruption, exactly because it was well known among Westerners although there is no evidence hereof.

468 Interviewed for the purpose of this research.

Hotlines

Interviewees in the governments of both the Emirates and Saudi Arabia claim to have opened hotlines for, among others, domestic workers in distress. Internet searches and inquiries of interviewed domestic workers have been fruitless; these phone numbers are very difficult to find. Therefore, even if the hotlines exist, they are effectively useless to domestic workers in distress.

Illegal Shelters

In both the Emirates and Saudi Arabia allegedly there are hidden, illegal shelters, but the problem is that runaways do not know if these places have been set up with good or bad intentions. Some shelters have forced women into prostitution, according to newspapers – although perhaps these stories are spread simply to stop domestic workers from running away. An interviewed diplomat, posted in Riyadh, did report having heard of a center using the name of the embassy's safe house, a place where the runaway domestic workers apparently were required to work on the black market to pay for the 'aid' they received.

Views on shelters

The Emirates and Saudi Arabia governments generally expect founders of shelters to have bad intentions. Harboring runaways is illegal in both countries and one can be fined thousands of dollars and up to six years in jail. If anyone helps these women despite these factors, personal financial gain is presumed, even at the embassies. The Minister of Social Affairs of Saudi Arabia told Human Rights Watch: "Foreign embassies go out of their way to rent safe houses to encourage workers to run away and then the embassies rent them out to new employers for a commission."[469]

Interviewed government officials, as well as several employers and lawyers (mainly Emirati), claimed not to understand the benefit of shelters. For instance, one interviewee stated: "No, we don't believe in shelters or NGOs. They are just there for the persons working there to look good, that's all. No, we don't believe in these things." Another interviewee stated: "Problems are there to be solved. Shelters will only perpetuate things." As discussed in chapter 4, according to the Palermo Protocol to prevent, suppress and punish trafficking in persons, many domestic workers in Saudi Arabia and the Emirates are victims of trafficking. Therefore each state party is obliged to consider implementing measures to provide for the physical, psychological and social recovery of victims of human trafficking, including appropriate housing.[470]

Merry states that the inability to see the value of shelters is rather common. For instance, in China activists stated that shelters do not mesh well with kinship systems in which a woman must live with either her husband's family or her natal family.

---

469 Report 18, P115.
470 Article 6 sub 3 Palermo Protocol.

Human rights are part of a distinctive modernist vision of the good and just society that emphasizes autonomy, choice, equality, secularism and protection of the body. It envisions the state as responsible for creating these conditions and the individual as responsible for making rights claims on the state. In the kinship system, in contrast, women are supposed to turn to their families for help,[471] but this system does not consider the fact that migrant domestic workers do not usually have family networks available in their country of destination.

8.3.4 Embassies' safe houses

Because of the lack of adequate shelters, certain embassies have decided to open safe houses themselves. According to several interviewed diplomats, both governments have tried to close these safe houses, but they are currently tolerated. In Saudi Arabia, permission was granted by the embassies to interview the women in these safe houses. The Emirates embassies, however, turned down the request. One diplomat explained that this was because they had been told by the Emirati government that the safe houses would be shut down if researchers or reporters were granted entrance.

Under article 3 of the Vienna Convention on Diplomatic Relations and its optional protocols (1961), one of the five functions of diplomatic missions is to protect the interests of nationals in the receiving state, within the limits permitted by international law. Under article 3 of the Vienna Convention on Consular Relations (1963), consular staff must protect, assist and help nationals (and must especially protect the interests of minors) and ensure that all nationals have appropriate legal representation to safeguard their rights and interests. Article 5H of the 1963 convention states that embassies must safeguard (within the limits imposed by the laws and regulations of the receiving state) the interests of minors and other persons lacking full capacity who are nationals of the sending state, particularly where any guardianship or trusteeship is required with respect to such persons.[472]

Because women in Saudi Arabia are supposed to be represented by their *mahram* (their unmarriageable guardian), under this rule, embassies are obliged to represent *all* female migrant workers. However, embassies completely lack the capacity to do so, and seem to be too understaffed to properly assist domestic workers. Calling employers to demand unpaid salaries and handling passports, exit permits and legal procedures often takes a very long time, and the domestic workers remain these shelters for months. During this time, they are not permitted to work. All domestic workers in Saudi Arabia and the over-stayers in the Emirates are not even permitted to leave the premises. Psychological help is rarely available, and those who are already traumatized by their experience and loneliness may get seriously depressed, as some of the interviewees showed to be.

---

471 Merry (2006) P152-220.
472 More hereon in Report 22, P26.

A labor attaché had an office in which the walls were covered with bookcases with endless piles of disorganized files. One diplomat observed: "There are so many law cases now, we cannot keep track." Furthermore, the diplomats admitted that they were not trained to do this work. Some were completely unfamiliar with the concept of Shari'a, did not know there was a labor law, or did not know that the domestic workers were not covered by this law (even though in both countries this is stated explicitly in the first articles). If the workers had trouble with the law, the diplomats were often not told about this by the police, contrary to the Geneva Conventions. Even if they are informed, they cannot do much because most diplomats are unfamiliar with laws like the Saudi criminal procedures act. They are thus incapable of providing assistance.

Corruption?

The embassies themselves generally state that they are proud of their achievements. For instance, one interviewed diplomat stated: "The welfare of the foreign workers is our primary mission. We have a network of community leaders in every Emirate to get in touch with them." This particular country of origin organizes pre-departure trainings for the domestic workers, telling them to come to the embassy's shelter in case of distress: "No, when they come here, we only give them information on how to find the consulate and the embassy. We don't give them information on police or the governmental bodies. You have to understand there are large language barriers." This was a rather strange remark given the fact that most people from this particular country are fluent in English, and the remark was made in the Emirates. However, there were many complaints from interviewed domestic workers about this embassy taking money for all sorts of services and suspicions about them taking money from the aggrieved employers. It is difficult to prove – but possible – that the embassy encourages runaways to come to them for help because they are a source of under-the-table income.

For many domestic workers, this is a reason not to ask the embassy for assistance. Domestic workers filled in the questionnaires with answers such as, "The only place to go really is the embassy, but they also sometimes help the Saudis; maybe they take some money under the table, you know." Other interviewees stated they never ran away because they worked for rich people who would be able to bribe the police as well as embassy personnel. Questionnaire responses to the question of whether domestic workers would go to the embassy in the event of a problem included, "They always hear the side of the employers and they are liars," and "They said I should stay with my employer; they can't help a lot of people there waiting for their help, and my problems are but little." Furthermore, when interviewees were asked which payments had to be made to embassies for new passports or papers, they often asked whether the question was about the official price alone or with the under-the-table bribes.

Other downsides

Another problem with the embassies' safe houses in Saudi Arabia and the Emirates is that they are overcrowded and dirty. This is not only very unpleasant for the runaways, but it also makes diplomats reluctant to welcome visitors. Domestic workers generally only ask for help here as last resort. Domestic workers who have less pressing problems – not large enough to run away, but serious enough to request advice and assistance – complain about this form of help not being available. "Try again tomorrow" is, so they state, the usual answer to calls. If their problem is serious enough to run away but not extreme, they might exaggerate the details to guarantee themselves a safe place to sleep. Anyone who has fallen in love with an employer and is pregnant has no choice but to tell the diplomats that they have been raped (which is in no way to deny that actual rape does occur).

Some embassies have opened their own hotlines, but these numbers are forwarded through friends and SMS and cannot be found on the web or in any directory. Others claim they cannot reach the embassy building. "My friend, she didn't have her passport or her *Iqama*,[473] so she cannot get into the Diplomatic Quarter. They catch you before you reach the embassy. And the employer doesn't allow her to go home, so she is forced to work secret jobs now." Yet others claim to have come to the diplomatic quarter without papers, upon which the guards called the embassy personnel to come and pick them up at the gate. The narratives are thus not consistent.

Last but not least, embassies' safe houses are used by some Emirati and Saudi government officials to justify the fact that they do not open more shelters themselves or do not offer any other aid. Several interviewed government officials made statements such as: "If there is a real problem, they can go to their embassies, they will follow up." This is most troublesome to those workers from countries that do not have safe houses, which are quite numerous. Nepal sends many domestic workers to Saudi Arabia and receives requests for help on a daily basis, but it does not have a place for them to stay. Likewise, some employers according to interviewed diplomats, use the existence of the safe houses at the embassies and the aid offered there as an excuse not to pay the worker's return ticket.

8.3.5 Redress back home?

The previous two sections describe how there are no effective conflict resolution mechanisms available to domestic workers. This could possibly be compensated by the availability of such mechanisms upon return in the home countries. To gain an answer to this question, returning domestic workers and NGO workers were interviewed in Jakarta and Manila. These interviews suggest that domestic workers have very little redress at home, either.

---

473 Residence permit.

Interviewed NGO workers explained that in exceptional cases they try to take action against the employer or the recruitment agency on behalf of the domestic worker, both through mediation and official conflict resolution mechanisms. However, the NGOs are practically powerless against the employers, who reside far away in the countries of destination. Against the agencies, there is – according to the interviewees – only a success rate of about 10% to 30%, usually in the form of settlements and usually thanks to pressure by publicity.

A cause to the low success-rate could be the fact that domestic workers are 'one-shotters' while the agencies are 'repeat players' (see next section). They are poorly educated, lack the resources to hire good lawyers, and cannot stay in the capital for the many months required to take legal action, as this hinders their ability to acquire income. Although one would expect the NGOs to compensate for the domestic workers' lack of legal knowledge, they do not. Interviewees at NGOs all explained that they had difficulties proving that a domestic worker had not received her salary; none of them said it was up to the agency to prove that she had indeed received it. Both in Indonesia and in the Philippines, from the discourse of interviewed government officials, it became clear that the governments themselves suggest to plaintiffs that they have to prove something that has not happened, which is logically impossible. Furthermore, the NGOs all stated to have been told that it is impossible or impermissible to contact any parties in the countries of destination directly. As one for instance stated: "No, we never contact the police there because it is out of our jurisdiction."

Because of the low success-rate in courts, the NGOs usually turn first to the recruitment agencies for redress and if they have no success, they may turn to insurance companies. Certain countries of origin have facilitated or stimulated insurances for migrant workers for unpaid salaries and other damages. Although these have officially been set up to protect the workers, they – according to the interviewees from the NGOs – function so poorly that they are suspected of having been set up for the sole purpose of extracting more money from the migrant workers. For instance, the insurance companies demand that they receive the passport on which the domestic worker has travelled to the Middle East, yet most employers take this passport away from the worker (see chapter 10). After she has run away, they often do not hand it over to the embassy upon request. Furthermore, several NGOs explained how the insurance companies often simply go bankrupt to avoid the obligation to pay anything, adding: "The owners, they are related to the people in the government, so what can we do?"

If domestic workers do not receive the help of an NGO, they are easily pressured by the agency into signing settlement documents. On one occasion, I myself observed an interviewee in Manila being pressured by her agency, inside a government shelter. She had not been paid for a year and had been severely abused. The agency offered one month's salary if she would sign a statement that they did not owe her anything else. They were very aggressive and, strangely enough, were admitted into the shelter.

A third problem is that domestic workers do not want to take legal action at home, as this will lead to their family finding out what has happened. Especially in rape cases, they will not take action back home, as this often leads to divorce requests from their husbands. As an interviewee stated: "The worker does not want her husband to know that she has been raped because if he knows, he will divorce her; they cannot accept that somebody else touched her. She is not clean, not pure anymore. If she has been raped and she gets a child, often the kid doesn't go to school. It is too shameful."

8.4 Getting your rights

Access to justice is essential for the effectiveness of rights. Based on the data in this dissertation, it can be concluded that domestic workers do not have proper access to law. The indirect result can best be explained in terms of the theory of Mnookin and Kornhauser.[474] They state that individuals act in the shadow of the law, meaning that even if individuals usually do not seek juridical redress, the fact that they can has an effect. Individuals negotiate with a mental image of what they and the other party are likely to achieve in court. It is interesting to compare the research of Macaulay (1963) and similar research performed in 1991 in the United States and in 2001 in the Netherlands on the use of contracts in business settings. These studies found that the parties referred less to rights, contracts, or legal discourse in general if a contract was more relational and less discrete.[475] In such cases, the parties preferred not to refer to rights; this would aggravate tensions, while longer-term business interests required good faith.

This is exactly what Saudi and Emirati families say: it is better not to talk about rights and the law within the family, because the employer and the domestic worker live in the house together and relations should not be tense. A major difference between the two situations, however, is that while Macaulay's research subjects were negotiating alternative outcomes in the shadow of the law, they knew that if these negotiations did not succeed, both parties had the option of going to court. In the case of the domestic worker, this is not true. Because neither the legal system of the Emirates nor the legal system of the Kingdom of Saudi Arabia provides them with proper access to courts run by unprejudiced judges, domestic workers do not negotiate in the shadow of the law. Their employers know that domestic workers have no judicial redress, and therefore the employers are in a position to enforce their preferred outcome.

---

474 Schwitters (2000) and Mnookin (1979) P950-997.
475 Hesselink (2004) P165-165 and Schwitters (2000) P200-209.

In no society on earth is access to law equal for all individuals. As the American legal sociologist Galanter pointed out, 'repeat players', individuals or legal entities that frequently visit court, stand a much better chance of winning than 'one-shotters'.[476] Other factors that influence domestic workers' legal standing include the fact that they are financially inferior to their employers; they can never afford a lawyer, whereas their employers most likely can. As foreigners, they have less knowledge of laws and procedures. They cannot receive compensation by seeking redress through organizations (such as workers unions or NGOs) because these organizations are not permitted in either Saudi Arabia or the Emirates. They could be compensated by appealing to the experience of their embassies, but in practice, this is not the case.

Not mentioned by Galanter as a factor that influences equal access to justice is knowledge of the language of the courts, but of course this is of the utmost importance in a case between a native Arabic speaker and an Indonesian woman who does not even speak her own official language. The governments of the Arabian Peninsula at the Abu Dhabi Dialogue agreed that the workers should learn the language of the country in which they live. However, most workers arrive on a two-year contract, and only very few people can learn the relatively difficult Arabic language in that time. Domestic workers have one comparative advantage over other migrant workers because their intensive interaction with their employers teaches them the basics of the language quickly. However, this knowledge is not nearly enough to understand court proceedings. Again, the embassies do not compensate for this imbalance, because most diplomats of labor-sending countries speak no Arabic and do not have the financial means to hire interpreters for all conflicts.

Furthermore, the level of education often differs significantly between the employer and the domestic worker. The low level of education of domestic workers, often no more than a few years of primary education, prevents them from asking for their rights. Many of them simply do not understand the concept of rights. They do not understand the interconnectedness of rights and duties, and therefore they are not likely to achieve the three steps described by Felstiner, Abel and Sarat: naming, blaming and claiming.[477]

Finally, financial considerations (and related time considerations) play an important role worldwide in the decision to take legal action,[478] but this is even more true for domestic workers in Saudi Arabia and the Emirates. If these workers invested all their resources to make the journey to the Arabian Peninsula and their employer never pays them, then the 20 dollars needed to start a case is an insurmountable hurdle.

---

476 As explained in Schwitters (2000) and Griffiths (1996).
477 Schwitters (2000) P205.
478 Schwitters (2000) P208.

Moreover, because they are not permitted to work during legal procedures, they cannot gain income for a few months, or sometimes a few years. They usually must remain in the embassies' shelters during the process, which most of them find a depressing place to stay.[479] For many of them, this is an impossible burden to overcome.

For these reasons, even if domestic workers had unencumbered access to conflict resolution mechanisms, they begin at a considerable disadvantage. But there are several more official mechanisms which limit their access to justice. As Bosniak explains, civil citizenship can be diminished because of the bureaucratic status of the person concerned. The civil citizenship of domestic workers in Saudi Arabia and the Emirates is indeed limited because of their bureaucratic status, through the sponsorship system as described in chapter 7. Based on the visa regulations, the employer can have the worker deported instantly, which severely limits her possibilities to request proper conflict resolution. The second cause to the limited citizenship of domestic workers, is the fact that they are women; they share limited civil citizenship with Saudi and Emirati women. This limitation operates through three concepts. The first is the concept of the private sphere of the household, the second is the concept of the *mahram* or male representative, and the third is the concept of *khulwa* or seclusion.

Private sphere of the house

As described in chapter 7, domestic workers are explicitly excluded from the protections of the statutory labor law. Horwitz (1982) states that the distinction between the private and public sphere as a concept has come into existence in the West as protective mechanism against the growing power of the state. Based on this theorem one could hypothesize that the strength of the concept of the private sphere currently in Saudi Arabia, could be related either to the relatively young age of the strong central state, or to the lack of other rule of law mechanisms that restrict the power of the state (or a combination of the two).

Mahram

The second concept which diminishes the access to justice of women in Saudi Arabia concerns the *mahram*. Women are supposed to be represented in law and at police stations by their *mahram*, a husband or unmarriageable male relative (a father, brother or son).[480] Women are officially not permitted to enter the courts because they are not allowed to mingle with men to whom they are not related. While some judges do allow women's entrance with a *mahram*, others refuse them entrance entirely. Most judges refuse to look at women's faces and ask for identification through the intervention of a male relative. Some judges refuse to let women talk entirely, and others refuse them as witnesses.[481]

---

479 Compare Report 18, P6.
480 The *mahram* then functions as a *wali*, which is the Arabic term for legal representative or guardian.
481 Compare Report 4.

The resulting position of women in court is not good, but the government remains quite hostile to the notion of gender related legal reforms, out of fear of instigating a rift between the royal family and the legal-religious class.[482]

Legal authorities thus essentially treat adult women as legal minors[483] who are
entitled to little authority over their own lives and well-being. The woman is treated as a symbol of honor and virtue, as an object that needs to be protected for its
childbearing functions, or that as a component of a family unit needs to be safeguarded against neglect.[484] In other words, women (according to most Saudi men)
need to be protected, not empowered to protect themselves, which undermines
protection against the protectors. Male guardianship over women makes it nearly
impossible for survivors of family violence to avail themselves of protection or redress mechanisms.[485]

This same problem applies to domestic workers, who are theoretically considered to be part of the family and are thus supposed to be protected by the employers, but in practice are protected only when this is convenient to the employer. As
she is usually not permitted to leave the house (see next section), usually the employer is the one she has a conflict with, but then the employers practically always
side with their family members, not with the domestic worker. Several interviewed employers reported problems between their domestic worker and the children or a spouse. While they admitted that the domestic worker was right, they
still refused to side with her. So the male employer will not protect her rights.
Domestic workers generally do not have a *mahram* around as they are migrant
workers. In the rare cases that domestic workers' conflicts are dealt with in official
conflict resolution mechanisms, they are represented by male diplomats from
their countries of origin, but the embassies are entirely incapable of representing
the estimated two million domestic workers in law.

Khulwa

A third important concept in Wahhabism is *khulwa*, or gender segregation. Women
are not allowed to be in one place with a man who is not her *mahram*, her father,
brothers, sons, or husband. This leads to the exclusion of women from the larger
parts of public life. This concept is worsened by the facts that women are not permitted to drive, are officially not permitted to share a car such as a taxi with somebody
who is not a *mahram* and thirdly the fact that there is barely any public transport in
Saudi Arabia. As many public buildings are restricted to men, women also do not
have that many places to go outside their own house and those of direct relatives.

---

482 Abukhalil (2004) P149.
483 Based on Sura 4 verse 34: Men are the protectors and maintainers of women, because God has given the one
more (strength) than the other and because they support them from their means.
484 Radtke (1994) P180 and beyond.
485 Report 18, P2.

Therefore, the lives of women remain largely restricted to the house. Domestic workers not used to this habit, are forced into this same rule by several means; by closing all doors and windows, by not providing her any information on the location of the house in relation to other locations and by making her afraid of the outside world.

8.5 Patriarchy and access to justice

Although discourse from Islam in general and Sharia in particular may be used to defend the three concepts that limit women's access to justice, they are not essentially Islamic. As stated, the exclusion of domestic workers from the labor laws based on the argument that they are employed in the private sphere of the household, is a phenomenon occurring worldwide. The concept that the woman should not defend her own rights, but should be defended in court by a male representative is also a common phenomenon that has been abolished in the Christian world only recently. The concept of *khulwa* is a Wahhabi concept, not an Islamic concept and is also something that has occurred in many other countries, including the United States.

What does influence the diminished citizenship of domestic workers, is the fact that in both countries but especially in Saudi Arabia, the patriarchal system still heavily influences the position of women. There are several possible answers to the question why this is the case. One answer would be to point at the relatively late industrialization on the Arabian Peninsula; this answer implies the theory that patriarchy disappears upon economic specialization. But the connection between patriarchy, the economy and the position of women may be more complicated than that. First of all, until quite recently the country consisted of small nomadic and sedentary tribes in which social control functioned perfectly well (see chapters 3 and 5). Secondly, the dictatorial ruling family does not have any incentives to rapidly build the legal system which is required since industrialization (see chapter 9). The result is, as social control is not functioning anymore, a deteriorating legal system and absence of the rule of law. In the absence of the rule of law, there is no anarchy, but other systems filling the void: tribalism, corruption, cronyism and patriarchy. Arab families still cluster around the pivotal authority of the *pater familias* as a source of security. The upside of this system, of course, is that in the absence of any other legal system, patriarchy and tribalism do provide protection to individuals. The downside is that as the family and the tribe are supposed to protect you, the model does not provide for protection – if needed – against your family. Several scholars have noted that as the human rights situation in the Middle East has deteriorated and in the absence of defenders of civil society, the solidarity of the extended family arises from the need for cooperation, at the expense of the weaker parties within the household: women.[486]

---

486 A list of references is given in Report 22, P164-168.

The connection between patriarchy, law and the oppression of women has been noted already in 1869 by John Stuart Mill, who wrote in *The Subjection of Women* that law and legal institutions in a number of cultures, if not all, have played a significant role in maintaining patriarchy.[487] Although one can question the extent to which Mill has based this theorem on empirical data, feminist theory generally agrees that law is deeply gendered. And while Mill can be seen as a liberal feminist or equal treatment theorist[488] in the sense that he promoted equal rights, other more radical feminists state that law reforms should be abandoned because of the essentially patriarchal nature of law.

Yet, as stated in chapter 7, there has never been a court ruling on this matter. No interviewees other than a few government officials had ever heard of CEDAW. Some interviewees were aware of the possible direct effect of international law, but upon hearing about the UN women's treaty, they nevertheless said they would not use it in court. The Committee on the Elimination of Discrimination against Women does not know of any case either in Saudi Arabia or the Emirates where a person appealed to the convention.[489] If someone did so, however, a positive court ruling would be unlikely for several reasons. The most important reason is that the legal system, especially in Saudi Arabia, does not function very well – a matter that will be discussed more extensively in chapter 9.

Secondly, some Western interviewees doubted the effectiveness of reference to CEDAW in court because both countries ratified the convention with the reservation that compliance with the convention may contradict Sharia law. The CEDAW committee is concerned that this reservation constitutes a failure to adopt the spirit of the convention.[490] However, in practice, the question of whether Sharia limits the intended effects of CEDAW, depends on which interpretation of Sharia is used. As discussed in chapter 5, this depends on who has the right to interpret. Therefore, it is of the utmost importance for the workings of CEDAW in both countries that women gain the right to (re)interpret Sharia[491] and the right to formulate fatwas.

The third reason why a domestic worker may not be likely to win a case demanding equal treatment based on CEDAW is that the principle that equal cases require equal rules is not as straightforward as it seems. Article 1 demands treatment "on a basis of equality of men and women" but what is equality, what are equal cases? Theoretically, two cases can never be exactly equal; there must at least be a difference in time or place, or the two cases would be the same case. Yet in law, both time and place are often used to apply different rules. The decisive issue, therefore, is who formulates the decision to apply a different rule.

487 Henderson (1991) P411.
488 Levit (2006) P18-22.
489 Report 14.
490 Merry (2006) P81.
491 Referred to as the reopening of the gate of Ijtihad.

On the Arabian Peninsula, domestic workers are not covered by the labor laws because they work in the home, which is considered to be in the private domain – the domain of women. Yet rules and court rulings are written in the public domain, the domain of men. It is men who define what a laborer is and legal realists say that as long as they continue to do so, change is unlikely.[492]

Therefore, it is important for domestic workers that Saudi and Emirati women gain the right to write laws and become judges.[493] Until quite recently in the West, women were not allowed to join the legal profession. The statement "God designed the sexes to occupy different spheres of action and that it belonged to men to make, apply and execute the laws" comes from an American, not an Islamic, court.[494] In the Emirates, the first female judges have recently been appointed. This is not the case in Saudi Arabia, but in March 2010 the National Society for Human Rights and the Human Rights Commission of Saudi Arabia stated that there are no objections in the Sharia to female judges.[495]

In Beijing in 1995, the simple statement that "women's rights are human rights" was incorporated in the declaration that ended the Fourth World conference on women, the largest meeting of women ever held and the largest conference ever convened by the United Nations.[496] Merry states that violence against women is not easily defined as a human rights violation because many forms of domestic violence and sexual assault are perpetrated by private citizens rather than by states. Yet, Merry continues, at the "beginning of 1990, activists argued that a state's failure to protect women from violence is itself a human rights violation. States are responsible for exercising 'due diligence' in the protection of women from the violence of private individuals. States that fail to protect their members from violence in a discriminatory way violate their responsibility towards these members." This is correct in the sense that governments are obligated under international law to protect women from rights violations committed by individuals. Merry notes that states are obligated to protect their members. Of course, as it concerns human rights attached to personhood, she does not mean 'members' but 'residents'.

"Women's rights are human rights" implies that the obligation of governments to protect individuals from rights violations includes the obligation to protect women, even if the violations come from family members. Strangely enough, this rarely leads to the recognition that states that disregard human rights do not protect women's rights either. The Chilean feminist and sociologist Julieta Kirkwood was one of the first to establish a correlation between peace within the home and peace within the nation.[497]

---

492 Among others, Domosh en Seager (2001) P38 and further.
493 Likewise, Fraser in Agosín (2002) P34.
494 Fraser in Agosín (2002) P35.
495 Doha Statement on women's rights and gender equality: www.aehrd.info.
496 Felice in Agosín (2002) P98.
497 Agosín in Agosín (2002) P11.

If the state in general does not offer much protection, women are generally the first victims; in war zones, the position of women deteriorates rapidly. After the dismantling of the Bath Party and the related decision to fire 1.5 million bureaucrats in Iraq, the legal system deteriorated and, with it, the position of women. This has nothing to do with ideology or religion, but with the simple fact that where the rule of law fails, the family becomes the prime protective unit. The family does not, however, offer women protection from itself.

8.6 Summary

Domestic workers are excluded from the Saudi and Emirati Labor Laws and therefore they officially have no access to the labor offices that are designated to deal with conflicts between employers and employees (although some labor offices in Saudi Arabia by exception do accept cases involving domestic workers). The Human Rights Commission of Saudi Arabia officially stated that domestic workers do have the right to go to the labor offices, but the office in Riyadh turned out to be unaware of this.

Other conflict resolution mechanisms do not compensate for this exclusion. Domestic workers in general are too afraid to go to the police and they seem to be right fearing them. They are regularly brought back by the police to their – possibly abusive – employers and apparently sometimes abused by the police themselves. In the Emirates this situation seems be improving though. In Saudi Arabia the Governor's office, the National Society for Human Rights and the Human Rights Commission function as some sort of ombudsman, but they are all three rather prejudiced against domestic workers. Another possibility would be to refer to the Saudi Sharia courts. Yet many Sharia judges apparently refuse to look into cases concerning domestic workers.

In the Emirates, in a conflict, domestic workers are officially supposed to turn to the mediation offices under the responsibility of the Ministry of Interior. In Abu Dhabi, this office did indeed exist, but in Dubai it did not. Diplomats in the Emirates also occasionally take cases to the Sharia Courts or the attached reconciliation committee if a rule of Islamic law has been broken. Yet they all complain about the very meager chances of winning a case. The evidentiary problems in the Sharia courts, language problems and a lack of knowledge of the legal system, could possibly be alleviated, in part, by lawyer representation, but there is practically no legal aid available to domestic workers.

Many domestic workers apparently use connections through friends or family to return home or to 'disappear' on the black market, but these workers are difficult to research. Other runaways turn to the agency of the employer for help. Some agencies replace the workers to another employer, but are also frequently reported to abuse domestic workers. Other places to turn to for help would be the two (or possibly three) government shelters in Saudi Arabia, although these are reported to be overcrowded, dirty and prison-like. Deportation usually follows swiftly. In the Emirates the government shelter is practically empty; no domestic worker is allowed to enter it. No other safe or corruption-free shelter has been found. Hotlines are also impossible to find. Several embassies have opened their own safe houses, which are also overcrowded and seem to be rather corrupt. Domestic workers have no proper redress in their countries of origin either.

The access to justice of domestic workers is thus extremely limited. The effect hereof is that they cannot bargain in the shadow of the law; their employers, in negotiations, do not have to consider what result a domestic worker could reach in court, as she cannot reach anything there. He can thus, based on his power, impose the result he wants. To provide further explanation of the inadequate access to law for domestic workers in Saudi Arabia and the Emirates, the next chapter describes the overall malfunctioning of the Saudi and Emirati legal systems.

9. Rule of Law and the rentier state theory

9.1 Introduction

Several interviewed employers and government officials made statements such as: "Why is the whole world so upset about these domestic workers? Nobody has rights in this country." That is the subject of this chapter. It places domestic workers' poor access to the law, as discussed in chapter 8, into the larger perspective of the overall poorly functioning legal systems of Saudi Arabia and the Emirates. First, three sections draw a picture of the poorly functioning legal systems. Section 9.2 describes how rules are regularly unknown or untraceable. Both inhabitants and citizens run the risk of being punished for not acting according to rules of which they did not know and could not have known. Section 9.3 describes the overall poor access to the law. Section 9.4 describes the lack of objectivity of judges.

Section 9.5 then moves on to a description of the legal system that is, by lack of the rule of law, not random, but a system of its own. It is locally described as *wasta* and maintained by nobility. Section 9.6 explain how oil is a cause to the poor functioning of the legal system, with reference to the rentier state theory. Section 9.7 explains why the situation is worse in Saudi Arabia than in the Emirates. Finally, section 9.8 describes attempts to improve the legal system, and why these attempts are more successful in the Emirates than in Saudi Arabia.

9.2 Unknown or untraceable rules

Both in Saudi Arabia and the Emirates, there are many ambiguous, hypothetical and secret rules, unknown or untraceable to the inhabitants who are supposed to abide by them. For instance, the rules concerning the retention of domestic workers' passports by their employers, is untraceable. In both countries, interviewed government officials stated that an employer is not allowed to take the passport from a domestic worker. Yet, neither in Saudi Arabia nor in the Emirates has any interviewee been able to provide evidence that such a law actually exists. An interviewed ILO official stated that in the Emirates, the matter is regulated in the Labor Law, but that law does not apply to domestic workers. In Saudi Arabia, the issue is supposed to be regulated in Council of Ministers Decision no. 166, dated 12/7/1421 H (2000), but no interviewee had a copy of this decree or knew where to find it. Therefore, because the rule may just as well be non-existent, it is discussed here under unknown and untraceable rules, not under formal legal norms in chapter 6.

Another example concerns the rules in Saudi Arabia on women and driving. Several interviewed government officials stated that there is no law prohibiting women from getting behind the wheel. Yet although women sometimes drive in the countryside, anyone who tries to do so in the capital is punished.[498] No le-

---

498 See for instance http://boingboing.net/2010/04/17/saudi-activist-wajeh.html and http://www.washingtoninstitute.org/templateC05.php?CID=2383 June 2010.

gal basis is ever requested, even though one does seem to exist: no one is permitted to drive without a license (presumably) and, according to two interviewees, the authorities have been instructed not to issue licenses to women. However, most rules discriminating against women have no basis in law at all. The religious police in Saudi Arabia arrest women for showing their ankles when stepping out of a car,[499] without clarifying the legal basis. The Mutawwa may even act contrary to known laws. Although in the spring of 2009 it was officially announced that women would be permitted to work in lingerie stores, Saudi interviewees reported that the women trying to do so were arrested.

Overall, national statutory laws are very difficult to find in either country. An interviewed Dubai-based lawyer stated: "The laws are available on paper only and in Arabic only. We have to call the Ministry concerned to get us a copy if there is a new law, but often when you call them, they don't know what you are talking about." Some Emirati lawyers subscribe to websites to acquire this knowledge, but anyone without funds or knowledge of such websites remains oblivious to the formal legal rules. In a bookstore in Abu Dhabi in 2009, a book on labor law that was presented as the latest version, contained no laws promulgated after 1996. Several embassies of labor sending countries, admitted to not having copies of important laws, such as the criminal procedures law and they did not know where to get them. One interviewee in Saudi Arabia who wanted to register a child with a foreign name was told this was not possible because of "a secret law."

Sharia law is just as obscure as the formal statutory law; no one knows the exact rules because they have not been codified. Nor is it clear to whom the rules apply or what the appropriate punishments are. For instance, one Christian interviewee who filed a complaint at the Dubai police for assault, was herself accused of drinking alcohol. When her lawyer contacted both the public prosecutor and the Sheikh's office to ask which rule stated that non-Muslims were not permitted to drink, no one knew the answer. In Saudi Arabia, almost all Saudi interviewees complained about the fact that punishment for the same crime can range from one to ten years of jail time, depending on the judge. For example, an interviewee stated: "There was a guy who killed a couple of sheep and he got three years and a thousand lashes. And another guy beat up and choked his wife to death and he got one and a half year only!" As Human Rights Watch summarizes the situation: "Saudi Arabia has not promulgated a penal (criminal) code. Accordingly, citizens, residents and visitors have no means of knowing with any precision what acts constitute a criminal offence. Previous court rulings do not bind Saudi judges and there is little evidence to suggest that judges seek to apply consistency in sentencing for similar crimes."[500]

---

499 As had happened to one female interviewee.
500 Report 17, P3.

Maneuvering space and power

The rule in the West considered to be fundamental, that persons can be held legally accountable only for rules they could have known,[501] is thus not applied by either government. The resulting obscurity of rules creates a maneuvering space that works to the advantage of more powerful parties (as discussed in chapters 3 and 7). It is thus not surprising that Emirati and Saudi citizens demand clarity on rules in their dealings with more powerful parties such as the government, but they refrain from doing so in their dealings with less powerful parties such as migrant workers. Many interviewed employers complained that domestic workers do not know what their rights are, yet it is not considered problematic that they, as employers, do not know this either. Although most interviewed employers did not know that the Labor Law is not applicable to domestic workers, they also did not know or care to know about its content.

The Saudi government is not inclined to clarify the rules. They distribute an English translation of the Labor Law, but concerning the rule that employers are not permitted to take domestic workers' passports, the Saudi Deputy Minister of Labor stated: "If the law is not imposed, it is not the fault of the Ministry" and "It's not our responsibility to make sure that the employers know." In response to the suggestion to set up a website with all Saudi laws in Arabic and English, an interviewee at the Saudi Human Rights Commission stated, "No, if we tell them all immediately about all the rights they have, it will be a disaster." The Emirati government does take action to spread information about new laws, but several government officials stated that it is better to make people accept a law than to actually enforce it. One of them summarized: "A lot of laws here are passed without the possibility or even the intention to enforce them."

9.3 Access to justice and legal aid

The unavailability of access to justice is a problem with which not only domestic workers but also most non-citizen residents of both countries struggle. Non-Saudis, even if they have been born in the country like many Palestinians, have no access to the law because they know that upon legal action, they will be deported instantly following to the sponsorship regulations (chapters 6 and 10). Even if salaries have not been paid for several months, as was the case with one interviewee, one cannot do anything but ask politely. One interviewee had been detained for defending a South African colleague. The latter had written a critical report on the finances of a hospital upon which she faced charges for doing 'magic' on the hospital equipment. A South Asian male interviewee who had been sexually assaulted explained that he was not going to report this to the police because his male colleagues who had done so in the past had all been deported, often that same day.

---

501 Which is considered to be included in the principle of legality: *nullum crimen, nulla poena sine praevia lege poenali.*

If one does take legal action, the number of available and well-qualified lawyers and judges is low.[502] The available lawyers usually choose to represent well-paying companies or rich individuals. Protecting the underdog actually entails large risks: Saudi lawyers can face charges[503] or lose their licenses for carrying out their duties as lawyers towards their clients. Furthermore, witnesses who report themselves to testify, or anyone else trying to help an accused, may end up in detention. Likewise, in the Emirates, lawyers are regularly prosecuted or slandered. However, the majority of judges and lawyers are not Saudi or Emirati but are of foreign origin. Because they are not exempted from the sponsorship system, they can also be deported instantly by either the sponsor or the government.[504]

The trustworthiness of lawyers is problematic, and there is no functional system to take action against mala fide lawyers. One interviewee claimed to have paid $20.000 dollars to her lawyer, but she thought that he had done nothing but come to court twice. Another paid a comparable amount but had the impression that instead of doing his job, the lawyer had simply used part of the amount to bribe the prosecutor. The quality of the lawyers and judges is not high either; a bachelor's degree in any legal system is usually enough to find employment.

According to all interviewees, free legal aid for the poor is not available – not for migrant workers, but not for citizens either. The only recourse the poor have is to write letters to organizations such as the Human Rights Commission or to a governor, hoping that these organizations and individuals will take up the cause. This situation is especially problematic for migrant workers in prisons and detention centers. An interviewee who had been there stated: "Some of them had been staying there for months already. I think you do have the right to a lawyer, but there is no free legal aid, so you need money for a trial. The other option is that you are just deported, but then you need money for the ticket home. So if you don't have money and you end up in jail, you just cannot go anywhere anymore." Another interviewee who had been detained stated: "The police didn't care if I was innocent. They said: Somebody has to go to jail."[505]

Another important problem for women is the unavailability of female legal aid and female judges. In Saudi Arabia, women are not permitted to become barristers, and they were only recently permitted to be solicitors. They are also not permitted to be judges. In the Emirates, women are permitted to become barristers, solicitors, and judges, but their availability is still low.

---

502 There are no statistics available concerning lawyers, but concerning judges see, for instance, http://www. nationmaster.com/graph/cri_jud_and_mag_percap-crime-judges-magistrates-per-capita.

503 Report 17, P 55. Likewise, Mr. Abdul-Rahman al-Lahem, who received the International Human Rights Lawyer Award from the American Bar Association (ABA), was jailed and banned from travelling.

504 2008 Country Report on Human Rights Practices in United Arab Emirates of the U.S. Department of State.

505 Compare Report 17, P95: A blatant example of the divergence of the Saudi criminal system from the rule of law is that judges have the capacity to punish a defendant "on a discretionary basis" even though the prosecution case before them is not proven. This is linked to the vague nature of charges and reflects an approach to justice that suggests that even if a defendant facing trial may be acquitted of an offense, they are surely "guilty of something."

This is problematic for many women who are not comfortable talking about physical or sexual abuse to a man. In Saudi Arabia, the problem is even more complicated, because neither bruises nor pictures of them can be shown to a male judge, who may therefore conclude that there is no evidence.

Unfamiliarity with legal systems

Another issue, comparable to the lack of knowledge on rules, is the ignorance about, fear of, or unfamiliarity with the police force and the judicial system. Because many migrant workers have had negative experiences with these organizations in their countries of origin, they do not ask for their help in the countries of destination. The complications of intercultural communication and the lack of interpreters add to their distrust and fear. Yet the Emiratis generally are not inclined to go to the police either, because the culture of shame prevents them from bringing conflicts out in the open. A woman who has been abused by her husband may have the right to legal protection, but she may refuse to ask for it due to her cultural background. Further, in the patriarchal system as present in both countries, a family member rather than a lawyer is supposed to represent a woman. Even though the strength of the patriarchal system is diminishing, Saudis and Emiratis are still not inclined to hire legal aid because the general trust in lawyers is close to zero, especially in Saudi Arabia. Furthermore, most people in Saudi Arabia do not even know where to start searching for information on legal aid or courts. In the Emirates, again, this is somewhat better.

Still, the police and the judicial system give many people a Kafkaesque feeling. Uncertainty about how long a trial can take or what the charges and penalties are, constantly changing charges, secret evidence and language barriers all add to the fear of the legal system. Another interviewee who had been in detention stated: "And it's really scary in there. I was there only ten hours, but it changed me, it changed my life; I will never be the same. You just don't know what is going to happen to you. You don't know what your rights are, you don't know if you can make a call, how long you are going to be there. Another girl was arrested while pregnant. The baby was seven months old now. They kept telling her 'Yes, your case will go before the judge soon,' but it never did."

Not only domestic workers but also many others are detained without a proper court ruling. In the spring of 2008, several arrests were made involving employees of the Dubai-based companies Deyaar, Tamweel and Dubai Islamic Bank. An American passport holder, Shahin, and several Emiratis were still imprisoned a year later, without any charges having been filed.[506]

---

506 See http://www.zimbio.com/Dubai+World/articles/23/Corruption+Dubai+Reaches+Epic+Proportions June 2010.

Likewise, in Saudi Arabia, an interviewed European diplomat responsible for a human rights file listed four dissidents whom he wanted to visit, only to find out that the third had recently been arrested for demonstrating against the detention of the first two without charges. In its 2008 Country Report on Human Rights Practices in United Arab Emirates, the U.S. Department of State summarized, "The constitution prohibits torture; however, there were unverifiable allegations of tortured political prisoners during the year. (...) The constitution prohibits arbitrary arrest and detention; however, there were reports that the government held persons in official custody without charge or a preliminary judicial hearing."[507]

9.4 Judicial bias

When a civil or criminal case reaches the courtroom, the situation does not necessarily improve, because many judges regularly disregard Sharia or statutory law. For instance, in the spring of 2009 the international media reported extensively on the Saudi case of an eight-year-old girl who had been given away as a bride by her father as payment for a debt. The mother went to court, but the judge refused to annul the marriage, even though Sharia requires that the girl (who can indeed marry at the age of eight) must agree to the marriage.[508] A female interviewee who filed for divorce lost custody of her four-year-old child (which occurs regularly in Saudi Arabia),[509] even though Sharia states that in a divorce, children must stay with their mother[510] until at least the age of seven (according to other interpretations, even longer). When the interviewee appealed to a higher court, she was told to go home and stop bothering the court: "You already have a court ruling, deal with it." Many migrants are sentenced to punishments of 3,000 or even 10,000 lashes, even though Sharia prescribes only 100 lashes for *zina*, extramarital sex. This same crime requires four witnesses, which judges rarely ask for. The examples are so common that the non-application of Sharia seems to be the rule instead of the exception.

According to all interviewees, the party that wins a case is usually the more powerful one. In both countries – but especially in Saudi Arabia – many interviewees complained about the fact that the elite seem to be above the law entirely. A Saudi prince allegedly killed a diplomat and assaulted his wife. His only punishment was that he was not allowed back in the country, but even this banishment does not take place if the victim is considered less important (such as non-Western laborers), or if the prince is more powerful (such as Prince Mishal Bin Abd al-Aziz[511]).

---

507 Report 31.
508 CNN April 10, 2009 http://edition.cnn.com/2009/WORLD/meast/04/12/saudi.child.marriage/.
509 Sasson (2004-2) P276-277.
510 Some say it is a right to custody, others say it is a right to take care. Among others, Schacht (1964) P167.
511 The elder brother of the king who allegedly shot seven mutawwa while intoxicated.

An interviewee stated, for example: "My uncle was a contractor here. He was doing very well, until he got a contract with a prince. He had all these subcontractors and when the prince didn't pay him, nobody helped him; no judge, nobody. So he went bankrupt." Other interviewees made more general statements like: "If you have a company and some prince decides he wants to have half the shares, there is nothing you can do to stop him." Well-connected non-royalty can also get away with many crimes. One interviewee stated: "If they like you, there are no rules. If they don't like you, there is nothing but rules."

Women

So more powerful parties allegedly usually win conflicts, while in the lower strata of society, many people seem to lose conflicts based on their background or a less powerful position. Women claim to often lose conflicts based on their gender. A Saudi female interviewee stated: "It all really depends on who is the judge. Some are very strict in the religion; they are always on the men's side." Extensive problems may arise. For instance, one interviewee stated: "My wife's sister has been trying for six years now to get a divorce because her husband is sleeping with the maids all the time. But they don't allow her to get a divorce. He plays the smart guy in court, educated, well-dressed, and then they refuse her the divorce. She supports the children on her own now, doesn't get alimony or anything and doesn't get a divorce either."

Likewise, according to two interviewees who were both experts on domestic violence, many judges refuse to take action upon accusations of abuse. One of them explained: "The judges, they don't even understand what is emotional abuse. They see no bruises so there cannot be abuse. With sexual abuse, shortly afterwards there is no evidence anymore. But they don't believe that, they just say she is lying. And if a child reports abuse, they say, it's only a child, why believe him? The judges say they know about Islam and Sharia, but they are lying!" Another interviewee stated: "And some in the way they look at women, it's very bad, it's with suspicion. If a man says one thing, they believe him, but if a woman says something, then no, then they are in doubt." Another female interviewee stated: "There is the principle of the *Ghulla*. If the woman wants to divorce because she doesn't like the man, she has to give back the dowry. But if there is abuse, she can keep the dowry. But if she is abused, she has to prove it. How? She cannot show her bruises to the judges, she cannot even show him a picture of her face, so how can she show her bruises? And it's impossible for her to talk with the judge about sex, so how can she talk of sexual abuse? This is not possible."

In Saudi Arabia, the position of women in court is worse than in the Emirates, as the government remains quite hospitable to the notion of gender related legal reforms, out of fear of instigating a rift between the royal family and the legal-religious class.[512] Women are officially not permitted to enter the courts because they are not permitted to mingle with men to whom they are not related. While some judges do allow women's entrance with a *mahram*, others refuse them entrance entirely. Most judges refuse to look at women's faces and ask for identification through the intervention of a male relative. Some judges refuse to let women talk entirely, and others refuse them as witnesses.[513] The Saudi legal system is an all-male judiciary, and the question of whether women will ever be allowed to become judges usually makes interviewees laugh out loud: "Female judges? Here? There should be women in the court to whom you can tell all this and show this and then the woman can write a report to the judge. We ask for something like receptionists in the courts. Already this would be a great improvement. But female judges? No, this is a great step and I think for now it is too far." In the Emirates, women are allowed to enter the court, and in Abu Dhabi the first female judge (the niece of the Minister of Justice) holds office. Furthermore, judges appear to be prejudiced against women to a lesser extent.

Lower citizens and foreigners
The legal systems are prejudiced not only against foreigners and women, but also against certain groups of the population. In Saudi Arabia, the Shi'a population usually loses in conflicts with the Sunni, like the Ismailis of Najran.[514] One interviewee, for instance, stated: "There are no written rules, it all depends on the judge, on his mood, does he like you, which sector are you from, which family. I am Shi'a, I can never win a case." The same is true for other minorities, such as the Palestinians. Those who also normally lose conflicts are the non-Western laborers. In a hospital, a baby disappeared: "All the nurses and all the domestic workers present in the hospital at the time were searched, they searched all our apartments, but none of the Saudi guards was ever questioned. Also, the family was never questioned. Then it turned out to be the grandfather who had taken the child." Likewise, certain items in a company were stolen: "The police questioned all the non-Saudi cleaners and helpers. We told them again and again, that only the Saudi guards had had the opportunity to steal the machines, but the police simply refused to question them. In the end they wrote a report that the thief must have been an outsider but if we had not insisted that the cleaners couldn't have done it, I am sure they would have thrown one in jail."

---

512 Abukhalil (2004) P149.
513 Compare Report 21.
514 See Reports 29 and 30 respectively.

An interviewee who regularly visited an embassy's shelter in the Emirates stated, "If you report that you have been raped they first ask: was he Emirati? And then they ask, was he Arab? If he was Emirati, you can't win; if he was Arab, you probably won't win." Likewise, a Saudi princess wrote: "In Saudi Arabia, liability for public disorder falls upon the foreigner, never upon a Saudi."[515] Another Saudi interviewee stated: "The labor courts, most are just very corrupt. They rule almost always in favor of the Saudis. Some not, some are actually still afraid of God and rule in favor of the one who is right, but most rule in favor of the one they know."

Westerners, with their protective embassies, business interests, and connections, do stand a chance of winning conflicts in court, unless they end up in conflict with a powerful opponent. Yet outside court the same rules apply to them; almost all Western expats (in both Saudi Arabia and the Emirates) complain about the fact that in a car crash with a citizen, the police usually decide instantly that the expat is at fault.[516] As an interviewed government official admitted: "Taxi drivers, they all go to jail if they clash with a Saudi and the Saudi is not honest enough to admit that it was his mistake. It comes down to the fairness of the individual Saudi, because the legal system doesn't do anything with equality." The situation in the Emirates in this respect is somewhat better than in Saudi Arabia. The difference in law enforcement can even be seen in the street: in Saudi Arabia large and expensive cars are never stopped by traffic police, while in the Emirates they are.

9.5 Wasta

The previous section suggests that although there is no rule of law, there is something of a hierarchy involved in the issue of who usually wins in a conflict. This hierarchy is shaped by how much power the parties concerned have. Their power, in turn, depends on connections, or *wasta*. *Wasta* is determined by patriarchy, tribalism, cronyism, and the power to corrupt or bribe.

Patriarchy

In the absence of a functioning rule of law, the most important system to protect one's position is the patriarchal status model. Arab families still cluster around the pivotal authority of the *pater familias* as a source of security.[517] Several interviewed employers stated that they side with their family no matter what, even if they do not agree with what has happened. Family members know they are required to provide support and protection, and they know that, in exchange, they receive the same. They are even considered to be breaking the dependency rules and acting unethically if they do not request such protection and support in times of need, or if they do not act in ways that would be considered nepotistic in the West.

---

515 Sasson (2004b) P204.
516 Likewise Ali (2010) P61.
517 Report 10, P166. See Chapter 8 above.

The upside of this system, of course, is that in the absence of any other legal system, it does provide protection to individuals. The downside of patriarchy is that the family is supposed to protect, and so the model does not provide for protection – if needed – against the family (as described also in chapter 8). Several scholars have noted that as the human rights situation in the Middle East has deteriorated and in the absence of defenders of civil society, the solidarity of the extended family arises from the need to cooperate, at the expense of women as the weaker parties within the household.[518] Women are supposed to be represented in law and at police stations by their *mahram*, a husband or unmarriageable male relative. Yet if the *mahram* is the one who violates a woman's rights or who poses a threat, little action is possible.

This same problem applies to domestic workers, who are generally considered to be part of the family only when this is convenient to the employer (see chapter 7). Several interviewed employers reported problems between their domestic worker and the children or a spouse. While they admitted that the domestic worker was right, they still refused to side with her. One employer who attempted to advise his mother on being kind to her domestic worker, received an angry yet common response that he was not allowed to "prefer the servants to her."

Tribalism
The extension of the patriarchal system is tribalism: people side with their tribe's members no matter what. Tribal loyalty arises from essential needs. As with patriarchy, when the state-enforced legal system weakens,[519] tribalism gains force as protective network. Because neither Saudi Arabia nor the Emirates has ever had a period in its history in which governments enforced rules equally for everyone, tribalism has a strong history. Arabs highly value bloodlines, and Muslims who claim to be descendants of the Prophet are held in high esteem. Offspring of foreigners, non-believers or bastards, no matter how devoted they are and no matter how often they have performed the Hajj, are generally considered dirty.[520] Pure blood needs to be protected, and therefore it has to marry pure blood. Every now and then a marriage is dissolved by male relatives if they consider the blood of their in-law not pure enough to marry into their family.

The ties between different tribes can go back centuries, which makes excellent sense in a nomadic, desert-based society where dried-up wells or sickness can wipe out entire herds. Generations-old debts can be called in to obtain new cattle and start a new herd. This extreme long-term thinking still heavily influences life, especially in Saudi Arabia, where many refer to the unbreakable deal closed between the family Saud and the family Al Sheikh in the eighteenth century and where several interviewees accused me, a twentieth-century Dutch researcher, of being guilty of the Crusades.

---

518 A list of references is given in Report 10, P164-168, as previously noted in Chapter 8.
519 For instance, as it did in Iraq after 1.5 million civil servants were fired based on their Bath membership.
520 Rugh (2007) P17.

In the tribal system, people side with those closest in bloodline or from a tribe strategically aligned with their own. While the system divests a man of his individual identity and obliges him to act in solidarity with blood loyalties, it also ensures that he obtains in return privileges within the same group. Several Saudis and Emiratis explained how, in the event of a legal problem, they would "call in a favor" from a distant cousin or uncle. This system works well for those from a large and powerful tribe, but whoever is without a tribe such as a migrant worker, is without recourse.

The better-organized and financed embassies (which are mostly Western embassies) function somewhat similarly to a tribe. Embassies provide legal assistance to their own citizens (tribe members), even if they have committed murder. They will make phone calls to powerful people upon a complaint by an important businessman. The Emirati government, who accused the owner of a shelter of corruption, for example stated: "The American embassy is backing her up. We can't touch her." Yet again, whoever is without a tribe or without a properly functioning embassy is without recourse.

Corruption

New to the system (since the spreading of the monetary system over the entire Arabian Peninsula) is corruption. While in the past, loyalty from another tribe and the possibility of calling in favors could be gained by providing new cattle in times of drought, loyalty is currently bought with money or anything that can provide money (assignments, orders, visas etcetera). While this is called corruption in the West, on the Arabian Peninsula it is actually the basis of both governments, as they buy the loyalty of their citizens with oil revenues. Upper-middle-class citizens who lack the right bloodline or the proper tribal connections can buy loyalty from more powerful tribes, and this loyalty can be very profitable over time. Short-term deals are closed as well. A small sum of money paid to a judge can work miracles. To put this 'corruption' into perspective: the Sharia on capital offenses often leaves the choice up to the victim to request either retaliation or blood money, so payments are often perceived not as a way of escaping punishment, but as punishment itself. "People pay big money here to the police and to the victim, but they don't see it as corruption, it's blood money, as you are supposed to pay under Sharia law." A problem with this is that nowadays the money does not always flow to the victim, but more often to the judge or the public prosecutor.

Cronyism

In the absence of an objective organization that will protect the individual, the fourth system that will do so is cronyism: friends and colleagues helping each other. In a rapidly changing society, an individual's dealings with tribe members diminish because many work in companies that create new ties and networks.

These ties may also be called on for protection. Several interviewees reported that they had called on a superior from work in the event of a conflict or legal problem. One explained that his son was arrested when he was in a neighborhood where a car had been broken into: "There was no evidence at all, but nevertheless they refused to let him go. So I called my boss and he called a prince, and then he was released."

Such connections are so important to social position or to the prospects of moving up in society that Emirati and Saudi men who try to seduce a woman talk about their connections to princes.[521] It very much resembles what social-psychologist Zimbardo writes about ghetto life: "it is all about surviving by developing useful 'street-smart' strategies. That means figuring out who has power that can be used against you or to help you, whom to avoid and with whom you should ingratiate yourself. It means deciphering subtle situational cues for when to bet and when to fold, creating reciprocal obligations and determining what it takes to make the transition from follower to leader."[522]

No wasta

The combination of patriarchy, tribal ties, cronies, and the power to corrupt or bribe, is what determines somebody's *wasta*. One interviewee said about not being able to get a scholarship, "No, it depends on your *Wasta*, the 'vitamin wow.' It's the people you know. There's no rules for these things, it all depends on whom you know." Migrant workers generally do not have *wasta*, which makes them lose conflicts. This is why an NGO (trying to promote the rights of workers) in the Emirates chose as its name "Ma Fi Wasta," meaning, "There are no connections" or "I don't have connections."[523]

Yet, *wasta*, the strength of tribalism and the Godfather-like system, should not be seen as the cause of a weak state. Rather, it is the other way around. In the absence of a strong state that protects individuals, a small-scale system of social protection (chapter 3), or civil society (chapter 7), people have no choice but to defend themselves through these systems. "In the absence of a viable civil society that could protect citizens' interests, exposed individuals turned their backs on the institutions of civil society and sought the rude shelter of the tribal and clan systems, with its feudal and organic bonds."[524] In this situation, the Arab world is no different from other countries: "In many countries laws favorable to the poor exist but are not implemented. Where the state is not effective, its residents must protect assets and resolve disputes pragmatically, by aligning with a political patron for instance."[525]

---

521 Or at least, all Saudi and Emirati men who tried to seduce *me* bragged extensively about their connections.
522 Zimbardo (2008) P xi.
523 www.mafiwasta.com.
524 Report 10, P166.
525 Report 27, P79.

An important clue that the relation is this way (and not the other way around) is the fact that of all the interviewees, only one was ready to defend tribalism and nepotism. All others were embarrassed about it and claimed not to have a choice. For instance, an interviewee stated: "Jeddah is much corrupter than Riyadh because for a long time we had a prince here as Governor who didn't do anything. That is the problem of a dictatorship; when somebody is incompetent, you cannot get rid of him. So everyone became completely corrupt and opportunistic. Now this is slowly changing, but it will take time before the damage is undone."

Several scholars confirm this and make the connection between on the one hand fundamentalization and the call for Sharia, and on the other the call for the rule of law:

This desire for Sharia is reminiscent of the reasons behind the early development of Islamic law, to create a rule of law as a shield against the power of the caliph or sultan. As Richard Bulliet notes in *The Case of Islamo-Christian Civilization*: "All that restrained rulers from acting as tyrants was Islamic law, Sharia. Since the law was based on divine rather than human principles, no ruler could change it to serve his own interest." Today, greater interests by the politically radicalized in the implementation of Islamic law, reflects their desire to limit the power of rulers and regimes that they regard as authoritarian, un-Islamic and corrupt.[526]

Likewise, in the Emirates and Saudi Arabia, the call for Sharia today should be interpreted as a call for the rule of law.

9.6 Rentier state theory versus domestic workers

The diminished access to justice of domestic workers and the consequential lack of effective rights, as discussed in chapter 8, heavily influence the conflicts between domestic workers and their employers. As the previous paragraphs show, this is better understood when placed in the larger context of the weakness of the entire legal system. With a lack of protection from the state, individuals protect themselves through the systems of patriarchy, tribalism, corruption, and cronyism. Whoever has the least clout, the least *wasta*, loses a conflict. This is usually the domestic worker, as she forms the bottom stratum of society; she has no family or tribe in the country of destination. She lacks funds to get legal aid or to bribe a judge, and she does not know any princes. Employers seem to know this, and they seem to act upon the knowledge that in case of a conflict, the domestic worker will always lose. This is an important part of the answer to the question of why there is a relatively high occurrence of conflicts involving domestic workers in both Saudi Arabia and the Emirates.

---

526 Esposito (2007) P93.

To provide solutions to this problem of a weak legal system, one needs to know why the system functions poorly. An answer to this question is provided by the rentier state theory.

9.7 Montesquieu in Saudi Arabia

The situation described in the previous sections is true both for the Kingdom of Saudi Arabia and the United Arab Emirates. Yet as can be deducted from the answers given by interviewees in both countries concerning the question if they had ever been in a more serious conflict and how this had been resolved, the state of the legal system is worse in Saudi Arabia than in the Emirates. The main reason seems to be the fact that, in contrast to the Emirates, Saudi Arabia has a class of religious leaders with a strong power base going back centuries. They are judges (*qadis*), lawyers (*muhama*) and prayer leaders (*imams*) who work in the Ministry of Justice and Interior and lead the religious police, Mutawwa. In 1792, the Al Sauds started to dominate politics while the scholars, most notably the decedents of Muhammad ibn Abd al-Wahhhab, the so-called 'family of the Sheikh' (Al Sheikh), remained an important pressure group that dominated the realms of religion, education and the administration of justice.[527] This division of power is often interpreted by Westerners in terms of the dichotomy of secular versus religious power, as for instance in the following sentence: "For nearly 300 years, the Al Saud has controlled the state while the Al ash-Sheikh, the descendants of Sheikh Muhammad ibn 'Abd al-Wahhab (1703-1792), has controlled the religious institutions."[528]

Yet this interpretation creates an incorrect image of the power relations because many Westerners, in light of their own society, presume religious institutions to be of lesser importance. As the same article correctly states: "The power of the *ulema* is missed by many observers in the West, who mistakenly assume that their influence is limited to the religious sphere." A more insightful framework of interpretation is the Trias Politica of Montesquieu. He proposed that power be divided between an executive, legislative, and judiciary branch. In this framework, the family Al Sheikh and their cronies occupy two out of three branches of power, which explains why no prince of the Al Sauds has thus far become king without their support.[529]

An interviewee[530] explained: "These judges, it is a class. It's certain families from the Najd, from Al Qasim. They protect their interests. It's not that they are only trained in the Najd, but all their families are originally Najdi families. And the courts are their main stronghold. ...

---

527 Steinberg in Aarts (2005) P13.
528 http://www.meforum.org/article/482 spring 2010.
529 Currently, Prince Nayef attempts to enlarge his power base by tying himself to the Ash-Sheikhs and the Mutawwa. His opponent, King Abdullah, on the contrary, tries to diminish the power of the Ash-Sheikhs and their cronies by installing an Allegiance Institution, a committee (consisting of male Sauds only) that can vote for one of three princes nominated by the current king to become the new king.
530 A Saudi male interviewee with fairly good connections to both the family Saud and the religious class.

"They protect it. They are not in solidarity with society, but only toward each other. They have a common agenda of self-preservation. And it is not like elsewhere, judges working together like a mine workers union; people with the same profession. Here it's certain families,[531] it's loyalty from birth, not from after you get appointed. It's a class really." This statement about the existence of a class or caste are confirmed by Rasheed,[532] who describes how this legal-religious nobility used to be entirely from the Najd-region. Since the 1920s, however, this has become slightly less true, as the Sauds have been trying to expand their power over the territory of Saudi Arabia while diminishing the power of the Al Sheikhs, by allowing a few other families entrance into this legal-religious class.

The power of this nobility over the judiciary is still strong though. Another interviewee stated: "It is not that one judge gives his position to a son, like a King does. But in certain families everyone studies Sharia and these people gain positions which are all connected. It is not just the judges who stop society from changing; more important are the imams in the Mosque. But they are all related." A third one stated: "Appeal is no use, the judges they just do what they want. Eighty percent agrees with the previous judges without looking at the case, even if it contradicts with what they usually do. They will never suspect each other or attack each other. They cover each other, will never remove each other from power, they will not change each other's verdicts. They feel they are responsible only to each other, not to the society."

An interviewee explained: "We need written rules here, but the judges, they don't want this because they will lose power then. Now they have all the power to say what the rules are. They can say whatever they want. The king appoints the judges but that is only officially. They appoint each other. It is a couple of families from Al Qasim." An interviewee who was himself member of one of these families stated: "The heads of the Sharia educational institutes, they decide who will become a judge, who will become a teacher. The King officially appoints judges, but it is the Al Sheikhs who decide. There is the Al Sheikhs and Al Ruhaidan and the Al Haidan, but the Al Ruhaidan supplies more Mutawwa leaders than judges. But Bin Baz[533] did not belong to this nobility. He was chosen for his reputation but that is an exception. And there is a couple more smaller families, they are all from the Najd, like we are. Only some judges they are Al Husain, they are from the Hijaz and not so severe." Note that the interviewee explicitly uses the word 'nobility' here. The existence of such nobility is officially denied. The Minister of Justice denied discrimination in the appointment of judges and that judges from certain regions of the Kingdom were being favored.

---

531 Among others, the family Al-Luhaidan was mentioned by three interviewees, of whom former Chief Judge Salih Al-Luhaidan is a member; quoted in Section 5.2.2.
532 Rasheed (2007) P27-47.
533 Former grand mufti.

"That is nothing but newspaper talk," he said. "The judiciary is open to anyone qualified to apply."[534] Interestingly enough, the family name of this same Minister is Al Sheikh.

Another interviewee who called himself nobility explained that it made perfect sense that almost all judges are corrupt: "The leaders decide who will be a judge, but many find the salary of a judge too low; only 30,000 Riyal per month.[535] That is not enough to maintain four wives and more than eight children. And as we are from this class, we have to have four wives, so they ask for bribes." Another interviewee explained: "The religious endowments, the Awqafs, they are administered through the courts. When somebody dies, the family doesn't always know about the endowments and the judges, they take the money. And also, with houses and land, property has to be transferred through the courts. The judges don't pass the paperwork unless they receive a bribe. That way they can stall major projects for months; people pay them because it costs too much money not to pay them."

Using Montesquieu's model, the religious class holds two out of three powers, which offers a variety of ways to gain wealth. They are slowly losing their grip on the legislative power as the government writes more and more statutory laws. As Merry states, laws establish the supremacy of the state over religious institutions.[536] The religious class fiercely resists this loss; they claim such statutory laws can only be written after they have studied all of the sources of Sharia to deduce what the Prophet Mohammed would have thought of, for instance, computer hacking. Because Sharia is, in their view, a complete law, they denounce the statement that there is nothing in the Sharia on computers. Like many government officials throughout the world[537] who appreciate their bureaucratic position as a source of power and their illegal income through bribes, kickbacks and other rent, they sabotage legal reform.

In the end, this obstruction can become very dangerous, as the commission on the legal empowerment of the poor notes: "This is not just unfair, it is short sighted. It may enable the rich to stay at the top of the pile for now, but at a huge cost. It erodes the state's power, shunts economic growth and breeds instability. Corruption and rent seeking are particularly costly. In the worst cases, failing states descend into conflict. But even in countries where matters have not deteriorated as far, unjust systems that undermine security and restrict opportunity ultimately harm not just the poor, but society as a whole, even the elites. Where formal laws and institutions do not serve the needs of the poor, politics gravitates towards informal channels. When governments are unable or unwilling to deliver protection and opportunity for all, the formal system's legitimacy and relevance are eroded. ..."

---

534 Arab News on the Internet, 31 March 2008.
535 About $6.000.
536 Merry (2006) P110.
537 Report 27, P80.

"A vicious circle develops, with the decay of legal institutions and the growth of makeshift informal arrangements feeding on each other. At best this results in a precarious state of arrested development, at worst, collapse."[538] The Saudi executive power seems to be aware of this and out of self-preservation pushes for some legal reform,[539] although the more common method to appease the population seems to remain distribution of funds.[540]

9.8 Reforms

The Saudi onion

Most Saudi interviewees openly stated that their legal system has many shortcomings. For instance, one of them stated: "The legal system is one of the biggest problems in this country, it's one of the weak points. Too long they have relied on Sharia only and on the traditional courts. All these types of new cases were piling up. We have about 800 judges only in the whole country."[541] A government official stated, "The country is only 80 years old. We started from tribes fighting each other in the desert. Education has started only 60 years ago." On the tradition of Sharia schools and Ulema, he said, "That was just a few hundred men who could read. Don't think too much of that."

In the wake of a decision to allow Saudi Arabia to join the World Trade Organization in December 2005, the government announced, "Saudi Arabia had committed to fully transparent legal regimes." By "demonstrating a fundamental shift within Saudi Arabia," reforms "will increase transparency and predictability," the announcement continues, emphasizing that "the Kingdom has committed to establish and maintain the rule of law in Saudi Arabia."[542] In 2007, Saudi Arabia again announced modernizations of its legal system.[543] The reforms were supposed to lead to the creation of a Supreme Court, an appeals court, and new general courts to replace the Supreme Judicial Council.

More importantly, the government intends to create all sorts of specialized courts: "specialized courts for criminal, commercial, labor and family matters," as one government official explained.

---

538 Report 27, P43.
539 See paragraph 7.4.2 for more reasons why the haves slowly start to have more interest in providing for the have-nots.
540 For instance upon the protests mainly in the East of Saudi-Arabia in 2011, following the uprisings in Egypt and Turkey and the protests in neighboring Bahrain, King Abdullah announced "another multi-billion dollar package, which included creating 60,000 jobs in the security forces and 500,000 new homes, to appease his citizens." http://www.idsa.in/idsacomments/ChallengesforSaudiArabiaamidstProtestsintheGulf_pkpradhan_250311 September 2011.
541 Eight hundred for 28 million inhabitants, compared to over 8000 for 16.5 million in The Netherlands: 17 times more. http://www.rechtspraak.nl/NR/rdonlyres/47CCB618-B8B8-4E90-9F4A-8C5C79166AAF/0/factsheet4personeelbijderechtspraak20002006.pdf.
542 Report 17, P51.
543 BBC News on the Internet, 5 October 2007.

An interviewed Shura[544] member stated: "But there are going to be all sorts of specialized courts, for instance for medical affairs." Another one mentioned the goal of establishing "trafficking courts and so on." One interviewee explained that this has to do with the power of the legal-religious nobility: "Because they are so powerful they want to reform the legal system by establishing all sorts of specialized courts; as the layers of an onion, they are going to peel off the power of the judicial establishment. They just see how far they can get; where they succeed, where they don't." Another interviewee confirmed, "The Sauds called the Bahrainis for advice. It's not just window dressing, they really want to improve their legal system now. In Bahrain they decided to have separate courts, Sharia is now restricted to family disputes, divorce, wills, minors." Asked if it was like peeling off an onion, he replied: "Yes, that is exactly what they did in Bahrain and what they try to do now in Saudi Arabia."

As can be expected from the previous section, the legal-religious class resists such change. Judging from the interviewees, they seem to be successful in doing so. No interviewee reported seeing improvements: "That's beyond repair. I have given up on our legal system." Another was more elaborate: "It's like with the shelter they built; they open a building but never think of who is going to run it, how women are going to find the shelter or how the conflict is going to be resolved. It's the same with these new courts; they build this big and expensive courthouse and somehow expect that to be enough." Another one confirmed: "They build new buildings and that's it." A third one concurred: "The money, well they put it in all these new buildings and the rest disappeared in their pockets, that doesn't change anything. Judges still arbitrarily send out lawyers, even though the law has stated for years that lawyers are always allowed to be present." Another interviewee mentioned judges receiving training in the United States, but according to the American embassy, this was the case for a hand full of judges. A human rights organization made an official statement concerning the increasing violations of human rights and concluded: "Despite a promising start to reforms in the reign of King Abdullah (...) the reforms have stalled."[545] The extent to which the proposed[546] reception centers for the identification and legal assistance of women have been established in the courts is unknown.

Reforms in the Emirates
In the Emirates, the situation of the legal system seems to be somewhat better. They have taken the shortage of proper courts and well-trained jurists seriously, possibly because the society was very small and there were no proper Sharia courts to begin with.

---

544 Advisory Parliament of Saudi Arabia.
545 http://www.google.com/hostednews/afp/article/ALeqM5ieWRIy4we-axmf3a4fAxntX075DA.
546 Arab News on the Internet, 31 March 2008.

Most interviewees were somewhat positive about the legal system. For instance, one lawyer stated: "Only the really big boys, we can't touch them, but the rest is under the law now." Yet he later on added, "Dubai police? They are nicely paid to prevent corruption. But sometimes they don't allow us to see our clients on behalf of the investigation and sometimes they make up evidence." Another interviewed lawyer stated: "I think 90 to 95% of the cases is fair now. There is not much corruption in the courts; only cases that are sensitive, that involve the state, then you don't win when you are right. The problem is execution of court rulings. The ones with *wasta* can avoid that."

9.9 Summary
The legal systems of both Saudi Arabia and the Emirates have many shortcomings according to almost all interviewees. The rule that persons can be held legally accountable only for rules they could have known, is not applied; there are many unknown and untraceable rules. The unavailability of access to justice is a problem with which not only domestic workers but also most non-citizen residents struggle. The number of available and well-qualified lawyers and judges is low and free legal aid for the poor is not available. An important problem for women particularly in Saudi Arabia, is the unavailability of female legal aid and female judges. The police and the judicial system give many people a Kafkaesque feeling. Uncertainty about how long a trial can take or what the charges and penalties are, constantly changing charges, secret evidence and language barriers all add to the fear of the legal system. Not only domestic workers but also many others are detained without a proper court ruling.

Non-application of Sharia seems to be the rule instead of the exception. According to all interviewees, the party that wins a case is usually the more powerful one. In both countries – but especially in Saudi Arabia – many interviewees complained about the fact that the elite seem to be above the law entirely. So more powerful parties allegedly usually win conflicts, while in the lower strata of society, many people seem to lose conflicts due to their background or a less powerful position. Although there is no rule of law, there is something of a hierarchy involved in the issue of who usually wins in a conflict. This hierarchy is shaped by how much power the parties concerned have. Their power, in turn, depends on connections, or *wasta*. *Wasta* is made up of a combination of patriarchy, tribalism, cronyism, and the power to corrupt or bribe, and was often translated by interviewees as 'connections' or 'clout.' Whoever has the least clout, the least *wasta*, loses a conflict. This is usually the domestic worker, as she forms the bottom stratum of society; she has in no family or tribe the country of destination. She lacks funds to get legal aid or to bribe a judge, and she does not know any princes. Employers seem to know this, and they seem to act upon the knowledge that in case of a conflict, the domestic worker will always lose. This is an important part of the answer to the question of why there is a relatively high occurrence of conflicts involving domestic workers in both Saudi Arabia and the Emirates.

To provide solutions to this problem, one needs to know why the legal system functions poorly. The answer to this question is provided by the rentier state theory: states that receive substantial amounts of revenues (rent) from the outside world on a regular basis, combined with a relative absence of revenue from domestic taxation, tend to become autonomous from their societies, unaccountable to their citizens and autocratic. Such states fail to develop in the direction of the rule of law. The point that this dissertation adds to the rentier state theory is that because the governments of Saudi Arabia and the Emirates have an independent source of income and thus cannot be forced into organizing a proper legal system, individuals have no choice but to protect themselves through ulterior systems including patriarchy, tribalism, cronyism, and corruption, collectively referred to as *wasta*. Because domestic workers form the bottom stratum of society, they do not have *wasta* and are the ultimate victims of the oil revenues. This is not simply because the oil revenues have made their employers rich enough to hire domestic workers, but because the oil allows the governments to ignore abusive individuals, including many domestic workers' employers.

Although the situation described in the previous sections is true both for the Kingdom of Saudi Arabia and the United Arab Emirates, the state of the legal system is clearly worse in Saudi Arabia than in the Emirates. The main reason seems to be the fact that, in contrast to the Emirates, Saudi Arabia has a class of religious leaders with a strong power base going back centuries. In the Trias Politica framework of Montesquieu, the family Al Sheikh and their cronies occupy two out of three branches of power. The power of this nobility over the judiciary is strong. The government therefore intends to create all sorts of specialized courts: as the layers of an onion, they intend to peel off the power of the judicial establishment. As can be expected from the previous section, the legal-religious class resists such change. In the Emirates, the situation of the legal system seems to be somewhat better; most interviewees were somewhat positive about the system or the reforms.

PART FOUR

HOUSEHOLD DYNAMICS

10. Unfreedom

10.1 Introduction

This chapter is the first one of Part IV, concerning the dynamics in the household: the power relation between the domestic workers and her employer and all related conflicts. Power has been researched because a power imbalance can lead to conflicts as it allows for one party to behave contrary to the norms of both parties without anyone interfering. As stated in chapter 7, the employer is the more powerful party who can therefore use the enlarged maneuvering space that legal pluralism provides him with. Part IV digs deeper into the question why the employer is more powerful and discusses the consequences hereof. Chapters 10 and 11 therefore concern research sub-question number three: which party is able, in a non-externally adjudicated conflict, to enforce its own norms or preferred outcome and what influences this power relation? Chapter 11 hereafter describes the total freedom the employer has to expel the domestic worker instantly. He does so regularly because of the complicated position the domestic worker finds herself in at the margins of the family; the employer needs this freedom to expel because the arising conflicts can be severe. Thus, chapter 10 describes by contrast the severely limited freedom of the domestic worker to leave her employer and the factors that influence this lack of freedom. Even though she needs the same freedom as the employer has, she has none.

The impediments for the domestic worker to leave, or the factors that create the employer's power, can be divided into four types: legal, economic, physical and psychological impediments. Section 10.2 briefly describes the sponsorship system, a set of government regulations prohibiting migrant workers from changing employers.[547] Section 10.3 discusses the economic impediments: salary retention, debts, needy family members and transaction costs. Section 10.4 concerns physical impediments, such as the fact that many workers cannot leave the house or the country. Section 10.5 describes psychological impediments: the patriarchal system, fear, indoctrination and the mental programming that rules cannot be broken. Section 10.6 briefly discusses the fact that domestic workers do resist the different impediments to their freedom, no matter how limited their possibilities are. Section 10.7 discusses if all these impediments to the domestic workers' freedom result in a situation that can rightfully be called modern-day slavery and section 10.8 discusses which preconditions for balanced labor relations can be deduced from this chapter.

The data for this particular chapter have been gathered through questionnaires filled in by domestic workers who were or had been employed in Saudi Arabia and the Emirates. Furthermore, the data stem from interviews with domestic workers, employers, diplomats and Emirati and Saudi government officials.

---

547 For more information on this sponsorship system, see chapter 7 on formal legal norms.

10.2 Legal impediments

The most important impediment for migrant workers is the *kefala* or sponsorship system. As described in chapter 6 on formal legal norms, this system concerns a set of visa regulations (both in Saudi Arabia and the Emirates) that tie the worker to one specific employer. A foreign worker cannot enter the country and work in it without a local guarantor, who may be a governmental or private institution or an individual. The system does not allow foreign workers to move from one employer to another without the approval of the employer/sponsor. The main difficulty for the domestic worker is the rule that as soon as the labor contract is no longer in place (for whatever reason), the visa automatically becomes invalid and the worker has to leave the country instantly. If labor laws do not offer sufficient protection against arbitrary dismissal or if labor laws do not apply (as is the case with the domestic workers), these regulations give immense power to the employer: he can have his workers deported at will.[548] Moreover, the worker can only leave the country with the employer's signature.

There are different rules in each country that add to the powerful position of the employer. In both countries, it is illegal to employ anyone for whom one is not the sponsor. It is not possible to transfer sponsorship to another employer even with the cooperation of the employer, within a certain time frame that depends on the country concerned and the educational level of the worker. In the Emirates, ex-pats can be sponsors only to a limited extent and in Saudi Arabia to a very limited extent.[549] Previously, transfer of sponsorship was only possible in the Emirates after the worker had returned home for a year (later, half a year). Exemption from the rules is given in the Emirates if the employer has not paid any salary for several months, but, as described in chapter 8, domestic workers have no access to labor courts and the Sharia courts usually ask the domestic workers to deliver evidence that something did not happen – in this particular case, that the salary has not been paid[550] – an impossible task. The most peculiar aspect of the sponsorship system is the fact that, in both countries, the employer/sponsor is responsible for renewal of visas and work permits of his employees. If he fails to do so, this makes the worker illegal. In other words, the employer has full power over the matter of whether the status of his domestic worker's residency in the host country is, and remains, legal. A domestic worker cannot renew her own papers, even if she can afford to.[551]

Many foreign workers are upset about the sponsorship system. For example, one interviewed domestic worker said: "Let them give us our freedom! They have to stop the sponsorship system. It gives so much power to the sponsor. If you think you go home on holidays and you do one little thing that your sponsor does not like then he will not let you go. You cannot do anything about it!"

---

548 Al Kitbi at Abu Dhabi Dialogue, Jan. 2008. Likewise, Report 22, P35.
549 Al Tamimi (2006) P7.2.
550 Several interviewed domestic workers, diplomats, caseworkers and even a judge stated that domestic workers are asked to prove they did *not* receive payment, did *not* steal, did *not* have a boyfriend or did *not* abuse the children.
551 Compare Anthias (2000).

Nowadays, the criticism about the sponsorship system is more widely shared: "Reactions first were very fierce when I called the sponsorship system a system of slavery, but now there are more people calling it like this. This is a major turn."[552] Several international organizations are pressing for the abolition of this system, including the WTO, ILO and EU. Finally, there is a growing awareness within both countries that the system is an obstacle to a properly functioning labor market,[553] which could be related to the fact that many Saudi and Emirati government officials have studied in the United States, the free trade defender. Yet there are several factors making abolition of the sponsorship system difficult, as described in chapter 7, section 3.

10.3 Economic impediments

Many domestic workers cannot leave their employer for financial reasons. This can be due to the employer's failure to pay the salary every month, debts made before departure, the financial needs of family members, transaction costs, or the lack of employment possibilities in the home country.

Salary retention

A common way to pressure domestic workers into staying is by postponing salary payments, sometimes for several years. An interviewed diplomat stated: "Often they do not start paying your salary until you have been working two months. Then if they want to get rid of you, they just do not pay these last two months; they accuse you of something and make sure you are deported." The ILO writes: "There is a tendency by some employers to withhold workers' wages, mostly in small companies. It goes far beyond even the 'customary' withholds of six to eight weeks for purposes of security and is essentially done to keep workers from running away. All these companies, including the largest, are using their workers as a source of interest free credit as well as cheap labor."[554]

Several domestic workers interviewed for this research confirmed that their employer used salary retention to force them to stay, or to behave a certain way. For instance, when a severely abused domestic worker was asked why she had not left earlier, she replied: "Because of the salary; they said they would pay everything in the end, so I had to stay." To the question, "If they had paid you every month, would you have run away?" she replied, "Yes, of course." Several interviewed domestic workers provided similar accounts: "When I left I had to train the new maid and they told me, do not tell anything to her because if you do, we will cut your salary in half." A similar trick, according to interviewees, is used in households with more than one domestic worker: if one domestic worker wants to go on holiday to see her children, the others are not permitted to leave and will not receive their salaries until the first has returned.

---

552 Dr Awadh at Abu Dhabi Dialogue, Jan. 2008.
553 Al Salman at Abu Dhabi Dialogue, Jan. 2008, and for instance Arab News 6-7-2008.
554 Report 5.

This way, the household avoids having to pay large amounts of money to the agency for a new worker.

Interviewed employers justified this behavior by claiming that the withheld money is kept safe until the worker goes home, so she cannot spend the money on "unimportant things" or "something haram."[555] When the employers were asked if they would agree to their own employer retaining salary payments for so long, no one agreed. The domestic workers are regularly perceived by these employers the way that people in the West view their children when they help them save money (as described in chapter 4). The government in the Emirates is now working on a system to have all employers transfer salaries to laborers through bank accounts, to make sure monthly payments are made. However, domestic workers do not fall under these rules as they are not considered to be workers (see chapter 7).

Debts

A second economic reason why domestic workers cannot leave their employer is debts incurred in the home country before departure. Many workers in the GCC countries have large debts upon arrival. Research commissioned by the ILO explained this situation:

> For Bangladesh, initial analysis of the cost of overseas migration shows high costs and wide variation. The average cost for men was around $1.400 and for women around half this amount. (...) Country-wise, the Emirates emerges on average as the most costly destination, followed by Kuwait. The high costs of recruitment are associated with the high level of indebtedness of many workers before leaving their country of origin, which in some cases can result in failure of the migration project, if the income generated is insufficient to repay these debts. Rates of interest charged by moneylenders are generally of the order of 10% per month, meaning that the outstanding debt can rapidly escalate if repayment is not achieved quickly. [556]

Yet interviews and questionnaires for this study revealed that most domestic workers (or at least the Indonesians and Filipinas old enough not to need false IDs) have some debt, but less than that of other groups of laborers.[557] The initiatives of the governments of certain countries of origin to reduce the placement fees thus seem to have their effects. Although there is officially no placement fee in either Manila or Jakarta, the average Indonesian or Filipina domestic worker in this research has paid about two months salary, an amount that most have borrowed from friends or family members. Only in exceptional cases, the debts are as high as $900.

---

555 In this context: forbidden, bad.
556 Report 6.
557 And not as large as it seems to have been; compare Heyzer (2006) P xxi.

As long as this amount has not been paid back, they cannot leave. The situation for workers from other countries, such as Sri Lanka, is more difficult. One interviewed domestic worker from this country for instance stated:

> Some women, they pay so much to the agency. If they run away from a bad employer, they cannot even go to the embassy. They have to work illegally first, to make enough money to pay their debts and all and then they can go to the embassy. They sell their land, they borrow for high interest rates and then if the salary is not paid, the debts just get larger and larger. In our country things are so bad; it's all corrupted. Agencies, the government, you have to pay so much everywhere. We married quite young; we borrowed 55,000 rupees[558] from friends to come here. I had to work so hard, but because we had to pay our friends, we could not leave. Then after six months, when we had paid them all back, we left. My hands were totally damaged from all the work by then.

Needy Family

Even if a domestic worker has an employer who does not use his position of power to stop her from leaving and if she has not paid a placement fee, there are usually other economic impediments. One of the items on the questionnaire was, "If you would want to go home now (for example, because you are really homesick), would you be able to go back home?" Thirty-four percent said yes, 7% said this was impossible because of debts, 9% said it was impossible because there was no money for a ticket home and 50% said this was impossible because there were family members depending on them.[559]

Several interviewed domestic workers stated that they had children and that they had to work in the Gulf after their husbands ran off. One domestic worker helped three cousins through college: "I cannot go home. This means my cousins will not have a future anymore." Some claimed to have worked for family members for a long time, and were now finally able to save some money for their own retirement. They do not want to ask for money from their children because these will need all their money for the next generation. The pressure from family members to send money home is intense: "There are strong pressures from the families of migrant women workers abroad to remit their earnings home, in order to support unemployed and underemployed male relatives, young children and the elderly, as well as to build up family security, assets and status."[560] Sometimes this pressure is so strong that migrant workers end contact with their families to gain some freedom; two interviewees admitted to having disappeared from their families for this reason.

---

558 $435.
559 Silvey (2006) rightfully states that the needs of a family are a matter of perception. On P25 she states that "transnational migration came to be viewed as necessary only after women's migration and higher levels of consumption became a widespread possibility." Nevertheless, now that this perception is established, family members who perceive themselves and are perceived as needy, form an obstacle for domestic workers to go home.
560 Andrees in Kuptsch (2006) P67.

Transaction costs

Several interviewed domestic workers do not leave their employers because the process of getting another employer is too costly. This is what is known as transaction costs: money actually spent as well as the money that could have been earned in the time spent searching for new employment. Workers usually need time and money to leave the house of the employer, wait for clearance to be able to leave the country (one interviewee had been in the embassy's shelter for three years with no income), fly to their home country (employers usually do not pay return tickets upon absconding), approach a recruiter, possibly pay for new (false) IDs, wait for placement (two or three months), fly back to the Middle East, and possibly not be paid during the first two months by their new employer. This makes changing employers so costly that many domestic workers, upon absconding, decide to find employment directly on the black market. Others pay their former employer to get him to sign a release. This No Objection Certificate is needed to move to another employer without leaving the country and without making all the travel expenses.

An interviewed domestic worker explained how the high transaction costs put her and her husband in a Catch-22 situation: "For a transfer we have to pay 8000 Riyal.[561] My husband is trying to get the money together now. If we do not find a new sponsor who wants to pay this amount, we must go home, but then we need money for the ticket. Either way we need money." Thereupon she burst out crying and added, "Please help me!" Because this problem of high transaction costs is known to domestic workers, they are ready to suffer a considerable amount of abuse to avoid incurring these costs. Alcid likewise writes about domestic workers in Hong Kong: "Fighting for their rights from the viewpoint of the worker, is not without risks and sacrifices, because they spend the equivalent of two to three months wages to find work again in Hong Kong. Workers are terrified to lose their jobs, so they are prepared to suffer considerable indignity and often inhuman working hours and conditions in order to keep them. Thus it is only in the most extreme circumstances that they will lodge an official complaint."[562] To avoid the high transaction costs, one could suggest that a worker finds employment in the home country. However, for most domestic workers who decide to leave their employers, the only alternative is to return to the Middle East on a new contract. In their home countries, unemployment is usually very high, which is the reason they signed a contract in the first place: "If I go back now, there is no food to eat, no nothing. I have to sign a new agreement immediately; I have to come back here." An interviewee from Ethiopia, when asked if the food crisis had had any effect on the supply of domestic workers, responded: "Yes, very much so. It's much worse than 15 years ago. We just have no choice now. So they can do whatever they want, they can really dehumanize us."

---

561 Ten months salary for her, or about seven months for him.
562 Alcid in Heyzer (1994) P175.

10.4 Physical impediments

Many interviewed domestic workers explained that they could not leave their employer because they could not leave the house. There are three ways to keep a domestic worker inside: an employer can lock all the doors; he can make sure that she does not know where to go outside; and he can stop her from leaving the country by keeping her passport, which in many cases leaves her with nowhere to go.

Keeping her in the house

The first possibility to prevent the domestic worker from leaving is simply to lock the door, which is what certain employers do. An interviewed diplomat in Abu Dhabi stated, "I think about 90% cannot leave the house without difficulty. The walls are too high; they have to climb on the garbage to get out." This seems to be an incorrect estimate; while doing door-to-door interviews in Sharjah, several domestic workers opened the door and these workers were all physically capable of leaving whenever they wanted. Yet confinement does occur. A runaway domestic worker stated: "And then one time he raped me. Immediately after this, I ran off. I took a taxi to the embassy. I could not get out first. He kept me locked in the house. However, there was a hammer, so I smashed a window and I ran." Another interviewee said: "The doors were locked all the time. I had to jump out the window, but it was very high. So I yell at this man in the street, so he put some old tires under the window so I would jump and he catch me."

A problem is that a vicious circle seems to occur here at two levels, individually and societally. If an employer has a small conflict with a domestic worker, he can get worried that she is going to run away. To prevent her from doing so, he starts to lock the doors, which can be a reason for the domestic worker to try to run away. Several interviewed domestic workers explained how doors were locked after salary conflicts began. Also at the societal level, if employers hear from friends and family that their workers have run away, it gives some of them a reason to introduce stricter rules, which again can be a reason to run away. One domestic worker, who only had to work four hours per day, ran away because she was locked in her room the remaining 20 hours: "What was I supposed to do all that time! The workload was not really a problem, but I was just looking at the walls all the time." Interviewed employers from their side confirmed that runaways in their social surroundings sometimes lead to stricter rules in their own house.

An important aspect of this problem is that prohibiting wives and daughters in an employer's own family from going outside is not unusual either, especially in Saudi Arabia: "Since the man is born, he is taught that sisters, wives and daughters are private property. (...) It is very common, for example, not allowing foreign domestic workers from leaving the house at any time. Some Saudi women are actually locked in by their husbands in their houses. There are many cases which are witnessed where university professors have locked their wives in their apartments and houses until they come back from work."[563] Saudi female interviewees confirmed that this still occurs.

Keeping her in the dark
A second technique to keep the domestic worker in the household against her will is by keeping her completely in the dark as to where she is. Many domestic workers arrive at the airport and are taken straight to the house of the employer in a car with darkened windows. They have no idea where they are or where the embassy or police station is. Some of them cannot read at all. Most cannot read the Arabic street signs. Many would not know how to read a map if they were given one. Embassies, according to interviewed diplomats, regularly receive telephone calls from domestic workers in distress who do not know where they are. They are asked to describe what they can see from the window or what they can see outside when they take out the garbage: "Can you see a mosque? What's the color of the mosque?" Then (if it concerns a better staffed and organized embassy) a car is sent to try to find her. Therefore, certain embassies now (claim to) require the agency or employer who requests stamps for passports, to not only give the name and address of the employer, but also a map where the household can be found.

Keeping her in the country
A third way to prevent a domestic worker from leaving is by taking her identity papers. All interviewed employers kept the papers of their domestic workers. Only one kept them in a place where the domestic worker could easily reach them as well. Most reasoned that it was safer this way, but the question is for whom; no one ever mentioned passports being stolen or lost. Some interviewed domestic workers did not mind their employers keeping their identity papers. They gave the same answer on the questionnaires as the employers: "It is safe this way." However, a majority of the interviewed domestic workers was upset about it: "They say they do not give me my Iqama[564] if I do not give them my passport. However, it just feels so wrong, it feels like they take not just my papers but part of my identity and certainly my freedom!" Likewise, a representative from an NGO stated at a conference in the Emirates: "Passports, papers are basic rights, a basic dignity; we cannot take that away when a worker crosses a border." However, this issue is not primarily a matter of emotions. Both in the Emirates and in Saudi Arabia, anyone walking around in the streets without a passport or Iqama risks being stopped by the police to be deported. As an interviewed domestic worker in the Emirates explained: "But when we were in the Agency, they gave us a copy of the contract, but now the employers took it, with

---

563 Stated by a professor at a Saudi University.
564 Residency permit.

our passport. They do not even let us have the labor card! So when the police catch us here, ah! Especially now, they become really strict, you know. If you do not have the labor card, they will bring you to the police station." Therefore, without papers, domestic workers cannot leave the house.

According to interviewed government officials, neither in Saudi Arabia[565] nor in the Emirates[566] are employers currently permitted to retain identity papers, although no law has been found that confirms this. However, there are two problems with these rules. The first problem is that in the Emirates few employers and in Saudi Arabia, very few employers, know that (according to these government officials) this is not permitted. Even members of the Commission for Human Rights in Riyadh did not know about this law, nor did any interviewed diplomat. The domestic workers do not know about the law either. To the question: "Do you know that the employer is not allowed to take your passport?" 26 replied that they knew and 24 replied that they did not know. When the question was later changed to "Do you know if the employer is allowed to take your passport?" 16 workers replied that he is allowed and only 4 said that he is not.

When the Deputy Minister of Labor of Saudi Arabia was asked why all employers retain the passports of their non-Western employees, he answered that the problem is that the workers know nothing about their rights. He said it is the duty of the governments of the countries of origin to educate them upon departure to the Middle East. When told that none of the employers interviewed for this research knew about the rule either, he answered: "It's not our responsibility to make sure that they know." In the Emirates, this situation is only slightly better; there is some governmental communication about the retention of passports, but it is rather limited. Furthermore, when domestic workers arrive in Saudi Arabia, customs officers immediately hand over their identity papers to the employers. In the Emirates, the agencies process the papers and then hand them over to the employers. Several agents visited for the purpose of this research, stated that if I was to hire a domestic worker, I should not let her keep her own passport (more on this part of the research in chapter 6). Furthermore, if the domestic worker runs away after abuse by the employer and the authorities arrive to collect her passport, many employers simply refuse to give up the papers and the authorities do not force him to do so.[567] In other words, no one clarifies to employers that this is not permitted. On the contrary, employers are encouraged from all sides to retain the passports.

---

565 Council of Ministers Decision no. 166 dated 12/7/1421 H (2000), which I have not been able to find anywhere, although I have searched and asked extensively; it may be non-existent.
566 It seems to be written solely in the Labor Law, which does not apply to domestic workers.
567 Report 18, P5.

10.5 Psychological Impediments

The fourth type of impediment for domestic workers to leave the house is psychological. There are three such impediments: the patriarchal system, fear, and mental programming about the symbolic power of the contract.

Patriarchy

As explained in chapter 4, many domestic workers think in patriarchal terms, not in terms of the contractual system. In the former, everyone has a position in a hierarchy with rights and duties attached to it, but these rights and duties are not dependent upon the rights and duties of others. As an interviewee in Jakarta explained: "And the people from Java have learnt that they always have to obey the master, whether the master is good to them or not."

Fear and indoctrination

Adding to the lack of knowledge about the outside world (as discussed in section 10.4) is the fear of the outside world. To the question of whether being locked in the house bothered her, one interviewee responded: "No, I was scared to be in another country. Not being allowed to go out did not bother me because it was scary outside." Certain employers seem to actively contribute to this fear, as several domestic workers explained how their employers had warned them about the risks of being raped, abducted, abused, or instantly deported upon going outside. One domestic worker was so afraid of the outside world that while waiting for an embassy's car, she hid in the garbage bin. Another interviewee stated about her employer, "She told me I am a slave. She told me if you run away I will call the police to shoot you, to kill you."

Several interviewees also stated that the agencies actively use such stories to indoctrinate the domestic workers: "They tell them, 'You have to obey. And if something happens that you do not like, you just have to think, this is my fate; otherwise, something bad will happen to you.'" Another domestic worker explained how her employer brought her to the agency. She was seriously harassed there, after which the employer came to pick her up again. He said that if she was disobedient again, he would bring her back to the agency permanently.

Likewise, upon my own arrival in the Kingdom of Saudi Arabia, the hotel staff informed me that I could only use the (very expensive) hotel's taxi service, because with any other taxi I would run the risk of being raped. Stories of women being raped when leaving the house "without permission" are frequently told: "Did you hear about this Bluetooth film going around of the *Mutawwa*[568] having sex with a woman in exchange for not arresting her?" "Did you hear about this domestic worker who was taken by security forces to what was supposed to be a safe house and then raped by forty-three men?" The truth of these stories could not be determined, but even if they are not (all) true, they have the effect of making it scary for women to leave the house. These

---

568 Religious police.

threats and stories, according to two interviewed diplomats, become more effective when a domestic worker is under emotional stress from solitude, exhaustion or sleep deprivation.

Other factors that could be at play here are paralysis, learned helplessness and Stockholm syndrome. Some rape victims become paralyzed with fear and are unable to display physical resistance.[569] Walker theorizes that women subjected to continual abuse may learn to be helpless and stop trying to leave. They acquire survival skills within the relationship but develop an inability to see escape alternatives. Walker's later works characterize this syndrome of learned helplessness as a type of post-traumatic stress disorder.[570] Likewise, victims of Stockholm syndrome develop a strong emotional tie with their captors and do not leave.

Fictive rules and contracts
Another way to tie domestic workers to their employers is the contract. The reason this is discussed in the section on psychological rather than legal impediments, is that there is no enforcement of the official contracts, and agents or employers regularly refer to stipulations that are not in the contract at all. The stated contractual rights are not delivered or protected, yet many domestic workers see the contract as the primary impediment to leaving; they feel they have a duty to stay with their employer for two years, regardless of whether their rights are respected and regardless of the fact that no authority enforces the stipulations of their contract.[571]

Both sociologists and anthropologists have noted the peculiarity of people following rules simply because they are rules. In Milgram's obedience paradigm, test subjects were asked to apply electric shocks to (what they did not know were) actors. Obviously, they wanted to withdraw from the experiment, but the experimenter continued to insist that they go on. He reminded them of the contract and of the agreement to participate fully, and they were told to follow the rules, upon which most of the subjects applied (or thought they applied) deadly shocks.[572]

Many explanations of why people in such situations follow rules focus on situations where those who do so are not victims themselves. Johnson states, "It is important to note how rarely it occurs to people to simply change the rules. (...) If we try to explain patterns of social behavior only in terms of individual people's personalities and motives (...) then we ignore how behavior is shaped by the paths of least resistance found in the systems people participate in."[573] Yet he discusses how men follow the rules of patriarchal society in which women are the primary vic-

569 Levit (2006) P183.
570 Levit (2006) P191.
571 So by the definition of Kelsen, it is not law. More on Kelsen in among others Brouwer (2004) chapter 1.
572 Zimbardo (2008) P270-273.
573 Johnson (1997) P35.

tims. Others discuss how Nazi soldiers followed the rules when harming others, not only as the path of least resistance, but also as a way of rejecting responsibility for their own actions, much like Milgram's obedience paradigm.

In the case of the domestic workers, however, the persons blindly following the rules are not the actors but the victims. Some interviewees who were victims of rape (both Indonesian and Filipina) said to have stayed with their employer "because of the contract." An illiterate (Indonesian) domestic worker who was ill and in serious pain stayed: "I had to wait until the contract was over." How can this be explained? Moreover, there is a difference between Indonesian and Filipina domestic workers concerning this issue. The Filipinas, when asked why they could not go home, gave diverse answers, such as: "I already talked to them about that when my son got sick; I could not go" and "I know they have paid money at the agency for me and for my ticket, so it's too much hard for them to release my papers." Very few referred to the contract. Indonesians, on the other hand, almost all referred to the contract.

There are two possible explanations for this phenomenon. One is the possibility that, as one interviewee stated, the agencies indoctrinate them that leaving prior to finishing the contract is impossible, and Indonesian agencies maybe do so more than Filipino agencies. The other explanation is offered by symbolic anthropology: the contract for domestic workers from a patriarchal society has some sort of supernatural force, and as there seems to be a stronger belief in Indonesian society in occultism (see chapter 11), this may also be an explanation. Further research is needed here.

Threats and violence
Sometimes violence is used to keep domestic workers obedient and inside. The most serious victim of violence interviewed for this research was the publicly known Nour Miyati. Whenever she asked for her salary, which was long overdue, her female employer smashed her fingers with heavy things, like an iron. The male employer once grabbed her by the hair and threw her against a wall. Nour needed medical aid but was not permitted to leave the house; she was locked up in her room after finishing her work. It was not until her fingers and toes started to smell bad from gangrene that they let her go. By then, amputation was the only solution left. Yet Nour was not the only one. Several interviewed domestic workers had stitches, bruises or burn marks. Domestic violence occurs all over the world and in all parts of society, but the problem in the Emirates and Saudi Arabia is that the perpetrators are usually not punished. This makes it easy for employers to use violence to make their employees (or women or children) obedient. Other interviewees stated that they received threats that if their behavior did not improve or if they ran away, the employers would go to the police to (falsely) report theft. In light of the fact that these accusations are usually treated by the police as true (see chapter 11), such threats are very effective.

10.6 Resistance

Obviously, not all domestic workers accept their situations. Some have the means to enforce their own norms as well. In continental Europe, domestic workers who did not agree with their employers could vote with their feet: they left. As explained in this chapter, however, for many workers it is impossible to leave the house, so they use another pressure method to resist the employer: they sometimes simply stop working. Some domestic workers have been given the explicit advice at the pre-departure courses: 'If you are unhappy with the employer, stop working as soon as possible." They can drive their employers crazy by doing so. One interviewed employer explained: "They will play all sorts of tricks to get their way. They will stop working, they lock themselves into their room, they stop eating, they cry all the time. They just do not want to be responsible. (...) They know they cannot go to the embassy if there is no reason, so they just force the employer to bring her to the airport." Patterson writes that these types of resistance were normal for slaves as well: "He might react psychologically, play the slave, act dumb, exasperate. He might lie or steal. He might run away. He might injure or kill others, including his own master."[574] Several anthropologists have studied the forms of resistance of domestic workers. See, for instance, Moukarbel on Sri Lankan domestic workers in Lebanon and their everyday forms of resistance.[575]

10.7 Slavery?

In the international press, the position of domestic workers is regularly described as modern-day slavery. As stated in chapter 3, the diminished civil citizenship of women has been referred to by Marilyn French as a form of slavery. As described in chapter 6 on contractual rights, certain agencies explicitly state that the domestic worker will be the employer's slave for two years. Moreover, several interviewed domestic workers report having been told that they were slaves: "They told me I'm a slave, that I do not have any right." Furthermore, the term used in the Gulf for domestic workers, Khaddamah, was used in the past for female slaves.[576] Slavery was, as elsewhere, a widely used practice. In the seventh century, high-class Chinese families bought African slaves through the market in Zanzibar, which was dominated by the Arabs from the eighth century on.[577] On the Arabian Peninsula, slavery was officially abolished under international pressure in the second half of the twentieth century by order of the respective rulers. Consequently, a switch has been made to paid, foreign domestic workers.[578]

---

574 Patterson (1982) P172.
575 Moukarbel (2009).
576 Strobl (2009) P165.
577 Wolf (1990) P42.
578 Several interviewed employers stated that they hired domestic workers since the seventies, when slavery was becoming rare but when quickly rising prices of oil allowed increasing numbers of Arabs to attain domestic help.

When analyzing the current position of these paid foreign domestic workers, is it correct to say that they are 'modern-day slaves' for a period of two years? Of course, it depends on the definition of slavery. The United Nations, which has formulated the most commonly used definition of slavery, has played an important role in the near extinction of legal property in persons, but the organisation has not succeeded – as discussed in chapter 3 – in eliminating the type of slavery that existed before the concept of property came into being: a power relationship in which one person has extreme control over another. Patterson states the following about what slavery is:

> Relations of inequality or domination, which exist whenever one person has more power than another, range on a continuum from those of marginal asymmetry to those in which one person is capable of exercising, with impunity, total power over another. (...) Slavery is one of the most extreme forms of the relation of domination, approaching the limits of total power from the viewpoint of the master and the total powerlessness from the viewpoint of the slave. Yet it differs from other forms of extreme domination in very special ways. If we are to understand how slavery is distinctive, we must first clarify the concept of power. The power relation has three facets. The first is social and involves the use or threat of violence in the control of one person by another. The second is the psychological facet of influence, the capacity to persuade another person to change the way he perceives his interests and his circumstances. And third is the cultural facet of authority, the means of transforming force into right and obedience to duty.[579]

According to this description, domestic workers in Saudi Arabia and the Emirates are indeed slaves. The employer holds extreme power over the worker; he (or she) can make her work all day and can decide how much and whether she eats or sleeps. He is considered to have the right to use a certain level of violence to make her obey (chapters 5 and 11) and he can deport her at will (chapters 7 and 10). Many domestic workers cannot leave the employer's sphere of influence either physically or psychologically, and the situation is described in terms of the employer's rights (based on the contract and payments to the agency) and it is the domestic worker's duty to fully obey him. Because the labour relationship is perceived as a private issue in which the government may not interfere (chapters 5 and 8), no one protects the domestic worker from the power of the employer. Therefore, using Patterson's description of slavery, that is what domestic workers are, albeit only for the two-year term of a contract. That is exactly what a researched recruitment agent in Riyadh stated: "She will be your slave for two years."

---

579 Patterson (1982) P1-2.

The fact that the women themselves sign contracts to become domestic workers does not change this situation to one of non-slavery. As pointed out by the historical precedent of Patterson:

> Poverty was, of course, one of the main reasons for self-sale and we have already noted that in several advanced societies such as China and Japan, it was at times a major source of slaves. In Russia between the seventeenth and nineteenth centuries, self-sale as a result of poverty was the most important reason for enslavement among the mass of domestic slaves. Richard Hellie goes so far as to call Russian (private) slavery a welfare system.[580]

For the domestic workers in Saudi Arabia and the Emirates, poverty is the main reason why they sign contracts. Some of them are lucky enough to find employment in a non-abusive family and as they can often sustain their entire families back home with their salary, this can indeed be referred to as an international welfare system. Thus, from a sociological point of view, despite the fact that some of the domestic workers are treated well, because of the extreme power the employer holds over the domestic worker this relation can be labelled slavery according to the pre-Roman concept of slavery. Since the invention of the concept of property over persons, it is referred to as bonded labour, but an also appropriate term is 'power slavery' as opposed to 'legal slavery'.

One could counter the argument that it is slavery by stating that parents also hold extreme power over their children, whereas children are not referred to as slaves either. Yet especially in Saudi Arabia and to a certain extent in the Emirates, it is considered to be forbidden for the government to interfere in domestic matters, to interfere in the private sphere of the house.[581] Interviewed male employers and government officials gave statements such as: "It's something from our house and it's not for somebody from outside to judge" and "even if there is a problem with my father like if he would beat me, even then, they have nothing to do with it; it's our house."[582] Therefore especially in Saudi Arabia, where men are allowed to treat the members of their family as they deem fit, interviewed female employers regularly referred to themselves as slaves as well – not because they are property, but because their fathers and husbands have almost unlimited power over them.

---

580 Patterson (1982) P130.

581 Compare Sasson (2004) P29: "The authority of a Saudi male is unlimited; his wife and children survive only if he desires. In our homes, he is the state."

582 Early Anglo-American Law was the same in this respect. Levit (2006) P180: "The notion of women as property also meant that men could never be guilty of raping their wives because men could treat their possessions, or 'chattel' in nearly any way they wanted. Indeed, the doctrine of 'chastisement' allowed husbands to beat their wives, in 'moderation' to make them obey. (...) When feminists challenged the laws on chastisement during the Reconstruction era, judges invoked the public-private distinction, reasoning that the legal system should not interfere in cases of wife beating, to protect the privacy of the marriage relationship and to promote domestic harmony."

Here the term 'slavery' could be deemed inappropriate as the women are not property of their husbands. 'Bonded labour' is not appropriate either, as there is no labour relation between the two. But the proposed term 'power slavery' articulates the point that the women concerned try to make. The power of employers over domestic workers is at least as strong, as this chapter has shown.

10.8 Summary

This chapter discussed the several reasons why it is often impossible and usually very difficult for domestic workers in Saudi Arabia and the Emirates to either change employers or return home. A paramount legal impediment to the freedom of the domestic worker is the sponsorship system. Economic impediments include salary retention, debts, needy family members and transaction costs. Some of these impede the worker's freedom because of the employer, while other impediments may occur without the employer's knowledge. Physical impediments include the impossibility of leaving the employer because the domestic worker cannot leave the house, because she does not know anything about the outside world, or because the employer retains her passport. Psychological impediments include the patriarchal system, fear, indoctrination and the mental programming that the contract cannot be broken under any condition. These impediments together create a situation in which the employer holds extreme power over the domestic worker. As the relation is not one of property but one of extreme power, it is usually referred to as bonded labour. Yet because it is akin to pre-Roman slavery, to slavery as it existed before the invention of the concept of property over persons, the labour relation can also be referred to as *power slavery* as opposed to *property slavery*. This term has an advantage over the term bonded labour, that is, it clarifies how connected the position of the domestic worker is to the position of women and children in these locations where the patriarch is considered to be the state within the private sphere of the household.

Whatever one's position on the question of whether it is modern-day slavery, it is clear that the situation cannot be referred to as a free labor market. The alteration of the sponsorship system, as discussed in chapter 8, will probably create somewhat more freedom. Although it will not create a fully free labor market, it could create an institutionalized setting that compensates for market failures caused by transaction costs, as will be further discussed in chapter 12.

11. Otherness and Expulsion

11.1 Introduction

This chapter is the second one of Part IV, concerning the power relation between the domestic worker and her employer. This power relation has been researched because a power imbalance can lead to conflicts as it allows for one party to behave contrary to the norms of both parties without anyone interfering. The previous chapter discussed the limited freedom of domestic workers to leave their employment. This chapter describes how employers to the contrary have every freedom to instantly end the labor relation. They do so regularly by means of different sorts of accusations. Their reasons hereto are connected to the fact that domestic workers find themselves in an ambivalent position in their employers' houses. They are part of the family, yet they are not family. They are women who are very close physically and yet not close at all mentally. This leads to specific conflicts related to different forms of otherness.

Section 2 discusses three types of otherness: (i) the domestic worker as a foreign woman, (ii) the domestic worker as the other woman next to the – often jealous – wife, and (iii) the domestic worker as a woman who is different from a man and therefore both fascinating and threatening. In this section about gender and gender-related conflicts, the male and female employers are sometimes referred to as the husband and the wife because these terms have emotional connotations that make the problems more easily understandable than the term 'employer'.

These three types of otherness can lead to conflicts that, due to the closeness of the domestic worker, can become extremely violent: psychological, physical and sexual violence occur regularly. The employer in these cases has the freedom to instantly remove the domestic worker from his family, something he often does by means of accusations. Section 4 describes these accusations that are generally presumed to be true by the Saudi and Emirati authorities. Section 5 discusses that the accusations seem to have the function of instantly expelling the marginal other.

This chapter is based on interviews with domestic workers, employers, diplomats, lawyers and two psychologists. The issues are rather sensitive and the relevant answers were usually given only after the interview had been going on for a long time or in a second or third meeting. Some information was gathered from people who had been told about this research and its purposes, but who at the moment of the relevant answers seemed to have forgotten about it. For instance, some men were interviewed, thereafter invited me for dinner and only there started to explain about their sexual relations with domestic workers. The questionnaires provided no information for this chapter.

The next three sections will show how the otherness of the domestic workers takes three forms in practice, all of which seem to be stronger in the Gulf than in many other societies.

II.2 Otherness

As explained in chapter 3, domestic workers are often perceived as 'the other' due to their position at the margins of the family. Both in Saudi Arabia and the Emirates, almost all of the interviewed employers stated their concerns that the workers would bring strangers into the house. Several employers also stated their concerns about gossip; this strange foreign woman enters the household where she learns all the secrets of the family. This is a large responsibility to carry in a culture where 'shame' and 'face' are such essential features.[583] She knows a lot and her level of loyalty can be too low. One interviewed employer for instance stated: "The maids, they know the secrets of the house. That is also why they cannot go out, they will tell the neighbors." Many domestic workers reported the same: "Some employers don't want us to talk to each other. They are afraid we are going to say bad things about their family."

To manage this complicated situation, domestic workers are regularly kept away from the family. In richer families in Saudi Arabia and the Emirates, the same pattern takes place; if possible, the domestic worker is kept physically apart as much as possible. Because dirt is contagious, it must be kept away, as in the Arabic saying: "If you stand near a blacksmith you will get covered in soot, but if you stand near a perfume seller you will carry an aroma of scent with you."[584] To deal with the fact that this dirty outsider may turn out to be very attractive, they are commonly portrayed as lusty sexual devils.[585] One Saudi interviewee stated, wording the opinion of many: "and the problem is, they are sexually very easy going. The Africans are not so easy, it's more the Asians. They don't have to be in love for this. Too many are pregnant and they leave the child or orphan here. You have to look after the maids all the time to protect your own sons. They want to be done, especially the Muslims. They pray and they think that then they are forgiven." This sexually charged dynamic might lead to untenable situations that cause employers to want to get rid of the domestic worker instantly or domestic workers to want to leave instantly.

This is problematic, however, because, though they are portrayed as unreliable, they are at the same time indispensable. In particular, female employers in Saudi Arabia and the Emirates complained that they were entirely dependent on their domestic workers and that they run the risk of her leaving. As one interviewed employer stated: "And you think they go and pick up your children, but they just disappear in thin air and you don't hear about it until the police bring your children home."

The data in this research show that this otherness of the domestic workers, a common phenomenon, actually takes the shape of three different forms of otherness. These three forms are all more severe in Saudi Arabia and the Emirates than what can be expected in many other countries.

---

583 More on the culture of shame in chapter 5 that discusses the position of domestic worker as part of the family.
584 Sasson (2004) P196-197.
585 Schama (1988) P460.

11.3 The foreign woman

Domestic workers are almost always migrant workers, usually from a quite different culture.[586] The workers and their employers therefore suffer from severe intercultural communication problems. Many women who arrive on the Arabian Peninsula speak Arabic poorly or not at all. But even when the workers are fluent in this language however, many misunderstandings occur. For instance, under Islam, one is religiously obliged to wash after having sexual intercourse, before one can pray again. Because showing one's hair to a man is regularly viewed as a sexual invitation, showing wet hair is sometimes interpreted as a very explicit sexual invitation.

Hair is also in other instances a problem; many Indonesian domestic workers, in particular, have a habit of gathering hair for different reasons. One such reason is the innocent superstition (as they themselves usually see it) that if they lose their hair on the Arabian Peninsula, they will not be able to return to their home country. Therefore, they gather their hair in little bags to bring home. Others believe that hair must be gathered during menstruation, to be burnt later as cleaning ritual. However, Arabic employers, many of whom are staunch believers in supernatural forces and occultism, may feel threatened by this custom as they think it involves the hair of the employer, to be used for voodoo-like practices. Several Saudi and a few Emirati interviewees explained how 'magic' can be used to steal the love of a man – their husbands or sons – and that hair is a common tool for occultism (more in the next section).

In Saudi Arabia, there is an issue that contributes to the foreignness of the domestic worker: the fear and dislike of others, taught by Wahhabi scholars[587] at schools and in mosques. As a Saudi interviewee stated: "We have been taught in school that Christians are *Kuffar*, that they are very dangerous. That is why we cannot look them in the eye, we cannot shake their hands and we certainly cannot laugh at them!" These teachings about 'others' reflect the Wahhabi worldview: a world divided into the believers and preservers of the true faith and the infidels. A defensive tone underlies the message about the 'other' projected in the demonization of the different. The defensive tone and projections of fear are reinforced by the various punishments for deviancy spelled out in textbooks in great detail. As a Saudi woman observed: "The mind of each of us has been programmed since school age that values and good deeds are ours only and that others lack them." Such teachings undermine the trust and confidence Saudis have in their domestic workers, as several interviewees stated.

These teachings may have a purpose. Non-Wahhabis, especially ones who reside within the household, can pose a threat to the power of the Wahhabi establishment by spreading information about all sorts of different worldviews such as Christianity or democracy.

---

586 See section 2.4 for a list of countries of origin.
587 More on Wahhabi scholars in chapters 2 and 9.

In that light, it is no surprise that the former Grand Mufti Bin Baz has provided the following *fatwa*: "It is not permissible to employ a non-Muslim servant, male or female, nor a non-Muslim driver, nor a non-Muslim laborer in the Arabian gulf, because the Prophet, peace be upon him, ordered the removal of all Jews and Christians from it and he ordered that none should remain in it except Muslims. (...) This is because bringing male and female disbelievers is a danger to the Muslims, their beliefs, their morals and the upbringing of their children, so it should be forbidden."[588]

So the Wahhabi teachings on the dangers of foreigners add to the otherness of domestic workers. Furthermore, as the average educational level is low and independent critical thought is not stimulated in schools, many employers believe urban legends. This is especially the case among interviewed female employers. Other interviewees denied that these are urban legends and insist that it was indeed their own cousin who was: "chopped up in pieces by the domestic worker while the husband went out for cigarettes. And the domestic worker said the woman had left with another man. But the husband didn't trust it and he went to search and found her chopped up in thousand pieces in the storage." Further questions about such extreme stories, such as asking about the specific punishment the domestic worker was given and whether evidence of her guilt existed, are always averted. One interviewee stated that there is a book with stories on domestic workers who used supernatural powers and occultism to kill their employers or the children, a book which he claimed is very popular among Saudi Arabian women.

Thus, the fear of the other in Saudi Arabia seems to be very strong, stronger than in the Emirates. This is compensated for by a different, fierce fear of the other in the Emirates caused by the fact that the original population has now been reduced to 10%.[589] One interviewed domestic worker commented on how she had been humiliated by her Dubai employer: "I think it's fear. There are too many foreigners. They are afraid of all the changes and they are afraid the workers will not want to go home." Another problem in both countries which possibly adds to the fear for foreigners, is unemployment among citizens, especially among young Saudis.

II.4 The other woman

The second type of otherness concerning the domestic worker comes from the fact that, in the eyes of the female employer or wife, she is 'the other woman' to whom the male employer or husband may be attracted. The wife can be either content or dissatisfied with that, though the latter seems to be the most common. Although this form of otherness exists worldwide, it could maybe have larger effects in Saudi Arabia and the Emirates, as men in both countries are permitted to marry up to four wives.

---

588 Prokop in Aarts (2005) P71.
589 See chapter 2.

Whereas Western women are sometimes confronted with their husbands having a mistress, Saudi and Emirati women can be confronted with their husbands marrying the mistress. The situation with the domestic worker is even more complicated. She can be the mistress of the employer (either forced or voluntarily) while living in the same household as her employer and his wife.[590]

Just the thought of that possibility makes many female employers behave differently – or even horribly – towards their domestic workers.[591] Several Saudi and Emirati interviewees complained about domestic workers wanting to steal their husbands. For instance, one stated: "The problem is that many men think they have the right to an affair, they think they have a right to the maid. But it also happens the other way around: the maid saying she has the right to the man, that she is the concubine, that therefore it is not *Haram*, not forbidden, but *Halal*. It can also happen that the master marries the maid."

Both women know that the female employer is not the ultimate authority in the household. Though the husband usually plays a small role in the details of day-to-day life, his position is pivotal because he decides how much freedom his wife has. Several female interviewees confirmed this: "No matter what we do, our future is linked to one prerequisite: the degree of kindness in the man who rules us."[592] From an early age, they learn to manipulate rather than to confront. They learn that they are born to be pretty and not much else. The female employer therefore feels very threatened as soon as she is not the prettiest thing in the house anymore.

Almost all interviewed domestic workers talk about their female employers being extremely jealous, even of their husbands saying a kind word to this other woman. One of them accounted: "If I was in the kitchen and the man would walk in there, she would go crazy! The male employer was very nice, he never asked for anything. She was very jealous." Another reported: "The female employer was very jealous and very temperamental. I ran away to the consulate when she threw hot porridge over my legs." This domestic worker admitted later in the interview that she had not protested when the male employer had entered her bedroom at night, adding, "The man was nice to me."

One domestic worker could not stop talking about the misery of coming between her male and female employer: "My employer said, you are so beautiful. I told him that I offer my service, that doesn't include my body! I didn't sign anything to offer my body! Then he took another woman home and he had sex with her in the living room. He said that if I'd tell the madam, he would kill me! He told me that he wants a divorce. Why he tells me that? It's not my business! I said Baba please stop and I cry but he says it's not your business. Baba says my wife doesn't give me any care, doesn't understand me, but that's not my business! They must divorce; it's too horrible."

---

590 On the Arabian Peninsula, in polygamous marriages every woman is supposed to have her own house.
591 Compare Patterson (1982) P175.
592 Sasson (2004) P162.

A few domestic workers reported about female employers cutting their hair off to make them look like boys, beating them for saying a word to the male employer, or even beating them for being thin. One Saudi interviewee reported the same: "I have a friend called Nada. She hates the maid, she admits that sometimes she hits the maid, just because the maid is skinny and Nada is not. Nada is really fat, like most Saudi women nowadays." However, other women seem to be pleased with the fact that the domestic worker can serve the needs of the men in their house. Two interviewed domestic workers who reported having been raped claimed that their female employers knew about it. One even said that it was the female employer who had removed the key from her room, so that she could no longer keep the male employer outside at night.

11.5 The woman

Third but foremost, the domestic worker is the 'other' simply because she is a woman who is both strange and attractive to the men in the household where she is employed. This may lead to a variety of situations.

Love and care
First, a love affair is possible. Despite the negative press about domestic workers being sexually harassed, some of them simply do fall in love and this may be mutual. For example, the following is an excerpt from an interview with a male employer:

> There used to be this girl from Indonesia with us and I liked her. She had a nice face: white and clean. So one day I was just passing by all the time, passing the room where she was working. And she asked, 'Abdullah, what do you want?' And I said 'What do you think?' So that was my first time. [*She didn't refuse?*] No, she liked me. But afterwards I felt really bad you know, I was so scared; if my father would find out, what would he do to me! So for some days I didn't look at her. And she asked me: 'Abdullah, aren't you hungry for me?' [*So it happened only once?*] No, a couple of times, but every time after some weeks. [*Weren't you afraid she would get pregnant?*] No, but I didn't ... she was still a virgin afterwards. I would never take that from her, that would have destroyed her life!

As an interviewed diplomat from a country of origin stated, an important factor is that many domestic workers, far from home, are lonely and long for some personal care and attention. An interviewed Saudi employer concurred: "They will have relations with the boys in the house or with the driver. That's why many families prefer to have a maid and a driver who are married to each other. Many who do have relations are happy with that. You have to understand: they are lonely, so they are not refusing." Such a situation becomes problematic when the domestic worker becomes pregnant or when she understands that the employer (or his son) will never marry her, despite her hopes or beliefs that this would happen, as in the following interview with an employer:

> We had a maid from the Philippines and she was in love with my brother. After he got married, she cried for days and then she ran away. [*Do you think something has happened between them?*] Yes, I don't have real evidence or something, but he was going to the roof a lot, you know, where her room was. And when I asked, he always said he had to adjust the satellite. Well, let's just say it needed a lot of adjustments! [*But he married somebody else. Do you know anybody who married the domestic worker?*] No! Of course their parents will never ever allow them to marry the maid! [*Because they don't even allow them to marry somebody from a lower tribe?*] Exactly![593]

But as soon as a domestic worker who has fallen in love runs away, pregnant or not, she has practically no choice but to accuse the employer of sexual abuse because otherwise, the black market is the only place to go: embassies' safe houses are overfull and refuse to help women who suffer from nothing but a broken heart.[594] Moreover, because extramarital sex is heavily punished in both countries, the worker cannot possibly admit to the Saudi or Emirati authorities that the sexual intercourse was consensual. Any domestic worker who is pregnant and not engaged, will accuse her employer of rape to save her life. The problem is that because the authorities realize this, they no longer believe the women who actually have been abused.

Prostitution

Other domestic workers enter into sexual relations with one or more men in the house for financial reasons. Many interviewed domestic workers reported having been offered money in exchange for sex, but because of the stigma attached, no one admitted to having accepted it. Nevertheless, it is clear that this does happen. One interviewee arrived at the safe house of her embassy with a large amount of gold on her wrists. She claimed to have run away because her life had become "too complicated" but refused to say anything else. Several Emirati and Saudi interviewees stated that they understood the reasons for prostitution: "They can make as much money in an evening as they normally make in a month. Of course some of them say yes." However, the majority of interviewed employers, especially older and female ones, were fierce in their rejection of prostitution and as elsewhere in the world, the blame falls on the female accepting (and usually needing) the money, not on the man who pays her.

---

593 Other interviews revealed that marriages with domestic workers do occur, although very rarely. It seems to be least common in the center of Saudi Arabia where this interview took place.
594 See chapter 8.

As Levitt and Dubner colorfully describe it,[595] sex is a matter of supply and demand. In sexually restrictive societies, the demand for sex is high and the price paid to prostitutes rises. Furthermore, depending on the usual income of women, when payments rise, the supply of prostitutes rises with it. In the Emirates – but even more so in Saudi Arabia – the demand for sex is high because the availability of 'casual sex' or 'friends with benefits' is very low. Prostitution is widely visible in the streets and hotels of Dubai. In Saudi Arabia it remains more hidden, but all younger interviewees who were asked about it, admitted that prostitutes were available everywhere. In Saudi Arabia, as several interviewees reported, Saudi women can be so poor that they become prostitutes – a very dangerous profession in light of the threat of being stoned to death. In the Emirates, prostitution seems to be an occupation entirely consisting of female migrant workers.[596] Prices differ greatly depending on the nationality of the prostitute, with differences comparable to the salary differences between domestic workers of different nationalities.[597]

Harassment, rape and sex slavery
Last but not least, domestic workers are regularly forced into sexual relations. As one of many interviewed domestic workers explained: "In the beginning he just tried, but this year he got what he wanted. He is very big you know, so what could I do? He raped me. I didn't tell his wife because my friends told me his wife will side with her husband no matter what. I had tried to contact the embassy before and I planned to run away, but then this incident happened. I threatened him I would tell his wife, but I didn't because it was no use. He came to the house when he knew all the others were out and he raped me."

Some men are perfectly aware of the fact that they are forcing the domestic worker because they apply physical abuse at the same time. However, other men do not seem to realize that for instance the uncomfortable smiles and silences of a young Indonesian woman mean no. Some of the culturally prescribed ways in which women typically respond to difficult situations – with silence, an uncomfortable laugh, or attempts to maintain friendly interactions – can be interpreted as consent or encouragement.[598] Thus, the intercultural differences between silent women and fervent men create a considerable problem. Furthermore, a lack of violence is often misinterpreted, as it is elsewhere in the world: many believe rape does not occur unless the offender uses violent physical force or a weapon. The typical rape, however, involves no weapons and little or no physical force. Many

---

595 Levitt (2009) chapter 1.
596 Which probably is related to the fact that poor Emirati women are very rare, while poor Saudi women are quite numerous.
597 See chapter 6.
598 Levit (2006) P69.

believe that rape does not happen unless the victim physically resists her at-
tacker, when in fact victims often suffer physical paralysis and mental disassocia-
tion, which cause silence and passivity and prevent them from resisting.[599]

An interviewed Saudi psychologist stated this as follows: "If a man tries to have
sex with the domestic worker, her reaction can vary enormously: 'Yes, I want this
too' or 'I have been abused all my life, so I guess this is normal' or 'This man is so
big and scary so how on earth can I say no?' Yet on the outside to the average
Saudi all these reactions will look the same; there is no fierce rejection, which will
be interpreted as a 'yes.' The problem here is a lack of education in what this absence of fierce rejection can mean; the concept of being paralyzed by fear is unknown to them." Secondly, male employers do not seem to realize that due to the
immense power the employer holds over the worker (as explained in the previous
chapter), domestic workers are usually not in a position to refuse. Whereas in the
West there is a minimal awareness that sexual relations should generally be avoided in power relations, none of the male interviewees in Saudi Arabia and the
Emirates seemed to have thought this over before they were asked about it.

Furthermore, although many believe that victims promptly report a rape to police or other local authorities, most victims around the world never report the sexual violence they suffer. In many communities, to report a rape is actually to risk
punishment, as the victim herself may be punished for admitting to having had
sexual intercourse outside of marriage. Formal and informal punishment of rape
victims ranges from public disgrace and social ostracism, to actual imprisonment
for fornication or prostitution, to becoming the victim of a so-called 'honor killing'
by the family members who believe the only way to cleanse the family name of the
stain of illicit sexual intercourse is the murder of the rape victim. Despite the massive social and public health crisis that it represents worldwide, sexual violence
continues to be shrouded in shame. Victims continue to be blamed and despised
within their own communities and the law continues to struggle to offer victims
justice.[600]

Seclusion and mystification

The sexual use and abuse of domestic workers has been commonplace throughout history and all over the world,[601] yet on the Arabian Peninsula – and especially
in Saudi Arabia – the situation is worse. Research shows that an excess of males in
the overall population encourages prostitution and sexual abuse, both outside and
within the servant class.[602] Both in Saudi Arabia and the Emirates the large majority (60 to 70%) of the population is male, as most migrant workers are male (working in production and construction).

599 Clark (2007) P1265.
600 Clark (2007) P1265.
601 Rollins (1985) P 24 & 29; and compare Patterson (1982) P173-175 for abuse of female slaves.
602 Rollins (1985) P43.

Furthermore, the (30 to 40%) minority of women is barely visible, due to the rules of *khulwa* or seclusion. For most Muslims, unrelated men and women cannot be together in private quarters, but they can be together in public spaces as long as they are respectful and keep decent manners. For Wahhabis, if a man and a woman are not related they should not be together, no matter what. Therefore, in conservative Saudi Arabia, women live largely segregated from men. This seclusion has become more severe over the last decades because many families now have enough financial resources to keep their women entirely in seclusion and to build large walls around their houses. As one interviewee explained: "In the old days you had to go to the market; now your husband makes you send the driver." Another factor is that, due to economic changes, families have diminished from extended families to core families. The number of women with whom the average man interacts is therefore extremely low. According to another interviewee, "70% to 90% of men have never been exposed to women other than their direct family." As another interviewee explained: "Women are in a very secret place, the men are elsewhere, we don't mingle at all. At least, in the upper classes we do, but the lower and middle class no, there they don't mingle at all. So men and women are both incapable of communicating with the other sex."

The effect hereof is, according to several interviewees, a form of mystification of "the woman." For instance, to the question of where he could meet girls, one interviewee responded: "I don't know. You don't. If you want a good wife, you can ask a friend about his sisters. But a girl who would want to talk to me, I would never marry her." No matter how much he wanted to talk to and was interested in girls, he could not understand that maybe girls felt the same and were interested in boys. If this was the case, she had to be a bad person. Many male respondents thought alike: the woman was not considered to be similar to or have feelings similar to those of men. She is perceived as entirely different and incomprehensible, which can lead to violence. As an interviewed Saudi psychologist explained: "There is more sexual violence in uneducated and in religiously strict families because there is less mingling. They don't learn to communicate."

In the Emirates, the *khulwa* rules are applied less strictly to Emirati women, but as domestic workers are usually not permitted to leave the house and as they form such a large part of the female population, the streets are filled there mainly with men as well.[603] This low visibility of women creates sexual tension with the few women who are seen. As an interviewed Saudi government official admitted, he had been completely accustomed to women while travelling in Europe and the United States, but now that he was back in his own country, just the sight of a female face (my face, unfortunately) made him lose all concentration and self-discipline.

---

603 Apart from the specific locations where Western tourists or prostitutes can be found.

Because of this sexual tension, even women who are permitted to leave the house prefer to stay inside, which creates a vicious circle: because there are few women visible and available, men become sex-oriented. Because they are sex-oriented, the situation is less safe for women in the streets and therefore there are fewer women available. The domestic workers, however, are permanently indoors; they are permanently visible and available to the men in the house. Some enjoy it, some use it and some hate it. Whatever their position, there is no chance of going elsewhere. As such they share their problems with many women in Saudi Arabia who are not permitted to leave the house. As a Saudi expert on domestic violence stated: "And many brothers touch their sisters because she is the only woman around. "There is a lot of sexual abuse, a lot!" She concluded: "Sexual violence is cultural, when considering how families live here; very closed. Inside the house one is not protected."

Opening up society
In the United Arab Emirates, sexual abuse of domestic workers seems to be less common.[604] Several interviewees in the Emirates explained that having a sexual relationship with the domestic worker used to be entirely common: "If you didn't do her, your friends said you were an idiot." Another one confirmed, "Well, about ten years ago, when our society wasn't so open as it is now, the houses were closed, the families were closed. And all of a sudden there was this strange woman in the house and some of them were really pretty. And for them, they were away from house, two years, three years, so they were lonely. And they have needs, like we have needs. It's natural. At that time, I think about 70% to 80% had an affair with the maid."

However, more recently this particular problem seems to be diminishing because Emirati men have so many other alternatives available: the bars are full of prostitutes and willing tourists. This could be related to the impression of interviewed diplomats of countries of origin, that sexual abuse of domestic workers in the Emirates is diminishing. To a lesser extent, prostitution seems to be on the rise as well in Saudi Arabia (as described above). Whereas the higher strata of society have had access to prostitutes in countries like Malaysia and Thailand for decades, the number of hidden prostitutes – even in extremely conservative Riyadh – seems to be rising rapidly, and visiting them is said to be frequent and accepted as normal among men.

The intention here is not to praise prostitution, especially in light of the fact that many prostitutes are likely to be pressured into this activity. However, it is possible that prostitution takes pressure off domestic workers by providing an alternative for men. Yet to the contrary it could also deteriorate the situation, as prostitution seems to have a very negative influence on the male perception of women in general and foreign women in particular.

---

604 Sabban (2005) P30.

Many Saudi and Emirati men visit brothels in their own country or in the Far East. Most of these men consider any woman who is not a Muslim a prostitute including their domestic worker.[605] Further research on the relation between the availability of prostitutes and sexual abuse of domestic workers would be helpful.

Patriarchy

In addition to the mystification, another problem is that both societies are very patriarchal,[606] to the point that sexual abuse is almost always blamed on the abused woman. For instance, one interviewee stated: "One friend got his maid pregnant. [*So what did he do?*] He got her the abortion pill. You cannot buy that here, but there are ways to get it. They bring it in from Egypt or Lebanon. [*But it's dangerous because if the police find out, you can go to jail.*] "Yes, *she* can go to jail." Likewise, a Saudi female interviewee stated that she would never tell anyone about sexual abuse: "They will destroy me, you know. After that, I will be trash for everyone. The only one who will want to marry me is some old ugly guy with one eye only and even he will treat me like trash because I am a prostitute because I have let myself get raped."

Sexual violence is connected to patriarchy because patriarchy legitimizes violence against women as a form of necessary discipline. Rape and battery are often seen as individual acts of sick or angry men rather than acts of patriarchy, but gender violence serves other more normalized ends, such as male control and domination.[607] Men resort to sexual violence not only out of a need of sex, but also because it works as a control mechanism. Thus, although patriarchy itself might be a deteriorating factor (both Saudi Arabia and the Emirates are still very patriarchal societies), a factor that might make matters even worse is that patriarchy is under pressure in both countries.[608] The fact that certain Saudi and Emirati men resort to sexual or other forms of violence against women could be related to the fact that these women no longer obey the way they used to. The fact that they no longer obey may have to do with social changes in economy that calls for smarter, higher educated workers, regardless of gender. In other words, sexual violence may (temporarily?) increase due to economic changes, although this hypothesis needs further comparative research, particularly from scholars trained in gender studies.

Sexual abuse and wasta

Intimate violence occurs across all races, classes, ethnicities, sexual orientations and religions.[609] The interviews for this research with domestic workers who claimed to have been raped, also suggest that sexual abuse is not limited to particular social groups or classes.

---

605 Compare Sasson (2004) P136-137.
606 See Levit (2006) P23 for the relation between patriarchal society and oppression of women.
607 Johnson (1984) P29 & 46.
608 See also chapters 2 and 3.
609 Levit (2006) P194.

However, what is striking is the large number of domestic workers who claim to have been abused by an employer who was, or claimed to be, either a police officer or a high-ranking army officer. The possibility should not be disregarded that police officers are more sexually violent than others; however, a more likely explanation seems to be that police officers expect not to be punished because those who would arrest them are their colleagues. As explained in chapter 9, the legal systems of both countries work on *wasta*, connections, not on rules equally applied to all.

Denial

The common occurrence of sexual abuse of domestic workers is generally denied in both the Emirates and Saudi Arabia. UNDP states: "Domestic violence is not a purely Arab phenomenon. It is found and condemned in many areas of the world. Nevertheless, what is disturbing is the persistent denial in some Arab countries that it exists."[610] However, this denial is not in any way particular to the Middle East. For instance, in the United States, stranger assaults comprise the minority of rape cases, although the common discourse is that acquaintance rape is an exception.[611] Just as these women prefer not to think about the fact that every acquaintance is a possible rapist, Saudi women prefer not to think about the fact that their husbands may be raping domestic workers. As long as the denial continues though, effective measures are not likely to be taken.

11.6 Expulsion

11.6.1 Accusations of occultism

Both in the Emirates and in Saudi Arabia, the belief in the occult is widespread. According to interviewed Saudis and Emiratis, it concerns "the unaccepted use of invisible forces to achieve something." A prayer for health to (the invisible force) God or Allah is not considered 'magic' and therefore forbidden, as calling on God or Allah is accepted. However, the use of other invisible forces, such as *ginnies*[612] to achieve either good or evil is not permitted under Sharia law. Occultism, under this definition, includes what is usually referred to as shamanism or (aspects of) witchcraft. Many interviewees stated that Westerners are wrong to deny the existence of the occult or to deny the fact that they believe in it. Several made statements like, "You also believe in magic; it's in the Bible you know, when Moses changed his stick into a snake." They furthermore emphasized that, unlike Westerners, Arabs do not make a distinction between good and bad occultism. For instance, another interviewee said: "We all know that there is three kinds of creatures: people, angels and ginnies. And people who do witchcraft, they communicate with ginnies. But they

---

610 Report 10, P116.
611 Stapleton in Agosín (2002) P220.
612 Spirits or ghosts.

are bad, so that's why you cannot talk of black magic, as you do in the West, because all magic is bad. Islam forbids this."

Occultism is, by the interviewees in both Saudi Arabia and the Emirates, considered to be practiced mainly by women. In these two highly patriarchal societies, women are supposed to obey the men in their family, and several male interviewees stated that occultism must be at play when a man falls in love so deeply that a woman controls him. This goes against what is considered the natural state of things and therefore the supernatural must be involved. These two countries are not exceptional: throughout the world and throughout history, women have primarily been accused of doing 'magic' and of being witches,[613] accusations that are strongly attached to the otherness of the woman, which creates both desire and fear. For instance, the English verb enchanting, can mean both bewitching and enthralling; charming can mean to cast a spell or to delight. Throughout Europe, women were accused of being witches until the Enlightenment in the eighteenth century, when people started to think about the world more scientifically. The unchangeability of the newly discovered laws of nature made the concept of witchcraft unlikely. This process of disenchantment, seems to be currently taking place in Saudi Arabia and the Emirates, possibly due to the spread of education in natural sciences, although more research is necessary on this subject.

As shown in the previous section, the otherness of the domestic worker is intimately connected to her femininity: she is the foreign woman, the other woman and the woman. She is both attractive and dangerous. Even more than other women, domestic workers undermine the 'natural' order of society when they make a man fall in love with them. Therefore, it is not surprising that domestic workers and female slaves have always regularly been accused of doing magic.[614]

Interestingly enough, several Saudi and Emirati men stated that a woman's hair is her most precious jewel; on other occasions, interviewees explained that hair is the most common tool used to practice occultism.[615] Many Indonesians in particular admitted to gathering their hair, although not to practice occultism on anyone else: "We believe that you have to gather it during menstruation, otherwise it brings bad luck; the evil spirit will follow you. My grandmother tells me this as well." The Filipina domestic workers generally do not gather hair and know nothing about practicing occultism with it. For instance, one interviewee who was accused of theft accounted, "And then they take this hair band and they pulled it from my hair, I don't know why. And they took the hair from it and put it in a tissue. And then when they finish my bag they say to take off all my clothes to see but I have nothing! And they wanted the police there but the police refuse, they say it's *haram*. And then they made me take off my clothes and they took pictures of

---

613 Zimbardo (2008) P9 and Crow (1968).
614 Patterson (1982) P62-64.
615 Compare Holton (2007) P238.

me without a dress. It was very ... they harass me really. Why do you think they take my hair?"

Most employers believe that domestic workers of particular nationalities practice occultism. For instance, an interviewed employer explained: "In Indonesia they all believe in this magic thing. They do magic at home to make the employer like them. The employers think it is magic against them. Magic is a big problem here, it is absolutely not allowed." Many employers confirmed the widespread idea that Indonesians practice occultism with bad intentions. Moroccan women (domestic workers or others) are generally accused of using super natural powers only to steal husbands. One exception was the following account from a Saudi interviewee: "If the worker is good, she will stay with a family for ten years or more. But some stay just a few months and then my mum says "Khalas, time for you to go home." Like for example a girl from Morocco. She had health problems, epilepsy. But this was not because of a disease, she would get it when talking about *ginnies*, about ghosts. So I told my mum I was scared of her and that I didn't want to eat her food anymore and my mother sent her home."

Accusations of occultism as tool

Many employers actually fear the (perceived?) occultism of their domestic workers, but often the accusation is nothing but a tool to have her removed from the household instantly. Magic accusations are often used to expel women who are perceived as creating problems. This is clear in the example of a South African woman who worked in Saudi Arabia. She wrote a report on the large-scale corruption and theft in a hospital, upon which she was accused of practicing magic on the hospital equipment. An interviewee close to the accused explained: "They just wanted to scare us, to make us shut up." A diplomat of a labor-providing country stated: "They just accuse them because they don't want to pay the salary or because of jealousy or something like that. By accusing them of occultism, they can refuse to pay, they can deny accusations, they can send them away. When they torture the maid, they accuse her of magic to legalize the torture so they get no prosecution." Human Rights Watch found the same pattern and writes of "spurious countercharges of theft or witchcraft from their employers in efforts to mask mistreatment."[616]

According to Douglas, accusations of magic and witchcraft are common against those at the margins and those whose position in the hierarchy is unclear: "Here are people living in the interstices of the power structure, felt to be a threat to those with better defined status. Since they are credited with dangerous uncontrollable powers, an excuse is given for suppressing them, they can be charged with witchcraft and violently dispatched without formality or delay."[617]

---

616 Report 18, P6.
617 Douglas (1966) P102.

The connection between an accusation of magic and its ability to have a marginal person expelled resounds in the Arabic language: the Arabic word for excommunication is *Takfir*, which means calling someone a *Kafir*. This word can mean a non-believer, but it also means a disloyal person or even a communist. Through *takfir* or accusations in general, people are removed from a community regardless of the truth of the accusation. More interesting for the analysis of the accusations is therefore not what has happened before, but what happens afterwards.

The advantage of magic accusations compared to other accusations is that the evidentiary rules concerning this crime are non-existent.[618] As an interviewed lawyer stated about a new case: "The employer raped the lady, then the wife comes here with the 'proof' that the maid was doing magic." The interviewee then showed a picture of two small plastic bags, one empty and one containing some unknown substance. A Saudi employer stated, "I also was a spiritual healer. I know it happens sometimes, but the problem is, magic is invisible, so you cannot be 100% sure. You cannot have real evidence." Another explained, "If somebody gets sick and a domestic worker is accused of having caused this by doing magic, finding ropes with knots therein may be evidence enough for a conviction. When the ropes are unknotted and the patient feels somewhat better, the conviction is guaranteed." No Saudi or Emirati who believed in magic seemed to know the meaning of the placebo effect (which, I agree, could be called magic). Not only the evidentiary rules, but also the rules concerning appropriate punishment are being disregarded. An interviewee stated: "Evidence is the problem; nobody can prove the magic. Some women they get sentenced to 10,000 lashes plus jail time. The Qur'an talks about 80 lashes or 100 lashes when it comes to alcohol abuse or extra marital sex, but 10,000? This is ridiculous."

The economics of occultism
Another problem is that certain people make money on magic. As one attentive interviewee noted: "Magic is a big problem. It has become like an industry here in Saudi Arabia. They have TV shows in which they discover the magic tools from domestic workers at people's houses." Many private practitioners also seem to be earning money on magic accusations: "If there is somebody in the family with some health problem, they go to the doctor. If he cannot find anything, than after that they go to a religious person. He may say it's magic. Then they go to the house and search if they find little things; like pieces of clothing of the person concerned with ropes around them. They untie the rope. If the pain goes away then, that's the proof that the magic was intended to harm and then people are sent to jail." [*Are these religious persons paid to do this?*] "Yes, they are very expensive."

---

618 Likewise stated in a Human Rights Watch letter to the King of Saudi Arabia, 12-02-2008: http://www.hrw.org/en/news/2008/02/12/letter-hrh-king-abdullah-bin-abd-al-aziz-al-saud-witchcraft-case.

Another interviewee stated: "Going to magicians is also a waste of money and a loss to the woman who seeks them." A third one said: "This book on witchcraft is a real bestseller, you know." This magic industry certainly is disadvantageous to domestic workers if magic is an accusation usually made against marginal women, because that is what domestic workers are.

11.6.2 Other accusations

Magic accusations are not the only accusations cast against domestic workers. The most common ones are theft, extramarital relations and the abuse of children. As with the magic accusations, not much evidence is generally demanded, as described in chapter 9. Deportation usually follows swiftly, but even a conviction without evidence is quite normal. An interview with an Emirati judge was particularly enlightening in this respect. When asked about cases he had judged involving domestic workers, he disregarded the possibility that their rights had been violated, by stating that all cases involving domestic workers concerned theft, boyfriends or violence towards the children. When questioned on the kind of evidence provided in such cases, he looked puzzled. His explanation was that employers have no reason to lie. Therefore, if an employer accuses a domestic worker, the accusation simply must be true.

According to an interviewee who had spent time in Dubai's detention center, many domestic workers there claimed to have been falsely accused. One illiterate Ethiopian was accused of stealing a computer, although she had no clue what to do with a computer. Another took care of a baby who hurt himself while playing, according to the domestic worker; she was accused of sexual abuse. In none of these cases did the police try to gather evidence.

There are several reasons for such accusations that apply, mutatis mutandis, to the magic accusations but which are more applicable to these three other types of accusations. First, the accusation might be true, or it might be believed to be true. There usually exists an enormous distrust between the employer and the domestic worker, which makes the employer suspect theft as soon as something disappears from the household. One domestic worker related how she had been accused of stealing something from the family while they were on vacation, although she had not even been allowed to join them on their trip. Second, the accusation may conceal violations of the rights of the domestic worker. In the famous case of Nour Miyati, who developed gangrene in her hands and feet due to daily beatings from her employer, Nour was accused of bringing strangers into the house who abused the children. No evidence was ever presented. As her lawyer stated, "But the shame over the fact that they had beaten her up this bad, was such a threat, that they would rather have her lose all her fingers and rot in jail than that anybody would find out."

Third, the accusation may conceal violations conducted by other family members. A Saudi psychiatrist stated that in cases of child abuse, the driver is usually blamed. Fourth, most contracts state that employers have to pay for the return ticket at the end of the contractual two-year period. If the domestic worker turns out to have committed a crime, however, she will be deported by the government: "If you get a big fight, you take her to the deportation center. Normally you pay, but if she has been wrong, then they pay." In other words, employers have a financial incentive to falsely accuse domestic workers of improprieties.

As Strobl concurs, there is often no hard evidence (particularly with the theft of money) to determine who is most likely telling the truth. However, discerning whether the domestic worker is guilty is irrelevant to the outcome of most cases. Under the law, if a sponsor wants to revoke sponsorship of a domestic worker, she has no right to contest this. Once the sponsor cancels the sponsorship, deportation proceedings begin.[619] Likewise, Human Rights Watch states that domestic workers risk spurious counter-accusations of theft, witchcraft and adultery if they try to bring charges of abuse against their employers.[620]

One must keep in mind that in Europe in the seventeenth and eighteenth centuries, the employer was similarly taken at his word when posing accusations against his personnel.[621] The types of accusations were even similar. Legitimate reasons to send servants away included mischief, wantonness, disobedience, fornication, theft, or drunkenness.[622] Certainly, some domestic workers do steal. They may think they are entitled to steal because the employer is not paying what the worker thinks he should.[623] They may do so simply because they want to have something, or they may do so to take revenge for bad treatment. Yet in light of the fact that (i) the police never ask for any evidence of theft; (ii) the employers rarely present the police with such evidence; and (iii) domestic workers are very consistent in their stories of being accused of theft when there are other conflicts occurring in the house, it seems safe to conclude that a false accusation of theft is regularly used to get rid of a domestic worker.

11.7 Summary

Domestic workers find themselves in an unusual position in their employers' houses. They are part of the family, yet they are not family. They are women who are very close physically and yet not close at all mentally. This leads to specific conflicts related to three different forms of otherness: (i) the foreign woman; (ii) the other woman; and (iii) the woman. As a foreign woman within the household, the domestic worker has a difficult position. On the one hand, her different way of communicating and her strange habits are threatening. On the other hand, she can be fascinating and enchanting.

---

619 Strobl (2009) P173.
620 Report 18, P4-5.
621 Molenaar (1953) P51.
622 Knegt (2008 a) P21.
623 See previous chapter.

This otherness as foreigner is especially significant in Saudi Arabia because of the Wahhabi teachings. The second form of otherness is the domestic worker as the other woman towards the wife. The domestic worker often forms or is perceived to form competition for the love of the husband and therefore the target of jealousy. This type of otherness is widespread in Saudi Arabia and the Emirates. Its pervasiveness is possibly related to the possibility of multiple marriages, as many women are concerned about having to share their husbands. As a third form of otherness, the domestic worker is a woman, and husbands or sons sometimes react to the domestic worker as they would to any other woman – as a woman who is different from a man and therefore both fascinating and threatening. This type of otherness is pervasive in the Emirates but even more so in Saudi Arabia, due to the segregation rules. These rules make interactions with women infrequent, which leads to a mystique about women and severe sexual tension.

As the husband and wife are at the same time employers with extensive power over the domestic worker, the usual conflicts between men and women can deteriorate into severe aggression, both physical and sexual. When this occurs (or threatens to occur), the 'other' is expelled from the family by means of all sorts of accusations. A historically common accusation used to expel the other from the inner circle is magic. This accusation is still common in Saudi Arabia and, to a lesser extent, in the Emirates. In other cases, accusations are made about boyfriends, theft, or abusive behavior towards the children.

The accusations are usually accepted as legitimate by the authorities without any further examination into the facts of the case. This demonstrates the employer's power to instantly end the work relationship, which stands in stark contrast to the domestic worker's inability to end her employment, as discussed in the previous chapter. By means of accusations the employer may end the work relationship at any time. Thus, the question of whether the accusations are true is, from a sociological point of view, as irrelevant as asking whether the claim of magic is true. Whether true or not, the accusations do something, they have an effect in reality: they expel the marginal other. At first sight, the crimes of extramarital sex and magic do not have much in common. However, this chapter shows that accusations of sex and magic are very much connected. They resemble practices from other places and other times because they perform a specific function relating to male desire, the fear of women and the restoration of peaceful family relations.

This chapter concerned the power relation between the domestic worker and her employer, because an imbalance in power can lead to behavior which is contrary to the norms of both parties and which is possible because nobody interferes. Rape is such a type of conflict: both employer and domestic worker agree that this is not allowed. Yet it happens. This chapter describes how the employer indeed holds very strong power over the domestic worker; he can have her deported at will, while the previous chapter described that she has no freedom to leave.

Such power can add to, among others, sexual harassment. Nobody interferes, because as discussed in chapter 5, customary norms prescribe that the government does not regulate what happens behind closed doors, a concept which, as discussed in chapter 8, is contrary to the Convention on the Elimination of all forms of Discrimination Against Women.

Yet rape not only has to do with power that allows it to happen, but also with the otherness of the domestic worker that can cause it. In such instances, the power of the employer to instantly remove her from the family prevents further aggravation of the situation. So the power of the employer over the domestic worker should be limited to diminish the possibility of abuse, but this should be done by enlargement of the freedom of the domestic worker, not by limiting the freedom of the employer to expel her. As described in chapter 6, both the Saudi and the Emirati governments propose alteration of the sponsorship system; in the future not the individual employer is to be the sponsor, but the Ministry of Labor or several large agencies. The data of chapter 10 suggest that such proposals are positive as they will enlarge the freedom of the domestic worker by limiting transaction costs. The data of this chapter suggest that the proposals are also positive because they limit the power of the employer over the domestic worker (he can no longer have her deported instantly), while his freedom to have her instantly expelled from his family is not limited.

PART FIVE

CONCLUSION

12. Summary, Conclusions and Recommendations

In this chapter, section one summarizes the results from this research and contains the answers to the five research sub-questions. Section two places these results into a single framework and provides an answer to the central research question: which factors influence the conflicts between domestic workers and their employers? It discusses the pivotal role of oil and point at three important point of theory developed in this dissertation. Section three extrapolates the results and discusses the extent to which this research provides answers to matters concerning domestic workers in other countries, and concerning other migrant workers and women in Saudi Arabia and the Emirates. As some of the research results led to new questions, section four offers suggestions for further research. Considering the aim of the research and its results, section five contains several policy recommendations for ways to improve the position of domestic workers both in Saudi Arabia and the Emirates.

12.1 Summary

12.1.1 Norms referred to in conflicts

Chapter one introduced a distinction in three types of conflicts. In the first type of conflict, there is disagreement from the outset regarding the norms that should apply. In such instances, the conflict is clearly connected to a preliminary disagreement over applicable norms. In the second type of conflict, the conflicting parties disagree as to behavior or a preferred outcome and only thereafter disagree over the norms that should apply. It is not a disagreement over the norms that leads to such a conflict, but disagreement over behavior or outcome, whereupon both parties refer to norms as discursive or justification tools. In the third type of conflict, both parties initially agree on the norms, but one party nevertheless acts contrary to these norms. Thereafter, the party that is in breach of the shared norm regularly refers to a norm that states that his behavior is a permitted exception. In short, type one conflicts commence with norm disagreement, type two conflicts commence without a clear concept of the applicable norms, and type three conflicts commence with a norm agreement.

This tripartite distinction has been useful for data analysis, in combination with the theory of legal pluralism. Legal pluralism, as described in chapter 3, is generally defined as a situation in which two or more legal systems coexist in one social field. Legal pluralism is the existence of more than one legal order, based on different sources of ultimate validity and maintained by organizations, including (but not limited to) the state, in one social location. Domestic workers in Saudi Arabia and the Emirates, as described in chapters 4 through 7, work in such a state of legal pluralism. There are customary, contractual, Islamic and formal legal norms to which both parties refer. By providing an overview of these norms, these chapters answered the following first three sub-questions: (i) In what way and to what extent do domestic workers and their employers refer to Islamic, customary, contractual and formal legal norms? (ii) Do conflicts concern disagreement over norms or disputes regarding behavior contrary to the norms upon which both parties agree? (iii) Which factors influence the Islamic, customary, contractual and formal legal norms that both parties (may) refer to in conflicts?

Chapter 4 described the Islamic norms to which both domestic workers and their employers may refer during conflicts. This chapter discussed how Sharia may be viewed as a collection of rhetorical tools or arguments that are used in power struggles throughout all strata of Islamic society, including conflicts between domestic workers and their employers. The result depends not on Sharia but on who is in power to decide which legal concept or normative tool will be applied. Such is the case with not only the position of domestic workers but also the position of women in general; their positions are both under attack and are defended through the use of Islamic discourse. Another argument regularly used to defend the proposition that Islam negatively influences the position of domestic workers is that female witnesses under Sharia only count as one half and that, in certain cases, non-Muslims are not permitted to testify at all. In practice though, the evidentiary rules are followed if the judges involved decide to do so. Thus, in the end, the result does not depend on an evidentiary rule, but on the judge. A third factor from Sharia that can theoretically deteriorate the position of the domestic worker, is that Islam (according to some interviewees) emphasizes that everyone has been given a place in society by God (Allah), which, therefore, must be accepted. Nevertheless, as with the position of women, Sharia also offers rhetorical or discursive resources that directly contradict this discourse which legitimizes and perpetuates inequalities.

Furthermore, there are several aspects of Sharia that can, theoretically, affect positively the position of domestic workers. The first is a view of Allah as a panoptic God who constrains the individual through the belief that God will one day punish him even for sins that no one witnessed. Another aspect of Sharia that Muslim interviewees regularly emphasized is the centrality to Islam of justice, basic human rights, dignity and equity. The concept of human rights, according to several interviewees, is not new to the Middle East, as it has already been introduced by the Prophet Mohammed. Apart from these general principles of Sharia that prescribe human rights and dignity, there are several specific Sharia rules for the proper treatment of slaves and workers. If all Muslims on the Arabian Peninsula followed these rules, the domestic workers would be doing rather well. Another possibly positive aspect of Sharia is the emphasis placed on the fact that contemporary domestic workers are neither slaves nor concubines. This distinction means that while slave owners are permitted to have sex with their slave, employers are not permitted to have sex with their domestic worker. In practice, though, employers are never punished for harassment and are rarely punished for rape. As domestic workers are migrants, their knowledge of Arabic is usually poor or non-existent, and as many are not Muslim, their capability to convince a decision-maker through use of Sharia rhetoric is very limited. In courts, domestic workers typically lose (see chapter 8). Within the house, the employer has more power than the domestic worker (see chapters 10 and 11). Therefore, he can easily enforce the to him more convenient interpretations of Sharia, using the normative tools that defend his preferred outcome.

Chapter 5 described customary norms and how they are changing because of the rapid economic changes taking place in both the Kingdom of Saudi Arabia and the United Arab Emirates. Over the last fifty years, both countries have undergone a process of industrialization in which production was moved from extended family units to companies and factories that are outside the family. This same transformation has taken place in Europe, but over a much longer period of time and in a different manner; thus, similarities could be deemed unlikely. Nevertheless, the similarities between Europe and the Gulf as to the customary norms that pertain to domestic workers are striking. Rollins describes three phases in the development of the position for domestic workers in Europe; a status-based phase, an intermediate phase, and a contractual phase. Domestic workers as well as employers in both Saudi Arabia and the Emirates make statements about the position of domestic workers that very much resemble these three phases. The difference between Europe versus Saudi Arabia and the Emirates is that, due to the speed of the economic changes, the three phases are recognized concurrently between families, within families and even in the discourse of one employer. At the same time, domestic workers expect or demand either a status-based or a contractual relation, depending on their country of origin and the issue at hand. The speed of these changes and the coexistence of different normative models can be referred to as anomie, as described by Durkheim.

Although both employer and employee maneuver between a patriarchal status model and a contractual model, the intermediate phase is never referred to as a normative model or an ideal to be followed. This phase is only acted out by certain employers, as it merely describes the situation in certain relationships. Therefore, an adjustment in Rollins' theory is proposed. Whereas Rollins presented her findings as three phases in the development of labor relations, the results from this research suggest that they concern two normative models: the status-based model and the contractual model. The intermediate phase concerns a labor relationship in which humiliation and even dehumanization are possible, as the enforcement mechanisms for the status model are disappearing, while the enforcement mechanisms for the contractual model are not yet in place. Rollins' description of the three phases is thus, in this dissertation, redefined as two models having an intermediate phase, wherein dehumanization is possible because the safeguards for the status model have disappeared, and the safeguards for the contractual model are not yet in place. The data from this research, furthermore, show that strategic maneuvering does not simply take place between the two models but between different subtypes as well. In addition, the data indicate that if parties have a preliminary, contradicting conviction as to the appropriate model, this can cause conflicts. The co-existing normative models are not only used for strategic maneuvering in (type two or three) conflicts, but they also cause (type one) conflicts.

Chapter 6 described both the contractual norms that domestic workers and their employers refer to in conflicts and the question where these norms come from. Because of a lack of information or incorrect information, domestic workers and employers often have very different perceptions as to the contractual norms that have been agreed to. These differences lead to many conflicts and raise questions regarding the binding force of these contracts. In the Philippines and Indonesia, middle men or agents do not provide important information such as exactly what the work entails, how many days and hours per week the domestic worker must work and the fact that most domestic workers are not permitted to freely leave the house. Domestic workers in these two countries regularly either must sign contracts they cannot read, contracts they are not permitted to read, multiple contracts, or they have no contract at all. Governments and other organizations use different standard contracts without an agreement as to which contract is binding or on the legal basis for such actions. During their training, domestic workers receive information that is incorrect, too vague and that should have been provided to the worker prior to her commitment to the job offer.

Agencies in Saudi Arabia and the Emirates also provide a great deal of incorrect information to the employers and regularly deny that the domestic worker signed a contract pre-departure. Often employers are not permitted to read the contract either. In addition, agencies regularly encourage employers to restrict the domestic workers' rights and freedoms. The result is a broad range of (type one) conflicts caused by disagreement over the applicable contractual norms. Such conflicts concern the most basic working conditions: salary, transaction costs, deductions, weekly days off, hours worked per day, confinement, tasks, experience, age and even the country in which a domestic worker will be employed.

Chapter 7 provided an overview of formal legal norms that concern domestic workers and that were either written or ratified by the Saudi or Emirati government. In both Saudi Arabia and the Emirates, domestic workers have been explicitly excluded from the protections of statutory labor laws because they work in the private sphere of the house that is still highly protected. The sponsorship system is a set of immigration regulations that allows for deportation of the domestic worker upon the wish of either the employer or government. Thus far, international protests against this system have been without much result, as the sponsorship system provides substantial financial means to both governments and several other parties. Moreover, it is perceived by Saudis and Emiratis as providing safeguards against the dangers of large migration flows.

Both Saudi Arabia and the Emirates have ratified several ILO treaties, but because neither country recognizes domestic workers as workers, these conventions are not applied to them. The most relevant and ratified rules of international law are the Palermo Protocol against human trafficking and the Convention on the Elimination of all forms of Discrimination Against Women (CEDAW). Many domestic workers, both in the Emirates and in Saudi Arabia, meet the definition for trafficking victims. The Palermo Protocol obligates states to offer assistance and protection to trafficking victims as well as to criminalize and prevent trafficking. However, this assistance and protection does not take place, probably because there is too much money involved in the maid trade. By prohibiting a distinction that has the effect of impairing the rights of women, the CEDAW prohibits both direct and indirect discrimination. As almost all domestic workers are female, excluding them from the protections of the labor law seems tantamount to indirect discrimination. However, CEDAW has practically no effect in either country.

The interplay of the four different types of norms, customary, contractual, Islamic and formal legal norms, can be referred to as legal pluralism. This interplay creates an unregulated arena or maneuvering space in which primarily the more powerful party, the employer, can tactically choose which norms to apply, which will usually be the norms more favorable for him. A larger maneuvering space or a larger reservoir of discursive tools, allows employers to enforce a larger range of outcomes that they prefer. This maneuvering space could be limited by formal legal norms, such as a labor law that protects the weaker party, the domestic worker, but they are excluded from the existing labor laws. However, even if domestic workers were covered by existing labor laws, their protections would be minimal; the formal legal protections for laborers are overall rather limited in both Saudi Arabia and the Emirates.

Therefore, chapter 7 described, primarily on the basis of the work of De Swaan, the way that Western labor law can be perceived as a collective good developed by the 'haves' to protect the 'have-nots' in their own interest. Under this analysis, labor laws emerged in Europe because the upper class was confronted with the problems created from the poor state of the underclass, such as crime, contagious diseases, the threat of strikes and revolutions, the need for (new) laborers to perpetuate wealth and the need for an economic level playing field. By improving the state of the underclass, the upper class also improved its own position. However, on the Arabian Peninsula, most lower class laborers are migrants who are generally deported for every possible (perceived) shortcoming. Thus, the societal factors that stimulated the upper class in the West to take protective steps toward the underclass barely exist on the Arabian Peninsula. This absence of incentives made effective labor laws unlikely to come into existence over the last decades. Currently, the societal stimuli for the upper class to protect laborers have, in part, come into existence. Still, substantial change cannot be expected, as the absence of a civil society further blocks the development of protective laws. The governments of Saudi Arabia and the Emirates are both dictatorial states. As such, they do not recognize either the freedom to unite, the right to collective action, or the freedom of expression. However, these rights all appear to be necessary for the creation of collective goods, such as protective laws. Therefore, even to the extent that the societal circumstances would stimulate labor protection for the poor to come into existence, this process barely takes place because of the lack of a civil society.

12.1.2 Conflict resolution mechanisms

Part III of this dissertation answered the fifth sub-question: which types of external conflict resolution methods are used, what are their usual outcomes and which factors influence these outcomes? The conflict resolution mechanisms were placed in the framework of the theory on citizenship, as formulated by Bosniak. She distinguishes three types of citizenship, which are helpful in analyzing the position of domestic workers. The right to legal protection can be referred to as civil citizenship. Political citizenship refers to the right to participate in public decision-making processes. Economic citizenship refers to the right to gain an independent economic existence on the market. Economic citizenship for domestic workers is not limited, and political citizenship is not what they seek. What they lack is civil citizenship, the right to legal protection by the government.

Domestic workers lack this type of citizenship because of two separate causes. Bosniak makes a distinction between (i) those who lack citizenship based on either their bureaucratic status or their lack of membership in a community and (ii) those who lack citizenship based on a lack of membership in the public community. The first category encompasses illegal migrants who have no official right to reside in a country. In many countries, they either have no rights or cannot enforce them, whereas in other countries, they have limited rights. The second category contains those members of the community who have a diminished membership in the public community, including women and others whose lives are largely contained within the private sphere of a household, such as children and domestic workers. Both in Saudi Arabia and the Emirates, these two causes strongly diminish the civil citizenship of domestic workers. The first cause is that they are migrants, working and residing under the sponsorship regulations as described in chapter 7 on formal legal norms. The second cause for limited civil citizenship is a status that domestic workers in Saudi Arabia and the Emirates share with domestic workers worldwide and, more generally, with all women worldwide: second-class citizenship. This gender-related limitation to civil citizenship in the two countries researched, works via three concepts: the private sphere of the house, the *mahram* (person who can function as male representative) and *khulwa* or seclusion. These three concepts are all related to the patriarchal system, not to Islam.

Chapter 8 described what this limited civil citizenship of domestic workers looks like in empirical reality: domestic workers are excluded from the Saudi and Emirati Labor Laws and therefore, they have no official access to the labor offices that are designated to deal with conflicts between employers and employees. Other conflict resolution mechanisms do not compensate for this exclusion. Domestic workers in general are too afraid to go to the police, and they seem to be correct in this fear. They are regularly brought back by the police to their, possibly abusive, employers and apparently are sometimes abused by the police themselves. In the Emirates, this situation seems be improving though. In Saudi Arabia, the Governor's office, the National Society for Human Rights and the Human Rights Commission function in an ombudsman role, but all three are rather prejudiced against domestic workers. Another possibility would be to refer to the Saudi Sharia courts. However, many Sharia judges apparently refuse to look into cases concerning domestic workers.

In the Emirates, in a conflict, domestic workers are officially supposed to turn to the mediation offices under the responsibility of the Ministry of Interior. In Abu Dhabi, this office did exist, but in Dubai, it did not. Diplomats in the Emirates also occasionally take cases to the Sharia Courts or the attached reconciliation committee if a rule of Islamic law has been broken. However, domestic workers and diplomats complain about the very meager chances of winning a case. The evidentiary problems in the Sharia courts, language problems and a lack of knowledge regarding the legal system could possibly be alleviated, in part, by legal representation, but there is practically no legal aid available to domestic workers.

Many domestic workers apparently use connections through friends or family to return home or disappear on the black market, but these workers are difficult to research. Other runaways turn to the agency of the employer for help. Some agencies place the workers with another employer, but they also reportedly abuse domestic workers frequently. Additional places to turn to for help include the two (or possibly three) government shelters in Saudi Arabia, although they are reported to be overcrowded, dirty and prison-like. Deportation usually follows swiftly. In the Emirates, the government shelter is practically empty; no domestic worker is allowed to enter it. No other safe or corruption-free shelter has been found. Hotlines are also impossible to find. Several embassies have opened their own safe houses, which are also overcrowded and seemingly corrupt. Domestic workers have no proper redress in their countries of origin either. The access to justice for domestic workers is, thus, extremely limited. The effect is that they cannot bargain in the shadow of the law; their employers, in negotiations, do not have to consider what result a domestic worker could reach in court, as she cannot reach anything there. Thus, he can, on the basis of his power, impose the result that he desires.

To provide further explanation for the inadequate access to law for domestic workers in Saudi Arabia and the Emirates, chapter 9 described the overall malfunction of the Saudi and Emirati legal systems and linked it to the rentier state theory. The legal systems in both Saudi Arabia and the Emirates have many shortcomings. The rule that persons can be held legally accountable only for rules they could have known is not applied; there are many unknown and untraceable rules. The unavailability of access to justice is a problem with which not only domestic workers but also most other non-citizen residents struggle. The number of available and well-qualified lawyers and judges is low and free legal aid for the poor is not available. An important problem for women, particularly in Saudi Arabia, is the unavailability of female legal aid and female judges. Non-application of Sharia seems to be the rule instead of the exception. According to all interviewees, the party that wins a case is usually the more powerful one, while in the lower strata of society, people seem to lose every conflict.

Although there is no rule of law, there is something of a system that regulates the issue of who usually wins in a conflict; the man with *wasta,* a word that can be translated as 'connections' or 'clout'. A person's *wasta* is determined from a combination of patriarchy, tribalism, cronyism, and the power to corrupt or bribe. Whoever has the least clout, the least *wasta,* loses a conflict. This party is usually the domestic worker, as she forms the bottom stratum of society; she has no family or tribe in the destination country. She lacks the funds to obtain legal aid or bribe a judge, and she does not know any princes. Employers seem to know this, and they seem to act upon the knowledge that, in the case of a conflict, the domestic worker will always lose.

To answer the question why the legal system functions poorly, chapter 9 referred to the rentier state theory, in the following way: states that receive substantial amounts of revenue (rent) from the outside world on a regular basis, combined with a relative absence of revenue from domestic taxation, tend to become autonomous from their societies, unaccountable to their citizens and autocratic. Such states fail to develop in the direction of the rule of law. This dissertation adds the following point to the rentier state theory. As the governments of Saudi Arabia and the Emirates have an independent source of income and, thus, cannot be forced into organizing a proper legal system, individuals have no choice but to protect themselves through ulterior systems including patriarchy, tribalism, cronyism, and corruption (which collectively determine somebody's *wasta*). As domestic workers form the bottom stratum of society, they do not have *wasta* and are the ultimate victims of the oil revenues. The fact that they are 'victims' of the oil revenues is not because the oil revenues have made their employers rich enough to hire domestic workers, but because the oil allows the governments concerned to ignore abusive individuals, including many domestic workers' employers.

Although this is true both for the Kingdom of Saudi Arabia and the United Arab

Emirates, the rule of law in Saudi Arabia is even less developed than in the Emirates. The primary reason seems to be the fact that, in contrast to the Emirates, Saudi Arabia has had a class of religious leaders with a strong power base for centuries. In the Trias Politica framework of Montesquieu, the Al Sheikh family and their cronies occupy two out of three branches of power. The power of this nobility over the judiciary is strong. The government (the family Saud and its cronies), therefore intends to create all sorts of specialized courts; as the layers of an onion, they intend to peel off the power of the judicial establishment. As can be expected, the legal-religious class resists such change. In the Emirates, the situation of the legal system seems to be somewhat better; most interviewees were somewhat positive about either the legal system or the reforms.

12.1.3 Dynamics in the house

Part IV of this dissertation answered the fourth sub-question: (iv) which party is able to enforce its own norms or to act contrary to norms on which both parties agree, and which factors influence this (im)balance of power? It addresses the dynamics in the house, the unequal power distribution and related conflicts. Considered from an economic perspective, the result from these constraints cannot be labeled a free labor market. Although recruitment may, to some extent, have been free (though severe poverty can reduce this freedom to nothing), as soon as the domestic worker arrives at the workplace, her freedom vanishes. The result is a phenomenon that economists call monopsony, a market form with only one buyer. This gives the employer the power to unilaterally decide on salary and the amount of hours to be worked. The welfare loss suffered by the domestic worker is larger than the gain for the employer, which is the reason that this situation can be considered Pareto inefficient.

In the international press, the situation is not described as monopsony, but as modern-day slavery. The most frequently cited definition is the one given by the League of Nations committee on slavery: "The state or condition of a person over whom any or all the powers attaching to the right of ownership are exercised." This right of ownership is what distinguishes slavery from all other forms of dependency and involuntary labor. According to this definition, domestic workers are not slaves in either Saudi Arabia or the Emirates, because they are not officially the property of the employer. However, this definition depends upon the concepts of ownership and property, concepts that are relatively new in history, while the institution of slavery is very old. The United Nations has abandoned the concept of property in persons, but the organization has not succeeded in abandoning the type of slavery that existed before the concept of property came into being: a power relationship in which one person has extreme control over another. Such extreme control is not possible where an organization protects individuals from being placed in such a position. According to Patterson's definition of slavery that he based on historic research concerning this phenomenon, domestic workers in Saudi Arabia and the Emirates are slaves. The employer holds extreme power over the worker; he can make her work all day and decide how much and whether she eats or sleeps. He is considered to have the right to use a certain level of violence to make her obey (chapter 5), and he can deport her at will (chapters 7 and 11). Many domestic workers cannot leave his sphere of influence, either physically or psychologically, and the situation is described in terms of his rights (based on the contract and payments to the agency) and her duty to fully obey him. As the labor relationship is perceived as a private issue in which the government may not interfere (chapters 5 and 7), no one protects the domestic worker from the power of the employer. Therefore, using Patterson's description of slavery, that is what domestic workers are, albeit only for the two-year term of a contract. As the relation is not one of property, but of extreme power, it is usually referred to as bonded labor. However, because it is akin to pre-Roman slavery, to slavery as it existed before the invention of the concept of property over persons, this labor relationship can also be referred to as 'power slavery' as opposed to 'property slavery'. This term has advantage over the term 'bonded labor', as it clarifies the similarity between the position of the domestic worker and the position of women and children, in such locations where the patriarch is considered the state within the private sphere of the household: in such locations where no organization is deemed to be allowed to protect individuals against extreme power of others over them.

Finally, chapter 11 described the unusual position domestic workers find themselves in within their employers' houses. They are part of the family, yet they are not family. They are women who are very close physically, yet not close at all mentally. This position leads to specific conflicts related to three different forms of 'otherness': (i) the foreign woman, (ii) the other woman, and (iii) the woman. As a foreign woman within the household, the domestic worker has a difficult position. On the one hand, her different way of communicating and her strange habits are threatening. On the other hand, she can be fascinating and enchanting. This otherness as foreigner is especially significant in Saudi Arabia because of the Wahhabi teachings. The second form of otherness is the domestic worker as the other woman toward the wife. The domestic worker often forms or is perceived to form competition for the love of the husband and therefore the target of jealousy. This type of otherness is widespread in Saudi Arabia and the Emirates. Its pervasiveness is potentially related to the possibility of multiple marriages, as many women are concerned that they will have to share their husbands. As a third form of otherness, the domestic worker is a woman, and husbands or sons sometimes react to the domestic worker as they would to any other woman: as a woman who is different from a man and, therefore, both fascinating and threatening. This type of otherness is pervasive in the Emirates and even more so in Saudi Arabia, because of the segregation rules. These rules render interactions with women infrequent, which leads to a mystique regarding women and severe sexual tension.

As the husband and wife are also the employers with extensive power over the domestic worker, small conflicts can deteriorate into severe aggression, both physical and sexual. When this occurs (or threatens to occur), the 'other' is regularly expelled from the family via all sorts of accusations. A historically common accusation used to expel the other from the inner circle is magic. This accusation is still common in Saudi Arabia and, to a lesser extent, in the Emirates. In other cases, accusations are made regarding boyfriends, theft, or abusive behavior toward the children.

These accusations are usually accepted by the authorities as legitimate, without any further examination into the facts of the case. This activity demonstrates the employer's power to instantly end the work relationship, which stands in stark contrast to the domestic worker's inability to end her employment, as discussed in chapter 10. Via accusations, the employer may end the work relationship at any time. Thus, the question of whether the accusations are true is, from a sociological point of view, as irrelevant as asking whether the claim of magic is true. Whether true or not, the accusations have a real effect: they expel the marginal other. At first glance, the crimes of extramarital sex and magic do not have much in common. However, chapter eleven revealed that accusations of sex and magic are very much connected. They resemble practices from other places and times, as they perform a specific function relating to male desire, the fear of women and the restoration of peaceful family relations.

Chapter 11 concerned the power relationship between the domestic worker and her employer, as an imbalance in power can lead to behavior that is contrary to the norms of both parties and is possible because no one interferes. Rape is such a type of conflict; both employer and domestic worker agree that this is not permitted. Yet, it happens. This chapter demonstrated that the employer holds a very strong power over the domestic worker; he can have her deported at will, while chapter ten established that she has no freedom to leave. Such power can add up to, among other issues, sexual harassment. No one interferes, because, as discussed in chapter 5, customary norms prescribe that the government does not regulate what happens behind closed doors. However, rape is related not only to the power of the employer that allows it to happen but also to the otherness of the domestic worker. In such instances, the power of the employer to instantly remove her from the family prevents further aggravation of the situation. Thus, the power of the employer over the domestic worker should be limited to diminish the possibility of abuse, but this should be done by enlargement of the freedom of the domestic worker, not by limiting the freedom of the employer to expel her.

12.2 Answer to the research question

12.2.1 Putting the pieces together

The central question underlying this research is, as stated in chapter 1, the following: which factors influence the (emergence and character of) conflicts in the Kingdom of Saudi Arabia and the United Arab Emirates between domestic workers and their employers, the norms both parties (may) refer to and the related (im)balance of power? This section aims to combine the research results as summarized in the previous section, to answer this research question. All of the results from will be visualized in a single framework, which is presented below in a stepwise manner. Allow me to add the remark here that, as this research methods did not concern Popperian falsification of one hypothesis but grounded theory methods, the arrows drawn below are not intended to stand for rock-solid conclusions. They merely draw the picture that, based on all the data gathered for this research, is the most likely answer to the research question.

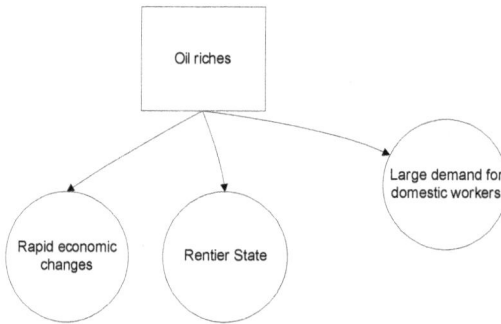

Large oil fields have been discovered both in Saudi Arabia and the Emirates, which caused three important issues. First, the oil revenues have created, as discussed in chapters 2 and 9, the rentier state, a state that has an independent source of income and, therefore, functions independently of its own population. Second, the discovery of oil caused, as discussed in chapters 3 and 5, extremely rapid economic changes. Third, because of the oil revenue, a large portion of the population is now able to afford domestic workers.

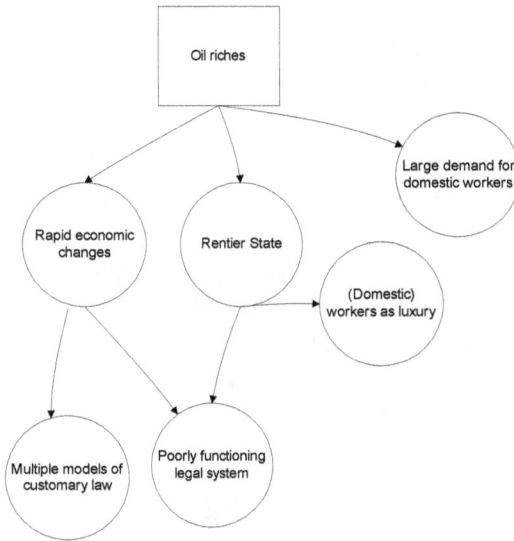

The rentier state has had two effects. For one, as the population has no means to force the government to actually govern the country and organize the necessary services, the rentier state contributes to a poorly functioning legal system (as discussed in chapter 9). In addition, the government has attempted to appease the population by providing luxuries (chapter 2) of which the domestic workers are an important part. The rapid economic changes, as discussed in chapter 5, have led to the co-existence of multiple models of customary norms. Furthermore, as the former legal system of social control is no longer sufficient, a top-down legal system has become necessary, but the government does not provide this, as it is a rentier state.

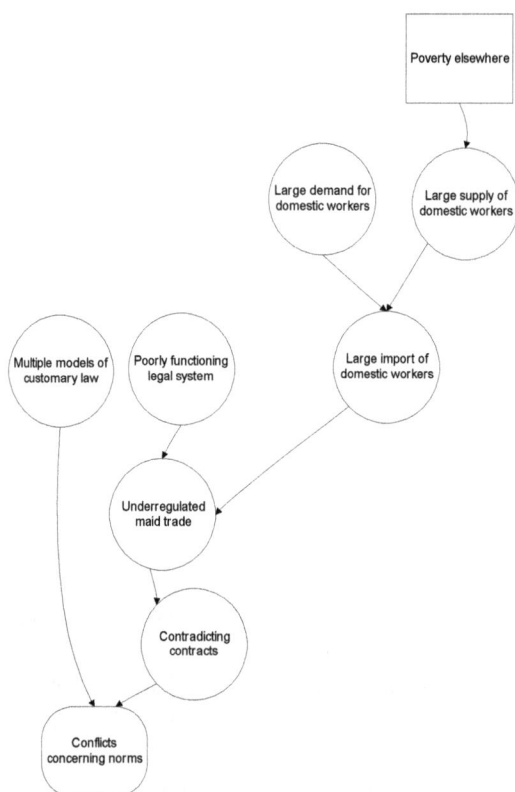

The picture becomes somewhat more complicated. Because of poverty elsewhere, there is a huge supply of domestic workers worldwide. Demand in Saudi Arabia and the Emirates, combined with the large supply from elsewhere, has created a large import of domestic workers. As the legal system functions poorly, the maid trade is under-regulated. This situation creates many conflicts concerning the contractual norms, as discussed in chapter 6. Furthermore, due to the rapid economic changes, there are multiple models of customary law: the status based model and various contractual models. This, as discussed in chapter 5, also causes conflicts concerning norms.

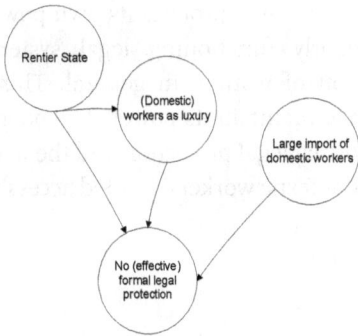

As discussed in chapter 7, based on the theory of De Swaan it is plausible that because of the rentier state and the large flow of migrant workers, the 'haves' do not
have much of an incentive to protect the 'have-nots'. To the contrary; the domestic
workers form part of the luxuries supplied by the rentier states to appease the
Saudi and Emirati population. Therefore, little or no formal legal protection has
come into existence.

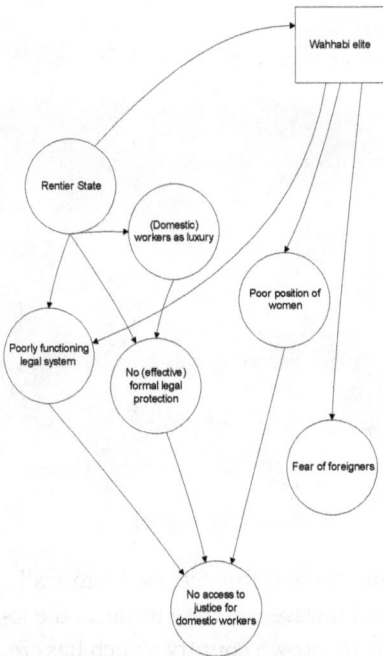

A societal factor, which primarily has an effect in Saudi Arabia, not in the Emirates,
is Wahhabism. The Wahhabis have a long standing agreement with the Sauds and
as long as the Sauds are kept in power with oil money, the Wahhabis are also likely

to remain in power. The Wahhabi legal-religious nobility protects its own power position and, as such, contributes to a poorly functioning legal system. Furthermore, its teachings weaken the position of women in general. Third, Wahhabism spreads a fear of anything foreign to maintain its power. The poorly functioning legal system, the lack of effective formal legal protection and the poor position of women in general all influence the domestic workers' limited access to justice.

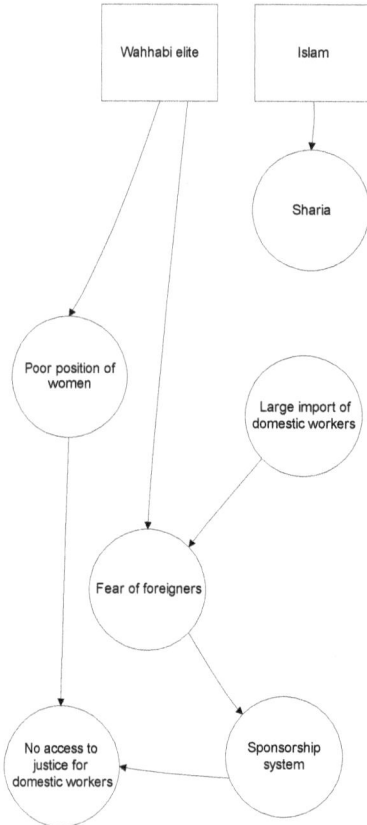

```
┌──────────────┐      ┌──────────────┐
│ Wahhabi elite│      │    Islam     │
└──────────────┘      └──────────────┘

                            Sharia

  Poor position of
      women
                       Large import of
                      domestic workers

       Fear of foreigners

  No access to        Sponsorship
  justice for           system
  domestic workers
```

In the Emirates, Wahhabism does not have this same influence, as, historically, there is no strong religious elite in power there. However, in the Emirates, the local population has become a very small minority in its own country, which has created the same fear of foreigners; the domestic workers already outnumber the citizens. This fear of foreigners keeps the sponsorship system in place, as discussed in chapter 7. The sponsorship system is another factor limiting domestic workers' access to justice.

Both the Emirates and Saudi Arabia are Muslim countries. Therefore, it is appropriate to consider Islam and Sharia (with the presumption that they can be separated, while in reality this is more difficult). As described in chapter 4, Sharia can be viewed as a collection of discursive tools. In practice, both men and women as well as employers and domestic workers, refer to Sharia to defend their positions. Therefore, in this depiction, it is not Sharia that influences the poor position of women, but the Wahhabi elite, which has the power to implement certain interpretations or discursive tools and discard others. Therefore, Islam and Sharia are in this picture not connected to the other societal factors.

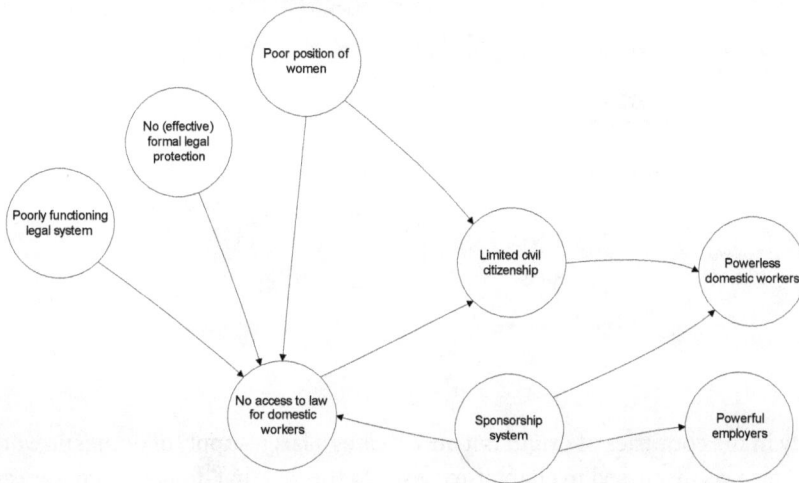

The sponsorship system adds to the domestic worker's lack of access to justice. These two factors, in addition to the overall poor position of women, result in an extremely limited civil citizenship for the domestic worker, as discussed in chapter 8. The limited civil citizenship leads to a powerless position for the domestic worker, while the sponsorship system creates, in contrast, a very powerful position for the employer (see also chapter 10).

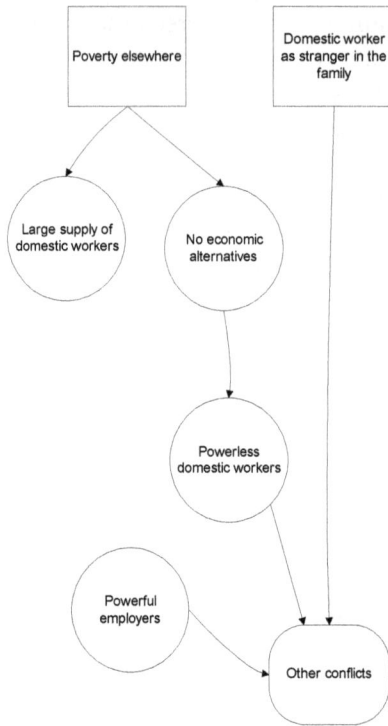

Poverty in the countries of origin not only creates a large supply of domestic workers but also, as discussed in chapter 10, leads to the fact that domestic workers are generally not in the financial position to leave their employer. This lack of freedom to leave their employer adds to her powerlessness. As discussed in chapter 11, the final complicating factor is the position of the domestic worker as a stranger in the family. This issue, combined with the very powerful position of the employer and the powerless position of the domestic worker, leads to many conflicts. Such conflicts in general do not concern norms. They are often more violent conflicts that are usually resolved by expulsion of the domestic worker from the family.

Combining all these illustrations, we get the following picture:

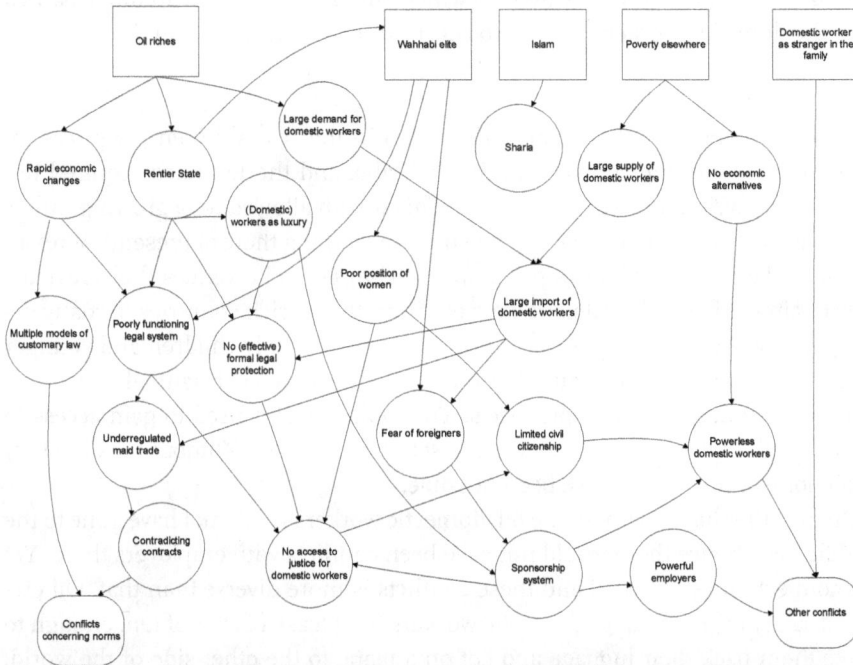

Many additional aspects could be included in this overview. For example, the discovery of oil has, as described in chapter 2, also created Dutch Disease. This concerns the phenomenon that, due to the export of oil, the currencies of both Saudi Arabia and the Emirates have risen, which results in a high level of difficulty for the development of other export-oriented sectors of the economy. This adds to unemployment among citizens, which contributes to a fear of foreign workers whom are perceived as threats on the tight job market. Furthermore, the variety in countries of origin leads, as discussed in chapter 5, to different expectations with respect to customary norms. This could have been added in the overview, but is not. Poverty in the country of origin leads to corruption, which adds to the underregulation of the maid trade. However, the picture, as painted above, is intended to summarize the most important factors, not to be complete. Furthermore, as stated before, not all the arrows are based on rock-solid evidence. It is the picture that, based on the data of this research, shows the most relevant aspects of the most likely answer to the research question.

On the basis of this overview of the most important factors that influence the (emergence and character of) conflicts in the Kingdom of Saudi Arabia and the United Arab Emirates between domestic workers and their employers, the next section will provide suggestions to reduce the occurrence of conflicts between domestic workers and their employers in Saudi Arabia and the Emirates. But first, this section will discuss the extent to which these results apply to other parties than the domestic workers in the two countries concerned.

12.2.2 Oil: the black curse

Oil was discovered on the Arabian Peninsula in the 1930s. When the prices increased sharply in the 1970s, both Saudi Arabia and the Emirates acquired unprecedented wealth in a very short time. This wealth allowed for a growing inflow of female domestic workers (about two million working there at present). With an average salary of around $200 per month per worker, oil revenues thus created a flow of almost five billion dollars per year from the oil rich countries to many developing countries where it feeds family members (mainly children and younger siblings). It educates, medicates and shelters them, which substantially raises the next generation's economic prospects. The money is also used to gain access to nations with higher salaries, and even to set up businesses. Without the discovery of oil none of this would have been possible.

On the other hand, without the oil, domestic workers would not have gone to the Middle East, hence there would not have been conflicts with employers there. Yet the connection between oil and these conflicts is more diverse than that. Oil created a salary differential for domestic workers by at least a factor of ten, enough to make them pack their luggage and get on a plane to the other side of the world. They don't (properly) speak the language, they don't understand the culture and the religion, or even the way they are supposed to do their household chores. Because of oil, young girls from the villages around Jakarta, girls who don't even speak proper Bahasa and who have never seen a gas stove or a microwave, get on planes and travel to Arab families, where they are expected to know how to prepare the traditional soup during Ramadan. This leads to conflicts.

Oil has also led to such unprecedented economic changes that both societies are rather confused and could even be called schizophrenic. Weddings are celebrated in twenty-first-century luxury hotels according to a complex mixture of long-standing traditions and new fashions. With one foot in Bedouin life and the other in a post-industrialized society, both Saudi Arabia and the Emirates suffer from substantial lack of clarity regarding their norms and behavioral patterns. Is the domestic worker supposed to be a family member (albeit with a somewhat lower position)? Do her actions bring shame on the family? Is her employer responsible for her good name, finances and immortal soul? Or is she merely a contract worker who should neither be patronized nor protected?

This lack of clarity in normative patterns can itself lead to conflicts, but rapid changes have also taken place in the (efficiency of) mechanisms for enforcement of norms. Social control no longer functions properly, yet no other adequate rule-enforcement mechanisms have been set up to replace it. Oil has changed society there from tightly knit smaller groups into anonymous metropoles. The grandmothers of today once assisted their husbands in maintaining peace among their extended families. Now they often have no idea what their grandsons are up to when they jump in their sports cars. Are they going to share a traditional *shisha* water pipe with friends, or are they visiting a former domestic worker who has been forced into prostitution? Social control used to be sufficient; now a police force is needed, but that force has not been properly set up.

Again, oil plays a role in this: proper law-enforcement mechanisms, the rule of law, they have not (yet?) come into existence. Both governments have had only a brief period of time to achieve this Herculean task, but in fact neither government has reason to do so. When governments need money from their populations (as in Europe and the United States), they are forced to listen to their taxpayers about how to spend it. Thanks to the discovery of oil, the Saudi and Emirati governments have independent sources of income. This allows them to behave in a dictatorial manner. If they do not feel inclined to set up a proper system for law implementation, or if they feel it is not in their interest, then they do not.

In other parts of the Middle East, 2011 was the year of the Arab Spring, but such was not the case in Saudi Arabia and the United Arab Emirates. Again, we have to look at the influence of oil: both governments basically bribe their citizens into acquiescence with oil revenues. Protests were comparatively negligible in the Emirates, where the government provides all the basics; housing, schooling and healthcare are available to citizens. In Saudi Arabia not all citizens are properly taken care of, and the Arab Spring did have an effect there. The king immediately promised new funding, and the unrest subsided. Among the luxuries provided by the dictators to appease their citizens are domestic workers. Neither government does much to improve the situation of domestic workers, who are migrants, vis-à-vis their employers, who are citizens. Migrants can be deported, but citizens cannot, or at least not on this scale.

Because of (a) Saudi Arabia's endless oil reserves, (b) production flexibility, which makes it of pivotal importance to the stability of oil prices, (c) the threat Iran poses to Saudi Arabia's stability (the oil fields are located in a region populated mainly by Shi'a Muslims), and (d) the geographically strategic position of the Emirates with regard to Iran and their willingness to host a U.S. military presence, it is unlikely that the West will put pressure on either country to ratify the Convention on Domestic workers, or to undertake other substantive projects to protect these migrant workers. Again, oil plays a pivotal role.

The flow of migrant workers will not stop as long as the oil flows. That raises another problem. In Europe's past the upper classes had incentives to provide various forms of aid to the less fortunate, but such is not the case in the Middle East, where every problematic worker can be deported instantly. There have been, of course, large migrant flows in Europe, but deportation was not as easy there as it currently is in the Gulf. The deserts that provide the oil also form an impenetrable barrier. Oil revenues finance extensive and technically sophisticated border patrols, including iris scans. Because of those revenues, the governments need neither the financial means of their citizens, nor their labor. All workers can be deported, hence there is no incentive for the upper class to improve the position of the lower classes.

A final connection between oil and the conflicts can be found not only in the billions of dollars per annum in remittances, but also in the substantial fees paid to the maid trade. These fees flow partly into the pockets of those who could fight human trafficking, and who could properly regulate the international maid trade. The red tape and resulting bribes (which ultimately come from the oil revenues) allow a situation to exist that can best be described as a spaghetti junction of contracts that contradict each other – and as such cause conflicts. The countries of origin have low per-capita GDPs and low government salaries, which makes their officials more susceptible to bribes from oil money, which in turn prevents both proper regulation of the maid trade and prosecution of traffickers.

The discovery of oil in Saudi Arabia and the Emirates has had a massive impact (even though oil reserves in the Emirates have since shrunk). In a myriad of ways – the speed of economic changes, the dictatorships supported by its revenues, the flows of remittances, the bribes and red tape – oil causes conflicts, and also severely weakens the position of domestic workers in these conflicts. If the question "What causes the high occurrence of conflicts between domestic workers and their employers in Saudi Arabia and the Emirates?" could be answered in one word, that word would be oil.

12.2.3 Theory development

Legal pluralism and conflicts

On a more theoretical level, what can we learn from conflicts involving domestic workers? One important lesson is the extension of the theory of legal pluralism. Current theories suggest that a plurality of normative orders allows flexibility in conflict resolution. The parties involved can maneuver strategically, choosing a conflict resolution mechanism and the norms they appeal to, in order to achieve their preferred outcome. This research shows that legal pluralism has more consequences. First, contradicting norms not only offer choices in existing conflicts, they can also lead to conflicts. Second, if one of the parties is more powerful than the other, legal pluralism works mainly to the advantage of that more powerful party. This research also shows that conflicts can usefully be divided into different categories: (i) conflicts about disagreement on norms, (ii) conflicts about behavior without preliminary norms, or (iii) conflicts about behavior contrary to shared norms. The division in categories moved the focus from the individual conflict to the broader question of what caused the disagreement over norms, and it may do the same in other research.

Rentier state theory

Three distinct contributions to rentier state theory, which describes how governments with independent income sources become unaccountable to their citizens and turn into dictatorships, are made by this research. First, this dissertation describes how dictators have no reason to set up properly functioning legal systems, which is a disadvantage to those at the bottom of the social hierarchy. Second, revenues other than taxes not only make governments independent of their citizens' financial means, but also of their labor force. This again diminishes the incentive to care for those at the bottom of the social hierarchy. Migrant workers are imported and deported on an unprecedented scale, especially in Dubai where migrants make up more than 90 percent of the population. As a result, the Saudi and Emirati governments are completely globalized in both their finances and their work forces. This obstructs not only the democratization processes, but also the development of rule of law in general and labor law in particular. The third contribution to rentier state theory could be called the export of the rentier state. The trade in humans, the migrant-worker industry, creates large flows of money from rentier states to the governments of countries of origin in the form of official fees, bribes and red tape, thus making those governments less accountable to their own populations as well.

Intersectionality and slavery

Female migrant workers in particular are in a vulnerable position because of their severely limited access to justice. They are largely excluded from the legal system based on the fact that they are both non-citizens and women, an intersectionality of gender and bureaucratic status. The concepts of *khulwa* and *mahram* and the strictly protected private sphere of the household all serve to limit women's access to justice, as does the sponsorship system for migrants. The concept of intersectionality highlights the fact that discrimination often occurs based on a combination of classifications such as gender, race, nationality, class and sexual orientation. Intersectionality has the advantage of emphasizing that double discrimination often leads to a greater than double disadvantage. The concept also has its limitations in that it creates an illusion of coherence and gives the false impression that discrimination under different regimes has more in common than just the end results. Limited access to justice for women is connected to the patriarchal system. Discrimination against migrants is better analyzed using neo-Marxist theories, for example, as the migrants' subordinate position is tied to the political economies of both countries. Does this intersectionality of discrimination against female migrants, their limited access to justice and the resulting lack of effective rights make them modern-day slaves, as is often claimed? One needs a proper definition of slavery to answer this question. To that end, this dissertation introduced the concept of power slavery, in which one individual holds extreme power over another, but does not hold property rights. This concept has an advantage over that of bonded labor. It clarifies how the domestic worker's position is connected to that of wives and children, in such situations where the patriarch is considered the head of state within the private sphere of the household.

12.3 Extrapolation

This section discusses the extent to which these research results are also applicable beyond the specifics of this research topic; to what extent are they applicable to domestic workers in other countries, to other migrant workers in the same countries and to women in general the same countries? The answer to this question can best be illustrated using the above drawing and the factors in it which are likely to have effect elsewhere or on others.

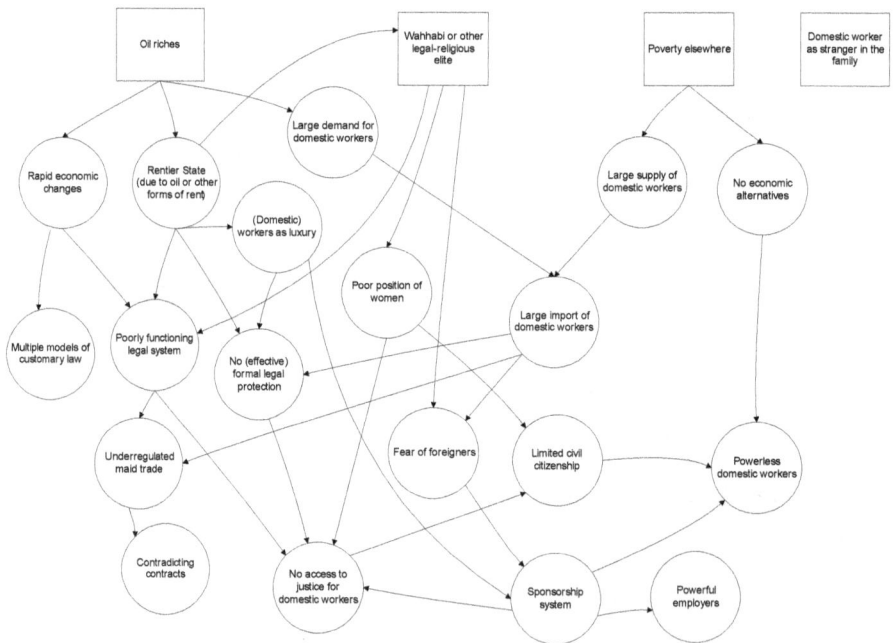

As Islam was of little consequence, that factor has been removed. Luckily, the Wahhabi elite has power only in Saudi Arabia, and therefore, this factor will be of little influence elsewhere. However, other legal-religious elites in power in other countries can, in the same manner, limit the protection of the lower classes in their own interest. For instance, in Iran, the legal-religious elite is likely to worsen the position of women and to enhance distrust toward foreigners to retain its power. While in Iran this has not led to visa regulations comparable to the sponsorship system, this factor influences the position of domestic workers in the other Gulf countries that do have this system. In these countries, access to justice is also limited, and therefore, civil citizenship is limited. This factor influences the position of all migrant workers. The discovery of oil, likewise, has its influence in other oil countries (such as the Gulf countries), but the rentier state may also be caused by other factors. If a country receives comparable large amounts of for instance donor money, this factor also renders governments less accountable to their residents and, therefore, will deteriorate both the legal system and formal legal protection. As such, development aid may actually diminish access to justice for several groups in society. Rapid economic changes may also be caused by other factors than oil. For instance, Hong Kong has seen an unprecedented growth, which may have led to comparable phenomena of the co-existence of multiple models of customary law or the poor functioning of the legal system. Additionally, of course, throughout the world, poverty is a factor that influences the lack of power for domestic workers and many other migrant workers; without viable economic alternatives, workers are vulnerable to abuse. Last but not least, the position of the domestic worker as stranger in the family, as discussed in chapter 11, also has an influence worldwide. However, whether this leads to violent conflicts depends on the power balance between the two parties and the freedom that both parties have to end the labor relation. Because of this precarious position, it should always be easy for the employer to hire another worker and for the domestic worker to find another employer.

The picture also clearly shows which factors will influence the position of other migrant workers and women in Saudi Arabia and the Emirates. Although they thank their job to oil, other migrant workers also suffer the consequences of oil, as they are equally affected by the sponsorship system, the poorly functioning legal system and the fear of foreigners. Saudi and Emirati women in general suffer from limited access to justice and limited civil citizenship. In the Emirates this is caused by the combination of rapid economic changes and the rentier state, while in Saudi Arabia the Wahhabi religious elite adds to that as a third factor undermining the position of women in general.

12.4 Suggestions for further research

12.4.1 *Quantitative research*
The introductory chapter states that the quoted Human Rights Watch report gives the impression that the position of domestic workers in the Middle East is worse than elsewhere. Reports 8, 17, 18 and 19 support this suggestion, as do several

interviewees from NGOs in Manila and Jakarta as well as interviewees from the International Labour Organization. Nevertheless, no hard quantitative data are available to confirm this. Hard numbers are available neither on the domestic workers that are actually employed in Saudi Arabia and the Emirates, nor on the number of runaways. No study has been able to quantify the reasons that domestic workers run away, nor the percentages of the domestic workers that should be considered victims of trafficking. This research has not been able to provide such quantitative answers either. Extensive multi-site, multi-method research is required for the correct answers. For the best results, such research should be executed by a team of both male and female researchers to limit researcher bias. Furthermore, cooperation of the governments concerned must be asserted to gain access to certain locations, such as detention centers and deportation centers. Funds are needed to hire translators from different backgrounds, to prevent sample bias based on nationality. Furthermore, it is recommended to interview domestic workers at airports upon arrival in their countries of origin, as this method provides access to large groups of domestic workers, both runaways and those who were satisfied with their employers. At the airports of the destination countries, if local authorities would allow this, researchers could determine to what extent the workers have been promised realistic work conditions and, thus, to what extent they are victims of trafficking due to deception by agents. Researchers from the same nationality as the domestic workers are likely to gain the best access to the black market, to assess the extent to which domestic workers employed there ran away because of conflicts with their employers or for other, possibly financial reasons. Researchers with the nationality of the destination countries are most likely to gain proper access to employers for interviews concerning conflicts. These interviews may be conducted individually, in discussion groups, through questionnaires, or via social networks such as Facebook.

12.4.2 Sociology of the Palermo Protocol

Although further quantitative research is needed, on the basis of the data in this research, it seems a safe estimate that at least one-third of the domestic workers in the Emirates and in Saudi Arabia meet the definition of trafficking victims. This portion is primarily for the following three reasons: (1) they regularly end up in situations of forced labor and exploitation; (2) they are regularly misinformed regarding important work conditions; and (3) they are often minors. Despite the fact that both Saudi Arabia and the Emirates, as well as many domestic workers' countries of origin have ratified the Palermo Protocol, there is barely any prosecution taking place against human trafficking.[624]

---

624 Vlieger (2011 c).

This deficiency is related to several obstructions to implementation of the UN's Palermo Protocol. Primarily, the human trafficking business is estimated to be approximately as large as both the illegal arms trade and the drug trade combined. This amount of money can buy a lot. In all four countries visited for this study (Saudi Arabia, the Emirates, Philippines, and Indonesia), interviewees stated that a legal case or action against a rich and powerful man cannot be won. Sometimes an agency's license will be temporarily suspended, but afterward, either the suspension is cancelled or the agent concerned simply begins a new agency under a different name. Government officials are said to be either bribed or connected to the agents by family ties. The potential penalties can be changed into fines low enough not to deter anyone.

Moreover, governments in labor-sending countries are more concerned with employment and remittances, which constitute a very large portion of their GNP. The IMF and the World Bank apparently use remittance flows in calculating sustainability of loans, and credit rating agencies such as Moody's, Standard & Poor's, and Fitch, do the same for their decisions on certain bond ratings. The governments in labor-sending countries understandably do not want these remittances to diminish and therefore, in general, do not make a strong stand for their overseas workers. Thus, neither the countries of origin nor the destination countries do much to prevent human trafficking. At international conferences, the destination countries state that the agencies in the countries of origin are the problem, whereas the countries of origin state that the agencies and employers in the destination countries are the problem. The result is that trafficking agencies in all countries continue their business virtually untouched. Given the amount of money and political interests involved, this system cannot be expected to change unless new implementation mechanisms are developed.

To design the proper implementation mechanisms, what is first necessary is research on the sociology of the Palermo Protocol. The questions underlying such research should include the following: Which barriers exist that prevent the effective prosecution of traffickers both in the countries of origin and destination? To what extent can this situation be expected to improve in low-wage countries of origin, or in rentier states? Are there implementation mechanisms existent that are immune to corruption? And, if such mechanisms cannot be found, does this justify lifting implementation of the Palermo Protocol to an international level? If so, then what should the implementation mechanisms preferably look like? And, finally, how likely is it that enough states will ratify a treaty with such international implementation mechanisms to render it effective?

12.4.3 Miscellaneous

There are a few more, smaller issues that deserve further research. The first issue concerns the data from chapter 9 regarding the legal system. The hypothesis posed there is that the differences between the Saudi and the Emirates legal systems can be explained through the existence in Saudi Arabia of an old legal-religious elite, which is trying to hold on to its power. Members of this legal-religious elite are generally not keen on granting anyone the right to interview them or providing access to courts and other legal institutions. Likely only Saudi researchers can ascertain the extent to which this elite blocks, to protect its power position, legal reforms that have become necessary because of economic changes. Only Saudi researchers can ascertain to what extent judges are indeed corrupt or generally apply what they feel is Allah's concept of Justice.

Chapter 7 also points to a larger scale of power politics. It proposes the hypothesis that the ruling families (executive, legislative or judiciary) do not offer proper protection to the lower strata of society because they have no incentive to do so. Necessary for conclusive answers to this issue, is comparative research in several countries on labor protection and the extent to which the five incentives set out by De Swaan exist. Such research should include countries with different religions. Singapore should preferably be included in this research, as it is also a labor-importing state that has a preoccupation with the employer-citizen, rather than with the employee-migrant worker.[625]

Another issue that deserves more attention is the fact that the data seem to suggest either that policemen more frequently rape domestic workers, or that rapists frequently pretend to be policemen. If the answer turns out to be the latter, then this could be related to the fear of domestic workers towards policemen, either caused in the countries of destination, or in the countries of origin. If policemen indeed more frequently rape domestic workers, one explanation could be the overall poor functioning of the legal system and the knowledge of policemen that they will go unpunished. Another explanation could be that policemen, either in general or in these countries, enjoy exerting control, with reference to the view that rape is not (only) about sex but about control. This last hypothesis would also explain why rape as social problem seems to rise in occurrence generally (also outside the police force) when the patriarchal system declines; as the power of men over women diminishes, rape could augment in an attempt to regain control. Thus, although patriarchy is a factor facilitating rape (as the rapists in this system is supposed to be the one protecting the victim), an additional factor that might make matters worse is patriarchy under pressure. The fact that certain Saudi and Emirati men currently resort to sexual or other forms of violence against women could be related to the fact that these women no longer obey the way they used to. The fact that they no longer obey may have to do with social changes in the economy that call for smarter, higher educated workers, workers that may as well be female.

---

625 Anggraeni (2006) P115.

In other words, sexual violence may (temporarily?) increase because of economic changes in the following manner: specialization of the economy raises the demand for higher educated workers – regardless of gender – which raises the demand for independent women, which undermines the power position of men, which may lead to a higher occurrence of sexual violence. This hypothesis is worthy of further comparative research, particularly from scholars trained in gender studies.

An interesting issue that could simultaneously be investigated is the extent to which the rise in aggression against homosexuality is also related to the decline of the patriarchal system and changes in the economy. This violence against homosexual men is relatively new; in the sixties, especially in Dubai, gay relations were accepted. This situation has changed, though not because of large numbers of gay tourists, a hypothesis regularly offered for countries such as Egypt and Morocco. Dubai has never seen comparable gay tourism, while aggression against homosexuals has nevertheless increased. One explanation could be that the economic changes undermine the patriarchal system, which undermines the power attributed to men based on their role as the masculine provider and protector. As the male power position is under threat, men may resort to violence against homosexuals because they deny the traditional role models which used to grant this power. Further research is needed on these possible connections.

Also possibly connected to gender violence, and potentially to economic changes, is the issue of occultism. In patriarchal societies, women are supposed to obey the men in their family, and several male interviewees stated that occultism must be at play when a man falls in love so deeply that a woman controls him. A woman in control goes against what is considered the natural state of things, and therefore, the supernatural must be involved. Throughout the world and history, primarily women have been accused of 'doing magic' and of being witches,[626] accusations that are strongly attached to the otherness of the woman, which creates both desire and fear. Also in Europe, mainly women were accused of witchcraft. It would be interesting to see if there has been a heightening in such accusations in regions where women gained power. During the Enlightenment in the eighteenth century, people began to consider the world more scientifically. The consistency of the newly discovered laws of nature rendered the concept of witchcraft unlikely. In Saudi Arabia and the Emirates the growing power of women may increase the occurrence of accusations of witchcraft, while the spread of education in the natural sciences to the contrary may lead to a process of disenchantment, which should diminish accusations of magic. More research is necessary on this subject.

Potentially connected to the issues of occultism and (the decline of) the patriarchal system is the issue of extreme adherence to contracts. Some interviewees who were victims of rape stated that they stayed with their employer "because of the contract."

---

626 Zimbardo (2008) P9 and Crow (1968).

How can this extremely strong adherence to a contract that is disregarded by the employer be explained? Moreover, there is a difference between Indonesian and Filipina domestic workers concerning this issue.

The Filipinas, when asked why they could not go home, gave diverse answers, such as the following: "I already talked to them about that when my son got sick; I could not go" and "I know they have paid money at the agency for me and for my ticket, so it's too much hard for them to release my papers." Very few referred to the contract. Indonesians, on the other hand, almost all referred to the contract. There are two possible explanations for this phenomenon. One is the possibility that, as one interviewee stated, the agencies indoctrinate them that leaving prior to finishing the contract is impossible, and Indonesian agencies maybe do so more than Filipino agencies. The other explanation is offered from symbolic anthropology: for domestic workers from a patriarchal and low-educated society, the contract may have some supernatural force. There seems to be a stronger belief in Indonesian society in occultism (see chapter 11), which may then explain this stronger adherence to contracts. Further research is needed here.

12.5 Policy recommendations

The four main incentives for the conflicts described in the second section to this chapter are oil revenues in Saudi Arabia and the Emirates, poverty in many other countries, Wahhabism and the awkward position of the domestic worker as an outsider within the family. Obviously, these four factors cannot be changed easily. The oil reserves will run out one day, which will force the Saudi and Emirati governments to find other means to collect revenues. According to the rentier state theory, this will most likely lead to improvements in their governing efforts. However, this process will take time and be accompanied by severe and unwanted economic problems for both countries.

To what extent the worldwide poverty problem will and can be resolved any time soon is highly controversial. I do not consider myself capable to provide an answer here. But more important, for all current domestic workers, action is needed sooner. The awkward position of the domestic worker is another issue that is difficult to improve; she will always remain a stranger who, as a marginal person within the privacy of the family, can be perceived as both attractive and threatening. The overview does discuss the factors Islam and Sharia, but as chapter 5 demonstrates, Sharia has little or no influence on conflicts, and therefore, there are no arrows coming out of the Sharia-circle. In contrast, Wahhabism is a factor of influence. However, the extent to which the Wahhabi legal-religious nobility will be able to maintain its power position is another question I do not consider myself capable of providing an answer to. Nevertheless, there are several factors between the four main causes and the resulting conflicts that can be addressed. This section, therefore, discusses four policy recommendations that I, on the basis of the data from this research, deem to stand the largest chance of success in improving the position of domestic workers in Saudi Arabia and the United Arab Emirates.

12.5.1 *Regulate the maid trade*

The first issue that could be changed to improve the position of domestic workers worldwide is the highly under-regulated maid trade. As described in chapter 7, there is so much money involved in this industry that large scale action against malpracticing agents cannot be expected either in the countries of origin or destination. One strategy could be to empower organizations above the governments. As discussed in section 12.3.3, research is needed regarding the sociology of the Palermo Protocol to assess the shortcomings in its implementation mechanisms and to draw up ameliorations. The ILO currently advises countries to set up a national licensing system. It is probably more effective to draw up an international treaty stating that anyone bringing a worker across borders must be internationally licensed by the ILO. This organization could randomly check into whether workers receive the conditions promised to them before departure. If this is not the case, the agency should receive a warning and its actions should be scrutinized more carefully. After two warnings and a misstep, the agency should lose its license, and the owners should be banned from applying for new registration. Anyone bringing a worker across a border without an ILO license should be subject to punishment in any country that has ratified the relevant treaty. Under this system, well-meaning higher officials could bypass corruptible lower officials.

This strategy makes sense given that other international problems, such as international commodity and capital flows, have been solved by empowering international organizations. Although world migration pressures have increased, progress towards a multilateral approach to migration management is far slower than in the management of trade and capital. Yet setting up such a system will take time, especially to advocacy ratification. Therefore, in the meantime, the ILO could develop a hallmark, an international mark of ethical quality, given only to those agencies that do not violate the ILO's basic treaties. Through media campaigns, employers could be stimulated to do business only with such hallmarked agencies, not only because of ethical reasons, but also to reduce the risk of hiring unsatisfied and disappearing workers.

Another strategy that may work is to empower those below government level, such as the individual employer and employee. As for the employers of domestic workers, they are simultaneously consumers of agencies. Therefore, an international consumer organization could be established, to unite the employers' forces against the agencies. This consumer organization could demand agreements between employers and agencies under the condition of payback of fees in the case that the workers have been misinformed as to essential work conditions. As both Saudi Arabia and the Emirates have strict laws against non-governmental organizations, the consumer organizations should be set up as commercial organizations. Another option, especially for Saudi Arabia where the Chambers of Commerce are comparatively powerful, would be to set up a department in the Chambers of Commerce that unites consumer interests against certain powerful producers. Such consumer organizations may turn out to have the additional benefit of stimulating the development of producer liability laws, which may improve protection of both housewives and domestic workers against health damaging cleaning products.

The domestic workers could also be united in an international organization. This arrangement has been suggested before, but it is now becoming feasible, as increasing numbers of domestic workers have mobile phones. Such a union could be set up via telephone-pyramids, with small units of domestic workers keeping an eye (ear) on each other and informing one another of rights and duties. In the forthcoming treaty on the rights of domestic workers, a stipulation should therefore be included stating that domestic workers worldwide have the right to the use of a mobile phone (outside of their 8 to 10 work hours). As use of the Internet and tools such as Facebook are also growing, these web-based communities could be actively used to improve the protection of domestic workers.

As the Internet is without borders, organizations such as the ILO can set up a system in which both employers and employees can give ratings on the agencies with which they have done business. Further, these websites, through data mining, could provide information regarding the connections between the agencies in the countries of origin and destination; joint liability for human trafficking, in the end, is pointless as long as there is no information on the business partners. Of course, serious intellectual investments are required to render such websites hacker-proof, as the agencies have a large financial interest in protecting their reputation.

The ILO treaty for domestic workers should, furthermore, contain rules for agents that obligate them to properly explain work conditions. In addition, it should state that parties be requested to include in their legal systems a rule governing the case where a worker has been misinformed regarding essential work conditions. In this circumstance, such a rule should require a judge to apply the contract that was signed in the country of origin. In this instance, the employer should be forced to pay the higher salary, after which the employer can collect this money from the agency with which he has done business. Likely, the agencies in the destination countries will then discontinue business with those agencies that lie to workers in the countries of origin.

Media campaigns could make the Saudi and Emirati public familiar with the salaries that the governments of the different countries of origin prescribe. Websites could provide all of the standard salaries prescribed by the different countries of origin. Although this publication could be undertaken by the ILO, the Saudi and Emirati governments are obligated to do so based on article 9 sub 5 of the Palermo Protocol, which states that both governments must take educational measures to discourage trafficking (see chapter 7). An alternative would include the policy recommendation discussed in 12.4.4, a standard contract for all domestic workers in the entire Gulf region that is widely published in all the countries of origin.

Non-governmental organizations have played an important and recognized role in exposing fraud, graft and corruption in the responsible administrative bodies and in assisting victims of such. However, as Saudi Arabia does not allow NGOs and the Emirates does so only to a very limited extent, this is rarely the case in these two destination countries. Therefore, the international treaty on the rights of domestic workers should include a specific stipulation that allows individuals to set up NGOs in the interest of domestic workers. The UN could play a role in uniting these NGOs via a transnational advocacy network. However, these networks should not organize the international licensing of agencies or the ethical hallmark, as NGOs in poorer countries are unfortunately but logically also susceptible to corruption. To summarize, as governments cannot be expected to proactively fight human trafficking, other solutions are necessary either below or above the government level.

12.5.2 Improve the legal system and access to justice

A second issue that needs to be addressed is that the Emirates and even more so Saudi Arabia suffer from a poorly functioning legal system (chapters 8 and 9). As neither the Emirati nor the Saudi population has proper means to force their governments to take action regarding the (near) absence of the rule of law, the international community must. Given the fact that the oil revenues will eventually dry up, both countries try to diversify their economies (see chapter 2). Both countries try to attract foreign investors and sign favorable treaties with organizations such as the WTO and the EU. In each of these instances, the international community should pressure both countries to improve access to justice for migrant workers in general and domestic workers in particular.

Furthermore, the international community could try to create better access to justice itself. Currently, non-governmental organizations are not or barely permitted in either country. There are other possibilities, though. Civil society is extremely poorly developed in the Gulf, as all governments are suspicious of anybody who claims to be doing something simply 'for the greater good'. What the governments concerned do understand or expect, is activism with private interests. Therefore, the potential for Corporate Social Responsibility projects is relatively large in the Gulf. What Westerners would call human rights meetings, are organized in the Gulf by private companies that operate under the name of 'event planner' or by companies that see CSR as a way of creating goodwill.

What thus seems possible in both countries is a Corporate Social Responsibility project, aiming at the provision of free paralegal services to migrant workers to strengthen the rule of law. Such a CSR project should be set up in close coordination with the Embassies of the labor-sending countries as well as the embassies of the United States and the European Union. These last embassies should be involved not only to provide means but also to minimize corruption through the establishment of computerized and depersonalized procedures, and use their clout to gain cooperation from the governments of the countries concerned.

The legal aid offices could be set up in cooperation with companies such as Microsoft that already have a good track record on Corporate Social Responsibility projects. Other companies that could be involved are those that profit from contacts with migrant workers, such as Western Union. Furthermore, law firms can be involved, as they can use the legal aid offices to find and train their future associates. Law schools can be involved, as the legal aid offices provide excellent training opportunities for students in their final year. The legal aid offices could take on the simple cases themselves and forward complicated cases to lawyers. In large parts of the world, lawyers work on cases for free, which is called *pro bono* (for the good) or *pro deo* (for God). As Islam prescribes Muslims to pay *zakat*, attempts could be made to involve mosques in a project to have lawyers pay their *zakat* by taking on cases *Lillah* (for Allah).

Another necessary measure is for both governments to exclude all lawyers, (para)legal advisors and judges from the sponsorship regulations, freeing them from the threat of deportation. Furthermore, many lawyers need additional training. One interviewed diplomat stated it as follows: "Usually it's not that they are unethical, but they are just very unprofessional and the result is unethical." If the governments do not take any action to better regulate their countries' lawyers, the international community could attempt to do so by directly contacting bar associations or similar organizations. Judges also need more training, particularly on topics that seem entirely unfamiliar to them, such as the sociology of law. Judges need training as to their own role in society, ways to perform this role, ways to reflect on their own role and self-regulation.

12.5.3 Alteration of the sponsorship system

The gulf countries receive extensive criticism from the international community regarding the sponsorship system (chapter 7). However, its abolition is not likely in light of the objections to the abolition of the system. These objections, therefore, need to be addressed. If not, if the support within the population in favor of abolition is low, then employers will find loopholes in the new laws or they will invent tricks to keep the situation as it currently is. For instance, they will continue to retain the passports of the workers to prevent them from leaving. Therefore, successful alterations need to address the existing objections to abolition.

In Saudi Arabia and the Emirates, two alternatives for the sponsorship system are being discussed that, to a certain extent, address the objections to abolishment. Both entail transfer of sponsorship to a larger organization. In the Emirates, according to two government interviewees and newspapers, there are plans is to put sponsorship in the hands of the government.[627] The Minister of Labor is stated to have sketched a blueprint of new procedures that would require laborers wishing to work in the Emirates to go through the Ministry of Labor, rather than recruiting agencies. In contrast, in Saudi Arabia, a limited number of agencies are planned to become sponsor, turning these contracted agencies into labor pools. These agencies are expected to recruit large numbers of foreign laborers, enabling employers to hire a worker on the spot, without the delay currently experienced by sponsors in both Saudi Arabia and the Emirates. In the event of dissatisfaction, a foreign worker would simply flow back into the Ministry's or agency's labor pool and the employer would instantly be provided with another worker.

If the adjustments are combined with a residency cap, a maximum stay of approximately 6 years, the issue of fear from large numbers of migrant workers is addressed. This residency cap has a downside though, which is the loss of trained and experienced workers. However, the Gulf countries themselves have suggested a solution, asserting that the caps do not prevent workers from moving on to another Gulf country after 6 years' employment. As such, the Gulf countries will profit from on-the-job education provided in the surrounding countries, without the downside that the workers might pose a (real or perceived) threat to their citizens.

The issue of high fees that are currently paid to the agencies (chapter 10), that create a sense of ownership over the worker, could be addressed by obliging the employers to pay wages to the sponsor (the government or the agency) that will, then, pay the worker after deduction of the transaction costs. As such, payment of fees would not take place in advance, but would be spread over the 24 or 36 months that the worker resides in the country concerned. Unfortunately, the Emirati government (which intends to create a labor pool in the Ministry of Labor, contrary to Saudi Arabia, which intends to create labor pools in a limited number of agencies) may decide not to do so. Such a regime could support the impression that the fees are a tax, which (as several interviewed government officials explicitly stated) could possibly lead to unwanted demands for political power.

As the altered sponsorship system will allow for easy transfer of a worker to a new employer, there is far less reason for workers to disappear on the black market, and, therefore, criminality is also likely to diminish. Furthermore, with the agencies or government as the new sponsor, these adjustments also support the idea, contrary to international law but widely shared in both countries, that everyone requires a local guarantor. As such, the proposed alterations address all the

---

627 This has been denied by an interviewee from the ILO who stated transfer of sponsorship to the Ministry of Labor would not be possible in light of the governmental structure of the UAE and the independency of the different Emirates. Nevertheless, reports that this is indeed the plan are rather consistent and therefore are here deemed to be correct.

objections against abolition of the sponsorship system (chapter 7). The adjusted visa system grants more freedom and, therefore, more power to the worker.

However, this system is not perfect and, therefore, not uncontested. If the worker gets into a conflict with the Ministry (in the Emirates) or the agency (in Saudi Arabia), he or she would, according to these critics, be just as powerless as now. But because the relationship in these scenarios is not one-on-one, the level of abuse might be lower. An interviewee in Riyadh clearly noted this, stating, "It is better to find a job in a large company, because, in a one-man company, typically the employer gets very abusive." Furthermore, these labor pool systems may be better for certain migrant workers than a completely free market, for the following two reasons.

The first reason that total abolition of the sponsorship system may not be the best solution, is that not all workers can handle total freedom. This may sound degrading or paternalistic, but many domestic workers are 14 to 20 year old girls from the countryside of, for instance, Mindanao. These workers have not seen much outside their village of origin, stem from a patriarchal society in which they have learned to always obey men, have had a few years of school education only, cannot read and do not speak proper Arabic. These workers cannot be expected to make well-informed decisions in their own interest and to close agreements in freedom and knowledge. Illustrative in this sense is the answer of one very young interviewee to the question why she had come to a for domestic workers dangerous place like Saudi Arabia: "Well my father needed a scooter, so I went."

Furthermore, many of the domestic workers are aware of their incapacity for handling full freedom and often do not want it. In the two countries researched, most domestic workers live with the family they work for. Others work on the black market and are so-called 'freelancers', as they work for several different households every week. As these freelancers are not dependent on a single employer for their income, they usually have the freedom to quit if they do not like the way that they are being treated. This freedom certainly has advantages, although there are also disadvantages, as the workers have to arrange for their own housing, food, transportation, medical care, phone bills, holidays and pension. For some domestic workers, this is a sufficient reason not to become a freelancer. One interviewee for instance stated: "I don't want to be a freelancer. Too much headache you know, with transportation and the house and all. I am good where I am." Some domestic workers that were interviewed had run away and became freelancers, but they gave it up when they faced problems that they considered too large to deal with themselves. They later returned to the Middle East as 'live-ins' again.

The second reason why complete freedom for migrant domestic workers may not be the best solution concerns transaction costs incurred by the workers when they change employers. Several domestic workers that were interviewed do not leave their employers because the process of getting another employer is too costly. This is what is known as transaction costs: money actually spent and the money that could have been earned during the time spent searching for new employment. Workers usually need time and money to leave the house of the employer, wait for clearance to leave the country (one interviewee had been in the embassy's shelter for three years with no income), fly to their home country (employers usually do not pay for return tickets upon absconding), approach a recruiter, possibly pay for new (false) IDs, wait for placement (two or three months), fly back to the Middle East, and possibly not be paid during the first two or three months by their new employer. This process renders changing employers so costly that many domestic workers, upon absconding, decide to find employment directly on the black market. Others pay their former employer to sign a release. This No Objection Certificate is needed to move to another employer without leaving the country and taking on all the travel expenses.

An interviewed domestic worker explained how the high transaction costs placed her and her husband in a Catch-22 situation: "For a transfer we have to pay 8000 Riyal.[628] My husband is trying to get the money together now. If we do not find a new sponsor who wants to pay this amount, we must go home, but then we need money for the ticket. Either way we need money." She then burst out crying and added, "Please help me!" Domestic workers are usually aware of the problem of the high transaction cost and it makes them ready to suffer a considerable amount of abuse to avoid incurring these costs. Alcid, likewise, writes about domestic workers in Hong Kong: "Fighting for their rights from the viewpoint of the worker, is not without risks and sacrifices, because they spend the equivalent of two to three months wages to find work again in Hong Kong. Workers are terrified to lose their jobs, so they are prepared to suffer considerable indignity and often inhuman working hours and conditions to keep them. Thus it is only in the most extreme circumstances that they will lodge an official complaint."[629]

The high transaction cost is one aspect that limits domestic workers' freedom and increases the power of the employer (chapter 10). Economic theory on this topic offers a suggestion for improvement. Transaction cost is the key point in the controversy between the neo-classical view on the labor market and the neo-institutionalists. Neo-classicalists view the labor market as a place where workers and producers, respectively, offer and demand (hours of) labor. When the price of an hour of labor goes up, the workers will offer more hours, while the producers will demand less and vice versa. The market will move to an optimal equilibrium if there is no interference. The neo-institutionalists claim that, in reality, the market does not work like this, and that, contrary to what neo-classicalists support, transaction costs are neither zero nor negligible, but are actually quite high. As this is the case, in certain instances, it is more cost effective to have workers organized in an institutional setting instead of a free labor market.[630]

---

628 Ten months salary for her, or about seven months for him.
629 Alcid in Heyzer (1994) P175.
630 Davies (2004) P28-29.

As described, sponsorship in Saudi Arabia may be transferred to a small number of private companies and in the Emirates to the government. From the perspective of the neo-institutionalists, this creates an institutional setting from which both workers and employers will benefit, as it will create a better allocation of resources; workers can be placed anew with other employers for comparatively low transaction costs. This system is in the interest of both employer and employee. Several interviewed diplomats and human rights activists claimed to prefer full abolition of the sponsorship system. However, entirely free labor relations, according to the neo-institutionalists, are economically unprofitable until the transaction costs are lower than the profit gained from a switch from one employer to another.

Alteration of the sponsorship system as proposed by the Saudi and Emirati government is also in the interest of the family of the employers. These workers have a somewhat different position from other migrant workers, as they work in the private sphere of the household. Here, they take the marginal position of an outsider who is very close, a foreigner who learns all the secrets of the house; the worker is an enchanting stranger who can be perceived as both extremely attractive and intensely dangerous. This marginal position and the attached combination of attractiveness and danger can lead to a variety of explosive situations (see chapter 11). A simple example concerns a young domestic worker who is lonely, far away from home, who falls in love with the son of her employer and starts an affair. As soon as she realizes that he will never marry her, tensions will rise. If she is not removed from such a family, the situation can explode and lead to situations involving rape, theft and severe violence from both sides. As the data from this research demonstrated, many severe conflicts began small, but turned into a downward spiral of diminishing trust and augmenting aggression.

In such situations, domestic workers are often instantly expelled from the household by the employer. In light of the explosive situations that result from the marginal position of the domestic worker, the freedom of the employer to expel the domestic worker should not be limited; on the contrary, it should be enlarged. The domestic workers are usually deported, but some are sentenced to jail upon accusations and without evidence. If the freedom of the employer to expel the worker is enlarged, such accusations are no longer necessary. An important reason to make false accusations seems to be that the employer does not have to provide for a return ticket if the domestic worker has committed a crime. Therefore, if the employer does not have to pay for a return ticket, but simply returns the worker to the large institutional sponsor, returns her to the labor pool, then the number of false accusations will likely diminish.

12.5.4 Standard contract for domestic workers

To target the problem of unregulated domestic workers, several countries in the Gulf have introduced a standard contract. The International Labour Organization is promoting such a contract as solution. Although everyone agrees that such standard contracts are a good attempt to improve the situation, there are currently several problems that need to be addressed. First, most domestic workers do not know the difference between the several Gulf countries. For many of them, the term 'Dubai' stands for the entire Middle East. They do not choose a country, but the recruitment agency places them in one of these countries. Some of them after two years of employment still do not know in which country they work. As the standard contracts are different per country, this does not make it easier for the domestic workers to find out what their rights are.

Second, as not only the destination countries but also several countries of origin currently write standard contracts, many domestic workers have several contracts. For instance, Filipina domestic workers sign a standard contract prescribed by their government, which states that their salary should at least be $400 per month. As soon as they arrive in the Gulf though, this contract is replaced (contract substitution) with, for instance, the Emirati standard contract, stating a salary of approximately $200. Although some domestic workers are aware that their contract will be replaced and that the Filipino contract is just signed "to get the paperwork processed", not all of them realize this. That they then receive only half the promised salary renders them a victim of trafficking under the Palermo Protocol (see chapter 7). If the entire Gulf would work with a single contract that is widely published in the countries of origin, this situation would be prevented.

A third problem with the current standard contracts is that many of them have been written in very complex language. They have been written from the perspective that domestic workers have been excluded from the labor law and therefore should be given certain rights via contract. However, a law and a contract are two very different things, as they are supposed to be read and used by different parties. Laws are meant to be used by jurists, while contracts are meant to be used by the persons who sign the contract. Awareness of the difference between the two is especially important in light of the meager possibilities for implementation of any rule or regulation inside the private sphere of the household (which prohibits labor inspections for domestic workers). In this setting, the only possibility for enforcement is if the domestic worker herself demands implementation of her rights and the employer acknowledges them. This is only possible where they both understand what the respective rights and duties are. In light of the fact that the domestic worker's level of education is generally very low, the contract needs to be written in a language that is 100% comprehensible especially to her.

A fourth problem with the current standard contracts is that they have been written largely on the advice of Western lawyers, who had the rights of the domestic workers in mind, not the rights of the employers. However, because it is a contract, not a law, the contract should, to gain acceptance among employers, be equitable. Therefore, they should also contain rules regarding the rights of the employer and the duties of the domestic worker. Currently, this is rarely the case. For instance, for many employers in the Gulf, it is very important that the domestic worker respects the culture of her employer and, therefore, does not start a love affair. Many domestic workers are not aware of how important this rule is to the employer, which, therefore, leads to many conflicts. If the contract also contained these rules, many conflicts would be prevented. Furthermore, the contract would gain acceptance among employers, as it also protects their interests.

These four issues could be targeted by a project that aimed to implement one standard contract for domestic workers in all Gulf countries. Such a project could be coordinated through the ILO office in Beirut. The contract would then need to be published widely both in the countries of origin and destination. It should be written in a language that is entirely comprehensible by both the employers and domestic workers. Furthermore, it must contain all rules that both the domestic worker and employer deem important. To achieve this, someone should sit down with both parties and determine the extent to which they fully understand the language of the contract and the extent to which the contract contains all of the issues that both parties believe should be in the contract. Thereupon, the ILO should insist that all Gulf countries prescribe this one standard contract through their visa procedures. At the same time and in connection to the previous policy recommendations, the governments should declare that the labor courts in their respective countries are the appropriate courts to deal with conflicts concerning this standard contract.

13. Bibliography

13.1 Literature

Aarts, P. & G. Nonneman (eds.) (2005) Saudi Arabia in the balance: political economy, society, foreign affairs. UK, London, Hurst & Company.

Abu-Habib, L. (1998) The use and abuse of female domestic workers from Sri Lanka in Lebanon. In: Gender & Development, Volume 6, Issue 1, March 1998, pp 52-56.

Abukhalil, A. (2004) The battle for Saudi Arabia: royalty, fundamentalism and global power. USA, New York, An open media book, seven stories press.

AFesh, M. A. (2008) Spiritually Oriented Quranic Psychotherapy. Unpublished paper, available from author, at Saudi Arabia's Human Rights Commission.

Agosín, M. (ed.) (2002) Women, Gender and Human Rights: a global perspective. USA, New Brunswick, Rutgers University Press.

Ali, S. (2010) Dubai: gilded cage. USA, New Haven, Yale University Press.

Anderson, B. (2000) Doing the dirty work? The global politics of domestic labor. UK, London, Zed Books.

Anthias, F. (2000) Metaphors of home: gendering new migrations to Southern Europe. In: F. Anthias & G. Lazaradis (eds.) Gender and migration in Southern Europe: women on the move. pp 15-47. UK, Oxford, Berg.

Anggraeni, D. (2006) Dreamseekers: Indonesian women as domestic workers in Asia. Indonesia, Jakarta, Equinox Publishing & ILO.

Arendt, H. (1951) The origins of totalitarianism. USA, San Diego, A Harvest Book, Harcourt Inc.

Asad, M. (2005) The road to Mecca. USA, Louisville, Fons Vitae Publishing and The Book Foundation.

Ashcroft, B. & G. Griffiths & H. Tiffin (1998) Key concepts in post-colonial studies. USA, New York, Routledge.

Auwal, M.A. (2010) Ending the exploitation of migrant workers in the Gulf. In: Flechter Forum of World Affairs, Vol. 34:2, Summer 2010, pp 87-108.

Bakan, A.B. & D.K. Stasiulis (1995) Domestic placement agencies and the racialization of women's household work. In: Signs, Vol. 20, no. 2, pp 303-335.

Bakan, A.B. & D.K. Stasiulis (1995) Negotiating citizenship: the case of foreign domestic workers in Canada. In: Feminist review, no. 57, pp 112-139.

Bales, K. (2004) Disposable people: new slavery in the global economy. USA, Berkeley, University of California Press.

Bales, K. (2006) Testing a theory of modern slavery. Available on the net: www.freetheslaves.net

Barber, P.G. (2000) Agency in the Philippine women's labor migration and provisional diaspora. In: Women's Studies International Forum, Vol. 23, No. 4, pp 399-411.

Baroody, G.M. (1980) The practice of Law in Saudi Arabia. In: King Faisal and the modernisation of Saudi Arabia. UK, London, Croom Helm.

Basu, K e.a. (2003) International Labor Standards: history, theory and policy options. UK, Oxford, Blackwell Publishing Ltd.

Bayly, C.A. (2005) The birth of the modern world 1780-1914. Global connections and comparisons. USA, Malden, Blackwell Publishing.

Beblawi, H. & G. Luciani (eds.) (1990) The Rentier State in the Arab World. In: The Arab State, UK, London, Routledge.

Benda-Beckmann, F. von (2001) Legal pluralism and social justice in economic and political development. In: IdS Bulletin Vol. 32 No. 1, pp 46-56.

Benda-Beckmann, F. von (red) (2005) Mobile people, mobile law: expanding legal relations in a contracting world. UK, Aldershot, Ashgate Publishing ltd.

Benda-Beckmann, K. von (2002) Globalisation and legal pluralism. In: International Law FORUM du droit international vol. 4, pp 19-25.

Berg, H. van den (2004a) Discoursanalyse. In: Kwalon 26, y9, nr2.

Berg, H. van den (2004b) Discoursanalyse in praktijk. In: Kwalon 76, y9, nr3.

Bergh, G.C.J.J. van den (1988) Eigendom: grepen uit de geschiedenis van een omstreden begrip. The Netherlands, Deventer, Kluwer.

Bin Laden, C. (2003) Het gesloten koninkrijk. The Netherlands, Amsterdam, Poema Pocket, Uitgeverij Mouria.

Bix, B.H. (2009) Consent in contract law. Paper presented at the University of Amsterdam June 2009, publication forthcoming.

Boal, W.M. & M.R. Ransom (1997) Monopsony in the labor market. In: Journal of economic literature, Vol. XXV (March 1997) pp 86-112.

Borg, J. (2007) Persuasion: the art of influencing people. UK, Harlow, Pearson Education Limited, Prentice Hall.

Bosniak, L. (2006) The citizen and the alien: dilemmas of contemporary membership. USA, New Jersey, Princeton University Press.

Botman, S. (2003) The informal economy of paid domestic labor in Amsterdam. Unpublished paper UvA/ASSR.

Boyd, M. & E. Grieco (2003) Women and migration: incorporating gender into international migration theory. Migration information course, migration policy institute, available online.

Bradley, J.R. (2005) Saudi Arabia exposed: inside a kingdom in crisis. USA, New York, Palgrave Macmillan.

Brettell, C.B. (2000) Theorizing migration in anthropology. The social construction of networks, identities, communities and globalscapes. In: C.B. Brettell & J.F. Hollifield (eds.) Migration theory: talking across disciplines pp 97-135. USA, New York, Routledge.

Brinkman, J. (2000) De vragenlijst. The Netherlands, Groningen, Wolters Noordhoff.

Briody, D. (2003) The iron triangle: inside the secret world of the Carlyle Group. USA, New Jersey, John Wiley & Sons Inc.

Brochmann, G. (1993) Middle East Avenue. Female migration from Sri Lanka to the Gulf. Boulder, Westview Press.

Brouwer P.W. (2004) Recht, een introductie. The Netherlands, The Hague, Boom Juridische Uitgevers.

Buijs, G. (ed.) (1993) Migrant women: crossing boundaries and changing identities. UK, Oxford, Berg.

Calandruccio, G. (2005) A review of recent research on human trafficking in the Middle East. In: data and research on human trafficking, a global survey. Switzerland, Geneva, IOM, P267-301. Available online.

Carling, J. (2005) Gender dimensions of international migration. Switzerland, Geneva, Global Commission of International Migration, Global Migration Perspectives No 35.

Chang, G. (2000) Disposable domestics: immigrant women workers in the global economy. Canada, South End Press.

Chang, H-J (2008) Bad Samaritans: the guilty secrets of rich nations & the threat to global prosperity. London, UK, Random House Business Books.

Charmaz, K. (2006) Constructing Grounded Theory: a practical guide through qualitative analysis. USA, Los Angeles, Sage Publications.

Chaudry, K.A. (1997) The price of wealth: economies and institutions in the Middle East. USA, Ithaca, Cornell University Press.

Clark, B. (1991) The Vienna Convention Reservations Regime and the Convention on Discrimination Against Women. In: the American Journal of International Law, vol. 85, Nr 2 (April 1991), pp 281-321.

Clark, D.S. (ed.) (2007) Encyclopedia of Law & Society: American and global perspectives (Parts 1, 2 & 3). USA, Los Angeles, Sage Publications.

Colen, S. & R. Sanjek (eds.) (1990) At work in homes; household workers in world perspective. USA, Washington DC, American Ethnological Society Monograph 3, American Anthropological Association.

Constable, N. (1997) Maid to order in Hong Kong: stories of Filipina workers. USA, New York, Cornell University Press.

Coulson, N.J. (1994) A history of Islamic law. UK, Edinburgh, Edinburgh University Press.

Crow, W.B. (1968) A history of magic, witchcraft and occultism. UK, London, The Aquarian Press.

Davis, M. (2006) Fear and Money in Dubai. In: New Left Review 41, Sept-Oct 2006. http://www.newleftreview.org/?2635

Dhaheri, Ahmed bin Shabib Al (2008) The temporary nature of employment of contractual labor in the GCC states. Paper presented to the third session of the Emirates Gulf Forum on the temporary contractual labor, 23-24 January 2008.

Davidson, C.M. (2008) Dubai: the vulnerability of success. USA, New York, Columbia University Press.

Davies, A.C.L. (2004) Perspectives on Labor Law. UK, Cambridge, Cambridge University Press.

Dieteren, F. & E. Kloek & A. Visser (1993) Naar Eva's beeld: de geschiedenis van de vrouw in de Europese cultuur. The Netherlands, Abcoude, Uitgeverij Uniepers Abcoude.

Domosh, M. & J. Seager (2001) Putting women in place: feminist geographers making sense of the world. USA, New York, The Guilford Press.

Doorn, J.A.A. van (1990) De wording van de waarborgstaat: De Swaan over collectivisering van sociale voorzieningen. In: Beleid van maatschappij nr 5.

Douglas, M. (1966) Purity and Danger: an analysis of concepts of pollution and taboo. USA, New York, Frederick A. Praeger Publishers.

Durkheim, E. (1897) Le Suicide: Etude de Sociologie. France, Paris, Presses Universitaires de France.

Eberly, D.E. (2000) The essential civil society reader: the classic essays in the American civil society debate. USA, Lanham, Rowman & Littlefield Publishers Inc.

Ehrenreich, B. & A. Russell Hochschild (ed.) (2002) Global Woman: nannies, maids and sex workers in the new economy. USA, New York, Owl books.

Ehrenreich, B. (2005) De achterkant van de Amerikaanse droom. The Netherlands, Amsterdam, Atlas.

Elias, N. (2001) Het civilisatieproces. Sociogenetische en psychogenetische onderzoekingen. The Netherlands, Amsterdam, Boom.

Ent, M. van der (2007) In betrekking. Herinneringen van een dienstmeisje dat in het begin van de vorige eeuw volwassen werd. The Netherlands, Amsterdam, Artemis & Co.

Erlich V. (1966) Family in transition: a study of 300 Yugoslav villages. USA, New Jersey, Princeton University Press.

Esim, S. & M. Smith (eds.) (2004) Gender and Migration in Arab States: the case of domestic workers. Regional Office for the Arab States, Beirut, International Labour Organization.

Esposito, J.L. & D. Mogahed (2007) Who speaks for Islam: what a billion Muslims really think. USA, New York, Gallup Press.

Eyffinger, A.C.G.M. (ed.) (1991) Compendium Volkenrechtsgeschiedenis. The Netherlands, Deventer, Kluwer.

Fadl, K. A. El- (2001) Speaking in God's name: Islamic law, authority and women. UK, Oxford, One world.

Fauve-Chamoux, A. (ed.) (2004) Domestic Service and the Formation of European Identity: Understanding the Globalization of Domestic Work, 16th-21st Centuries. Bern, Germany, Peter Lang.

Fisk, R. (2005) De grote beschavingsoorlog: de verovering van het Midden-Oosten. The Netherlands, Amsterdam, Ambo Manteau.

Friedman, T. L. (2006) The first law of petropolitics. In: Foreign Policy, May/June 2006, http://www.foreignpolicy.com/story/cms.php?story_id=3426

Gamburd, M.R. (2000) The kitchen spoon's handle: Transnationalism and Sri Lanka's migrant housemaids. USA, New York, Cornell University Press.

Gardner, K. (1995) Global migrants, local lives: Travel and transformation in rural Bangladesh. UK, Oxford, Oxford University Press.

Geertz, C. (1973) The Interpretation of Cultures, USA, New York, Basic Books 2000.

Glenn, H.P. (2004) Legal traditions of the world. USA, NY, Oxford University Press.

Gluckman, M. (1972) The ideas in Barotse jurisprudence. UK, Manchester, Manchester University Press.

Gommer, H. (2011) A Biological Theory of Law: Natural Law Theory Revisited. Publication forthcoming.

Grabham, E. & D. Cooper, J. Krishnadas & D. Herman (eds.) (2009) Intersectionality and beyond: law, power and the politics of location. UK, Oxon, Routledge-Cavendish.

Grantham, G. & M. MacKinnon (ed.) (1994) Labor market evolution: the economic history of market integration, wage flexibility and the employment relation. UK, London, Routledge.

Griffiths (1996) De sociale werking van het recht: een kennismaking met de rechtssociologie en rechtsantropologie. The Netherlands, Nijmegen, Ars Aequi Libri.

Groot, A.D. de (1975) Methodologie: grondslagen van onderzoek en denken in de gedragswetenschappen. The Netherlands, The Hague, Mouton & Co.

Guild, E. & S. Mantu (ed.) (2011) Constructing and imagining labour migration: perspectives of control from five continents. UK, Burlington, Ashgate Publishing Company.

Guzman, O. de (2003) Overseas Filipino Workers, Labor Circulation in Southeast Asia and the (mis)management of overseas migration programs. Kyoto Review of South East Asia, Issue 4; regional economic integration. http://kyotoreview.csaes.kuoto-u.ac.jo

Habachy, S. (1962) Property, right and contract in Muslim Law. In: Columbia Law Review, Vol. 62, No. 3 (March 1962), pp 450-473.

Hamacher, W. (2004) The right to have rights: four-and-a-half remarks. In: South Atlantic Quarterly Volume 103, Number 2/3, p 353.

Henderson, L. (1991) Law's patriarchy. Law & Society Review, Vol. 25, nr 2.

Hesselink, M.W. (2004) Contractenrecht in perspectief. The Netherlands, Den Haag, Boom Juridische Uitgevers.

Heyzer N. & G. Lycklama à Nijeholt & N. Weerakon (eds.) (1994) The trade in domestic workers; causes: mechanisms and consequences of international migration. UK, London, Zed Books Ltd.

Hochschild, A.R. (2000) The global nanny chain. In: the American Prospect 11(4) pp 32-36.

Holton, P. (2007) Mother without a mask: a Westerner's story of her Arab family. UAE, Dubai, Motivate publishing.

Hondagneu-Sotelo, P. (2001) Domestica: immigrant workers and their employers. USA, Berkeley, University of California Press.

Horwitz, M.J. (1982) The history of the public/private distinction. In: University of Pennsylvania Law Review, Vol. 130, pp 1423-1428.

Jansen, C.J.H. (2003) Rechtshistorische beschouwingen omtrent het moderne arbeidsovereenkomstenrecht. Rede in verkorte vorm, uitgesproken bij aanvaarding van het ambt van bijzonder hoogleraar in het Romeins recht aan de Universiteit van Amsterdam op donderdag 23 januari 2003. The Netherlands, The Hague, Boom Juridische Uitgevers.

Jansen, S. (2008) Het pauperparadijs: een familiegeschiedenis. The Netherlands, Amsterdam, Uitgeverij Balans.

Johnson, A.G. (1997) The gender knot: unraveling our patriarchal society. USA, Philadelphia, Temple University Press.

Jureidini, R. (2002) Women migrant domestic workers in Lebanon. Switzerland, Geneva, International Migration Programme, International Migration Papers No. 48.

Jureidini, R. & N. Moukarbel (2004) Female Sri Lankan Domestic Workers in Lebanon: A Case of 'Contract Slavery'? In: Journal of Ethnic and Migration Studies 30, No. 4, pp 581-607.

Jureidini, R. (2010) Trafficking and Contract Migrant Workers in the Middle East. In: International Migration Vol. 48 (4), pp 142-163.

Kamali, M.H. (2002) Freedom, equality and justice in Islam. UK, Cambridge, Islamic texts society.

Keesing, R.M. (1981) Cultural Anthropology: a contemporary perspective. Orlando USA, Holt, Renehart and Winston Inc.

Klare, K.E. (1982) The public/private distinction in labor law. In: University of Pennsylvania Law Review Vol. 130, pp 1358-1422.

Knegt, R. (2008a) Normative structures of pre-industrial wage labor. Paper submitted to the European Social Science Conference, Portugal, Lisbon, 2008.

Knegt, R. (ed.) (2008b) The employment contract as an exclusionary device: an analysis on the basis of 25 years of developments in The Netherlands. Belgium, Antwerpen, Intersentia.

Krishna, S. (2009) Globalization & Post-colonialism: hegemony and resistance in the twenty-first century. USA, Lanham, Rowman & Littlefield Publishers Inc.

Kronman, A.T. (1983) Max Weber. Jurists: profiles in legal theory. UK, London, Edward Arnold.

Kuijer, A. & K. Steenbergen (2005) Nederlands vreemdelingenrecht. The Netherlands, The Hague, Boom Juridische Uitgevers.

Kuptsch, C. (ed.) (2006) Merchants of labor. Switzerland, Geneva, ILO.

Kurczewski, J. (2009) Bronislaw Malinowski misunderstood – or how Leon Petrazycki's concept of law is unwittingly applied in anthropology of law. In: Societas/Communitas, issue 1(7) / 2009, pp 47-62.

Leezenberg, M. (2002) Islamitische Filosofie; een geschiedenis. The Netherlands, Amsterdam, Bulaaq.

Leezenberg, M. & G. de Vries (2005) Wetenschapsfilosofie voor geesteswetenschappen. The Netherlands, Amsterdam, Amsterdam University Press.

Leun, J. van der & L. Vervoorn (2004) Slavernij-achtige uitbuiting in Nederland. Een inventariserende literatuurstudie in het kader van de uitbreiding van de strafbaarstelling van mensenhandel. The Netherlands, The Hague, Boom Juridische Uitgevers.

Levit, N. & R.R.M. Verchick (2006) A primer: feminist legal theory. USA, New York, New York University Press.

Levitt, S. & S. Dubner (2009) Superfreakonomics. USA, NY, Harpercollins Publishers.

Lindio-McGovern, L. (2003) Labor Export in the Context of Globalization. The Experience of Filipino Domestic Workers in Rome. In: International Sociology, 18(3), pp 513-534.

Locher-Scholten, E. (1994) Orientalism and the rhetoric of the family: Javanese servants in European household manuals and children's fiction. In: Indonesia 1994, Vol 58, pp 19-39.

Lutz, H. (ed.) (2008) Migration and domestic work: a European perspective on a global dilemma. UK, Aldershot, Ashgate.

Mahar, R.D. (1990) Dignity of Labor in Islam. In: Al Farooq, Islamic Monthly Journal, pp 28-29, December 1990, Karachi Pakistan.

Maine, H.S. (1913) Ancient Law: its connection with the early history of society and its relation to modern ideas. UK, London, George Routledge & Sons.

Manning, A. (2003) Monopsony in motion: imperfect competition in labor markets. USA, New Jersey, Princeton University Press.

Manseau G.S. (2007) Contractual solutions for migrant laborers: the case of domestic workers in the Middle East. Available online: http://www.nottingham.ac.uk/hrlc/documents/publications/hrlcommentary2006/migrantlabourers.pdf

Marzouqi, I. A. Al- (2000) Human Rights in Islamic Law. UAE, Abu Dhabi, unknown publisher.

Mattar, M. (2003) Trafficking in persons, especially women and children, in countries of the Middle East: the scope of the problem and the appropriate legislative responses. In: Fordham International Law Journal 2003, pp 721-770.

McKinley, B. (2008) Introductory statement to the ministerial consultations on overseas employment and contractual labor in countries of origin and destination in Asia. 22 January 2008 Abu Dhabi, UAE.

Merry, S. E. (1988) Legal pluralism. In: Law & Society Review, Vol. 22, No. 5, pp 869-896.

Merry, S. E. (2006) Human rights & gender violence: translating international law into local justice. USA, Chicago, University of Chicago Press.

Merry, S.E. (2006b) Anthropology and International Law. In: Annual Review of Anthropology pp 99-116, available at: anthro.annualreviews.org

Michaels, R. (2009) Global legal pluralism. In: Annual review of law & society 2009, pp 342-262.

Mnookin, R.M. & L. Kornhauser (1979) Bargaining in the shadow of the law: the case of divorce. In: Yale Law Journal Vol. 88, pp 950-997.

Mohammed, N. (1988) Principles of Islamic Contract Law. In: Journal of Law & Religion, Vol. 6, No. 1, pp 115-130.

Molenaar, A.N. (1953) Arbeidsrecht. The Netherlands, Zwolle, Tjeenk Willink.

Momsen, H.M. (ed.) (1999) Migration and domestic service. UK, London, Routledge.

Moore, S.F. (ed.) (2005) Law and Anthropology: a reader. UK, Oxford, Blackwell Publishing.

Moors, A. (2003) Migrant domestic workers: Debating transnationalism, identity politics and family relations. In: Comparative studies in society and history (2003) Vol. 45, pp 386-394. UK, Cambridge, Cambridge University Press.

Moukarbel, N. (2009) Sri Lankan housemaids in Lebanon: a case study of 'symbolic violence' and 'every day forms of resistance'. The Netherlands, Amsterdam, Amsterdam University Press.

Munif, A. (1987) Cities of salt. USA, New York, Vintage International.

Munif, A. (1993) The trench. USA, New York, Vintage International.

Nader, L. (ed.) (1969) Law in Culture and Society. USA, Berkeley, University of California Press. (Paperback version of 1997)

Najjar, S. Al (2002) Women migrant domestic workers in Bahrain. Switzerland, Geneva, International Migration Papers 47.

Nasr, S.H. (2004) The heart of Islam, enduring values for humanity. USA, San Francisco, Harper San Francisco.

Neyrey, J.H. (1986) Witchcraft accusations in 2 cor 10-13: Paul in social science perspective: http://www.nd.edu/~jneyrey1/2CorWitch.htm.

Nichols, R. (2008) Asian Labor Subordination and Resistance in Dubai, 2006. Paper presented at the conference on inter-Asian connections, Dubai, United Arab Emirates, February 21-23 2008.

Oomen, B. (2005) Chiefs in South Africa: law, power and culture in the post-apartheid era. Law & Society Association dissertation award winner. USA, New York, Palgrave.

Otto, J.M. & A.J. Dekker & L.J. van Soest-Zuurdeeg (eds.) (2006) Sharia en nation-aal recht in twaalf moslimslanden. The Netherlands, Amsterdam, Amsterdam University Press.

Ozyegin, G. (2001) Untidy gender: domestic service in Turkey. USA, Philadephia, Temple University Press.

Palmer, D. (1998) Filosofie voor beginners. The Netherlands, Utrecht, Uitgeverij Het Spectrum B.V.

Pampanini, A.H. (2005) Saudi Arabia: moving towards a privatized economy. USA, New York, Turnaround Associates Inc.

Parreñas, R.S. (2001) Servants of globalisation, women, migration and domestic work. USA, California, Stanford University Press.

Pattadath, B. (2008) Intersections of gender, religion and labor: Muslim migrant women domestic workers from Kerala to UAE. Paper presented at the confer-ence on inter-Asian connections, Dubai, United Arab Emirates, February 21-23 2008.

Pattanaik, B. (2006) reflections on initiatives to address human trafficking. In: Forced Migration Review, 24 May 2006, pp 4-5.

Patterson O. (1982) Slavery and social death, a comparative study. UK, London, Harvard University Press.

Pingol, A. (2008) Filipino Muslim women in Saudi Arabia. Paper presented at the conference on inter-Asian connections, United Arab Emirates, Dubai, February 21-23 2008.

Pool, C. (2011) Migratie van Polen naar Nederland (in een tijd van versoepeling van migratieregels). The Netherlands, The Hague, Boom Juridische Uitgevers.

Power, S. (2008) Chasing the flame: Sergio Vieira de Mello and the fight to save the world. USA, New York, Allen Lane, Penguin Group.

Prakash, B.A. (1998) Gulf migration and its economic impact: the Kerala experi-ence. In: Economic and Political Weekly, Vol. 33, No. 50 (Dec. 12-18, 1998), pp 3209-3213, available online: http://www.jstor.org/stable/4407474.

Radtke, L.H. & H.J. Stam (eds.) (1994) Power & gender: social relations in theory and practice. UK, London, Sage.

Rasheed, M. Al (2003) A history of Saudi Arabia. UK, Cambridge, Cambridge University Press.

Rasheed, M. Al (2007) Contesting the Saudi State: Islamic voices from a new generation. UK, Cambridge, Cambridge University Press.

Regt, M. de (2006) Mapping Study on women domestic workers in Yemen. Available online: http://bravo.ilo.org/public/libdoc/ilo/2006/106B09_159_engl.pdf

Regt, M. de (2008) Employing migrant domestic workers in urban Yemen: a new form of social distinction. Paper provided by de Regt to author mre@iisg.nl.

Regt, M. de (2009) Preferences and prejudices: employers' views on domestic workers in the Republic of Yemen. In: Journal of Women in Culture and Society 2009, Vol. 34, No. 3.

Rhode, D.L. (2004) Access to Justice. Oxford, UK, Oxford University Press.

Rollins, J. (1985) Between women: domestics and their employers. Temple University Press, Philadelphia, USA.

Romany, C. (1993) Women as aliens: a feminist critique of the public/private distinction in international human rights law. Harvard Human Rights Journal No. 6, pp 87-125.

Romero, M. (1992) Maid in the USA. USA, New York, Routledge.

Rooij, B. van & K. Fürst (2011) Rights based empowerment, a concept note on rights mobilization and power. Working paper.

Rugh, A.B. (2007) The political culture of leadership in the United Arab Emirates. USA, New York, Palgrave, Macmillan.

Sabban, R. (2002) Migrant women in the Emirates: the case of female domestic workers. Geneva, Gender Promotion Program, ILO, Genprom working paper nr 10.

Sachs, J. (2005) The end of poverty: how we can make it happen in hour lifetime. UK, London, Penguin Books.

Said, E.W. (2005) Oriëntalisten. The Netherlands, Amsterdam, Mets & Schilt.

Santos, M.D.P. (2005) Human rights and migrant domestic work: a comparative analysis of the socio-legal status of Filipina migrant domestic workers in Canada and Hong Kong. Netherlands, Leiden, The Raoul Wallenberg Institute Human Rights Library, Vol. 24.

Sasson, J.P. (2004) Princess, the true story of life behind the veil in Saudi Arabia. London, UK, Bantam Books.

Sasson, J.P. (2004b) Daughters of Arabia. London, UK, Bantam Books.

Schacht, J. (1993) An introduction to Islamic Law. Oxford, United Kingdom, Clarendon Press.

Schama S. (1988) Overvloed en onbehagen. De Nederlandse cultuur in de gouden eeuw. The Netherlands, Amsterdam, Uitgeverij Contact.

Schacht, J. (1964) An Introduction to Islamic Law. UK, Oxford, Clarendon Paperbacks.

Schwitters, R.J.S. (1991) Riskante aansprakelijkheid. In: recht en kritiek 17 (1991) 1, pp 5-39.

Schwitters, R.J.S. (2000) Recht en samenleving in verandering. The Netherlands, Deventer, Open Universiteit, Kluwer.

Shadid, W.A. (2003) Grondslagen van interculturele communicatie: studieveld en werkterrein. The Netherlands, Alphen aan de Rijn, Kluwer.

Silvey, R. (2006) Consuming the transnational family: Indonesian migrant domestic workers in Saudi Arabia. In: Global networks 6, 1, pp 23-40.

Soto, H. de (2000) The mystery of capital: why capitalism triumphs in the West and fails everywhere else. USA, New York, Basic Books.

Stanley, A.D. (1998) From bondage to contract. Wage labor, marriage and the market in the age of slave emancipation. USA, New York, Cambridge University Press.

Steinfeld, R.J. (1991) The invention of free labor; the employment relation in English and American law and culture 1350-1870. USA, Chapel Hill, University of North Carolina Press.

Stienen, P. (2008) Dromen van een Arabische lente: Een Nederlandse diplomate in het Midden-Oosten. The Netherlands, Amsterdam, Nieuw Amsterdam Uitgevers.

Strauss, A.L. & J.M Corbin (1990) Basics of qualitative research: grounded theory procedures and techniques. USA, Newbury Park, Sage.

Strauss, A.L. & J.M Corbin (1998) Basics of qualitative research: techniques and procedures for developing grounded theory. USA, Thousand Oaks, Sage.

Strobl, S. (2009) Policing housemaids: the criminalization of domestic workers in Bahrein. British Journal for Criminology 2009, nr 49, pp 165-183.

Swaan, A. de (2004) Zorg en de staat: welzijn, onderwijs en gezondheidszorg in Europa en de Verenigde Staten in de nieuwe tijd. The Netherlands, Amsterdam, Bert Bakker. Title of English version: In care of the state: health care, education and welfare in Europe and the USA in the modern era.

Tacoli, C. (1999) International Migration and the restructuring of gender asymmetries; continuity and change among Filipino labor migrants in Rome. In: International Migration Review, Vol. 33, No. 3 (Fall 1999) pp 658-682.

Tamanaha, B.Z. (2006) Law as a Means to an End: Threat to the Rule of Law. USA, New York, Cambridge University Press.

Tamimi, E. Al (2006) Setting up in Dubai: a comprehensive handbook on the legal aspects of establishing a business in Dubai. Business Investor's Guide, 4th edition. United Arab Emirates, Emirates Printing Press.

Tyner, J.A. (1994) The social construction of gendered migration from the Philippines. In: Asian and Pacific Migration Journal 1994, 3(4), pp 589-617.

Veen, R. van der (1994) De wankele verzorgingsstaat: een vergelijkende analyse van verzorgingsstaten in het licht van internationaliseringsprocessen. In: zorgen in het Europese huis: verkenningen over de grenzen van nationale verzorgingsstaten; Beleid & maatschappij jaarboek 1992/1993. The Netherlands, Amsterdam, Boom.

Vergrote, A. (1987) Religie, geloof en ongeloof: psychologische studie. The Netherlands, Kapellen, DNB/Uitgeverij Pelckmans.

Vlieger (2010) Sharia on domestic workers: legal pluralism and strategic maneuvering in Saudi Arabia and the Emirates. In: Journal of Islamic Law and Culture, Vol. 12, Issue 2, pp 166-182.

Vlieger (2011a) Transnationalism, legal pluralism and types of conflicts: contractual norms concerning domestic workers. In: Socio-legal studies on transnationalism, The Netherlands, Boom Juridische Uitgevers, forthcoming.

Vlieger (2011b) Dienstbodes in Saoedi-Arabië; intersectionaliteit en toegang tot het recht. In: Recht der Werkelijkheid 32 (2), forthcoming.

Vlieger (2011c) Domestic workers in Saudi Arabia and the Emirates: trafficking victims? In: International Migration, forthcoming.

Waal F. de (ed.) (2001) Tree of origin: what primate behavior can tell us about human social evolution. USA, Cambridge, Harvard University Press.

Waardenburg J.D.J. (ed.) (1994) Islam: norm ideaal en werkelijkheid. The Netherlands, Houten, Fibula.

Walsum, S. van & T. Spijkerboer (2007) Women and immigration law: new variations on classical feminist themes. UK, Oxon, Routledge-Cavendish.

Walzer, M. (1983) Spheres of Justice: a defense of pluralism and equality. USA, New York, Basic Books.

Wolf, E.R. (1990) Europe and the people without history. USA, Berkeley, University of California Press.

Zachariah, K.C. & B.A. Prakash & S. Irudaya Rajan (2002) Gulf migration study: employment, wages and working conditions of Kerala emigrants in the United Arab Emirates. Working Paper No. 326 Center for Development Studies Thiruvananthapuram, available online: http://cds.edu/download_files/326.pdf.

Zakaria, F. (2001) The politics of hate: why do they hate us? Newsweek 15-10-2001 available at http://www.fareedzakaria.com/ARTICLES/newsweek/101501_why.html

Zakaria, F. (2007) The future of freedom: illiberal democracy at home and abroad. USA, New York, Norton & Company.

Zimbardo, P. (2008) The Lucifer effect: understanding how good people turn evil. USA, New York, Random House Trade Paperbacks.

Zlotnik, H. (2000) Migration and the family: the female perspective. In: K. Willis & B. Yeoh (eds.) Gender and migration pp 27-45. UK, Cheltenham, Edward Elgar.

Zogby, J. (2007) Defining the middle class, Bahrain, Saudi Arabia and the Emirates. Zogby International. Submitted to McKinsey and Company, supplied to researcher by author.

Zubaida, S. (2005) Law and power in the Islamic world. Library of Modern Middle East Studies, 34. UK, London, Tauris.

Zubair, A. (1989) Concept and protection of labor under Islamic Law. In: Islamic Order Quarterly, third quarter, volume 11, No. 3, pp 18-24.

Zweigert, K. & H. Kötz (1992) An introduction to comparative law. UK, Oxford, Clarendon Press.

13.2 Reports

1. Towards a fair deal for migrant workers in the global economy. ILO Conference, 92nd session, 2004.
2. United Arab Emirates: A Country Study. Federal Research Division. Washington USA, Library of Congress, 1993
3. The Emirates' draft labor law, Human Rights Watch' comments and recommendations. 2007.
4. Life and Health on the Move: the sexual and reproductive health status and needs of Filipino women migrant domestic workers. Action for Health Initiative & UNFPA, Quezon City, Philippines, 2006.
5. Protection of expatriate workers in the United Arab Emirates. A summary report based on a study commissioned by the ILO for the Gulf Forum on Temporary Contractual Labor, Abu Dhabi, 23-24 January 2008.
6. Temporary contract labor in the Gulf States: perspectives from two countries of origin. Roger Plant, head special action program to combat forced labor, ILO Geneva. A summary paper based on studies commissioned by the ILO for the Gulf Forum on Temporary Contractual Labor, Abu Dhabi, 23-24 January 2008.
7. Foreign Labor in the GCC countries: low-wage workers. Dr. Baker Al-Najjar, prof. of sociology, University of Bahrain. A report based on a study commissioned by the ILO for the Gulf Forum on Temporary Contractual Labor, Abu Dhabi, 23-24 January 2008.
8. Swept under the rug: abuses against domestic workers around the world. Human Rights Watch, July 2006, volume 18, nr 7C.
9. Exported and exposed; abuses against Sri Lankan domestic workers in Saudi Arabia, Kuwait, Lebanon and the United Arab Emirates. Human Rights Watch, November 2007, volume 19, nr 16c, available at: http://www.hrw.org/reports/2007/srilanka1107/3.htm
10. Arab Human Development Report 2005: towards the rise of women in the Arab world (2006) UNDP regional bureau for Arab States, AFESD and AGPfUNDO, New York, USA.
11. The first report on Human Rights conditions in the Kingdom of Saudi Arabia (2006) National Society for Human Rights, Riyadh, Saudi Arabia.
12. Comments on the first human rights report in the Kingdom of Saudi Arabia (2007) National Society for Human Rights, Riyadh, Saudi Arabia.
13. Guidebook for Expatriates recruited for work in the Kingdom of Saudi Arabia (2006) Ministry of Labor, Riyadh, Saudi Arabia.
14. Concluding observations of the committee on the elimination of discrimination against women: Saudi Arabia. Advanced unedited version, February 2008, committee on the elimination of discrimination against women, CEDAW/c/sau/co/2.

15. Considerations of reports submitted by States Parties under article 18 of the Convention on the Elimination of All Forms of Discrimination against Women, combined initial and second periodic reports of States Parties, Saudi Arabia. March 2007, Committee on the Elimination of Discrimination Against Women, CEDAW/C/SAU/2. And Addendum 1.

16. The Shadow report for CEDAW, prepared by 'Saudi women for reform'. Executive Summary, December 2007, Saudi Arabia.

17. Precarious Justice. Arbitrary detention and unfair trials in the deficient criminal justice system of Saudi Arabia. Human Rights Watch, March 2008, Volume 20, No.3(E) available at: http://www.hrw.org/reports/2008/03/24/precarious-justice.

18. As if I am not human. Abuses against Asian Domestic Workers in Saudi Arabia. Human Rights Watch, July 2008, 1-56432-351-X, available at: http://www.hrw.org/en/node/62143/section/1

19. United States Annual trafficking in persons report 2007 on Saudi Arabia and the United Arab Emirates, available at: http://www.state.gov/documents/organization/82902.pdf

20. Organizing the Association of Employment Agencies in Asia: Moving Forward on Ethical recruitment (3&4 April 2008, Manila) Welcome Message Mr Harns, IOM.

21. Perpetual Minors: human rights abuses stemming from male guardianship and sex segregation in Saudi Arabia. Human Rights Watch 2008, available at: http://www.hrw.org/fr/node/62251/section/6.

22. Protection of migrant domestic workers in destination countries. ILO Human Rights training manual for consular officials and labor attaches. ILO Jakarta 2006, available at: http://www.ilo.org/jakarta/whatwedo/publications/lang--en/docName--WCMS_122313/index.htm.

23. National Report submitted in accordance with Section 15(A) of the Annex to Human Rights Council Resolution 5/1 of Saudi Arabia. A/HRC/WG.6/4/SAU/1, prepared for the human rights council working group on the universal periodic review, fourth session, 2-13 February 2009.

24. Decent work for domestic workers. ILO Geneva, report IV(1), fourth item on the agenda 99th session 2010.

25. Report on irregular migration and human trafficking. Centre for Migrant advocacy Philippines (CMA) and Mujeres Inc. Women United for Justice and Equality toward a Responsive and Empowered Society. 2007 CAM Philippines, Quezon City

26. Guiding the public in understanding irregular migration. A seminar-symposium series for migrant resource centers, NGOs and the Media, 2008 IOM, Manila, Philippines.

27. Making the law work for everyone. Volume 1, report of the commission on legal empowerment of the poor. USA, New York, 2008

28. Bridging the Gulf Feasibility Study: into the set up of an educational human rights institute in and for the states of the Gulf Cooperation Council, by Mauritius Wijffels, Melba Middle East Legal and Business Advice. UAE, Fujeirah, 2009.

29. Denied dignity, systematic discrimination and hostility toward Saudi Shi'a Citizens. 2009, Human Rights Watch, USA, New York. Available at: http://www.hrw.org/sites/default/files/reports/saudi0909webwcover.pdf.

30. The Ismailis of Najran, second-class Saudi citizens. 2008, Human Rights Watch, USA, New York. Available at: http://www.hrw.org/sites/default/files/reports/saudiarabia0908web.pdf.

31. 2008 Country Report on Human Rights Practices in the United Arab Emirates of the U.S.A. Department of State. Available at: http://www.state.gov/g/drl/rls/hrrpt/2008/nea/119129.htm

32. Combined initial and second periodic report of State Party Saudi Arabia to the Convention on the Elimination of Discrimination against women. 2008, available at: http://www.un.org/womenwatch/daw/cedaw/reports.htm.

About the author

Antoinette Vlieger was born on June 19, 1973 in Hillegom, the Netherlands. After completing secondary school (VWO) at the Fioretti College in Lisse, she studied at the University of Amsterdam where she completed a master's degree both in Dutch law and international law. In addition, she completed a minor's degree (propedeuse) in cultural anthropology and sociology of the non-Western world. She followed one-year courses in Arabic and the politics of the Middle East, economics (including development economics) and language studies, focusing on argumentation theory. Her final thesis concerned the Egyptian investment act. During her studies, she fulfilled an internship both at the International Dialogues Foundation in The Hague and at the Dutch permanent mission to the United Nations in New York. She held several positions in student organizations, rowed at national level, and won several prizes for writing short stories and columns.

She worked in corporate law for several years, first as a lawyer, later for the Dutch government, and finally in a private company. She returned to the University of Amsterdam in 2005. Since then, she has lectured several courses, primarily corporate law, introduction to law, argumentation theory and contract law from meta-legal perspectives. She attained her basic teaching qualifications. She has guided many students in writing papers and masters theses. With groups of motivated students, she organized conferences on the unsustainable debts of certain developing countries, human trafficking, and the limits of corporate social responsibility. From December 2006, she worked on this research project, within the Hugo Sinzheimer Institute for the sociology of labor law. She is an expert member of the workgroup on migrant workers in the Arab European Human Rights Dialogue. Her research has been published in academic and legal journals, in English and Dutch. In 2011 she publicly defended this dissertation and earned her Ph.D. from the University of Amsterdam.

Dutch is her mother tongue. She is fluent in English, proficient in French, and speaks some German and Arabic.

www.ingramcontent.com/pod-product-compliance
Lightning Source LLC
Chambersburg PA
CBHW080228270326
41926CB00020B/4187